CW01066862

SAMUEL JOHNSON AND THE MAKING OF MODERN ENGLAND

Samuel Johnson, one of the most renowned authors of the eighteenth century, became virtually a symbol of English national identity in the century following his death in 1784. In *Samuel Johnson and the Making of Modern England* Nicholas Hudson argues that Johnson not only came to personify English cultural identity but did much to shape it. Hudson examines his contribution to the creation of the modern English identity, approaching Johnson's writing and conversation from scarcely explored directions of cultural criticism – class politics, feminism, party politics, the public sphere, nationalism, and imperialism. Hudson charts the career of an author who rose from obscurity to fame during precisely the period that England became the dominant force in the Western world. In exploring the relations between Johnson's career and the development of England's modern national identity, Hudson develops new and provocative arguments concerning both Johnson's literary achievement and the nature of English nationhood.

NICHOLAS HUDSON is Professor of English at the University of British Columbia. He is the author of *Samuel Johnson and Eighteenth-Century Thought* (1988), *Writing and European Thought, 1600–1830* (Cambridge, 1994), and of numerous essays on eighteenth-century literature, thought, and culture.

SAMUEL JOHNSON AND THE MAKING OF MODERN ENGLAND

NICHOLAS HUDSON
The University of British Columbia

PUBLISHED BY THE PRESS SYNDICATE OF THE UNIVERSITY OF CAMBRIDGE
The Pitt Building, Trumpington Street, Cambridge CB2 1RP, United Kingdom

CAMBRIDGE UNIVERSITY PRESS
The Edinburgh Building, Cambridge, CB2 2RU, UK
40 West 20th Street, New York, NY 10011–4211, USA
477 Williamstown Road, Port Melbourne, VIC 3207, Australia
Ruiz de Alarcón 13, 28014 Madrid, Spain
Dock House, The Waterfront, Cape Town 8001, South Africa

http://www.cambridge.org

First published 2003

Printed in the United Kingdom at the University Press, Cambridge

Typeface Adobe Garamond 10/12.5 pt. *System* LaTeX 2ε [TB]

A catalogue record for this book is available from the British Library

Library of Congress Cataloguing in Publication data
Hudson, Nicholas.
Samuel Johnson and the making of modern England / Nicholas Hudson.
p. cm.
Includes bibliographical references (p. 264) and index.
ISBN 0 521 83125 3
1. Johnson, Samuel, 1709–1784. 2. Johnson, Samuel, 1709–1784 – Homes and haunts – England. 3. Nationalism – England – History – 18th century. 4. National characteristics, English, in literature. 5. Authors, English – 18th century – Biography. 6. England – Civilization – 18th century. 7. England – In literature. I. Title.
PR3533.H79 2003
828′.609 – dc21
[B] 2003046265

ISBN 0 521 83125 3 hardback

For Emilie and Alex

Contents

Acknowledgments *page* viii

Introduction 1

1 From "rank" to "class": the changing structures of social hierarchy 11

2 Constructing the middle-class woman 43

3 From "Broad-bottom" to "party": the rise of modern English politics 77

4 "The voice of the nation": the evolution of the "public" 108

5 The construction of English nationhood 133

6 The material and ideological development of the British Empire 170

Conclusion 221

Notes 227
Bibliography 264
Index 283

Acknowledgments

The research for this book was financed in large part by the Social Sciences and Humanities Research Council of Canada, an organization to which I later belonged as a committee member and chair, and which I consider one of the great funding organizations in the world. My thanks as well to the University of British Columbia for the generous distribution of smaller grants. Parts of chapter 1 first appeared as "Samuel Johnson and the Politics of 'Standard English'" in *Year Book of English Studies* 28 (1998): 77–93. My thanks to the Modern Humanities Research Association for permission to republish this material. At Cambridge University Press, I have benefitted from the insight of an editor, Linda Bree, who knows my field very well, and has been encouraging from the first proposal of the manuscript. Among Linda's contributions was the appointment of two readers, Fred Parker and an anonymous scholar, who knew a lot more than I did about important things, and who patiently slogged through early manuscripts that owed more to bardic afflatus than careful rereading. Many thanks to my copy editor, David Watson, for his skilled and patient work on my typescript. At UBC I have been blessed with wonderful graduate students and research assistants, Sharon-Ruth Alker, Dan O'Leary, Ray Siemens, and Greg Morgan, who have made eighteenth-century studies seem all the more exciting. And the support, patience and friendship of many people in my department are remembered with enormous gratitude. Thanks particularly to Titi Adepitan, Miranda Burgess, John Cooper, Pamela Dalziel, Claire Grogan, Ron Hatch, Ira Nadel, Tiffany Potter, Mike Wells, and Gernot Wieland. Among the greatest pleasures of an academic life is the creation of international communities of brilliant people with similar obsessions. Some of these scholars have contributed to my knowledge and to my recent career in substantial and tangible ways, including Fraser Easton, David Hensley, Nancy Johnson, Paul Korshin, Jack Lynch, Anne McDermott, Adam Potkay, Maggie Powell, Claude Rawson, and Howard Weinbrot.

But finally even academic books are made at home, and it is there that emotional debts become most weighty and, curiously, most joyful. To my step-sons – Abel, Abram and Axel – I say thank you for your patience during a time of enormous change. And to Emilie and Alex, to whom this book is dedicated, the gratitude is heart-felt and the word "thanks" strangely insufficient.

Introduction

In a depiction of a famous story in Boswell's *Life of Johnson*, the Victorian artist Eyre Crowe portrays the aging literary hero standing, head bowed, in Uttoxeter market-square, doing penance for a wrong committed many years before against his father. As a young man not long returned from Oxford, Johnson had refused to take his dying father's book-stall to Uttoxeter on the usual day. Significantly, modern scholars have tended to focus entirely on Johnson's act of penance: this is the "Johnson Agonistes" favored in our post-Romantic and Freudian age, a figure tormented by family-induced guilt, religious doubts and congenital melancholia. Curiously detached from his era and place, he stands for mental suffering, human courage and literary greatness at all times. Yet the Victorian artist presented Johnson on a wider canvas and in a specific social context. Around him bustles a rather idealized but recognizably eighteenth-century village market. At the author's right a book-seller points out Johnson as a salutary lesson to his son, reminding us that Johnson's sin was as much against the trading class and his own book-market as against his father on earth or in heaven. To Johnson's left, a merchant gestures with a goose in his direction, market-women and shoppers glance towards him curiously, a deputy prepares the stocks for the day's malefactor, and the vigorous orbit of English life and economy whirls on. To the mental eye of the Victorians, Johnson was at the center of that orbit, inseparable from his time and situation. In the case of scholars over the last fifty years, on the contrary, it often seems that this enveloping social context is exactly what they want to leave out.

This is not to disparage the remarkable achievements of much modern scholarship: Johnson has been effectively psychoanalyzed and deconstructed; his thought has been convincingly traced to Renaissance humanism, seventeenth-century homiletics and the classics.[1] And indeed, over the last decade, scholars have begun to awaken, though only slowly, to Johnson's importance in cultural history, particularly in connection with his role in fashionable areas of print culture, gender studies, and post-colonialism.[2]

But even in this scholarship, as I will have many occasions to point out, the aim has been less to understand Johnson within the cultural developments of his own age than to justify his canonical status in the context of the currently prevailing morality of the Anglo-American academy. According to a certain implicit assumption, Johnson must be recovered as acceptable according to *our* values as a socially progressive thinker who nobly opposed, against the currents of his time, misogyny and all kinds of racism, prejudiced nationalism, slavery and imperialism. In other words, to the extent that Johnson has been belatedly folded within the aegis of "cultural studies," the goal has been, despite appearances, too often *not* to understand how Johnson was shaped by or helped to shape the social world around him (except in the broadest sense), but rather to tailor intellectual history to our own ideological agendas. In contrast, the underlying aim of the following book is to reposition Johnson within the specific and transforming historical events of his lifetime, accepting all that might make him morally uncomfortable to us as well as admirable. I will be interested not just in the general tenor of English eighteenth-century culture with regard to social class, gender, nationalism, imperialism, and other topics, but in Johnson's evolving reactions to events as they occurred during the course of this dynamic and pivotal period of Anglo-American history. In other words, I examine Johnson not just in his "context" but as part of a *process* that was changing England from a pre-modern into a modern society, finally vaulting him into the iconically English figure imagined by the Victorians and even in popular culture today.

The slowness of recent scholarship to situate Johnson in the specifically eighteenth-century context can be attributed in part to the peculiar historical pattern of this field. A century ago, even Johnson's admirers acknowledged that he was more important as a "man" than as a "writer."[3] For scholars raised in the heyday of American New Criticism, on the contrary, it seemed important to prove just the opposite. In an era of expanding undergraduate education, professors felt obliged to prove that Johnson was a "great author" who deserved a place in the English literary canon, that select club of literary geniuses whose significance could not be confined to any particular time or culture. In an age that was rushing towards humanist alternatives to religion, similarly, it seemed best to treat Johnson's Christian devotion, so long admired, as the kind of neurosis suffered by peculiarly insightful and "modern" people. And in political terms, Johnson's old reputation as a "Tory," a patriotic conservative who stood for tradition, stability, and hierarchy, seemed unpalatable at a time when Anglo-American campuses were galvanized by anti-militaristic and civil-rights liberalism. The leading scholar of Johnson's political thought, Donald Greene (who as a Canadian Tory may well rank as a liberal beneath the forty-ninth parallel), fastened with interesting insistence on one of the most polemical Whigs of the nineteenth century, Thomas Babington Macaulay, as if this author's harsh criticism of Johnson in the early nineteenth century represented the whole history of attitudes about Johnson before 1960. Evidently, as an early progenitor of a Whig, "progressivist," and "liberal" tradition favored in late twentieth-century humanities, Macaulay's hatred of Johnson was particularly galling. He had to be proved wrong, or rather, Johnson had to be refashioned into the kind of "egalitarian" liberal, a hater of kings and advocate of "democracy," that Macaulay *should* have liked.[4]

As often in modern scholarship, however, this response is significant for what it ignores or hardly notices at the edge of the canvas. Some of Macaulay's harshest words against Johnson as an archetype of Tory "prejudice" and regression were delivered in a review of an 1831 edition of Boswell's *Life of Johnson* by Macaulay's most hated political adversary, John Wilson Croker. Croker was the Tory politician who coined the very term "conservative" to name his revived party and its political philosophy.[5] And it was certainly Croker's warm admiration for Johnson as one of the principal forerunners of conservative thought, not Macaulay's Whiggish disdain, that resonated throughout the Victorian period that followed. The admiration for Johnson among professed Tories such as Scott, Disraeli, and Kipling was summarized by Christopher Hollis in 1929: "Everything that we admire in Toryism we have crowded on to Johnson, the Tory."[6] In the view of these admirers, Johnson's benign version of Toryism had very little to do with Jacobitism, a red herring that has recently misled Johnson scholarship.[7] What authors praised was rather a modern form of this philosophy whose origins I will explore: it designated a conservative acceptance of the social order from the perspective of an emergent middle class which believed that its interests were best protected by the maintenance of a traditional, though flexible, social order. It resisted neither change nor progress, which seemed as undeniable to Victorians as the howl of a passing locomotive, but rather the careless uprooting of English cultural institutions. It stood for English nationhood, which most Victorians believed, with good reason, that Johnson had articulated with great energy, and for the Empire, which to a surprising degree Johnson had strongly defended. This was the Toryism meant by a great historian of eighteenth-century thought and culture, Sir Leslie Stephen: "If some leant towards freethinking, the general tendency of the Johnson circle was harshly opposed to any revolutionary movement, and authors were satisfied with the creeds as with the institutions amid which they lived."[8] For Stephen and his contemporaries, Johnson's significance lay not so much in the originality or distinctiveness of his thought (though we shall encounter many elements of originality in his reflections) as in his considerable and lasting impact on the development of English culture. In the words of Thomas Carlyle, Johnson was a "great English soul,"[9] and the same sentiment was amplified at the beginning of the twentieth century by Thomas Seccombe, who lauded Johnson for exemplifying "a common English ideal."[10] Walter Raleigh put the same sentiments more dramatically: "he has almost become the tutelary genius of the English people. He embodies all that we admire in ourselves. When we pretend to laugh at our national character, we call it John Bull; when we wish to glorify it, we call it Samuel Johnson."[11]

How then did Johnson attain to this status as an embodiment of Englishness? To answer this question we need to consider him both as the product of important social forces in his time and as a figure who influenced how these forces were interpreted by his contemporaries and later readers. In other words, I will examine Johnson's life and work as taking part in a dialectic between material and ideological developments. First, with respect to his context in material history, some observations on the economic conditions of the eighteenth century might be usefully laid out as the backdrop to the following portrait. The eighteenth century, once regarded as characterized by economic and social stasis rather than change, has more recently been rediscovered as a time of historic development in its own right. The remarkable statistics that measure this change reveal a society adjusting to a significant increase in population, particularly as compared with population growth on the continent. Between 1550 and 1820, England's population grew by 280 percent, as compared to the growth of 50 to 80 percent experienced in France, Spain, Germany, Italy, and the Netherlands.[12] But the rise of population from about 5 to 9 million during Johnson's lifetime does not tell the full story, for this growth occurred largely in cities rather than the country, and in London more than any other city. The Age of Johnson marked, as Peter Borsay memorably expressed it, an "Urban Renaissance."[13] London almost doubled in size, becoming the first European city to reach a million inhabitants in the early nineteenth century, and the proportion of English people living in expanding provincial urban centers such as Birmingham, Bristol, and Leeds also grew dramatically. The urban sprawl in English society reflected changes in the structure of the economy. Long before the "industrial revolution" (which may in fact have been less of a "revolution" than was once assumed) more and more English workers were employed in manufacturing rather than agriculture, many driven from self-sufficiency and traditional rural lifestyles by accelerated enclosure after 1750. England was generating wealth at an unprecedented rate. The economic historian W.A. Cole has observed that "in the eighteenth century industrial output nearly quadrupled and home consumption roughly trebled, while exports increased more than sixfold."[14] This wealth was not being evenly distributed, for historians have discovered a widening gap between rich and poor. On the one hand, the enriched middle ranks experienced unprecedented access to "luxuries" of all kinds. Whether or not this actually constituted a "consumer revolution," as Neil McKendrick has controversially claimed,[15] we will see that endowments that had previously provided a reliable index to social rank (fine dress, a sword, a passable fluency in literary culture) became so widely distributed that eighteenth-century moralists experienced a sense of collapsing social order, of disintegrating relations between deference and service, leisure and work. Meanwhile, the lower ranks worked ever harder for diminishing real income, as Britain's wars pushed up the price of corn and helped to cultivate the seed-ground for radicalism in Johnson's later years.[16] Hence, the economic expansion of England was not without enormous social, political, and emotional costs. Although the nation rose between 1700 and 1800 from being a minor European power struggling with its identity to being a great imperial and industrial power, the intervening century of change was, as I will stress throughout the book, filled with anxiety and painful adjustments to a new social reality.

It is to this dynamic social reality that Johnson responded throughout his life in tremendous detail and with considerable force and complexity. Yet his career not only charts this process of change, but also helped to give "the making of modern England" meaning and direction – for his contemporaries were reacting not only to new material forces but also to how these forces were being represented and interpreted by writers and public figures. Hence, in examining Johnson's writings and conversation with regard to a series of key concepts – class, gender, political party, the public, nationhood, and empire – we will explore not only how this influential writer was *made* by the evolving social circumstances of his age but also how he helped to *construct* the meaning of what it was to be "English." And it is for this reason that Johnson's rise to the status of the "typical" Englishman offers an especially promising field of inquiry.

That I should start this book with the issue of "class" might surprise my reader as curiously retrograde. Although modern scholars have never analyzed Johnson at any length with regard to his place in the English social-class system, now might seem an odd time to start, as we have allegedly passed into a "post-Marxist" era. My point is not, however, that social class represents an eternal verity of political economy: it is rather a constructed category that Johnson himself helped to define. Rank and class stand at the head of any thorough understanding of Johnson's social orientation because he was so consistently sensitive to his own modest social origins, the rank-inspired prejudices of those around him, and his own fairly shaky claims to respectability. Such a view is of course a mile distant from the popular belief that Johnson was an "elitist" who dangled on aristocrats and the *jure divino* pieties of a passing era. The alternative reading I offer here portrays Johnson, first, as a typically upwardly mobile figure during an era that, recalling Raymond Williams, we might call the "Long Revolution" of the eighteenth century.[17] No less than the bourgeois ideologues who led the French Revolution, Johnson represented a social stratum, the incipient middle class, that was transforming the nation, though this insurgency was storming the halls of power through the press, the banks, and political institutions below the cabinet. They were appropriating the wealth of the old elite, and also its visible symbols of rank and privilege. By 1789, a now self-conscious middle class had indeed accumulated sufficient wealth and influence that it reacted with alarm to further pressure for change from below, adopting a predominantly conservative political and social stance. This was the stance taken with imposing firmness in the writings and popular image of Samuel Johnson. Johnson was, that is, as responsive to the social, political, and economic transformation of Georgian England as the most "progressive" Whig of the day. His reactions and solutions to change were simply different – more skeptical, more cautious, more balanced.

The skepticism is shown by Johnson's discomfort with radical and opposition appeals to the "public" or the "people." He typically insisted instead on the myriad and individualized motives of the eighteenth-century masses. Donald Greene was right to identify Johnson's "individualism,"[18] but this individualism did not make him a Whig or liberal, for it tended instead to strengthen his belief in the need for a vigorously legislating state. Here indeed Johnson represents a particular stream in the watershed of modern English conservatism that must be distinguished from that of his friend Edmund Burke, whatever sources these men had in common.[19] Burke's conservatism was founded on belief in national communities with common traditions and institutions, a vision that led him to reject important versions of pan-global human values. He argued that America must be respected as a society fostered under special social and political circumstances; he campaigned passionately against Warren Hastings's despotic and roughshod contempt for Indian customs; he hated the abstract universalism of French revolutionaries. Johnson was far less confident about the existence of "cultures" or "societies," or about the organic national evolution articulated by Burke. As a moralist, he tended to dismiss the capacity of "public spirit" to overwhelm personal aims, and this attitude evidently influenced his late reactions to the American Revolution and the investigation of Warren Hastings, Governor-General of Bengal. He insisted that the Americans were merely self-seeking, and should be brought to heel politically and militarily; he remained loyal to his friend Hastings even in the face of the serious charges raised not only by Burke, but by men whose careers in India Johnson had promoted. Far more than Burke, that is, Johnson came to uphold a highly practical rather than idealistic outlook on Britain's emerging empire, attitudes that would remain important and even predominant into the time of Disraeli's "New Imperialism."

On the issue of nationalism, similarly, Johnson profoundly distrusted the blanket labels so typical of modern political discourse. Johnson's resonant remark that "patriotism is the last resort of a scoundrel"[20] echoed the skepticism of a whole generation who had grimly witnessed Patriots betray their friends and beliefs for a share of power. Johnson himself had been a Patriot of a kind in his early career: I will link him politically in the 1730s and 1740s with the "Broad-bottomed" Patriotism led by Chesterfield and his literary circle, which included Johnson's friend Robert Dodsley, along with Lyttelton, Warburton, Akenside, Fielding, and others he remembered well in later life. This political affiliation may indeed have earned Johnson the contract for the dictionary, though he evidently became deeply disillusioned with Chesterfield and his circle by the time the *Dictionary* was published in 1755. He came to hate this group's snobbish condescension, its expectation of overweening gratitude from impoverished "men of merit" such as himself. In later years, he also disdained the increasingly militant nationalism of the lower-middle ranks, recoiling from "the howl of plebeian patriotism" (10:385)[21] which was the shrill legacy of the Patriot cause that he himself had supported during his first years in London. His rising suspicion of the tendency of patriotism to arouse misleading and violent passions is reflected as well by his skeptical reaction to Scottish patriotism, most famously during his trip to the Highlands in 1773.

The irony of Johnson's discomfort with patriotism is, of course, that he himself contributed so much to constructing the English national identity. His very trip to Scotland suggests his warming interest in ethnic identities, national customs, and the British past. Johnson, who had once seriously considered writing a history of the English hero King Alfred, spent his last years eagerly promoting antiquarian researches into Irish, Welsh, Scottish, and Anglo-Saxon history. But Johnson's nationalism did not rely on a mythology of the past. The "nationalism" he came finally to propound represents a combination of a strong belief in "progress" and "civilization" – important ideological features as well of his mature outlook on the British Empire – with a moderate, though very real, interest in ethnicity and national history. To this extent, indeed, Johnson contributed to the emerging ideology of a *British* nationalism, for his moderate and balanced understanding of nationhood was in fact eminently consistent with the pro-British cultural philosophy of the "moderate literati" of Edinburgh, especially Hume and Robertson, who did so much to articulate a national identity that could be shared by all the peoples of Great Britain. Nonetheless, as my title indicates, it is more useful to understand Johnson as "English" rather than "British," not only because he continued to think of himself as specifically English to the end of his life, but also because he had been shaped by peculiarly English cultural, political, and economic forces.

A second characteristic of Johnson's conservatism, as I have mentioned, is its *balance*, as demonstrated by his response to that overwhelming golden tide transforming all in its wake, capitalism. Johnson's contribution here was to provide a calm voice of reason and moderation, of stability and acceptance in the face of change, during a time when the social upheaval impelled by prosperity had filled many Britons with anxiety. Recent studies that portray commerce as an undisputed source of pride for the English, "a polite and commercial people," highlight only one side of the story, often obscuring the extent of popular consternation at the rise of luxury and greed.[22] The commercial class, whatever its acknowledged importance to the economy, was in many ways isolated, both ideologically and geographically, in the City of London and other centers of trade like Bristol and Birmingham. Johnson's own essays represent indeed a good example of a widespread suspicion among the gentry and professionals towards merchants and traders, who were frequently disparaged for debasing traditional values and upsetting the social order. Johnson often lamented the supplanting of traditional values by a preoccupation with money, becoming particularly concerned with the upward mobility and political pretensions of people near the bottom of the trading classes. "As we once had a rebellion of clowns," he wrote during the Wilkite agitations in 1770, "we have now an opposition of pedlars" (10:341). His anxieties about men devoted only to lucre, the golden idol that justified an unlimited range of moral transgressions, also strongly informs his reactions to Britain's colonial wars during his lifetime. We often find Johnson supporting a moral (even "glorious") empire over a mercantile empire, in this way anticipating the strongly moral hue of Victorian imperialism. Again, however, there is another side to this story. Johnson's sense of national "progress" was strongly linked with material and economic development, as made very clear by his reactions to the relative poverty of northern Scotland. Modern scholarship has rightly noted Johnson's defense of luxury in Boswell's *Life* as economically beneficial, a point of view also expressed at many points in his writings. I will argue, for example, that *Rasselas* (1759) can well be understood as a defense of "luxury" understood in a philosophical sense (as defined by Mandeville, most famously) as the pursuit of excess above bodily needs. Significantly, this work was written during a vigorous debate concerning the "effeminizing" consequences of luxury, as in John Brown's highly popular *Estimate of the Manners and Principles of the Times* (1757). Taken together, Johnson's work bridges the gap between those who extolled trade and those who decried the influence of commerce and consumerism.

Ambivalent reactions to commerce and luxury, as feminist scholars have shown, became inseparable from similarly divided and mobile attitudes towards women. Commerce had given middle-rank women a new, even "masculine" agency and subjectivity as consumers, while allegedly debasing men into "effeminate" hedonists. But to recognize the seriousness of this concern among English authors might also lead us to question, as I will in this book, the assumption in much feminist scholarship that women were increasingly driven from active participation in the economy and into the shades of "domesticity." This thesis, which is often linked to a conviction in some preceding "Golden Age" for women, has been recently challenged and Johnson's career makes this challenge all the more compelling. It is well known that Johnson advanced the careers of women authors, and that his life was filled with intellectual acquaintances with women such as Elizabeth Carter, Charlotte Lennox, Hannah More, and many others whom he knew through his *public* life as a writer and man of society. Like so many of his contemporaries, male and female, he regarded his century as a time of remarkable achievement for women, a feminine "coming out" into the literary, social, and even political life of the nation. That he also upheld what we now consider regressive views concerning women's sexual freedom or their role in the church represents a very general pattern in all his thought: Johnson often strikes us as deeply resistant to "progress" at those points where he wished not to stop but to slow and limit the revolutionary pace of change. In later life, his foot pressed ever harder on the brake opposed to social transformation – a pattern of deepening conservatism nicely mapped by Robert DeMaria.[23] But the overall drift of his career, on issues of gender as on other issues, was towards the management of change rather than its extinction.

In summary, the purpose of this study is to reposition Johnson firmly back in the English culture of his own lifetime. It might well be said that my argument is "revisionist," for I will underscore the importance of Johnson's impact on English people of the Romantic and Victorian eras, whose perspectives on Johnson I consider extremely significant. On the other hand, my approach is not intended to confine Johnson's relevance to the past. To return to Eyre Crowe's portrait of Johnson that begins this book: Johnson was among the chief figures in Georgian England who made sense of the swirling and amorphous canvas of English culture, giving literary and ideological shape to the experience of life in his day. In this way, he took part in a dialectical process through which the social-economic "facts" of his time gave rise to certain interpretations of that experience that were themselves by no means necessary or pre-determined, and which helped to generate new material changes (through, for example, political and economic reactions and strategies) in an unfolding legacy of value-creation that extends even to our own time. This is why it is self-deluding to measure Johnson against what we consider "politically correct": at least in the Anglo-American tradition, our own values and forms of interpretation derive from the same process of material and ideological change that Johnson took part in and influenced. Our judgments of Johnson will therefore always be, to some extent, circular, for we judge him by criteria that he helped to create. To appreciate this circularity, I suggest, is to experience the historically situated Johnson as still alive among us.

CHAPTER I

From "rank" to "class": the changing structures of social hierarchy

JOHNSON AND THE FORMATION OF THE "MIDDLE CLASS"

Georgian England has presented serious problems for modern social historians who wish to understand its systems of social privilege and status. These difficulties have been perhaps particularly unsettling for scholars loyal to the historiographic tradition of Karl Marx, for a rigid division between three classes – aristocracy, bourgeoisie, working class – can hardly do justice to the subtle and changing gradations of eighteenth-century English society. Beneath the 160 or so officially "noble" families in England lay the subtly graded expanse of the "middling orders," stretching from the great City merchants to the artisans and shop-keepers whose feelings of political exclusion fueled the Wilkite protests of the 1760s. Wilkes had little interest in liberating the poor and lower orders who, as E.P. Thompson acknowledged, themselves seemed more intent on protecting the comforts they enjoyed under the old system of manor and tenant than protesting against the harsh new realities of enclosure in the country and exploitation in the city.[1] It was only after about 1780, with the advent of industrialism and later the panic sown by the French Revolution, that we can speak adequately of an English "class" system.[2] For it was only then that English people themselves began to speak and write a language of "class," consciously identifying themselves with causes, publications, and organizations formed on behalf of the upper, middle or lower classes.

Samuel Johnson, therefore, belongs to the prehistory of "class," a time that can at best be seen as an age in transition towards the class consciousness that begins to materialize near the end of the century. Indeed, his own *Dictionary* (1755) indicates how society was categorized throughout most of the eighteenth century. Johnson's only relevant definition of "class," "a rank or order of persons," is illustrated not by a reference to the social order, but to types of readers: "Segrais has distinguished the readers of poetry, according to their capacity of judging, into three *classes*." The most socially relevant definition seems to be "degree," which designates "Quality; rank; station; place of dignity." Notable here is that Johnson does not seem to be thinking primarily of economic categories: "dignity" seems totally abstracted from wealth or function in the economy, and to describe what Peter Laslett has called "social status" derived mostly from one's heredity or profession.[3]

To most historians, indeed, Johnson has seemed very much an artifact of this passing world of privilege and rank, even, as recently claimed, an advocate of a social hierarchy inscribed in the "Great Chain of Being."[4] Even among some good social historians, Johnson plays the walk-on part of truculent villain, the pompous defender of a system of social elitism, the eminently quotable adversary of all that is progressive and liberating in class history.[5] A main claim of the following chapter is that this portrait is profoundly unfair and based on little evidence. I will present Johnson as a far more complex, significant, and even forward-looking figure than historians have generally acknowledged. He certainly recognized that he belonged to a society that was being revolutionized by trade and commerce: this was a process that he accepted, and even welcomed in many respects. A man of modest origins who had benefitted from a changing order, he knew that social status and privilege were increasingly based on wealth rather than birth, a process that was at once liberating and potentially disruptive, as demonstrated by the Wilkite agitations of the 1760s and 70s. In the face of these changes, Johnson's most significant effort was to define the values and social role of what later became known as the "middle class," the stratum of professionals, writers, and men of commerce distinct from both the nobility and upper gentry above and the lower orders below.

In examining Johnson's role in this process, I will avoid the misleading and anachronistic model of the "rise of the middle class."[6] A "class" cannot "rise," obviously, if it does not yet exist, and what eighteenth-century people called "the middling orders" were internally divided by income, social function, birth, and innumerable other factors.[7] Even less satisfactory is the favorite Marxist term "bourgeois," an official rank division in France, where rigid social stratification finally exploded under the pressure of economic change. The same explosion did not occur in England because here there was an important measure of flexibility in the language and symbols of social status, particularly at the hotly contested zone traditionally dividing the nobility from the commonality – the rank of the "gentleman." In what I suggest was a slow-burning "revolution" in English society, a whole new mass of men – including Johnson's father and his early employer Edward Cave – claimed this status without the previously necessary advantages of birth or substantial property. From this gradual reclassification of the social order, facilitated by the general enrichment of the upper and middle orders, we can trace the later emergence of a self-conscious middle class.

Johnson's work helped to consolidate two main features of this reconfiguration. First, he made clear that the advantages of birth had become subordinate to the power and dignity of wealth. Second, he promoted an ideal of learning and virtue that, while derived from the older model of the "gentleman," came to characterize a new understanding of middle-class respectability. As I will go on to emphasize with relation to Johnson's *Dictionary*, it is indeed quite deceiving to identify this writer with the ruling class *tout court*, for he came to embody values of an English middle class that was self-consciously distinct from the nobility and upper classes, but which, at least among the majority of its members, ultimately believed that its own and the nation's interests were best protected by excluding the lower classes from political power.

The Marxist division of society into three ranks has, in fact, a long intellectual pedigree, and was developed in the nineteenth century on the basis of older and more traditional divisions. In 1707, Guy Miège rehearsed a conventional division of the people into "*Nobility*, *Gentry*, and *Commonality*."[8] And this ranking was also repeated almost half a century later by Henry Fielding in his *Enquiry into the Causes of the Late Increase of Robbers* (1752): "One known Division of the People of this Nation is into the Nobility, the Gentry, and the Commonality."[9] Neither Miège nor Fielding assumed that these three groups were based on wealth; wealth represented, traditionally, only an outward *sign* of a rank founded principally on heredity, education, and social function. By Fielding's time, however, the influx of wealth into the nation through trade had begun seriously to challenge this form of social classification, throwing into doubt the adequacy of the old divisions. As Fielding observed, "nothing has wrought such an Alteration in this Order of People, as the Introduction of Trade. This hath indeed given a new Face to the Whole Nation, [and] hath in a great measure subverted the former State of Affairs."[10] The major changes were occurring not at the top or the bottom, but at the middle of the social hierarchy. Interestingly, Fielding had trouble articulating this phenomenon: while he signals awareness of what he calls "the middle Rank,"[11] he generally lumps this ill-defined middling group into the "commonality." Hence, while noticing anxiously that society had begun to reconfigure itself along lines based on wealth rather than birth, he remained conceptually dependent on old categories founded on hereditary rank. Himself a legitimate "gentleman" by birth, particularly by virtue of noble blood on his father's side, Fielding was deeply discomforted by the recognition that this old criterion for gentility was being widely challenged by men who claimed to be "gentlemen" not by birth, but on the basis of wealth and "luxury." In Fielding's view, this disruption, fomented by "trade," had corrupted the whole social hierarchy: "while the Nobleman will emulate the Grandeur of a Prince; and the Gentleman will aspire to the proper State of the Nobleman; the Tradesman steps from behind his Counter into the vacant Place of the Gentleman. Nor doth the Confusion end here: It reaches the very Dregs of the People, who [aspire] still to a Degree beyond that which belongs to them."[12]

What was threatened by this "Confusion" was a social order largely taken for granted a century before. Works of the early seventeenth century reject wealth as a foundation for gentility, depicting trade as inherently vulgar and degrading.[13] The "gentleman," as William Higford put it, was a "minor" nobleman,[14] and should be educated to fill a post of leadership and to act as the exemplar of the highest accomplishments and virtues. For this reason, the mere pursuit of money was beneath his dignity, for the gentleman must have a refined and elevated soul, cleansed of "*selfe-love*, or *self-gaine*."[15] As Henry Peachum observed in *The Compleat Gentleman* (1634), "the exercise of Merchandize hath beene . . . accounted base, and much derogating from Nobility."[16] Opposing a practice already started, the purchasing of coats-of-arms, most writers insisted angrily that the right to wear a sword, symbol of the gentleman's continuing role as defender of the nation's glory, could only be bestowed by the King. The rejection of trade and commerce as sources of gentility reflects, as well, the conviction that intellectual labour was inherently superior to work performed with the hands. Professionals like lawyers and doctors could make some claim to the status of "gentlemen" by virtue of their superior learning, but those enriched by "Machanicall Arts and Artists, whosoever labour for their livelihood or gaine, have no share at all in Nobility or Gentry."[17]

In the era after the Civil Wars, however, tracts on the gentleman are characterized by a profound change of tone, particularly an irreverent hostility against the upper ranks in general. There are several explanations for this tone of indignation. For many, the Civil Wars marked the failure of the nobility and gentry to fulfil their allotted roles as guardians and exemplars of the nation. Exiled gentlemen who had supported Charles I, such as John Evelyn, expressed profound dismay with the alleged vulgarity and passivity of the gentry that remained in England under Cromwell.[18] Puritanism, moreover, had left its mark, stiffening popular disgust with the idleness and decadence of the upper ranks, a glaring feature of the Restoration court. "Idleness is become the badge, as it were, or distinguishing mark of

Gentility," complained William Ramsey in *The Gentleman's Companion* (1672), and he went on to denounce the gentry for excelling in consumption of drink rather than virtue or arms.[19] This attack on the morals of gentlemen was not, however, exclusively "Puritan." The English Jesuit William Darrell declaimed similarly against the idleness and corruption of the gentry and nobility in *A Gentleman Instructed* (1704), observing bitterly that "many who hang at Tyburn, are often less Criminal, than some of those who stand Spectators of the Tragedy, or perchance who sate on the Bench."[20]

From this kind of complaint arose the preoccupation with social inversion so typical of popular works of the early eighteenth century such as Gay's *The Beggar's Opera* (1728). Gentlemen had become criminals; criminals had become gentlemen. In the context of this disillusionment, the increasingly wealthy community of merchants and traders could make a strong case that they were wrongly disparaged, and that they were just as qualified to claim the title of "gentleman" as those idle and drunken coxcombs who claimed superiority by birth. Defoe hated "the numerous party of old women (whether male or female)," who thought that birth should be considered more important than the intrinsic attributes of gentlemen, as celebrated in handbooks of genteel behavior.[21] As Defoe complained, these traditional "gentlemen" by birth were failing to fulfil their true role as social exemplars, a function much better performed by virtuous, learned, and wealthy men of mean birth: "The son of a mean person furnish'd from Heaven with an original fund of wealth, wit, sence, courage, virtue, and good humour, and set apart by a liberal education for the service of his country . . . shews himself to be an accomplish'd gentleman, in every requisite article, that of birth and blood excepted."[22] This statement contains a challenge far more radical than might at first appear. Anticipating the much later language of "class," Defoe was reimagining social hierarchy as based on money rather than rank, wondering, in privately underscored lines, whether mere wealth "*may at the Bottom be the essence of that Distinction*" between the gentleman and the mere commoner.[23]

Nevertheless, Defoe's reflections on the "gentleman" also contain significant and revealing ambiguities. If, on the one hand, he wished to redefine this status in economic terms, on the other he clearly coveted the honors and insignia attached to the hereditary gentry. "I am resolv'd . . . to give antiquity its due homage;" he wrote, "I shall worship the image call'd antient lineage as much as possible without idolatry."[24] The ideal of ancient dignity and inherited honor clearly attracted a man who appended the elegantly Norman "De" to his family name of "Foe." As we will see, this ambiguity persisted right through the evolution of the "gentleman" and its later permutation, the middle class. The goal of the commercial middle class seemed, in many respects, to gain entrance into the traditional dignities of the gentry – to become, in effect, indistinguishable from the traditional elite. Yet it is doubtful that a full integration of the old and emergent elite ever occurred to the extent that Defoe liked sometimes to imagine, for the merchants and tradesmen, beginning with Defoe himself, developed pragmatic values antagonistic to the effete standards of the traditional gentry. As a result, the middle class emerged as an intensely conflicted group, socially and often politically divided between practical men of business and the professional or literary community represented by Samuel Johnson. Yet this band of English society, divided in values and manners, found common economic and political cause in opposing the agitations of the lower class and in their shared sense of separation from the traditional nobility.

This is not to deny that Georgian England *did* experience a historic transition in social standards that removed much of the stigma traditionally associated with self-interest and the pursuit of profit.[25] In 1674, Edmund Bolton complained harshly that, according to popular conceptions, "apprenticeship extinguisheth gentry" – that is, the children of gentlemen who went into trade were so sullied by its dishonor that they lost their genteel status.[26] Yet, to read Guy Miège's account of the gentleman in 1707, one would think that merchants and traders had quickly overcome this barrier to acceptance by the gentry. "Formerly Trading degraded a Gentleman," he observed, "but now a thriving Tradesman becomes a Gentleman by the happy Returns of his Trade, and Encrease of his Estate." Miège's work suggests that the title "gentleman" had come to describe not birth but rather merely "good Garb, genteel Air, or good Education," largely *outward* qualities rather than the disinterestedness and elevation of soul demanded by the traditional ideal.[27] And indeed conduct books of the early eighteenth century aimed at newly prosperous merchants and traders suggest similarly that gentility referred to how one looked and behaved, not to one's pedigree or even one's learning and virtue. A late work in this genre, John Constable's *The Conversation of Gentlemen* (1738), echoed the common advice that it was in fact highly impolite for a gentleman to refer to his "Advantage of a Family."[28] It was also rude to speak Latin, dispute academic points, or display the kind of learning traditionally given to gentlemen: this behavior was "pedantry," and broke the cardinal rule of merely blending in with the crowd of fashionable men distinguished by an elegant air and witty conversation.[29] As the distinguished settings of Constable's dialogue imply (formal gardens, drawing rooms), wealth remained a prerequisite for the gentleman, for only the wealthy could afford the pleasures and estates that defined a genteel life. Otherwise, however, the aim of Constable's book and others like it was to create a new ruling class that seamlessly melded the landed and monied elite through the medium of wealth and common manners.

That such a ruling class was forming in reality is evidenced, as social historians have noted, by the rising frequency of inter-marriage between the landed gentry and prosperous families in business.[30] Marrying into mercantile wealth was an attractive way to repair the damaged fortunes of the nobility. And it also became usual for the younger sons of noblemen to embark on a career in the City. This inter-penetration of the gentry and wealthy merchant community was increasingly regarded, indeed, as one of the distinguishing characteristics of English life. One of the most astute observers of British society at mid-century, Josiah Tucker, contrasted the rigid separation of the nobility and merchants in France with the mingling of these orders in England. In France, there were officially three "different Ranks, or Orders; The *Noblesse*, the *Bourgeois* [*sic*], and the *Païsans*"; trade was considered a disgrace, and bourgeois who bought their way into the nobility left the counting-house behind as quickly as possible.[31] In England, by contrast, "the Profession of a *Merchant* is esteemed full as *honourable* as that of an *Officer*. And no man need leave off Trade, when he finds himself rich, in order to be respected as a Gentleman."[32]

Yet there are also indications that the political and economic marriage between the gentry and the merchant community was not quite so peaceable and loving as Tucker and others suggested. Indeed, even Tucker would argue in a later work that only the *landed* classes could be trusted to keep the nation's general interest foremost in their thoughts; as important as it was to the economy, the monied classes could not be relied on in political decisions about, for example, the war with America.[33] Moreover, as the merchant community grew in wealth and power, it increasingly moved away from the ideals of behavior and manners inherited from the gentry. Consider the developing theory and practice of education during the eighteenth century: a marked trend in education was the decline of the classical grammar school, the institution established in the English Renaissance to train the aristocracy and gentry. Increasingly, rich merchants and tradesmen questioned the value of sending their sons to school to learn Latin, Greek, and classical poetry. They wanted their heirs to learn to count, to write clear English with a good hand, and to know enough of geography, history, and politics to compete economically on both the national and world stages. Hence, the number of schools designed for non-classical education multiplied by two-and-half times during the eighteenth century. The classics in general suffered a serious decline in English schools until the nineteenth century.[34] The following rhetorical questions posed in James Barclay's *A Treatise of Education* (1743) echo widely expressed attitudes in educational treatises of Johnson's era:

> The merchant, after five or six years study, hath he neither time or [*sic*] inclination to enjoy the reward of his labours in a narrow review of the classicks? Would he not rather wish so many leisure-hours had been employed in a greater practice of writing and arithmetick, the knowledge of history, antiquity, geography, the several branches of trade, and other things which are often the subject of conversation?[35]

This trend in education was also reflected in the century's book-market and press, as evidenced by *The Gentleman, Tradesman, and Traveller's Pocket Library* (1753). Written by "a Gentleman of the Bank of *England*," and published by the book-selling entrepreneur John Newberry, this one-volume encyclopedia gives a very different impression of what is expected of a "gentleman" than we find in the writings of Ramsey, Darrell, or even an older generation of "gentleman-merchants" like Defoe: its contents are entirely confined to practical, political, and commercial subjects – "a Short System of Geography," "the Political History of Europe," a "History and Rationale of the Stocks or Public Funds." There is not a hint of classicism in this book, and it reveals no interest in emulating the life and manners of the nobility or gentry.

It was during this age of transition in English society that Samuel Johnson emerged from relative obscurity as a teacher and later a journalist for *The Gentleman's Magazine* to become one of the great arbiters of taste and morals in the age. The collected *Rambler* essays, as Paul Korshin has noted, reached twenty editions by the end of the century;[36] they would continue to be standard reading for middle-class people throughout the nineteenth century. As we have already considered, moreover, Johnson would come virtually to epitomize the blunt common sense of the conservative bourgeois Englishman, a "John Bull" figure who helped to define a middle-class sensibility. How then did Johnson react and contribute to the evolution of the social values that I have described?

To tackle this question is to confront directly the paradoxes and tensions that we have considered in the transition from "rank" to "class." On the one hand, Johnson often seems to deserve his reputation among many modern historians as the truculent defender of the old order, "an enthusiastic supporter," as a recent historian writes, "of rank and hierarchy."[37] This impression cannot be ascribed, as has been sometimes suggested, merely to the biased portrait of Johnson by the elitist Boswell. Johnson's repeated advocacy of "subordination" in the *Life* is, if anything, *less* passionately conservative than the furious attacks on "low-born railers" and "the desire of levelling" (10:341–2) that fill his political writings of the same era. This impression is also corroborated by Johnson's ardent classicism, which reveals his self-conscious loyalty to the tradition of the Renaissance grammar school for "gentlemen." In starting his school at Edial, near Lichfield, in early 1736, he defied the overwhelming educational trend of his era towards non-classical schools profiting from merchants and tradesmen. Here is the advertisement that he placed in *The Gentleman's Magazine* in June 1736: "AT EDIAL, near *Lichfield* in *Staffordshire*, Young Gentlemen are Boarded, and Taught the *Latin* and *Greek* Language, by SAMUEL JOHNSON."[38] His plan of education was not quite so conservative as this advertisement suggests: a careful examination of his handwritten "Scheme for the Classes of a Grammar School," reproduced by Boswell, suggests that he generally followed the revised classical curriculum outlined by a moderate reformer of education, John Clarke.[39] It is hardly surprising, however, that Johnson's effort to buck the educational trends of his age failed, and his school was abandoned after less than a year. Even this failure did not lessen Johnson's loyalty to the classical grammar school, for he never gave more than qualified and lukewarm support for the new schools that reduced or eliminated the classics. As he said of a school established by Johnson's friend and admirer James Elphinston, "I would not put a boy to him, whom I intended for a man of learning. But for the sons of citizens, who are to learn a little, get good morals, and then go to trade, he may do very well."[40]

Striking and typical in this statement is Johnson's willingness to give "gentlemen" and "tradesmen" different kinds of education, and to treat them as essentially different groups. Johnson by no means opposed a practical education for merchants and tradesman, and indeed showed a personal interest in the world of business. Yet Johnson's essays show considerable scorn for merchants and tradesmen who, in the tradition of Defoe, attempt to emulate the fashions and manners of the gentry. A typical example is Misocapelus in *Rambler* No. 123, who makes a fortune as a haberdasher, but is mortified to discover that his conversation is scorned by gentlemen. In an attempt to gain the respect due to rank, Misocapelus dresses in high fashion and attempts to join the literary talk at genteel coffee-houses – but all for nought, as he is always "detected in trade" and ridiculed as "Tape the critick" (4:293–4). The *Idler* is filled with satiric sketches of tradesmen who attempt to behave like gentlemen, such as Sam Softly the wealthy sugar-baker, who buys a splendid chaise, fine clothes and tours fashionable estates. In Johnson's eyes, the punishment for Sam's vanity is utter absurdity: "Misapplied genius most commonly proves ridiculous. Had Sam, as nature intended, contentedly continued in the calmer and less conspicuous pursuits of sugar-baking, he might have been a respectable and useful character" (2:289). And the same absurd incongruity of status and pretension characterizes a gallery of figures in the *Idler* – Tim Ranger, Dick Shifter, Dick Minim – all tradesmen who in their various ways have "turned gentlemen" (2:287).

These essays suggest a determined effort to make a clear separation between mere wealth and the knowledge and conduct required of the "gentleman." Nonetheless, we are on thin ice in assuming that he wished merely to reinforce an old system of social hierarchy, for this assumption seems, indeed, entirely inconsistent with his own background and conduct. As Johnson's early biographers often noted, Johnson's father signed himself "Michael Johnson, gent." in the registry of his eldest son's baptism at St. Mary's Church, Lichfield.[41] Michael's pretension to the title of "gentleman" could be partly justified by his status as sheriff of Lichfield, and by his modest prestige as a (still) prosperous book-seller (traditionally considered the most "genteel" of trades on account of its demand for some learning).[42] In 1709, however, calling oneself a gentleman was a daring and even defiant act by a man of such lowly birth as Michael, the son of a field-laborer. In other words, Johnson's own father is a good example of the kind of ambitious, lower-order man who was challenging the old hierarchical divisions. This fact was not lost on the effete Boswell, son of a Scotch laird. "The truth is," he sniffed, "that the appellation Gentleman, though now lost in the indiscriminate assumption of *Esquire*, was commonly taken by those who could not boast of gentility."[43] Yet Boswell's own subject seems to have harbored some of his father's pretensions, an interesting possibility tucked away in a note appended by the biographer to his record of Johnson's doctoral diploma:

> I once observed on his table a letter directed to him with the addition of *Esquire*, and objected to it as being a designation inferiour to that of Doctor; but he checked me, and seemed pleased with it, because, as I conjectured, he liked to be sometimes taken out of the class of literary men, and to be merely *genteel*, – *un gentilhomme comme un autre*.[44]

The famous "Doctor Johnson," it would seem, actually preferred to be called "Samuel Johnson, *Esquire*." And in this respect he resembled both his upwardly mobile father and another new-style gentleman, the man who gave Johnson his break into the London literary scene, Edward Cave, editor of *The Gentleman's Magazine*. *The Gentleman's Magazine* was, indeed, the literary vanguard of the defiant new concept of the gentleman as a man not of birth but of knowledge and civilized manners. Its eclectic contents mirror a readership of men (and even women, who were employed by Cave) with an appetite for a vast range of subjects from politics to natural science, geography to history, literary criticism to the occasional Latin poem. Nor is commerce entirely omitted from the subjects of this journal, though "getting money" evidently played only a secondary role in this new ideal. As for Cave himself, he epitomized the middle-class gentleman who was challenging the domination of this status by the old landed gentry. As described in Johnson's warm biography of Cave, he was a self-made man who, rather like Johnson, spent much of his early life struggling for a career. In his early days as a printer's apprentice he stood clearly as an advocate for the underdog, "a tenacious maintainer though not a clamorous demander, of his right."[45] The same insistence on his "right" evidently inspired the determination of this ambitious but socially graceless man to link his name closely with a new idea of the gentleman. He even designed a coat-of-arms for himself (showing his offices at St. John's Gate), which he displayed on the door of his newly purchased carriage.[46]

Unlike Cave, Johnson himself did not affect the trappings or manners of gentility, a practice he satirizes in his essays. Yet his essays often express considerable contempt for the traditional nobility and gentry. A large number of his periodical essays are devoted wholly or in part to attacks on the ignorance, vanity, hedonism, and uselessness of the upper classes. In *Rambler* No. 39, he portrays "Cotylus, the younger brother of a duke, a man without elegance of mien, beauty of person, or force of understanding" (3:215). *Rambler* No. 132 describes the vain efforts of a tutor to educate a young nobleman to become "a wise and useful counsellor to the state" (4:337): spoiled and pampered by his mother, the tutor's charge instead becomes an idle rogue who knows nothing but "the rules of visiting," and "the names and faces of persons of rank" (*Rambler* No. 194, 5:249). The fashionable lady Peggy Heartless, in *Idler* No. 86, summarizes much that Johnson evidently thought about the polite inhabitants of Westminster: "Our fortune is large, our minds are vacant, our dispositions gay, our acquaintance numerous, and our relations splendid" (2:267). In his scathing portraits of upper-class mindlessness and triviality, Johnson seems to echo the satire of the traditional elite which characterized the conduct books of Ramsey, Darrell, Defoe, and others who promoted access to the privileges previously confined to those of proper birth.

Johnson belonged, that is, not merely to a genteel "elite," but to an emergent middle-class "push" into the lower levels of the gentry. "Middle-class" seems, indeed, *almost* the appropriate term, for men like Michael and Samuel Johnson or Edward Cave were carving out an identity based on knowledge, virtue, and financial independence, a social status that cannot be conflated with the values and expectations of the nobility or traditional gentry. We must also keep in mind, however, that members of the new middle class were fond, to varying degrees, of emulating the fashions and traditions of the elite: to a large degree, the gentry continued to furnish the models of "symbolic capital," Pierre Bourdieu's useful term for the currency of social prestige only indirectly related to economic status and advancement.[47] Johnson the teacher, as we have seen, remained loyal to the traditional gentleman's education, and often reacted with scorn to the awkward efforts of merchants and tradesmen to emulate the gentry. Hence, in examining this era of social transition, we inevitably confront the paradoxes exemplified by Johnson, a man who can seem alternately the social "rebel" described by Donald Greene and, especially later in life, a vocal ally of the traditional hierarchy crowned by the nobility and gentry. How can we explain these apparent contradictions?

What does seem certain is that Johnson was no believer in a "natural" hierarchy inscribed in the "Great Chain of Being." That he adhered to such a doctrine has, indeed, been widely affirmed by historians who apparently know little of his thought except what they have gathered from a shallow reading of Boswell's *Life of Johnson*. To link Johnson with the Chain of Being is indeed astonishing, for this was the writer whose review of Soame Jenyns's *Free Inquiry into the Nature and Origin of Evil* (1757) represents the century's most powerful attack on the logical and religious soundness of this very doctrine. Among other concerns in this review, Johnson excoriates Jenyns's glib and self-serving assumption that God had wisely allotted the poor a fixed place at the bottom of the scale of social rank, a disadvantage allegedly compensated by the ignorance of the poor about what they were missing. As Johnson objected, however, "to entail irreversible poverty upon generation after generation, only because the ancestor happened to be poor, is, in itself cruel, if not unjust." Such a restriction on social movement would, in any event, contradict "the maxims of a commercial nation, which always suppose and promote a rotation of property, and offer every individual a chance of mending his condition by his diligence."[48]

This is only one of many places in Johnson's writing and conversation where, despite his snipes at merchants and tradesmen, he recognizes the liberating and civilizing impact of commerce on society. During his travels with Boswell in the Scottish Highlands, for example, he often welcomed the first incursion of commerce into a feudal society that he disdained, in some important respects, as backward and barbaric: he complains about the drafty buildings, the miserable huts and even the lack of shops on the Isle of Skye. Yet his reactions to this living process of historical change were not simple. It is significant that the transition from a society based on hereditary rank to one that respected only wealth left him with divided emotions:

> When the power of birth and station ceases, no hope remains but from the prevalence of money. Power and wealth supply the place of each other. Power confers the ability of gratifying our desire without the consent of others. Wealth enables us to obtain the consent of others to our gratification. Power, simply considered, whatever it confers on one, must take from another. Wealth enables its owner to give to others, by taking only from himself. Power pleases the violent and the proud; wealth delights the placid and the timorous. Youth therefore flies at power, and age grovels after riches. (9:94)

This is a generally balanced analysis of the phenomenon that a Marxist historian might call the early stages of capitalism in a feudal economy: whereas most of the passage seems to favour the benefits of "wealth" over "power," the final reference to "age" groveling after riches is hardly uplifting. This ambiguity reveals Johnson's conflicting emotions at the loss and gain entailed by the historical process driven by commerce. On the one hand, he was certainly no indiscriminate admirer of the feudal charm of the Highlands, which he often compares unfavorably with the modernity and convenience of modern England. As I will argue at length in a later chapter on Johnson's nationalism, however, historians have been quite wrong to conclude that he merely despised Highland culture, for he admitted, more than once, to feeling the tug of the old heroic spirit of the ancient clan: "To lose this spirit, is to lose what no small advantage will compensate" (9:91). What *A Journey to the Western Isles of Scotland* (1775) shows, in fact, is Johnson's conviction that the historical changes occurring in the Highlands and, at a later stage of development, in England and Lowland Scotland entailed social readjustments that were both irresistible and morally ambivalent. By no means did he think that some "natural" order of hereditary rank was being destroyed by the evils of wealth. Rather, he regarded the increasing authority of wealth at the expense of rank as a necessary part of the modernization of society.

In thus treating this change as an essentially historical phenomenon, Johnson was perfectly in step with the thought of contemporary thinkers like John Millar, whose *Observations concerning the Distinction of Ranks in Society* (1771) can be called, without much qualification, the first British work devoted primarily to the issue of social hierarchy and its history. That Millar's history should appear so late is an indication of how intellectuals of Johnson's time were awakening for the first time to "class" in ways that no longer took the traditional hierarchy for granted. A Lowland Scot who viewed the Highlands largely from the perspective of the British and Continental Enlightenment, Millar shared Johnson's ambivalent feelings about the passing of birth and family as the primary bases of authority and prestige. In past times, Millar argued, social prestige was bestowed for military heroism. This form of honor was not only, by its nature, an unstable and transient basis for social order, but also promoted various evils such as, particularly, the denigration of women and children – the alleged characteristic of "primitive" societies such as the indigenous cultures of America. Only wealth, principally in the stable form of land, could lend continuity to the social order, raising the importance and prestige of women, whose virtue ensured the proper transferal of properties and titles. Yet riches also create disruptions of a new kind. Millar finally riveted on the following paradox of his own times: traders and artisans, newly empowered by wealth, felt increasingly impatient with the authority of the hereditary monarch, whose power, in turn, had been augmented by his control of a standing army paid from public funds. In Millar's view, in short, contemporary society teetered precariously between two possible disasters, civil insurrection on the one side and regal tyranny on the other.

In these observations on the increasing dissatisfaction and restlessness of traders and shop-keepers, Millar's anxieties echo Johnson's of precisely the same period – the period, significantly, when Wilkes was inflaming the agitation of mobs consisting largely of precisely these groups. As Johnson wrote in *The False Alarm* (1770), "we once had a rebellion of clowns, we have now an opposition of the pedlars" (10:341). Such a remark may well strike us as very curious coming from a man who once helped his father peddle books in the markets of Uttoxeter and Derby. Yet, like Fielding, Johnson is concerned that the opportunities for social and political advancement made possible by trade were theoretically without limit: if his father or Edward Cave could claim the privileges of being "gentlemen" without the advantage of birth, why should the same claim be denied the well-to-do sugar-baker or mercer? Unlike Fielding, however, Johnson was not merely hanging on to the hereditary privileges of the past era. Himself the benefactor of a changing social order, Johnson evidently supported "subordination" and the maintenance of traditional rights as an essentially *arbitrary* curb on the disruptive effects of a commercial society, changes that he nonetheless regards as historically inevitable. It is this conviction in the need for traditional buffers against modern change, and *not* veneration for the upper classes or belief in a "natural" order, that informs his arguments for subordination in Boswell's *Life*. Respect for "old families," he said to Boswell, is only "a matter of opinion." Nevertheless,

> it is a matter of opinion, very necessary to keep society together. What is it but opinion, by which we have a respect for authority, that prevents us, who are the rabble, from rising up and pulling down you who are gentleman from your places, and saying "We will be gentlemen in our turn"? Now, Sir, what respect for authority is much more easily granted to a man whose father has had it, than to an upstart, and so Society is more easily supported.[49]

In Johnson's view, it is more easy to grant authority to inherited rank because it is *accidental* and, for this reason, not open to competition and envy. As he is recorded saying in Boswell's *London Journal*, the "fixed, invariable rules of distinction of rank . . . create no jealousy," for "they are allowed to be accidental."[50] It is significant that in the passage above Johnson speaks *not* as a "gentleman" but as a member of the "rabble" addressing Boswell, the "gentleman" by birth. In other words, he implicitly includes himself in the feelings of envy for mere "upstarts," an emotion that he consistently regarded as natural and inevitable to some degree. Living in what he recognized to be a time of profound social transformation, Johnson favored the maintenance of traditional hierarchy and the political authority of the upper gentry as means of controlling natural, yet profoundly unsettling, ambitions released by a commercial society.

In remaining loyal to some aspects of the older social system, however, Johnson aimed to do more than merely control the forces of change also described by Fielding and Millar. Johnson was also anxious about the general degradation of social manners caused by the worship of money. Johnson's opening paragraph in *Idler* No. 73, published in September 1759, may almost be taken as summarizing the major theme in his essays written in 1750s. "In a nation like ours, in which commerce has kindled an universal emulation of wealth . . . money receives all the honours which are the proper right of knowledge and virtue" (2:227). The same theme underlies the many stories in the *Rambler*, *Adventurer*, and *Idler* that follow a strikingly consistent pattern: men and women of respectable pedigree, but little money, wander with naive optimism into a society in which, finally, wealth counts far more than rank. In *Rambler* No. 12, Zosima, "the daughter of a country gentleman," is left penniless and must search for a job as a servant: her claims of genteel birth are consistently scorned by the rich women she approaches for employment: "Such gentlewomen!" exclaims "the great silk-mercer's lady," "people should set their children to good trades, and keep them off the parish . . . Pray, Mrs. gentlewoman, troop down stairs" (3:63–4). Constantius in *Rambler* No. 192 is "the son of a gentleman, whose ancestors, for many ages, held the first rank in the county" (5:239). Constantius is nonetheless left poor by the neglect and luxury of his predecessors, and is accepted as a suitor for the hand of Flavia only so long as it is believed that he will inherit a fortune from his uncle, a wealthy merchant. In these essays, Johnson paints a world where all values seem extinguished except greed for wealth. It is a world without, to cite one of his favorite words, "reverence" ("Veneration; respect; awful regard"). Time and again in his writings and conversation, Johnson laments decline of the "reverence" for the social institutions and religion that preserve peace and order. "He that encourages irreverence, in himself or others," he instructed in Sermon 24, "weakens all the human securities of peace, and all the corroborations of virtue" (14:259).[51]

This anxiety to deter the erosion of "reverence," of non-mercenary and disinterested values, helped to motivate Johnson's continuing and loyal support for classical learning and the traditional education of gentlemen. Indeed, it is hardly an exaggeration to claim that Johnson's *Rambler* essays are dedicated, above all, to the defence of traditional learning and virtues in a society that increasingly finds dignity and merit only in riches. To this extent, Johnson does sound very like an advocate for the values preached in seventeenth-century conduct books, with their disdain for avarice and their glorification of scholarship and military valour. As Johnson writes in *Rambler* No. 118, "The man whose whole wish is to accumulate money, has no other care than to collect interest, to estimate securities, and to enquire for mortgages." Among such narrow and ignorant men, "The adventures of valour, and the discoveries of science, will find a cold reception" (4:268). Against authors like John Constable, who advised his "gentlemen" to avoid any show of learning, and simply to conform with those around them, Johnson indignantly defends "pedantry," "a censure which every man incurs, who has at any time the misfortune to talk to those who cannot understand him" (*Rambler* No. 173, 5:151). And if he seems often a partisan of "polite" society, it is usually because he believes that, at least here, people still have some value for "wit," an accomplishment utterly contemptible to the man who "never had any other desire than to fill a chest with money" (*Rambler* No. 128, 4:318). For Johnson, however, this is more than just an issue of social manners or the protection of those learned achievements that he valued in himself. He repeatedly associates a failure of generosity, compassion, and social responsibility with a narrow obsession with money.

A good example is Squire Bluster in *Rambler* No. 142: descended from an "ancient family" that exhibited the traditional gentry virtues of benevolent care for their tenants and neighbors, Bluster is brought up by his grandmother, who teaches him to care only about saving and wealth. As the result, Bluster becomes a tyrant, indulging constantly "in a contentious and a spiteful vindication of the privileges of his manors, and a rigorous and relentless prosecution of every man that presumed to violate his game" (4:392). He comes to embody "the depravity of mind" characteristic of a mercantile age, becoming a man who "has birth without alliance, and influence without dignity" (4:393).

In these essays, Johnson may seem only an advocate for the passing values of the traditional gentry, a man vainly attempting to buttress society against a capitalist order that was threatening to engulf all of society. Yet Johnson was in fact more a man of the "future" than he is usually credited with being. Significantly, he was defending ideals that would be integral to the formation of a self-conscious middle class late in the century. During the last quarter of the century, there was an important resurgence of the belief that classical education was indispensable in the formation of the true gentleman. This resurgence was led not by the aristocracy or the very wealthy. Rather, the ideal of the traditional gentleman's education was expounded by educators of the middle ranks such as Vicesimus Knox, a writer of conduct books and master of Tunbridge School: "But I will venture to assert, that classical learning tends most directly to form the true gentleman . . . it is not a fashionable dress, nor a few external decencies of behaviour, which constitute the true gentleman. It is a liberal and an embellished mind."[52] The same ideal of "liberal education" was expounded by contemporaries of Knox such as James Beattie, Joseph Cornish, and Percival Stockdale.[53] This ideal of a liberal education was not meant to challenge or even emulate the upper classes. Intended for the children of the middling ranks, this education promoted the belief that mere practical training was insufficient, and that the child must be endowed with "a susceptible and feeling heart," "a fine imagination and acquaintance with the world,"[54] in order to fulfil his or her duties in society. This idea of education would lead to the historic revival of classical education in English public schools of the nineteenth century, and the widespread belief in the value of literary education that lasted until the end of the twentieth century.[55]

Even within the middle classes, this notion of education did not go unchallenged. The merchant community was never, as we have noted, completely at home with the genteel values traditionally associated with wealth and power. Near the end of the eighteenth century, City authors such as the surveyor William Stevenson were still insisting that "classical learning has no connection with the primary object of a good education: the knowledge of facts and habits of reasoning."[56] And this prejudice against the classics extended to *belles-lettres*, which seemed of little use to many practical people of business, as Johnson had observed. Stevenson's attitudes reveal a persistent fault line in the middle classes between the commercial and professional/literary communities. Particularly in the latter group, however, there was wide consensus that respect for the traditional manners and attributes of rank, including a heart and mind shaped by liberal education, constituted an essential and unifying basis for middle-class consciousness. The first author to use the term "middle-class" in any systematic way, Thomas Gisborne, was strongly critical of the narrowing influence of avarice on the community of merchants and traders. "Of all the professions which are in the hands of the higher and middle classes of society," he wrote, "none perhaps lead more directly to contracted ideas than those which consist in buying and selling, in casting up accounts, in calculating pecuniary risks and advantages, and in the uniform transactions of the counting-house and the shop." Gisborne then went on to expound the principles of a liberal education. "To guard the youth destined for such a situation from falling into the trammels of prejudice, and habituating himself to partial and confined views of things, it is peculiarly desirable that his mind should be cultivated, his faculties expanded, and his ideas taught to expatiate in a wide and ample range, by a liberal and learned education."[57]

It cannot be stressed too much that Gisborne's version of a traditional gentleman's education, based on the classics and *belles-lettres*, virtue and good manners, does not represent merely an adulation of the landed gentry or a nostalgia for a past order. His underlying assumption was rather that the political interests of the middle class were best preserved by the status quo. The nobility offered a buttress against the common threat of the "swinish multitude," as Burke infamously labeled the lower orders in *Reflections on the Late Revolution in France* (1790). Aristocratic tradition also provided a useful social example to preserve unity and coherence within the middle class itself, minting a common currency of symbolic capital that could be exchanged between merchants and the literary/professional community. Keeping the merchant community loyal was indeed a high priority during the 1790s, as their alienation was seen as a central source of the disruptions in France.

It is this sense that the most famous conservative document of this era, Burke's *Reflections*, also represents a signal document in the history of an

English middle-class revolution. For those familiar only with the *Reflections*, such a claim will probably seem obtuse or paradoxical: Burke's treatise is rightly famous for its aggressively revisionist celebration of inherited rank and monarchy over "upstart insolence" and "dealers in stocks and funds," the groups he blames for leading the uprising against the throne, nobility, and church in France.[58] Like other English writers of his era, however, Burke was most intent on showing that the interests of the middle class, that testy union of the commercial and professional/literary communities, were best preserved by accepting the existence of a strong and privileged nobility, guardians of taste, learning and virtue. Burke customarily positioned himself among the "middle sort of men . . . who, by the spirit of that middle station, are the fittest for preventing things from running to excess."[59] This "middling" perspective is visually invoked in some of the most memorable passages in this work. We will recall, for example, Burke's lyrical reminiscence of Marie Antoinette shining "just above the horizon, decorating and cheering the elevated sphere she just began to move in,"[60] a resonant passage written, not accidentally, from the perspective of someone in an audience looking *up* from "just" below the horizon. Indeed, "horizon" seems a quintessentially middle-class image, locating Burke's precisely at his familiar, lifelong position *below* the balcony of power, the untitled advocate for middle-order interests and opinions. No wonder Tom Paine was surprised that Burke had written the *Reflections*: further "left" than Johnson himself, Burke had been among a handful of MP's who had opposed Wilkes's expulsion from parliament in 1769. Yet even the *Reflections* is very much a defense of the middle-class revolution that had already taken place in England over a long period of time. Burke's historically compelling diagnosis of the cause of the French Revolution echoes the views of Josiah Tucker almost half a century before: France had not permitted the intermixing of the noble and commercial sectors that might have diffused the pressure that finally exploded in France:

> Those of the commons, who approached to or exceeded many of the nobility in point of wealth, were not fully admitted to the rank and estimation which wealth, in reason and good policy, ought to bestow in every country; though I think not equally with that of other nobility . . . This separation, as I have already taken the liberty of suggesting to you, I conceive to be one principal cause of the destruction of the old nobility.[61]

Burke echoes a highly liberal and even "Whiggish" opinion: the French nobility, like the English, should have relaxed its demand for high birth to accommodate the social and political aspirations of the *nouveaux riches*.

As so often in his later writing, Burke speaks as a "new man," someone who argues not to defend his own hereditary privilege, but as someone of the untitled ranks who believes in a traditional social order because it is *theoretically* in the national interest. The brogue of Burke the upstart Irishman can always be heard just beneath the surface of his impassioned and patriotic prose. While hardly obvious in the *Reflections*, the indignation of a man insulted for his undignified origins and lack of title burns throughout *Letter to a Noble Lord* (1796), a work that virtually defines a distinctively middle-class conservatism.

English middle-class consciousness, that is, was marked by its trust in the inherently stabilizing ballast of traditionally aristocratic manners and education in a society increasingly propelled by the headwind of commercial wealth. That the structure of this society was more and more founded on wealth, not birth, is implicit rather than obvious in Burke's *Reflections*, but this observation is front and center in other conservative works of the same era. Alarmed by the insurgence of *sans-culottes* in the French Revolution, middle-class authors of this era were anxious to find economic and political justifications for existing political and social inequalities, and the standard justification was not reliant on traditional ranking but rather *economics*. The lower classes were told that their own welfare depended on the prosperity of the upper and middle classes. This argument implied a vision of society dominated by the relations of employment and labour. As maintained by Sir Frederic M. Eden in *The State of the Poor: or, an History of the Labouring Classes in England* (1797), "it is not the possession of land, or of money, but the command of labour, which the various circumstances of society place more or less within their disposal, that distinguishes the opulent from the labouring part of the community."[62] In other words, people formed a single class as a result of their performing a particular kind of *work*. The same understanding of the social hierarchy characterizes a more famous book of the same era, Thomas Malthus's *An Essay on the Principle of Population, as it Affects the Future Improvement of Society* (1798). According to Malthus's chillingly utilitarian defense of the free market, the lower classes had to be kept poor and struggling, their weakest and most idle members culled by the competition for survival, in order to facilitate their utilization by the higher classes as a cheap and pliable corpus of labor. Attempts to erect a Utopian society based on abstract principles of compassion and justice, such as proposed by William Godwin, would ultimately settle back towards the natural and inevitable division of economic roles, "I mean, a society divided into a class of proprietors, and a class of labourers, and with self-love for the main-spring of the great machine."[63]

During the 1790s, in short, middle-class authors had begun to speak the unmistakable language of class. This is a language interested primarily in relations of wealth and labour rather than heritage and family, and its classic formulation in tracts of the 1790s was spurred most significantly by the anxiety of middle-class authors like Burke, Gisborne, and Malthus that social upheaval in France would spread like a plague across the Channel. As we have seen, however, the language of class was not merely a phenomenon of the 1790s, for it evolved throughout the eighteenth century. In this evolution, Johnson's writings and conversation represent a major, and influential, step towards a class-based understanding of English society and, in particular, the formulation of middle-class attitudes and values. Johnson himself had benefitted from a transformation of social standards, even a kind of slow "revolution" of the hierarchy. This change is signaled by the emergence of a new kind of gentleman qualified for this status not by birth but by social success, wealth, and education. Johnson's classicism and insistence on the dignity of scholarship and virtue, while it seemed "unfashionable" in the 1750s, became a particularly important ingredient in the emergent middle-class consciousness of the 1790s and after. In the late century the kind of learning championed by Johnson – what came to be known as "liberal education" – was widely recognized as the training that characterized the middle class, consolidating its vast range of incomes and employments through a common set of values. Johnson's writings confirm the dignity and independence of the middle class, insisting on the fundamentally intellectual nature of its social role, and distinguishing this function from the physical labor of the emergent working classes. In the decades after Johnson's death, as Dror Wahrman has shown, the ideology of middle-classness became increasingly conservative. By the time of the debate surrounding the Reform Bill of 1832, conservative politicians and writers were more determined than ever to distinguish the middle class from its supposed inferiors, whose radical spokespersons widely regarded the newly enfranchised levels of the population (including now more prosperous tradesmen and middling officials) as antagonistic to the political and social ambitions of the still disenfranchised groups below them (including not only the workers, but what we might now call "the lower-middle class" of shopkeepers, artisans, and so forth).[64] As argued in 1839 by that pre-eminent arbitress of middle-class values, Sarah Stickney Ellis, "a time seems to be approaching, when the middle-class of society in England will have to be subdivided; and when the lower portion of this class will of necessity have to turn their attention to a different style of living, and to different modes of occupation, thought, and feeling."[65] The question, that is, remained *where to draw the line* at the bottom of the middle class, the same issue that had preoccupied conservative authors like Johnson half a century before.

It is little wonder, therefore, that Johnson became a posthumous hero for proponents of an increasingly hegemonic conservatism. His support for "subordination," such a visible theme in the conversation recorded in Boswell's *Life* (1791), was perfectly in tune with the frightened reaction to the French Revolution in the upper and middle classes and with the consolidation of middle-class identity and power that characterized the Regency and Victorian eras. As we will go on to consider, Johnson's *Dictionary* should be also regarded as a formative work of this middle-class consciousness.

THE SOCIAL RANGE OF JOHNSON'S *DICTIONARY*

"Johnson's notion of language, as of government, is quite openly and frankly one in which the majority should be idle and helpless spectators, while the customs of the polite are converted into law."[66] John Barrell's depiction of the *Dictionary* as a vehicle of upper-class privilege, a view repeated in later studies,[67] exemplifies the widespread but misinformed perception of Johnson as an "idolater of rank" and loyal supporter of the ruling class. Here is a view, as we have seen, that ignores Johnson's own pugnacious rise from the family of a tradesman, a struggle marked by his determination to be financially independent from the upper ranks and by his frequent attacks on the decadence and idleness of the elite. If Johnson was a gentleman, a status that he sometimes claimed, then it was certainly in a different sense than described by Barrell. Equating the "gentleman" with "polite" society, Barrell argues that works such as the *Dictionary*, Thomson's *The Seasons*, and novels like *Tom Jones* adopt a lofty, panoramic perspective of society that was meant, at a time of social and economic disintegration, to perpetuate the fiction that the upper ranks wielded authority from a position of comprehensive and objective knowledge. Ruling-class literature exhibited the gentleman as a figure of general and indiscriminate knowledge, as reflected by the encyclopedic scope of Johnson's *Dictionary* or *The Gentleman's Magazine*, when in fact this comprehensiveness authorized the exclusion of the language and arts of the lower-classes as "improper."

This analysis is problematic because the status of "gentleman" was, as I have contended, itself a zone of social conflict and challenge at a time when wealth was overtaking birth as the foundation of authority and privilege. People like Johnson's father or Edward Cave who appropriated this title were part of a slow "revolution" of the middle orders as profound in its social impact as the revolution in France, where social mobility had been more strictly confined. Barrell's argument also takes for granted what is simply not true about the *Dictionary* – that it systematically excludes idioms that are not judged "polite" or belong to lower ranks. In fact, the *Dictionary* was criticized by Johnson's erstwhile patron Lord Chesterfield and other upper-rank people for *failing* to give proper ascendence to "polite" language. As contemporaries saw, Johnson had composed a dictionary of quite remarkable social range, for he refused to be bound by the ancient principle that the best language is spoken by the social elite. Just as his essays attempt to relocate the sources of dignity from rank or wealth to virtues attainable by the middle order – notably virtue and learning – so the *Dictionary* adopts non-class-based criteria for excluding or stigmatizing words. Chief among these criteria was the attempt to determine an etymologically "pure" English or what he called "the genius of our tongue."[68] By thus wresting language *away* from the "polite," and placing it instead under the control of linguistic scholars like himself, Johnson again contributed to the gradual process that I have described as the formation of a middle class. As defined by authors of the late century, the authority of this middle class derived not from birth or riches, the acknowledged endowments of the upper class, but rather from their liberal education and exclusive responsibility for "intellectual" rather than physical labor.

This distinction between intellectual and physical labor plays an important role in Johnson's notion of social dignity and ranking. In *Rambler* No. 145 (written while he was laboring on the *Dictionary*), Johnson refused to accept that the most generally "useful" work in a society, that of the lowly "artisan" or "manufacturer," was for that reason more estimable than the work of the scholar or professional. As he maintained, "That work, however necessary, which is carried on only by muscular strength and manual dexterity, is not of equal esteem, in the consideration of rational beings, with the tasks that exercise the intellectual powers, and require the active vigour of imagination, or the gradual and laborious investigations of reason" (5:9). This statement bears a curious and ambivalent relation to Johnson's work as a lexicographer, for in the first paragraph of the Preface to the *Dictionary* he apparently ranks *himself* with the "drudges" of manual labor, those "who toil at the lower employments of life."[69] Nevertheless, in a later paragraph, he seems to insist, at least on first view, on the inferior status of language used by those occupied solely with work depending on "muscular strength and manual dexterity":

Of the laborious and mercantile part of the people, the diction is in a great measure casual and mutable; many of their terms are formed for some temporary and local convenience, and though current at certain times and places, and in others utterly unknown. This fugitive cant, which is always in a state of increase or decay, cannot be regarded as any part of the durable materials of a language, and, therefore, must be suffered to perish with other things unworthy of preservation.[70]

This passage has served as the main evidence that Johnson's *Dictionary* played an important role in the elitist cause of making "polite" language the only "proper" English, excluding working-class idioms as inferior or "improper." Yet it is surely of significance that in the dictionary that follows, Johnson does *not* exclude all terms of manufacture and commerce. As John Hawkesworth observed in a review of the *Dictionary* for *The Gentleman's Magazine*, "as this dictionary was not designed merely for critics, but for popular use, it comprises the peculiar words of every science, art, and profession, even to mechanical trades."[71] This apparent inconsistency will seem less puzzling when we consider that Johnson's primary concern in the above passage was not the supposed lowness or inadequacy of words used by "the laborious and mercantile" part of the people. His concern was rather that much of this idiom was "cant," a term that, in Johnson's vocabulary, has a specific technical significance having little to do with social origin.

In conversation with Boswell, for example, he reproved what he called "modern cant," such as the use of "idea" to mean "non-visual concepts," or the use of "make money" to mean "get money" instead of "coin money."[72] As these examples suggest, Johnson did not equate cant with lower-class language, though it did originally have this association.[73] "Cant" could still mean "a corrupt dialect used by beggars and vagabounds," as he noted in the *Dictionary*, yet this word had widened its extension to denote "a particular form of speaking peculiar to some certain class [i.e. group] or body of men." Such jargon certainly included the "fugitive cant" used by "the laborious and mercantile part of the people," that is, those who made their money (or, rather, *got* their money) from trade and commerce – by no means a universally downtrodden or marginalized segment of the British population. In the Preface to the *Dictionary*, Johnson singles out commerce as a prime culprit in the generation of cant. This was because "they that have frequent intercourse with strangers, to whom they endeavour to accommodate themselves, must in time learn a mingled dialect, like the jargon which serves the traffickers on the Mediterranean and Indian coasts." Such mercantile cant included "flimsy", which "crept into our language from the cant of manufactuers."[74] The trading and commercial communities posed a special threat to the stability and purity of language, thought Johnson, because it was overwhelmingly literate. This literacy was significant because Johnson laid most of the blame for linguistic corruption not on speakers but on "penmen" and those he called, confusingly, "illiterate [i.e. unlearned] writers."[75] Quite logically, he concluded that new words, however contrary to the general "analogy" of English, gained authority and official currency when introduced into books and pamphlets. Johnson's views on the influence of "print culture" were therefore more complicated and paradoxical than is sometimes assumed: he valued print as an indispensable resource to stabilize language through dictionaries and other books, yet he also recognized that, by increasing the dissemination and authority of neologisms, print had accelerated linguistic disruption.[76]

Given this reasoning, cant words were not those that normally arise from the speech of the lower orders, who remained predominately illiterate in Johnson's time.[77] Johnson insightfully pointed out that the language of "common people" tends to be highly conservative and traditional: "A great part of their language is proverbial. If anything rocks at all, they say *it rocks like a cradle.*"[78] As modern linguists have shown, popular speech generally resists innovation, a phenomenon he understood. And for this reason the most stable period of any language occurs before the rise of commerce and the proliferation of books: "The language most likely to continue long without alternation would be that of a nation raised a little, and but a little, above barbarity." The infamous "chaos" that Johnson found in modern English, and which he set out to order and control, was most characteristic of a society that had achieved a more advanced level of cultural and economic sophistication. Accordingly, linguistic disorder springs not from people at the lower end of the social spectrum, but from those who have had some education and leisure to think: "Those who have much leisure to think, will always be enlarging the stock of ideas; and every increase of knowledge, whether real or fancied, will produce new words, or combinations of words. When the mind is unchained from necessity, it will range after convenience."[79]

Those with much leisure to think included, of course, the "polite." So far from attempting to endorse a "polite" standard, Johnson recognized that the idle upper ranks were one important source of the cant and improper innovation that he sought to correct: "As politeness increases, some expressions will be considered as too gross and vulgar for the delicate; others as too formal and ceremonious for the gay and airy; new phrases are, therefore, adopted, which must, for the same reasons, be in time dismissed."[80] Fashionable society was the main conduit for the influx of French words and syntax into English, regarded by Johnson as perhaps the greatest scourge of the modern tongue. The *beau monde* also delighted in neologisms, as brought directly to Johnson's attention by none other than the aristocratic patron he finally rejected with famous indignation, Lord Chesterfield. As is well known, just before the publication of the *Dictionary* in the spring of 1755, Chesterfield wrote two papers in the *World*, throwing advice at Johnson with the postured aplomb of a man who really had fulfilled his function as the lexicographer's gracious patron. Johnson stiffly rebuffed Chesterfield's approaches in a letter that marks an important milestone in the rise of the professional author, free from dependence on the patronage of the great. In addition, as we will consider in a later chapter, there is probably an important political dimension to Johnson's outburst against Chesterfield: Johnson had been closely connected with a political circle, including his friend Robert Dodsley and aspiring contemporaries such as Henry Fielding, who had shared certain ideals concerning the ideally "Broad-bottomed" or non-party basis of English politics, and the need to support even obscure men of genuine "merit." In Johnson's case, at least, this ideal had been betrayed, for he had slaved in his attic with no support from Chesterfield, who meanwhile retired from politics, built a magnificent London house, and pursued his favorite pastime of shining in the company of people worth the effort. About the upper ranks, Johnson fumed publicly in his essays of the dictionary years: his scathing portrait of Prospero in *Rambler* No. 71 is almost certain leveled at Chesterfield.[81] It should come as no surprise that Johnson finally lashed out against Chesterfield when this supposed "patron" deigned to advise him on how to make his work more palatable to London's genteel inhabitants.

For this, indeed, was the gist of Chesterfield's papers in the *World* (which no one now, apparently, bothers to read): Johnson, advised the lord, should include words current in the *beau monde* in order to please people of fashion, especially fashionable ladies, to whom Chesterfield offers oily homage as the true arbiters of language. These words include "to fuzz" (a card term meaning to deal "twice together with the pack of cards, for luck's sake"), "vastly" (used as an intensifier, as in "vastly glad," "vastly sorry," or even "vastly little") and "flirtation" (which Chesterfield personally heard "coined . . . by the most beautiful mouth in the world").[82] Of these terms only "flirtation" made it to Johnson's *Dictionary*. Yet, significantly, Johnson seems also to have misunderstood what "flirtation" had come to mean, for Chesterfield's explanation makes clear that this word had already gained the significance which it retains to this day. "Flirtation" was not exactly "coquetry," observed Chesterfield, but rather something "short of coquetry," intimating "only the first hints of aproximation" [*sic*]."[83] Johnson's definition entirely misses this new sense, though he does know that it is upper-class cant: "FLIRTATION. A quick sprightly motion. A cant word used by women."

Johnson's unfamiliarity with the new sense of "flirtation" is hardly surprising. He himself was an unlikely target for this kind of attention from genteel women, as Chesterfield takes care to remind him.[84] Nor was there easy access from his smoky attic in Gough Square to the candle-lit halls of the rich. He was, as he replied to Chesterfield, "a retired and uncourtly Scholar,"[85] and the *Dictionary*, like his essays, was received by many in the "beau monde" as the work of a plodding pedant. "Well-bred" readers widely re-echoed Thomas Edwards's criticism that Johnson had crowded his work with "monstrous words . . . which never were used by any who pretended to talk or write English."[86] Particularly ungracious were the many "inkhorn" words such as "aedespotick", "turbinated", "perflation", and so forth that, as the blue-stocking Jemima Campbell, Marchioness Grey, complained, "really break my teeth."[87] Johnson himself was unapologetic, even defiant, in his alleged pedantry, as we have already discussed with relation to *Rambler* No. 173. It is notable, indeed, that Johnson's determination to speak as grandly as he wished, even in the best company, was often viewed as a sign of his bumptious scholasticism (echoing the old humanist complaint that the scholastics were vulgar and ill-bred).[88] In Archibald Campbell's farcical satire of Johnson, *Lexiphanes* (1767), for example, Johnson is portrayed lumbering through low-life London, declaiming on prostitutes, street-brawls, and tavern games in a crude parody of the *Rambler*'s Latinate prose: "It was impossible for me not to succumb under the conjunct importunities of so many illustrious associates, who all simultaneously obsecrated me to accompany them in an ambulatory project to the wakeful harbinger of day at Chelsea, and there to recreate and invigorate our powers with buns, convivial ale, and a sober erratick game at skittles."[89] Campbell's ostensible purpose in this satire (beyond denigrating the "anti-Scottish" Johnson) was to halt what he considered the dangerous drift of English towards the "absurd *Lexiphanick* style." He contrasted Johnson's "uncouth trash" with a style of "true taste," associated with the genteel prose of Lord Lyttelton (whom Johnson knew in his Opposition days) and other well-bred authors.[90] Indeed, many eighteenth-century readers criticized Johnson's style as stilted and opaque, preferring the graceful style of "gentleman-authors" like Lyttelton, Adam Smith, Hugh

Blair, and (foremost) David Hume. These were authors whose stylistic ease conveyed that they, unlike Johnson, did *not* write for a living.[91]

Neither Johnson nor his *Dictionary*, in short, was "polite." Barrell's opinion that he set out to convert "the customs of the polite" into "linguistic law" misrepresents both the considerable inclusiveness of Johnson's lexicon and his personal and intellectual isolation from the upper ranks. As I have indicated, Johnson is best regarded as defining a middle-class sensibility that cannot be simply conflated with the gentry or the ruling class. His separation from ruling-class or "polite" standards is signaled by his insistence on being guided only by "reason" or "virtue" in his moral essays, and by his analogous reliance on supposedly objective standards of linguistic purity in the *Dictionary*.

For what Johnson rejected in his *Dictionary* was the old humanist attitude that, as the eighteenth-century grammarian James Greenwood wrote, language should be adjusted by "the Custom and Use of the best Speakers."[92] This appeal to polite usage had a long history stretching back to classical rhetoricians such as Quintilian, who maintained that usage, "the surest pilot in speaking," must not be understood as the language of the majority, but as "the agreed practice of educated men."[93] Amongst the Renaissance humanists who revered Quintilian's teachings, such as Bembo, Valla, and Castiglione, there was a similar contempt for *lo volgare* and a tendency to associate proper speech with the best writing and most elegant speakers at court.[94] The court provided the standard of "bon usage" for many French grammarians of the seventeenth century, such as Vaugelas and Bouhours.[95]

There were, however, alternatives to merely authorizing "the Custom and Use of the best speakers." In France, the major alternative was *raison*, to use the essentially technical term employed in the French tradition of "rational grammar." The fountainhead of this movement was the *Grammaire générale et raisonnée* by the Port-Royal authors Arnauld and Lancelot. These Jansenist authors were isolated by class and theology from courtly circles, and they set out to overturn the criteria of "polite" usage associated primarily with the grammar of Vaugelas.[96] The Port-Royal grammar exerted a considerable influence in Britain, though the battle-lines between "reason" and "usage" were somewhat less clearly marked on that side of the Channel. The conflict is detected when we compare a grammar like Greenwood's *Essay towards a Practical English Grammar*, the source of our quote authorizing "the Custom and Use of the best Speakers," with Michael Mattaire's *The English Grammar* (1712), which places the emphasis instead on the rule of "analogy." Mattaire borrowed this term from the tradition of classical grammar, where (most famously in the work of Varro) "analogy" stands for the regular declension and morphology of Latin.[97] As Mattaire makes clear, analogy could not be separated from an accurate record of usage: a "word is called Analogous or Regular, which followeth the general rules of the Grammar, grounded upon observations drawn from that general use."[98] Nonetheless, analogy could also be deployed to judge the correctness or "purity" of even "polite" idioms. In contrast with Greenwood's definition of grammar as polite usage, Mattaire called grammar the "Art which teacheth the way of writing and speaking *truly* and *properly* [my italics]."[99]

Did the principle of "analogy" or "reason" have significance with relation to the politics of social rank? It seems important, indeed, that this standard could be used to correct the impropriety of even upper-class language. The "leveling" tendency of rational grammar no doubt helped to promote its immense popularity among the *lumières* of pre-Revolutionary France. In England, the correspondence between "rational" grammar and liberal politics was less consistent: it was more common there to object to the impropriety of upper-class English without implying some defiance of the ruling order. The Tory Jonathan Swift, for example, was profoundly disillusioned with the language of the court. Since the Restoration, Swift maintained, upper-class English had been corrupted by the wicked morals and affectation of fashionable society. As he declared in *A Proposal for Correcting, Improving, and Ascertaining the English Tongue* (1712), "the Court which used to be a Standard of Propriety, and Correctness of Speech, was then [at the Restoration], and, I think, hath ever since continued the worst School in *England* for that Accomplishment."[100] Swift's conservatism is revealed by his solution to linguistic corruption – the creation of an academy, modeled after those in France and Italy, for restoring English to the purity that he believed it once possessed in the court of Elizabeth. Although the academy would judge English according to a standard independent of current polite usage, its purpose would be to re-establish the linguistic authority of "the learned and polite Persons of the Nation."[101]

In the more populist climate that prevailed in England after the Hanoverian Succession, this proposal for a linguistic academy attracted little favor. Writing in 1761, Joseph Priestley maintained that "a publick *Academy*" was "not only unsuitable to the genius of a *free nation*, but in itself ill calculated to reform and fix a language."[102] A leading dissenter and campaigner for political and religious liberty, Priestley exemplifies how the use of "analogy" could be used not to authorize upper-class idioms, but indeed to guard against the imposition of a rank-bound standard. He did concede that the best writers and speakers of the language possessed "authority." But where the authorities differed from each other, grammarians and lexicographers should appeal to the autonomous principle of "analogy," the internal logic of a language which rightly determined the propriety of individual locutions: "the *analogy of language* is the only thing to which we can have recourse, to adjust these differences; for language, to answer the intent of it, which is to express our thoughts with certainty in an intercourse with one another, must be fixed and consistent with itself."[103] Consistent with Priestley's liberal politics, therefore, all usage, as found even in the "best" authors and the most educated speakers, was subject to a common standard adjusted by the particular "genius" of the tongue.

Significantly, Priestley refers approvingly throughout his discussion to "Mr. Johnson." For, indeed, Samuel Johnson, despite his supposed allegiance to the upper ranks, objected to the creation of an academy for reasons very like those of Priestley: the "spirit of English liberty," he declared, would surely resist the creation of such an institution, which had not, in any event, hindered the natural transformation of French or Italian.[104] Secondly, like Priestley, Johnson upheld the general "analogy" of the language or the "genius of the tongue" without considering whether a word derived from a particular social milieu. Indeed, he never appealed to "the Custom and Use of the best Speakers." In the *Plan of an English Dictionary*, he acquiesced in Lord Chesterfield's encouragement "to interpose my own judgment" only in the sense of preferring "what appears to me most consonant to grammar and reason."[105] At this stage, as he later confessed, he dreamed ambitiously of making words conform to "the nature of every substance,"[106] in the manner of John Wilkins and other seventeenth-century planners of a "universal" language. Upon awaking as a humble lexicographer, however, Johnson confined himself to the principles of etymology and analogy. He regarded etymology as the primary test for "cant," whether "low" or "polite." Cant is cant not because it is used by the lower orders, but because it lacks roots in the history of the language, and thus runs contrary to "the general fabrick" of the tongue.[107] Hence, "higgeldy-piggeldy", "Tory", and "flirtation" are "cant" because they cannot be traced by a regular series to a genuine English source; on the other hand, "filch", "helter-skelter" and "grudge" have roots in the Teutonic heritage of the language, and are thus accepted as legitimate English words, for all their "lowness." Such reasoning, we should note, is quite contrary to that followed by contemporary advocates of "polite" usage such as George Campbell: in his influential *Philosophy of Rhetoric* (1776), Campbell explicitly challenged Johnson on the issue, denying that cant could be equated with "want of etymology." It was rather "baseness of use" that fixed this "disgraceful appellation" on a word.[108]

The appropriate conclusion here is not that Johnson's appeals to "reason," "analogy," and the "fabrick of a language" prove that he was a radical like Priestley. On the contrary, I have already started my argument that Johnson is properly seen as a conservative in his opposition to radical political upheaval, particularly as emanating from the ambitious class of artisans and tradesmen who followed Wilkes and other radicals in the later century. But it is inaccurate to confuse this conservatism with an allegiance to the aristocracy or upper gentry or with opposition to change of any kind. Just as Johnson's essays appeal beyond rank or wealth to the superior dignity of "knowledge" and "virtue," so his *Dictionary* adheres to criteria of linguistic propriety and purity that are theoretically independent of social origin. By relying on standards of etymology and analogy, Johnson facilitated the independence and self-definition of what came to be called "the middle class." The "gentleman," in his updated guise as the respectable member of the middle ranks, could turn to Johnson's *Dictionary* as a basis for "proper" language that had nothing to do with high birth and polite society, and was by this means liberated to claim an independent place in the English class hierarchy. Late in the century, the middle class that Johnson helped to consolidate and authorize generally found its interests best protected by preserving the political power of the aristocracy and upper gentry. Yet through their appropriation of many of the titles, symbols and privileges of the ruling class (including, crucially, authority over language), the middling orders gradually transformed English society in ways that were as "revolutionary" as the more sudden and dramatic social conflagration that occurred in late eighteenth-century France.

Among the changes wrought by the middling ranks was a profoundly new role for women – the creation of a new middle-class "lady" to match the new middle-class "gentleman." In the last year of the century, Hannah More would claim indeed that a "revolution" had occurred in the manners and status of middle-rank women, referring to their increased literacy and participation in English letters, and to their more visible and "public" role outside the confines of household duty.[109] "The world has grown less domestic, and more self-engrossed," wrote another conservative woman author of the middle class, Jane West, in 1806.[110] That these women could make such a claim should cause us to reconsider the view that the eighteenth century witnessed the increasing confinement of women to the "domestic sphere," a position that was, until very recently, unchallenged in feminist histories. A re-examination of women's changing status in the middle ranks may, on the contrary, lead us to conclude that More and West were expressing the widespread feeling of women and men in their time, views foreshadowed and influenced by the writings and conversation of Samuel Johnson.

CHAPTER 2

Constructing the middle-class woman

MIDDLE-CLASS IDENTITY AND THE NEW PUBLIC WOMAN

The creation of that monolithic category "the middle class" resulted from a lengthy process, as we have seen, bringing together, in uneasy alliance, the groups that had profited most from the great enrichment of England during the eighteenth century – the gentry, wealthy merchants and manufacturers, and professionals, all of whom ultimately found their common interests best protected through maintaining political union with the crown and the traditional nobility. This complex and fundamentally restive union required as well that the daughters and wives in these groups adopt a new role in the emerging social-political order. According to influential recent scholarship on the history of women, this role was, above all, *domestic*. Endorsing previous claims concerning the supposed expulsion of women from the world of work outside the home during the eighteenth century, this scholarship has maintained that women became increasingly confined to the "domestic sphere," losing all influence over the public world of politics and professions that were now engrossed entirely by men. In the words of Leonore Davidoff and Catherine Hall, whose *Family Fortunes: Men and Women of the English Middle-Class* lent substantial authority to this thesis, "the equation of women with domesticity came to be one of the fixed points of middle-class status."[1] A weighty body of scholarship has since accumulated that portrays the eighteenth century as a time when women were increasingly confined to kitchen and drawing room, their heightened visibility as writers of novels and popular literature being small recompense for the hardening assumption that females were inherently destined to tend hearth and home.[2]

Belief in some lost "Golden Age" of women's public involvement has, however, recently faced strong challenge. For the evidence that women were driven from the work-force, or that the nature of their work underwent any substantial transformation during the century is, in fact, highly uncertain.

Amanda Vickery's recent and controversial contention that women tended to occupy the same kinds of trades and jobs in 1850 as they had in 1650 rests on a strong foundation of sociological analysis by historians of the middle class like Peter Earle and Margaret Hunt.[3] As shown by these and other historians, there was little change in the clustering of women in the service and hospitality sectors, along with certain "women's trades" in textile manufacture. Even unconventional business remained a possibility for women in straitened circumstances like Laetitia Pilkington and Charlotte Charke, neither of whom provoked any surprise among men when they opened a print shop and a grocery, respectively.[4] In *A Sentimental Journey* (1768), similarly, Laurence Sterne portrayed vigorous husband-and-wife teams behind shop-counters as "typically" English: "In London a shopkeeper and a shopkeeper's wife seem to be one bone and one flesh: in the several endowments of mind and body, sometimes the one, sometimes the other has it, so as general to be upon a par, and to tally with each other as nearly man and wife need to do."[5] On the other hand, the enrichment of English society meant that fewer and fewer married women *needed* to work in order to contribute to the support of a family. The traditional privilege of aristocratic and genteel women, to live without the need to work in either shop or kitchen, opened itself to an increasingly broad stratum of middle-rank wives, becoming a badge of respectability for both men and their wives. As Jane West observed in 1806, "the potent decree of fashion determined it to be unfit for the wife of men in reputable circumstances to employ herself in domestic arrangements."[6]

West meant this comment to be read with a disdainful shake of the head – for like other conservatives of this era, she was determined to enforce nature's alleged decree in favour of female domesticity. We should recognize, however, that such diligent promotion of domesticity by conduct book writers of the late eighteenth and early nineteenth centuries reflects a reaction against the increased *publicness* of women's lives that, as everyone of that time seemed to agree, had been among the most visible changes in middle-rank life during the eighteenth century. West recalled when, early in the eighteenth century, even "the heiress of large possessions" would ensure that she was caught by an eligible suitor "in the great hall clear-starching lawn ruffles." "I need not multiply anecdotes of this kind;" she went on, "the archives of every family can supply various attestations in point."[7] In the interval, however, even tradesmen's daughters had abandoned the confines of the household to mingle in the apparently endless variety of public events that characterized eighteenth-century social life – pleasure gardens and masquerades, mixed social assemblies, operas, card-parties, clubs, libraries, and plays.

There seems reason, indeed, to go even further than previous scholars who have challenged the "Golden Agc" thesis of women's decline into domesticity during the eighteenth century. So far from becoming more "domestic," women's lives in the eighteenth century became strikingly more *public*. This change resulted in part, as I have suggested, from the flooding down of wealth into ever-lower strata of the English social hierarchy: hence the distress of conservative women like Jane West, who was echoing a more general middle-class alarm that not only lowly tradesmen, but the lowly tradesmen's daughters, were neglecting the sober duties of shop and household for public frivolity. Yet the release of women from the houses and into the assemblies and parks of the nation had been, from the beginning, part of West's own middle-rank legacy, promoted even by its sturdy patriarchs. Since at least the beginning of the century, male conduct book authors were virtually unanimous both in conceding to women greater access to social activities and in promoting a range of educational opportunities that women had never enjoyed before.[8] The question we need to address is *why*? Why did the increased freedom of women to participate in English social life correspond with a sharp rise of female literacy, which became virtually universal in the higher middle ranks? Why did the number of schools for girls, though still a minority option even among the wealthy, go up in Roy Porter's words "by leaps and bounds"?[9]

When we turn to Samuel Johnson's surprisingly numerous discussions of women, in both his writings and conversation, we find important evidence towards answering these questions. In the relatively small body of well-informed scholarship about Johnson's attitudes to women,[10] he emerges as an open-minded figure on "feminist" issues, particularly as a warm advocate behind the literary careers of Elizabeth Carter, Charlotte Lennox, Anna Williams, Hannah More, and many other women. His social circle included many women, and he was unstinting in his praise for women whose learning and intelligence exemplified the improved state of female education. Yet Johnson was no more remarkable in this support of women's public role or female education than he was in his more notorious disparagement of women's preaching ("like a dog's walking on his hinder legs") or his rigid views on female chastity.[11] As Johnson's work indicates, the emerging middle class had good practical reasons both for allowing women access to public events and for making them more literate. Young women were on the front line of the middling-order invasion of genteel privileges and its effort to merge, through marriage, with the ruling elite. Few male commentators seemed to doubt that at least some education for women made them more attractive to eligible young men and, just as important, more able to utilize their new independence responsibly and in the best interests of their families.

On these issues Johnson was, characteristically, more reflective and complex than virtually all his contemporaries: we will find that he valued education for women not merely because he thought it made them more attractive or chaste but more especially because he believed that wisdom and literature made their lives richer, deeper, and more bearable. Yet he stands again as an important figure in the engineering of middle-rank opinion. His surprisingly broad popularity among intellectual women during the century after his death – he was admired by both the conservative Hannah More and the radical Mary Wollstonecraft, enthusiastically read and reread by women as different as Jane Austen, Elizabeth Barrett Browning, George Eliot, and Virginia Woolf[12] – suggests his significant influence on the construction of gender values in modern England.

To open a seventeenth-century lady's conduct book is usually to enter the narrow and stifling kitchen of female domestic duty: *The Whole Duty of a Woman* (1695), written by "A Lady," begins by rehearsing a few dreary tips about female submission and shame-facedness, and then moves on to the more interesting business of recipes for stews and syllabubs, herbal ointments and furniture polish. This is also basically the recipe for John Shirley's *The Accomplished Ladies Rich Closet* (1687), though, as we will see, Shirley already directs the jealous eye of his woman reader toward the drawing room and card-table. These tracts look back to an earlier generation of conduct books such as Samuel Torshell's *The Woman's Glorie: A Treatise, First, Asserting the Due Honour of that Sexe* (1645) and John Heydon's *Advice to a Daughter* (1658), works that alternately wheedle and hector the young lady with promises of masculine approval and eternal salvation for those who fulfilled their destiny to be "modest" and silent on the rare occasions that they emerged in public.[13] There were certainly differences in the expectations placed on women of different social ranks; it is unlikely that aristocratic women were ever expected to stir roux or scour pots. Lord Halifax's *The Lady's New-Years Gift* (1688) makes no requirement that his well-heeled daughter ever see the inside of a kitchen. That Puritan gentleman of academic leisure, John Milton, portrays the first woman as fatally disobeying her husband in her over-zealous desire to tend the garden, for Eve's role is not to work but rather to delight and soothe Adam: "Not equal, as thir sex not equal seem'd / For contemplation hee and valor form'd, / For softness she and sweet attractive Grace."[14] A hundred years later, Johnson would cringe at Milton's "Turkish contempt of females, as subordinate and inferior beings."[15] Yet Milton was expressing the widely vented views of his time. The obvious weakness of Eve's reason, the alluring though disabling sway of her passions, correspond with Lord Halifax's frank advice to his daughter that "Your *Sex* wanteth our *Reason* for your *Conduct*, and our *Strength* for our *Protection*: *Ours* wanteth your *Gentleness* to soften and entertain us."[16] Such homey duties did not, clearly, require that the lady open any book except the Bible, and while the seventeenth-century patriarchy did relent on the benefits of female literacy, which increased considerably during this time, "the over-riding aim of such education was a religious one – the fostering of a God-fearing and deferential clientele."[17]

Yet things were not entirely well in the paradise of seventeenth-century domesticity. Like their gentleman counterparts, ladies of the upper classes were deeply resented in the post-Civil War era, coming virtually to symbolize the decadence that even many supporters of the Restoration agreed in blaming for the nation's ills. Consider Richard Allestree, best known for his phenomenally popular *The Whole Duty of Man* (1658), but also the author of a solemn attack on the idleness and luxury of upper-class gentlemen, *The Gentleman's Calling* (1671). Allestree (despite his dour reputation) was no "Puritan": he was a genteel priest who strongly supported the royalists in the Civil War and was rewarded after the Restoration with a place in court. His political preoccupation was the reform of elite manners with the aim of making the upper orders more secure and responsible in their restored authority. These same concerns later inspired his *Lady's Calling* (1673), where Allestree describes the frivolous and irreligious course of a rich lady's day:

> The morning is divided between sleep and dressing, nor would the morning suffice, but that they are fain to make a new computation to measure it not by the Sun, but their time of dining, which is often as late as the stationary hours of the Primitive Fasts, tho upon a differing motive . . . so that whole round of her time seems to be a magic circle, wherein nothing that is holy must appear.[18]

The Lady's Calling is an early shout in the sustained chorus of contempt towards luxurious upper-class ladies that lasted well into the eighteenth century, still echoing in Wollstonecraft's *Vindication of the Rights of Woman* (1792). In *The Ladies Dressing-Room Unlock'd* (1700), Mary Evelyn lamented the passing of a supposed golden age when "our Fore Fathers . . . courted and chose their Wives for their Modesty, their Frugality, keeping at Home, Good-Housewifery and other Oeconomical Virtues."[19] Sadly, "the World is alter'd among us." As the result of "Foreign Manners," "Luxury . . . has universally obtain'd among us."[20] This threnody is followed by a ludicrous poem entitled "A Voyage to Marryland or, The Ladies Dressing Room" which, like Allestree's description of a fashionable lady's "magic circle," contributed to the shimmering reservoir of images later conjured by Pope in *The Rape of the Lock*:

> A new Scene to us next presents,
> The Dressing-Room and Implements
> Of Toilet Plate Gilt, and Emboss'd,
> And several other things of Cost:
> The Toilet *Miroir*, one Glue Pot,
> One for *Pomatum*, and what not?
> Of *Washes*, *Unguents*, and *Cosmeticks*,
> A pair of Silver Candlesticks;
> Snuffers, and Snuff-dish, Boxes more,
> For Powders, Patches, Waters store.[21]

Thus, when Pope described the glittering frivolity of the wealthy Belinda's private and public worlds, he was building on a well-established tradition of middle-rank satire against the idleness and luxury of upper-class women. And when, in the final 1717 version of the poem, he added a long speech on the need for Belinda to cultivate virtues of mind and character ("How vain are all these Glories, all our Pains, / Unless good Sense preserve what Beauty gains"),[22] we sense an important shift in attitudes towards the ideal attributes of women between Milton's epic and Pope's mock-epic. Women, evidently, could no longer be satisfied with "softness" and "sweet attractive Grace."

For Pope was addressing a society where access to the public spaces where Belinda reigns was no longer the exclusive privilege of the noble and very wealthy (despite the impression given by Pope). Emulation of polite society by middle-rank women had become such a norm, quipped the *Connoisseur* in 1754, that "The sex consists almost entirely of LADIES . . . there is scarce one woman to be met with, except among the lowest of the vulgar."[23] The widening public presence of middle-rank women (everyone above "the lowest of the vulgar") struck people of the early eighteenth century as a development of revolutionary significance, as suggested by an essay that the novelist Samuel Richardson wrote for Johnson's *The Rambler* in 1751. In the time of his youth, grumbled Richardson, "excepting sometimes an appearance in the ring, sometimes at a good and chosen play, sometimes on a visit to the house of a grave relation, the young ladies contented themselves to be found employed in domestic duties." But all, all was changed, for the modern woman had the choice of attending "routs, drums, balls, assemblies, and such like markets for women" (*Rambler* No. 97, 4:154). Richardson was repeating testimony given earlier by Eliza Haywood, who commented on the "Love of Company" that "makes our Ladies run galloping in Troops every Evening to Masquerades, Balls and Assemblies in Winter, and in the Summer to *Vaux-hall, Ranelagh, Cuper's Gardens, Mary le Bon, Sadler's-Wells*, both old and new, *Goodman's Fields*, and twenty other such like Places." These public areas were not restricted, scolded Haywood, to "the Beautiful and High-born," but were frequented by women who "ought to have the Care of a House and a Family at Heart," the families of Tradesmen who "affect to be, above the Thought of such Oeconomy."[24] Even at the end of the century, the anonymous author of the *Female Aegis* (1798) still wondered at the innumerable "scenes of public diversion" in which ladies were "whirled, day after day, and year after year, in a never-ending round of giddiness and dissipation."[25] Yet not all the new public activities available to women were so "decadent." If women had only limited access to the male institution of the coffee-house, there were ladies' clubs and salons such as the Ladies' Coterie at the Almack House and Elizabeth Montagu's blue-stocking circle at her houses in Hill Street and Portman Street. Women had access to the new public libraries and public lectures. For the first time, women became stars on the stage and, particularly at the beginning and end of the century, successful playwrights. Hannah More's *Percy* (1777), for example, ran twenty-one nights and made the author 600 pounds. Such activities were virtually unimaginable to women a century before.[26]

So far from being more "domestic," in short, the life of an increasingly large number of women had become "public" – at least in the way this word was understood in the eighteenth century. Johnson, for example, defined "publick" as "General; done by many," and as "Open for general entertainment," making no suggestion that "publick" was the opposite of "domestick," or that it implied the worlds of politics and business. In the contemporary sense, in fact, domesticity was actually on the decline: "Houswifely accomplishments are now quite out of date among the polite world," observed the *Connoisseur* in 1755. Unlike "the good dames of old," the modern young lady had no interest in learning how to starch linen or bake a flaky pie-crust.[27] If, at mid-century, this development generally provoked reactions ranging from outrage to scornful amusement, by the end of the century even the conservative Hannah More could, with certain reservations, share in the sense of "triumph" that the lady's responsibility for domestic chores belonged to a musty time of yore:

Among the boasted improvements of the present age, none affords more frequent matter of peculiar exultation, than the manifest superiority in the employment of the young ladies of our time over those of the good house-wives of the last century. It is a matter of general triumph that they are at present employed in learning the polite arts, or in acquiring liberal accomplishments; while it is insisted that their forlorn predecessors wore out their joyless days in adorning the mansion-house with hideous hangings of sorrowful tapestry and disfiguring tent-stitch.[28]

The "revolution of the manners of the middle class" described by More did not imply, of course, that the woman's life was no longer "domestic" in another sense.[29] Yet the *new* domestic ideology that More helped to develop must be seen as, in large part, a reaction to the greatly increased publicness of female life, at least for women of the upper-middle and middle classes. Indeed, the great central issue in eighteenth-century writing about women became what to do about the fact that women had unprecedented access to the temptations of the public world. For some writers of the era, the dissipation of female public life seemed intolerable: Mary Astell's *Serious Proposal to the Ladies* (1694) urged young women to renounce the decadent glitter of public pleasure for the wholesome shades of monastic retirement. Yet Astell's plan for learned nunneries was surely the desperate reaction of a pious woman to an evolution that could not be reversed. Indeed, for all the claims made today for Astell's "feminism," most contemporary young women could not, and did not, take her *Serious Proposal* very seriously at all, for they were increasingly tasting the unfamiliar adventure of social freedom. And this freedom was being promoted by middle-rank parents who sought the advancement of their own fortunes and social dignity through matching their daughters with "bachelors of fashion" in the "public market."[30]

"Market" is the right word. Through the combined enrichment of the merchant class and the beleaguered finances of the aristocracy, meteoric social advancement through marriage had become possible, even common. Daniel Defoe's *The Complete English Tradesman* (1725–7) boasted of the good marriages recently made by merchant-class girls to noble boys, crowing over "the number of daughters of tradesmen, adorn'd with the ducal coronet, and seen riding in the coaches of the best of the nobility."[31] Conduct books of the late seventeenth and early eighteenth centuries could be shameless in their prodding of middle-order girls to use the affections of young men as a lever for their families' social advancement. In *The Accomplished Ladies Rich Closet* (1687), John Shirley promoted women's wearing "sumptuous Attire," attending plays and reading novels of "Gallantry." "Dancing," as he saw it, was useful in displaying a shapely form, "the best and readiest way to put the Body, upon all occasions, in a graceful position."[32] So far as Shirley recommended traditional female virtues like modesty, he regarded them as instruments of seduction: "Blushes . . . let your Lover know the little Flames of Love are playing about your Heart."[33] Later authors like John Essex, in *The Young Ladies Conduct* (1722), came close to advising hypocrisy in urging modesty solely as a means of "recommending us to the Esteem of Persons of Distinction."[34] Act "modest" and "lowly," by all means, Essex instructed women, if that is what a shy gentleman seemed to like. Otherwise, "awkward Bashfulness"[35] could no longer be a virtue for young women who were, after all, expected to be efficient agents of middle-order ambition. According to Wetenhall Wilkes in *A Letter of Genteel and Moral Advice to a Young Lady* (1740), the elegant woman should accost the male interlocutor by looking "straight in the face without staring."[36] Ironically, these encouragements to the social ambition of young ladies had the peculiar down-side of disqualifying middling-rank males *themselves* from serious chances in the marriage-market. Hence, writers like Erasmus Jones promoted middle-order ambition while also bemoaning that "There is nothing more ridiculous than the double PRIDE of the *Ladies* of this Age, with respect to marrying what they call *below their birth*." How dare these ladies refuse to marry even rich tradesmen (like Jones), whom they very "improperly" dismissed as "*Mechanicks*."[37]

To send your daughter to "market" at an opulent assembly was, nonetheless, a gamble fraught with danger. The predatory Lothario who destroyed the marriageability of young women became such a standard of villainy in eighteenth-century theater and literature because he attacked the fortunes of aspiring middle-rank families. Hence, eighteenth-century gender discourse became obsessed with mediating the following crucial dilemma: how to give young women the access they needed to the public zones of courtship while also restraining them from making disastrous choices in that dazzling and bewildering market of silk breeches and enchanting promises. The increasingly accepted answer was what Hannah More, in a previous quote, called "liberal accomplishments." The amazing success of the *Tatler* and then the *Spectator* early in the century marked a revolution in attitudes to gender characterized by a new acceptance that the "understanding" of girls should be cultivated along with their physical attractions. As Richard Steele wrote in *Spectator* No. 66, this was the optimum balance of prudence and ambition: "there is a middle Way to be followed; the Management of a young Lady's Person is not to be overlooked, but the Erudition of her Mind is much more to be regarded."[38] The rationale of this advice was, above all, that women who had at least moderate education would be more virtuous and less vain. "I must again and again urge the Culture of your minds," wrote James Fordyce in his immensely popular *Sermons for Young Women* (1765), "Your Virtue, your sobriety, is intimately concerned in it."[39] Despite his reputation as one of the great fuddy-duddies of the eighteenth century, Fordyce actually encouraged a surprising broad range of learning for the young woman – from classical languages to modern history, mathematics to astronomy.[40] Yet Fordyce had no intention of prying women from the pleasures of the "world," in the manner of Mary Astell: "I would not rob your sex of a single advantage they possess from nature, providence, or legitimate custom . . . On the contrary, I would willingly add to your allurements."[41] Female learning, so long as it was not "pedantic," would encourage "rational conversation" and "the intercourses of real friendship."[42] Sparkling intelligence and the patter of "suitable" learning, as Wetenhall Wilkes instructed, would dazzle suitors far more than gaudy dress. "To cultivate and adorn your understanding with the Improvements of Learning (I mean such as is suitable to your Sex) is a Matter vastly more worthy of your Attention than any external Grace you can put on."[43]

The "suitability" of female learning was of course paramount. The author of the *Female Aegis* evoked, comically, the terrifying prospect of a learned wife "sallying forth from her books only to engage in literary disquisitions, and to stun her wearied mate with sonorous periods, and cumbrous terms of science."[44] Even an accomplished woman, that is, should *not* behave like Samuel Johnson. An exemplar of elegant female accomplishment in the late eighteenth century, Anna Laetitia Barbauld, contrasted French women, decked out in their rouge and pedantry, with her ideal of the wifely rose of England, "endowed with talents and graces to draw attention in polite circles," yet possessed of that steadiness of affection appropriate to a spouse and mother.[45] Learning of a polite and literary sort was nonetheless regarded as a *sine qua non* of late eighteenth-century middle-class femininity. The cultivation of "taste" (a trait that Hume believed women possessed naturally)[46] guarded young ladies against the lures of superficial beauty and false wit. As James Fordyce observed, woman of wider education and deeper insight would be likely to prefer a gentleman with "a plain coat, a cultivated understanding, and a manly deportment"[47] – precisely the sort of middle-class "gentleman" that the masculine ideal of "liberal education" was attempting, just at that time, to create.

This was the gentleman that Johnson, as we have seen, played an important role in forming. And he also had much to say about forming the middle-class lady. As usual, however, Johnson did not merely rehearse the emerging conventions of his time. Much of his significance derived from his ability to co-ordinate potentially hostile tendencies within the emerging ideology of English womanhood. The eighteenth-century woman had to be public and also domestic; as Barbauld suggested, she should shine in "polite circles" but also dispense care to crying children and fraught husbands. She should be "new" in her ability to talk and think (almost) like a man, yet be very "unmale" in her disapproval of the vices that lubricated male pleasure.

Johnson's remarks on women are commonly characterized by a sense of historical change, of a real "revolution" in the role of women since they were encouraged to converse on equal terms even with the most learned men. In *Rambler* No. 173, for example, he berated men who believed that they must avoid displaying "pedantry" around women, indicating that such men "form their notions of the present generation from the writings of the last, and are not very early informed of those changes which the gradual diffusion of knowledge . . . produces in the world." The modern scholar, he said, need not hesitate to show his learning even at the "tea-table," "Whatever might be the state of female literature in the last century" (5:153). Boswell recalled similar plaudits for the developing state of women's knowledge in the *Life*: "He praised the ladies of the present age, insisting that they were more faithful to their husbands, and more virtuous in every respect, than in former times, because their understandings were better cultivated."[48] As this observation suggests, Johnson fully agreed with contemporaries who considered the new public and educated woman as not less but *more* virtuous than her unlearned, domestic predecessor of a previous age.

Indeed, the housebound matron who continued to spend her days baking pies and sewing quilts seems to have provoked little else than Johnson's impatience and contempt. In *Rambler* No. 51, Lady Bustle is at best "a kind of neutral being" with regard to virtue and vice. "She has no crime but luxury, nor any virtue but chastity," desires no praise "but for her cooking" and wishes no ill to others except that "their custards may be wheyish, and their pye-crusts tough" (3:278–9). Amidst the steaming pots and jam-jars of Lady Bustle's kitchen, we find the wilting Cornelia, a visitor from London who wonders whether this could really be her proper destiny: "I am now very impatient to know whether I am to look on these ladies as the great pattern of our sex, and to consider conserves and pickles as the great business of my life" (3:279). Such is also the frustration of Myrtylla in *Rambler* No. 84, who submits to the dull domesticity of her aunt's house until she meets Flavia, a vivacious and self-confident modern lady from London who opens the girl's mind to the golden horizons of literature.

These essays form a sharp contrast to Richardson's fusty contribution, *Rambler* No. 97, where this allegedly "feminist" novelist waxes nostalgic about those days when "young ladies contented themselves to be found employed in domestick duties" (4:154). In the broader analysis, however, Johnson and Richardson were allied in their belief that literature offered important correctives to the frivolity, superficiality, and moral danger of the fashionable world that had increasingly opened its doors to women of the middling sort. The rigid virtue of Richardson's great middle-rank heroine, Clarissa Harlowe, is closely connected with her eloquence and rationality, virtues that guard her against the superficial charms of her aristocratic and highly literate assailant, Lovelace. A few years later, in *The Vanity of Human Wishes* (1749), Johnson followed with an analogously cautionary tale to "Ye nymphs of rosy lips and radiant eyes / Whom Pleasure keeps too busy to be wise" (ll. 323–4, 6:106–7). The "harmless Freedom" (l. 238, 6:107) of life in the fashionable world, as these nymphs find out, leads finally to a kind of enslavement to vice and false lovers – an irony that Johnson pursued in his depiction of a harem in the oriental tale, *Rasselas* (1759). When Pekuah is carried off by a rich Arab chieftain to his harem, she finds herself surrounded by trivial women who bear a remarkable resemblance to fashionable young ladies in a West-end drawing room. "The diversions of the women . . . were only childish play," recalls Pekuah, virtually echoing contemporary conduct books, "by which the mind accustomed to stronger operations could not be kept busy" (16:138). The irony of this episode would not have been lost on contemporary readers. The oriental harem was incessantly held up as the very antitype of the freedom enjoyed by English women. Yet were not vacuous beauties, competing with pretty rivals for the favor of a rich man, very like a stable of captive girls in an Eastern seraglio?

At least for the dramatic purposes of this tale, Johnson seems willing to corroborate conduct-book advice concerning the deeper and lasting attractions of women able to appeal to men with their intelligence rather than physical charm. The rich and intellectual Arab captor singles out the serious-minded Pekuah from this gang of disposable beauties and, to our heroine's distress, falls in love with her as they gaze through his telescope. But Johnson's talent was always to deepen and complicate the straightforward ideologies that inspired the books and talk of even his most up-to-date contemporaries. Many of Johnson's essays seem determined to disabuse his readers of the impression that learning necessarily helped women to attract eligible young men. "The most attractive beauty of the person," promised Vicesimus Knox, "results from the graces of the mind,"[49] But Johnson's Hymenaeus, in *Rambler* Nos. 113 and 115, is a man who is looking for a wife with some intellectual substance, and four times he discovers that depth of character can present as many obstacles as vacuous charm. Ferocula has wit and spirit, but finally reveals a corrosive penchant for petty dispute; Misothea allures Hymenaeus with her profound learning, but finally dispels this attraction in a cloud of fashionably impious abstractions; Sophronia is a personality who strongly anticipates the Victorian middle-class matron, an unforgiving supervisor of leger-books and pantries who fires servants for broken combs and spilled porridge. But Hymenaeus's final disaster is Camilla (recalling Virgil's Amazonian heroine), who professed "a boundless, contempt for the folly, levity, ignorance, and impertinence of her own sex" (4:249), confounding sexual roles in a way that, as we shall later consider, Johnson found distressing.

Some of these essays even suggest, contrary to the promises of conduct books, that learning could be a definite *disadvantage* to the social or marital fortunes of young women. Zosima in *Rambler* No. 12 finds that her genteel education provokes spiteful envy in the rich women whom she approaches for employment as a servant after her family falls into poverty. Johnson was too much a man of the world, similarly, to doubt that airy-headed young men would prefer women as silly as themselves. In *Rambler* No. 191, he is scolded for promoting learning by a fictional correspondent, the rich and spoiled Bellaria, who complains that "if I had not dropped all pretension to learning, I should have lost Mr. Trip, whom I once frightened into another box" (5:236). As the world went, learning was certainly less useful than a fine face or rich inheritance in gaining a husband. On the other hand – and this is Johnson's main point – knowledge and good sense endowed their possessor with deeper and more valuable riches of the mind and spirit. For Melissa in *Rambler* No. 75 the greatest gift of her unusually bookish education is not, finally, the respect she once received from eligible young men and even scholars, for this deference strangely dissipates after she loses her fortune in a bad fund. What she gains is, more important, equanimity and good humor in the face of misfortune, along with the knowledge of who among her supposed friends had real admiration for her learning and character (only an old priest and an army officer). The real dignity of Melissa contrasts with the numerous ignorant and simpering beauties in Johnson's essays who are paralyzed with boredom once they are carried from the constant physical stimulation of the town, or who are finally left to corrode in empty fashionable marriages with ignorant men.

In valuing female letters and reason primarily as means to personal fulfilment, dignity, and strength, and *not* as ornaments for the snaring of eligible husbands, Johnson earned the esteem of even radical women in later decades. *Rambler* Nos. 130 and 133, reprinted by Mary Wollstonecraft in her *Female Reader* (1789), concern a girl named Victoria who loses her beauty to small-pox and, abandoned by her suitors and her trifling mother, discovers that she was a being intended "to know, to reason, and to act." "Rise at once from your dream of melancholy to wisdom and piety;" she is advised by a worthy female friend, "you will find that there are other charms than those of beauty, and other joys than the praise of fools" (4:345). Wollstonecraft's admiration for Johnson is indeed interesting, for these two authors, so divided in their political outlooks, came to certain shared conclusions about women that discomforted conservative authors like Hannah More or Jane West. Like Wollstonecraft and the Whig historian Catherine Macaulay, Johnson placed little importance on the supposed "natural" differences between the characters of men and women: like those authors, he usually traced gender distinctions to "custom" rather than nature. Writing about the "Amazons" of old and their modern counterparts, the spirited "Amazons of the pen" in England, Johnson observed that "National manners are formed by chance" (*Idler* No. 87, 2:270). While he disliked the martial character of the legendary Amazons, he clearly avoided the implication that they were any more "unnatural" than modern women who had rejected domestic servitude in favor of literary ambition. Strikingly, Johnson seems not to have considered even that most quintessentially "female" instinct, maternal love, as especially powerful. The Countess of Macclesfield, whom Johnson decried for abandoning her alleged illegitimate offspring Richard Savage, is condemned not because abandoning children is "unnatural" (a term he does not use) but because her malignity towards Savage seems so motiveless. The Countess had no "interest" in spurning and even persecuting her supposed son. Yet where an actual "interest" did exist, Johnson makes clear, it was by no means unusual for women to abandon their children, a fact confirmed by the number of foundlings scattered on the streets of eighteenth-century London, the victims of male insouciance and female desperation.[50]

Nevertheless, Johnson and the later radicals took quite different lessons from this observation on the "customary" foundation of female character. Like her fellow radicals Macaulay and Hays, Wollstonecraft championed equal education for women and men, for she despised customs ("prejudices," as she called them) that had prohibited even unmarried women from entering the professional, political, and economic leadership of the nation. Johnson, on the contrary, showed a constant concern to maintain sexual distinctions, as well as the authority of "custom" in matters of social behavior that he considered morally or socially beneficial.

His outrage against the Countess of Macclesfield was venomous, even self-deluding. And here his views pointed in the direction of Hannah More and later conservative women authors, even if they were more inclined than Johnson was to found gender roles on supposed differences of "nature."

Johnson's considerable interest in the construction of gender identity can be detected even as early as *Irene*, the tragedy he carried with him in an unfinished form when arrived in London in 1737. The catastrophic problems dramatized in this play arise from the eponymous heroine's ambition to achieve political power by becoming the courtesan of the Turkish conqueror of her Athenian homeland, Mahomet. Mahomet embodies the oppressive attitudes towards women that allegedly prevailed in the "Orient." His belief that women were only "Form'd to delight" (II, ii, l. 16, 6:146) strongly recalls Johnson's later criticism of Milton's "Turkish contempt for females."[51] Indeed, everything in Johnson's play suggests that Irene and her friend Aspasia are right to believe that they possess the same rational natures as men. Aspasia even rejects the very common assumption in Johnson's age that women were more sensitive and delicate than men: "The weakness we lament, our selves create, / Instructed from our infant years to court / With counterfeited fears the aid of man" (II, i, ll. 26–8, 6:134). Again like Wollstonecraft, Johnson showed very little patience with women who claimed the privileges of fine "sensibility." Nevertheless, the more sensible Aspasia strongly rejects Irene's "amazon" desire to exercise "masculine" power. "When social laws first harmoniz'd the world," she insists, men were given "The scale of Justice, and the sword of Pow'r" (III, viii, ll. 70 and 72, 6:164), evidently by virtue of their superior physical strength. And Aspasia's warnings about women's mixing in the masculine contest for power are borne out by the play's tragic finale, which finds Irene, stripped of her virtue and religion, the hapless victim of murderous machinations in the Sultan's court. But Johnson's message to the women and men in the theater was not that women could exert no influence at all: Aspasia survives as the true feminine exemplar in the play because she confines her influence to giving frank and wifely counsel to her lover, the Greek hero Demetrius, couching her advice in a delicately measured language that Johnson seems to consider a sign of her virtue: "Think – but excuse a woman's needless caution, / Purge well thy mind from ev'ry private passion, / Drive int'rest, love and vengeance from thy thoughts" (IV, i, ll. 5–7, 6:172).

Aspasia's role as the moral counselor, distributing her virtuous influence within the limits of private conversation and personal relationships, is consistent with the social role for women generally advocated in Johnson's writings. As he wrote of women in *Rambler* No. 34, "so much of our domestic happiness is in their hands, and their influence is so great upon our earliest years, that the universal interest of the world requires them to be well instructed in their province" (3:185). This delineation of a woman's "province" reflects Johnson's determination to maintain what we might still call independent "spheres." Everywhere in his work, he reacts with dismay to confusions of gender identity, returning again and again, for example, to the Amazonian image of warrior women. In *Idler* No. 5 he facetiously suggests that fashionable ladies join their beaux in the war against the French, a ludicrous reflection on the notorious "effeminacy" of England's polite gentlemen. In *A Project for the Employment of Authors*, published in April 1756 for the *Universal Visitor*, he rehearsed much the same joke, observing that if "ladies of the pen" were sent to the battlefield they would be useless for domestic duties, and should therefore "form a regiment of themselves."[52] As he would write in *Idler* No. 87, "the character of the ancient Amazons was rather terrible than lovely; the hand could not be very delicate that was only employed in drawing the bow . . . and their example only shews that men and women live best together" (2:272).

It is important to recognize that Johnson's reaffirmation of gender divisions did not represent merely a return to the domestic ideals and constructions of femininity characteristic of the seventeenth century. Even among conservative male writers in the late eighteenth century, many of whom took direct inspiration from Johnson, the ability to make pies and embroider fire-screens was allotted very little importance, at least for women of the upper and upper-middle ranks. Vicesimus Knox was, for example, no rebel against his time's conventional ideology, yet we read in his essay on female education that "I ever thought it the most valuable recommendation of a wife to be capable of becoming a conversible companion to her husband; nor did I ever conceive that the qualifications of a cook-maid, a laundress, or a housekeeper, the most desirable accomplishments in a partner for life."[53] Knox's traditional vision of the educated woman merely as a "companion" is less ambitious than, for example, Fordyce's argument that women of sense and virtue played an essential role in modern culture. They were necessary in "civilizing" the male. The presence of women, declared Fordyce, "converts the savage into a man, and lifts the man into a hero."[54] Similarly, Thomas Gisborne gave women the role of "forming and improving the general manners, dispositions, and conduct of the other sex, by society and example."[55] These were the opinions summarized by Hannah More in her pious riposte to Jacobin femininity, *Strictures on the Modern System of Female Education* (1799): "The general state of civilized society depends," wrote More, "more than those are aware who are not accustomed to scrutinize into the springs of human action, on the prevailing sentiments and habits of women, and on the nature and degree of the estimation in which they are held."[56] More and her predecessors differed from more radical writers in generally wanting to confine female moral influence to the home and immediate neighborhood, for they remained highly resistant to the suggestion that women should wield "the scale of Justice, and the sword of Pow'r," to recall the words of Johnson's Aspasia. What radicals like Wollstonecraft or Hays called the "prejudice" which prohibited even unmarried women from political and professional leadership, they celebrated as the reign of salubrious "custom" and "tradition."

In articulating just this balance between innovation and "custom," change and tradition, Johnson stood as a major and influential precursor to attitudes towards women in the late eighteenth and nineteenth centuries. This observation does require some qualification: as we have seen, Johnson anticipated the radicals in certain key respects, placing almost no importance on "natural" differences between men and women. Conservatives like Fordyce, Gisborne, and More, on the contrary, tended to maintain a belief in women's inherent inclination to moral and "economical" virtues, even if they had clearly moved far from the rigid essentialism that prevailed in the seventeenth century. On the other hand, Johnson was a strong believer in the authority of "custom" in most areas of life, condemning "pride of singularity" and "a voluntary neglect of common forms" (*Adventurer* No. 131, 2:484, 486). Unlike the radicals, with their commitment to the rule of "reason" against "prejudice," Johnson accepted as an inexorable fact of humanity that "most minds are the slaves of external circumstances, and . . . roll down any torrent of custom on which happen to be caught" (*Rambler* No. 70, 4:6). This, he argued, was particularly true of women: "It may be particularly observed of women, that they are for the most part good or bad, as they fall among those who practice vice or virtue; and that neither education nor reason gives them much security against the influence of example" (2:6). In this pragmatic conviction in the insuperable power of custom, Johnson's views led to the conservatism of Burke and of writers such as Gisborne and More who were extending anti-Jacobin ideology to the problem of how to educate women.

It was, moreover, this conservative line of argument that would predominate in the gender ideology of Victorian England. If we look ahead to that doughty arbitress of Victorian womanhood, Sarah Stickney Ellis, we find an amplification of the view that women exerted their appropriate influence not in political affairs but in the home and neighborhood. Again, however, we should not confuse this form of "domesticity" with the much different form preached in the seventeenth century. As Ellis maintained in *The Women of England, Their Social Duties and Domestic Habits* (1839), the place of middle-class women was certainly *not* to labor at domestic chores. "Household avocations," as Ellis called them, had "now fallen into disuse from their incompatibility with modern refinement."[57] The woman's place was, first, to *manage* that labor as performed by the household staff of servants. Second, and just as important, women wielded considerable power over the moral and cultural life of the nation. Indeed, "a nation's moral worth is in your keeping,"[58] for women tended to the spiritual uprightness of men from diapers to breeches, administering their feminine balm on all the mundane and practical anxieties of life. Although this role was served in the salon and sick room, the local charity and church-hall, it was just as crucial to "public" welfare, she insisted, as the role played by their husbands on the more national stage of parliament, bench, and pulpit. Even here women should understand the public duty exercised in private: she urges women to master the principles of political economy so that they could shed their rational influence on men, leading "them away by imperceptible degrees, from those partial views which are the result of prejudice."[59] What Ellis represents, that is, is a historic mediation between the two tendencies that we have traced from the late Renaissance – the increasingly public and active role of women in eighteenth-century English society, and the continuing insistence of most writers on the need to keep gender roles distinct. It is little wonder that, for the majority of Victorian women trained to embrace this compromise, Johnson's essays made for such congenial reading. "My dear Dr. Johnson," as Jane Austen called one of her favorite authors, had articulated precisely this mediation of old and new in gender ideology.[60]

Hence, these developing, even revolutionary, attitudes toward the position of women in society were not just "small change," to quote Harriet Guest's recent term.[61] Literally speaking, they concerned massive transfers of money in a society adjusting uncomfortably to the reality of its new prosperity, "the vast Torrent of Luxury," as Henry Fielding wrote in 1752, "which of late years hath poured itself into this Nation."[62] As we have already suggested, there was an extremely important relationship between the evolving status of women and an expanding capitalist economy that required the financial adrenalin of "luxury."

WOMEN, LUXURY AND "OECONOMY"

In a fascinating comedy published in 1757, *The Tryal of Lady Allurea Luxury*, old and new attitudes towards both gender and the economy are brought before the bench of "Lord-Chief Justice Upright." Lady Allurea seduces her alleged victims in three interconnected ways – she is noble, she is French, and she is a "bewitching" woman. According to the leader of the prosecution, "Mr. Manly," she has fatally debased the morals of the entire nation, or of all except the Crown witness Henry True-Briton, who has removed himself to the Welsh island of Anglesey, where he eats roast-beef and drinks nothing but home-brewed porter. Yet a series of witnesses, mostly from London's financial community, testify that they have given their heart totally to the lovely Lady Allurea. It would be, argues her lawyer Mr Burgamont, "a Contempt to your Understanding" to deny that "she finds Markets for all Sort of Manufactures – encourages the Arts, and every Branch of ingenious Science – and maintains the Poor and Industrious of every Nation that she takes under her Protection."[63] In the end the judge retires to make a decision that is never delivered, for "a Mob of Nobility and Gentry" rescue Lady Allurea as she is being carried away from court.[64] "*God Save the King*," the play ends, apparently sending this whole contentious question back to the dour monarch who presided over both courtly luxury and the nation's general welfare.

On trial in this play were not only current ideas of "luxury" but also new and unfamiliar forms of femininity. The shockingly public allurements of luxury, which had spread like a golden cancer from the nobility even to "the trading Families in the great Cites of *London* and *Westminster*,"[65] seemed to fulfil the Babylonian prophesy that gaudily alluring women would dominate at the end of the world. Yet the inconclusiveness of the play seems to acknowledge that a final condemnation of luxury was self-defeating in a nation where this vice had become central to the economy, for it "finds Markets for all Sorts of Manufactures." *The Tryal of Lady Allurea Luxury*, that is, reflects a historical moment when ambivalent and tortuous reactions to wealth gave rise to similarly fraught and uncertain ruminations on gender.

Consider that "economy," traditionally, was both the diametric *opposite* of "luxury" and a virtue associated specifically with women. As defined in Johnson's *Dictionary*, "oeconomy" (as it was usually spelt) meant exclusively "the management of a family; the government of a household," connoting not luxurious profusion but rather, "frugality; discretion of expense; laudable parsimony." In this sense, oeconomy was closely connected with female domestic government over servants, the kitchen and many household expenses, precisely the activities threatened by the rise of luxury and the new public role of women. In the face of these changes, it is hardly surprising that many men and women continued to look back to a supposed Golden Age of both national and female virtue when women still reigned over household economy. "No Woman in the World," protested Edward Watkinson in his *Essay upon Oeconomy* (1762), "ought to think it *beneath* her to be an OECONOMIST."[66] Watkinson's claim that oeconomy had always been "an *Indispensable Part of Female Employment*"[67] is indeed borne out by any survey of conduct literature a hundred years before, where the management of household expenses and service was conventionally presented as the appropriate realm of femininity.[68] Nor did the ideal of female oeconomy disappear in the late eighteenth and nineteenth centuries, as evidenced by the pronouncement of Johnson's friend, Hester Chapone (*née* Mulso), in her *Letters on the Improvement of the Mind* (1773): "Oeconomy is so important a part of a woman's character, so necessary to her own happiness, and so essential to her performing properly the duties of a wife and of a mother, that it ought to have the precedence of all other accomplishments, and take its rank next to the first duties of life."[69]

If oeconomy was integral to "a woman's character," however, luxury as well had strong and traditional connotations as a characteristically female evil. An obsessive theme in diatribes against luxury, which reached a crescendo in the 1750s and 1760s, was that this vice was sucking out the nation's masculinity, leaving it "effeminate." That luxury was emasculating England was, for example, the lament of John Brown's highly successful *An Estimate of the Manners and Principles of the Times* (1757): softened by affluence and self-indulgence, the robust English males of old had dwindled into "money-getting Cowards,"[70] vain, hedonistic, and flabby, unable to compete with the still hard-chested French, who seemed indeed to be gaining the upper hand in newly commenced hostilities. Even after the British male had presumably proved his masculinity in a string of victories against the French in 1759, moralists continued to taunt the girlish luxury of the upper- and middle-rank men. "Our national effeminacy," wrote Samuel Fawconer in 1765, "seems to have extinguished our national spirit."[71] "The robust and hardy generation of ancient *Britons*," he bemoaned, "is dwindling into a degenerous [*sic*] and puny race of emasculated invalids."[72] This association between luxury and effeminacy belonged to a long tradition of thought that deemed excessive concern for physical pleasure, personal beauty, and dress as inherently "feminine" traits. The peculiar insistence of the association between luxury and effeminacy also disclosed a deep anxiety among many men concerning the unfamiliar boldness of women, who, in the extravagant finery of the enriched middle orders, had converted public assemblies into hot zones of sexual competition. The new public woman sidles towards John Brown with a brazen sensuality that, clearly, he can barely withstand:

In ancient Days, *bare* and *impudent Obscenity*, like a common Woman of the Town, was confined to *Brothels*: Whereas the *Double-Entendre*, like a modern fine Lady, is now admitted into the *best Company*; while her *transparent Covering* of Words, like a *thin* and fashionable *Gauze* delicately thrown across, *discloses* while it seems to *veil*, her *Nakedness* of Thought.[73]

Particularly interesting in these works is the close association between luxury and female publicness. Females who consumed luxuries, as well shown by Elizabeth Kowaleski-Wallace, provoked the same misogynist reaction as commonly directed against women who consumed indelicately at table or who were insufficiently lithe.[74] And luxury had a natural connection with public spaces (the ball, the masquerade, the park) where fineries were brandished with such sexual authority. Hence, the notorious enrichment of the English economy became deeply intertwined with a disruption of gender identities. The highly public "modern fine Lady" presented problems of gender identity because she seemed highly "male" in her willingness to engage with men on equal terms in the sexual market-place previously controlled exclusively by men. As Erasmus Jones complained in an earlier polemic against luxury, "Let no body tell me of the *Respect* that is due to *the Ladies*: – There are no *Ladies*: They have renounc'd and abandon'd whatever is *tender*, whatever is *amiable*, in Woman: and the *Rights* of the SEX are Advantages, which *They* are too *Mannish* to support any Claim to."[75] And John Brown was haunted by the same nightmare of womanish men and masculine ladies, "the one Sex having advanced into *Boldness*, as the other have sunk into *Effeminacy*."[76]

On the other hand, the anxiety of these men was fraught with contradiction, for the new visibility of women belonged, as I have argued, to a program of middle-rank ambition. The young virgin who allured the eligible gentleman at a dance, like her mother dickering over dress-material with a mercer on Ludgate-Hill, was playing an essential role in the new economy. For such a keen social observer as Bernard Mandeville, there was a laughably obvious link between the sexual and economic aggression of the middle ranks:

A young Lady of refin'd Education keeps a strict Guard over her Looks, as well as Actions, and in her Eyes we may read a Consciousness that she has a Treasure about her, not out of Danger of being lost, and which yet she is resolv'd not to part with at any Terms. Thousand Satyrs have been made against Prudes, and as many Encomiums to extol the careless Graces, and negligent Air of virtuous Beauty. But the wiser sort of Mankind are well assured, that the free and open Countenance of the Smiling Fair, is more inviting, and greater yields Hopes to the Seducer, than the ever-watchful Look of a forbidding Eye.[77]

Mandeville's favorite metaphor of a woman's chastity as a "treasure" was of course far from idle, for it marked the intersection between the economic and sexual aspirations of the middle ranks. Luxury, that infamous female vice, had become consistent with oeconomy, that hallowed female virtue, in the newly affluent society that he described. Hence, in conduct books of the middle and late eighteenth century, we find a considerably increased tolerance for female luxury, at least as confined within certain moral limits. "Articles of luxury," wrote John Gregory to his daughters in 1774, were "useful and agreeable when judiciously used."[78] There would always be "gay assemblies," confided James Fordyce, though the accomplished young woman should approach this luxurious vista with "just discernment" rather than "foolish wonder."[79]

This reassessment of the supposed evils of female luxury corresponded with a total rethinking of pleasure and money in Western society. The wind of economic/gender change was blowing strongly from the north, from Scotland, where David Hume, at a very early stage, was translating Mandeville's smirking economic satire into the "easy philosophy" of the newly leisured British middle orders. Hume was pro-luxury, and his views articulate a whole new way of viewing the relationship between luxury and the common good. Luxurious indulgences, he wrote in an essay "Of the Refinement of the Arts" (1742), "are only vices, when they are pursued at the expense of some virtue, as liberality or charity," or "when for them a man ruins his fortune, reduces himself to want and beggary."[80] Within these limits, luxury was not only innocent but even commendable, for it marked the progress of the arts to a higher level of sophistication. Luxury promoted, as well, a society of greater political freedom, benevolence and sociability, where "Both sexes meet in an easy and sociable manner."[81] From these ideas (not exclusively Hume's, but most cogently expressed in his work) can be traced two branches of later Scottish commentary on luxury. One branch is represented by the social histories of Adam Ferguson and John Millar, who portray luxury as the historic mark of societies that have achieved their highest point of affluence and sophistication.[82] Particularly in Millar's *Observations concerning the Distinction of Ranks in Society* (1771), the progress of luxury is linked closely to the liberation of women. Echoing the views of many in his time, Millar dwelled on "the servile condition of the fair sex, in barbarous countries,"[83] waxing eloquent on the dignity and freedom of the British "fair" in comparison not only with female "savages" (who allegedly spent their days skinning animals and hauling fire-wood for the lazy male "savages") but with women everywhere else.[84]

The other branch of ideas stemming from Hume's defense of luxury was the political oeconomy of James Steuart and Adam Smith. Evidently, it was Steuart who first started using "oeconomy" in its modern sense of the theory of wealth in a nation, beginning his *Inquiry into the Principles of Political Oeconomy* (1767) with an analogy between household and national oeconomy. Significantly, this introduction totally omitted any mention of women's traditional role virtue of oeconomy.[85] This "masculinizing" of oeconomy is indeed highly revealing of evolving ideas towards gender. Particularly as used by Adam Smith in *The Wealth of Nations* (1776), oeconomy signified not the direct *management* of a nation's finances, as on the model of the female-run household, but rather the theory of how, in fact, not to manage or interfere with economic processes that should be left to run on their own. Women represented over-management, the tendency to control too directly; men, who saw more widely, understood the need to leave well alone. And within the logic of this new male oeconomy, luxury played an important role in generating and disseminating wealth throughout the whole freely running system.

Hence, the invention of the science of economics had two major ramifications for the role of British women. First, the traditional female vice of luxury gained an important measure of tolerance as a genuine economic *good.* This development implied a significant degree of acceptance of the new, more public role of women in a society transformed by the middle-class revolution. On the other hand, the traditional female virtue of oeconomy was officially demoted to a secondary and lower place as the art of managing practical affairs, in contrast with the higher, abstruse and intellectual science of "economics." Ideologically, women were allotted the role celebrated by Sarah Stickney Ellis and her Victorian milieu – the earth-bound role of managing the immediate moral and physical needs of the family and the neighborhood. Men, on the other hand, were untethered to float in the stratosphere of abstract reasoning.

These changes in the linked concepts of gender, luxury, and economy constitute an important context for understanding Johnson's perspectives on both women and commerce. As copiously recorded by the pleasure-loving Boswell, Johnson liked to challenge more dour and conventional-minded friends, like Oliver Goldsmith, who echoed the old laments about the plague of modern luxury. "Luxury, as far it reaches the poor," he told Goldsmith "will do good to the race of people; it will strengthen and multiply them."[86] These typical comments by Johnson belong to the tradition of ideas from Mandeville to Smith that stressed the broader economic benefits of luxury, the theme as well of Johnson's *Adventurer* No. 67. In this essay, Johnson marveled that "custom, curiosity, or wantonness, supplies every art with patrons, and finds purchasers for every manufacture." "Not only by these popular and modish trifles," he went on, "but by a thousand unheeded and evanescent kinds of business, are the multitudes of this city preserved from idleness, and consequently from want" (2:385). This was a prosperity that he contrasted with the hardship and ignorance of the life of a "savage" (2:388–9), a distinction he took with him in 1773 to the country of Hume, Millar, and Smith. In Scotland, Johnson saw everywhere signs of a people just emerging from barbarous penury to the convenience, prosperity, and fashion of a modern, "civilized" society like England. Luxury, he agreed with its defenders, was the glittering badge of refinement and culture.

To this extent, Johnson was merely piling the building blocks of that durable modern edifice, capitalist ideology. In other ways, however, his contribution to this ideology was more original and distinctive, shaping as well his views on gender. First, Johnson had very little good to say about the traditional female virtue of oeconomy. He even, we might say, "deconstructed" the old binary of luxury/oeconomy. In the *Idler*, written just in the wake of John Brown's polemic against luxury in 1757, he repeatedly portrays exemplary "economical" women as heartless, absurd and, oddly, "luxurious." The fictional correspondents in *Idler* Nos. 13 and 100 both marry painstaking housekeepers and prudent managers, only to find their sensible wives dull and loveless. "Peter Plenty" in *Idler* No. 35 has a more peculiar problem with his wife. "Whatever she thinks cheap," he observes, "she holds it the duty of an oeconomist to buy; in consequence of this maxim, we are incumbered on every side with useless lumber" (2:109). This prosperous middle-rank gentleman finds himself served cheap salted meat in a parlour crowded with the useless chairs and extra china that his wife has bought at bargain prices. The obsession with saving money leads, absurdly, to superfluity. It is indeed a peculiarity of Johnson's portrayal of women that, in his view, they are far more inclined to be faulted in the direction of avarice than luxurious extravagance. The money-grubbing men in Johnson's essays, from Squire Bluster in *Rambler* No. 142 to Captator in *Rambler* Nos. 197 and 198, have in common that they were transformed into mean-spirited devotees of Mammon by the money-grubbing females who reigned over their families.

This intense distrust of female oeconomy was not really typical of his time, and must have perplexed prudent-minded female friends like Hester Chapone and Hannah More. On the other hand, Johnson's satire of *excessive* oeconomy in the traditional sense is consistent with the suspicion of economic management that would characterize the founders of *laissez-faire* capitalism, Hume, Steuart, and Smith. To this powerful tradition of modern thought, moreover, Johnson added a justification of luxury as a *natural* human drive – a drive shared by both men and women.

In this respect, *Rasselas* (1759) may well be regarded as a significant, even historic, work in the evolution of both economic and gender ideology. Two years after *The Tryal of the Lady Allurea Luxury* and two years after John Brown had charged that "our present exorbitant Degree of Trade and Wealth"[87] had reduced England to "effeminacy," Johnson created the very embodiment of luxury, the Happy Valley. This is a world devoted entirely to the pursuit of pleasure. Contrary to the assumption of "Estimate" Brown, Erasmus Jones or Oliver Goldsmith, however, it is a world entirely without "trade" or commerce of any kind, being a carefully mummified relic of a feudal past (like its symbolic equivalent, the catacombs at the end of *Rasselas*). From this hedonistic place, the son of a merchant, Imlac, leads one male and two female travelers into a distinctly modern world ruled by commerce. Only money talks here, not rank, as the princess Nekayah discovers at the outset to her prickly, class-conscious dismay. But there is certainly nothing "effeminate" about this modern world. Indeed, it is Nekayah who seems to grow most towards unsentimental and "masculine" rationalism. She finally doubts even the happiness of that all-consuming *telos* of eighteenth-century womanhood, marriage, and then resolves, like Mary Astell, to found a college for women. Similarly, her companion Pekuah sharpens into a highly rationalistic individual, mastering astronomy and resolving at the end to retire to a convent, also like Mary Astell. The effect of a capitalist world, that is, seems not to "effeminize" men but to encourage women towards more intellectual and spiritual pursuits.

Yet, paradoxically, even these rather Spartan women display a *kind* of luxury, at least as this idea was usually understood in the eighteenth century. What they pursue is fulfilment beyond mere physical necessity and that, according to the monastic standard brandished provocatively by Mandeville, is what luxury should *strictly* mean. Johnson, anticipating Adam Smith and others, in fact deemed this signification far too rigid: in his *Dictionary*, he defined "luxury" not as mere superfluity, but as "Voluptuousness; addictedness to pleasure." For, as Johnson so often stressed, the urge to go beyond mere physical need was the origin of all improvement, all art, all knowledge. This is the message of an *Idler* essay written in late December 1758 when Johnson was conceiving *Rasselas*.[88] "Even of knowledge," he wrote, "those parts are most easy, which are generally necessary. The intercourse of society is maintained without the elegancies of language. Figures, criticisms, and refinements are the work of those whom idleness makes weary of themselves" (2:116). Could not, that is, the pursuit of knowledge be construed itself as a kind of pursuit of "pleasure," as facilitated particularly by the physical leisure permitted by modern economic affluence? This is the suggestion made by Imlac in his long autobiography near the beginning of *Rasselas*: "Knowledge is certainly one of the means of pleasure, as is confessed by the natural desire which every mind feels of increasing its ideas" (16:49). In contrast with his merchant father, who was characterized by "diligence and parsimony," Imlac would not be boxed within the leger-sheets of middle-order prudence, but insisted on being non-"economical" (in the traditional sense) by sailing around the globe to glut his appetite for knowledge. Prefiguring his royal charges, he left certain physical prosperity to drink luxuriously "at the fountains of knowledge, to quench the thirst of curiosity" (16:34). And having made the mistake of passing through the gates of the Happy Valley, Imlac now shares the desire of the prince and princess to throw himself once more onto the tempestuous river of the outside world, a river impelled by the "choice of life."

Rasselas, that is, erects a powerful philosophical foundation for an essentially "free-market" understanding of human nature and social development. The pursuit of greater and greater gratification, thought Johnson (exemplifying what Marx would consider a central myth of capitalism), represented an inherent, "natural" drive of humankind. By their very nature, capitalist economies reflect the supposed realities of human nature, for the desire for superfluity, for gratification beyond mere physical need, could only be hindered through such a decidedly *unnatural* system as the "Happy Valley." The endlessness of the human drives for fulfilment is dramatically symbolized in *Rasselas* by the pyramids, which Imlac presents as monuments to the "hunger of the imagination." As he tells the travelers, "A king, whose power is unlimited, and whose treasures surmount all real and imaginary wants, is compelled to solace, by the erection of a pyramid, the satiety of dominion and the tastelessness of pleasures, and to amuse the tediousness of declining life, by seeing thousands labouring without end, and one stone, for no purpose, laid upon another" (16:119). There is certainly nothing "effeminate" about this excess of kingly power and self-indulgence. As readers of the time would have seen, Johnson was rejecting both the recent critiques of luxury and their obsessive association between luxury and effeminacy. Men and women, he thought, shared equally in this hunger for excess. Elsewhere, he drew a direct link between the "consumer" aspirations of women and their increasing mental cultivation. In *Idler* No. 39 he begins by describing a new fashion article, bracelets designed by women with pictures on them, and then goes on to deliver an encomium on "female erudition":

> This addition of art to luxury is one of the innumerable proofs that might be given of the late increase of female erudition; and I have often congratulated myself that my life has happened at a time when those, on whom so much of human felicity depends, have learned to think as well speak, and when respect takes possession of the ear, while love is entering at the eye. (2:122)

In short, modern affluence and luxury had not made women more wicked or men more effeminate. The changes had made women more learned and more virtuous. Perhaps no writer of the eighteenth century, male or female, made this argument so fully as did Samuel Johnson.

Once again, however, we must avoid the temptation of concluding that Johnson was a "radical" or a "progressive" on either of those interconnected fields of eighteenth-century social discourse, gender and economics. We have already seen that he ultimately supported a version of the traditional division of gender roles, even if he thought these divisions were *arbitrary* rather than "natural." Even in *Rasselas*, the possibility that the princess, like the prince, might like to govern a kingdom is never considered. And when the travelers encounter the melancholy-mad astronomer, Nekayah and Pekuah go into action in the traditional female role as healers of the tormented male soul, mollifying the lonely astronomer with their conversation and pulling him back to "earth." Similarly, Johnson's acceptance of the acquisitive and socially ambitious nature of all human beings did not diminish his commitment to "subordination" and the strict division of social classes, for he was convinced that this division was necessary to control and channel the destabilizing forces that modern affluence had unleashed. As would become increasingly apparent in the course of the century, indeed, the maintenance of gender divisions and of class divisions were closely interconnected with the aims of specifically middle-class interests.

CLASS POWER AND NATURALIZING THE MIDDLE-CLASS "WOMAN"

Virtually all the women portrayed in Johnson's writing belong to the middle orders, the exceptions being some satirical sketches of noble women in the *Rambler* and a single woman from the lower orders, Betty Broom in *Idler*

Nos. 26 and 29 (whose desire to be literate Johnson treats with genuine respect). Even the princess Nekayah seems mostly to represent the middle ranks, for she must adjust to a world where her royal origins mean little, and where she must experience the usual questions broached in female conduct books – to marry or not to marry, the nature of good female education, the silliness of women who set their minds only on fashion and men. In general, Johnson's women suffer *not*, as the modern reader might expect, from thwarted ambition in a male-dominated world, but from uncertainties and conflicts of social rank. For example, Zosima, in *Rambler* No. 12, is the daughter of an impoverished gentleman. Due to a financial crisis in the family, she is forced to seek employment below her rank and education in the homes of rich women in both the City and the West End. Because she has been raised in the manner of a gentlewoman, however, she is envied and despised by these ladies as "too fine" for service, and is finally left teetering on the precipice of indigence and prostitution, saved only at the last moment by another gentlewoman of "fine sense" (3:67). But the abyss of prostitution is what finally engulfs Misella in two fine essays, *Rambler* Nos. 170 and 171. Misella is another daughter of a gentleman in straitened circumstances who leaves her dependent on a wealthy relative. The slippery slide into the alleys of Covent Garden begins when her adoptive guardian loses interest in her welfare, relegating her to domestic labours not appropriate to a young lady of her rank and education. As Misella recalls, she was "degraded from my equality and enjoyed few privileges above the head servant, but that of receiving no wages" (5:137). Direct abuse begins when the relative becomes aroused by the presence of a blossoming gentlewoman helplessly in his power, and from there Johnson leads us down the gutter of a conventional tragedy.

In these essays, we witness the tragedy of middle-rank women forced down into a station that did not belong to them. The burgeoning lower-world of female servants, on the other hand, who weathered their fate at the bottom of many a polished stairwell of the eighteenth century, is very seldom the subject of Johnson's writing or conversation. But the ambition to climb *up* this stairwell to the level of the master and mistress's dining room filled him with anxiety. A revealing essay is *Idler* No. 53, the story of an anonymous gentleman disconcerted by the social ambitions of his wife. Though a man "of a fortune by no means exuberant" (2:165), he has the "misfortune" of moving into a street close to the residences of the nobility. Here his wife, once notable for her oeconomy, becomes obsessed with squeezing her way through the doors of her opulent neighbours, finally sneaking to the elbow one Lady Biddy Porpoise. While her hapless husband is left to care for the household accounts, this lady spends her days and nights at the card-parties and assemblies of the great, where she is barely tolerated. The worse effect of this ambition, we are told, is the deprivation of her "understanding": "She has no rule of action but the fashion. She has no opinion but that of the people of quality. She has no language but the dialect of her own set of company" (2:166).

The tendency of Johnson's essays is, in brief, to portray the troubled fate of middle-rank women who drift either up or down the social scale. These are women who have tragically left (willingly or unwillingly) the social space for which they were intended – the middle. As we have seen, this is also the appropriate station of the new gentleman, whom Johnson instructs and shapes in numerous essays. For both gentlemen and gentlewomen, the badge of middle-rank people is their learning and intelligence, traits that Johnson often contrasts with the air-brained hedonism of the *beau monde*. What we find, therefore, is that Johnson forges habitual and close links between gender and class. And in this habit of thinking about gender and class simultaneously, Johnson both reflects his time and looks forward to the end of the century and beyond.

For a highly significant characteristic of later writing about and for women, especially after 1790, was its obsessive linking of gender and social class. A revealing and interesting example of this trend is Priscilla Wakefield's *Reflections on the Present Condition of the Female Sex* (1798). Wakefield divided society in a fairly conventional way into four classes, the nobility, the untitled rich, the "self-sufficient" middle ranks and the "labouring poor."[89] Each corresponded in her view with different female duties and the need for a different kind of education. She was particularly indignant that "Tradesmen and millinners are fond of bringing up their daughters in what they term a genteel manner." Such socially ambitious citizens, she insisted, should not be encouraged to give their daughters skills like music, dancing, drawing, and foreign languages.[90] Instead they should be taught the "well-ordered oeconomy" suited to their partnership with a man of trade.[91] Within her four-class division, therefore, Wakefield was drawing a more subtle distinction between the upper- and lower-middle ranks. The daughters of merchants and professions are allotted a very different set of duties and a different kind of education than their sisters lower down the traditional middling orders. These were young women, she indicated, whose "refinement of manners unfit them from any occupation of a sordid menial kind."[92] What they required instead was "liberal cultivation," particularly "an intimate acquaintance with the best authors, who have excelled in history, biography, poetry, and morality."[93]

Wakefield's approach to gender and class thus closely parallels developments in the education of middle-class gentlemen during precisely the same period. As we have seen, the liberal education prescribed for the sons of merchants and professionals was meant similarly to distinguish them from the vulgar spawn of shop-keepers and mechanics, who had been trying in the later eighteenth century to catch the rising coat-tails of people like Samuel Johnson and Priscilla Wakefield (wife of a well-to-do Quaker merchant). The significance of this parallel development is that both men and women of this group were being enlisted in the late eighteenth-century campaign to forge a union between the upper-middle and upper orders, while stopping the downward slide of "gentility" to "pedlars," as Johnson called Wilkite protesters in *The False Alarm*. Indeed, young women performed absolutely crucial work in this consolidation of middle-class identity. Most obviously, their wise selection of spouses determined the tribal coherence of the middle orders, and could even forge real family links between the nobility and their upper-middle-class allies. Furthermore, the elegant chit-chat of a polite "mixed" assembly, seasoned with allusions to Milton, Pope, and Samuel Johnson, constituted the atmosphere of elite social hegemony, an atmosphere designed to be unbreathable by shop-keeping riffraff like the widow Prune in *Rambler* No. 182. The exemplary description of this company of learned men and women was, indeed, Boswell's *Life*, where the literary hero interacts to a degree unprecedented in biography with socially legitimate people of both sexes.

The use of women as the agents of class-definition and social control is most obvious in the work of politically conservative writers like Hannah More, whose career and reputation were indeed gilded by Boswell's portrait of her friendship with Johnson. More's proclamation that the "very existence" of modern civilization relied on the virtue, taste, and learning of "women of the superior class" is only superficially addressed to the upper crust of English womanhood.[94] In fact, More's *Strictures on the Modern System of Female Education* defines "women of rank and fortune"[95] in such a nebulous way as to make any lady of adequate income, taste, and learning (such as herself) the arbitress of civilization's moral and religious welfare. In contrast, the woman of the trading class is consigned to the less glamorous role of being the "narrow minded vulgar economist" filling out the household leger and attending to the practical duties of the kitchen.[96] As lower-class writers like Ann Yearsley found out, More's patronage of women further down the ranks was patronizing to a withering extreme. While More is an easy target of modern liberalism, even the Whig ladies of the late eighteenth century seem, in fact, only fractionally better as promoters of social equality. The Whig historian Catherine Macaulay, who was once challenged by Johnson to let her servant sit at the dinner table,[97] would make no apologies for addressing her *Letters on Education* (1790) to the relatively few women in families able to afford the course of erudition that she recommended. "Cavillers may raise objections to the author's rules of education on the following grounds," she wrote, " – That the plan can alone be carried into general practice by the opulent." In her defense against this "cavil," Macaulay sounds little different from More in maintaining that wealthy women need a special education because they were responsible for the moral progress of civilization: "To these objections the answer is plain and fair. – That it is men of opulence alone who can reap the choicest fruits of the industry and ingenuity of their species – That the education of the great, were it properly attended to, and pursued on the best rules, would be felt in the improved virtues of all the subordinate classes of citizens."[98]

Mary Wollstonecraft's views on class and gender present more knotty difficulties. This fiery veteran of Revolutionary Paris could hardly have been unaware of demands among laboring-class women for inclusion in the general progress of women's rights, as demonstrated by her trenchantly realistic portrait of an abused laboring-class woman, Jemima, in her posthumously published novel *Maria*. Moreover, Wollstonecraft linked social and gender change in a way that is precociously Marxist, for she believed that women could never be convinced of their interest to be rational and independent so long as they witnessed upper-class ladies wallowing in prolonged and luxurious childhood. For Wollstonecraft, as for Marx and Engels, gender relations would be rationalized only when the hereditary class-system was destroyed. On the other hand, the "woman" whose rights are defended in *A Vindication of the Rights of Woman* seems to possess decidedly middle-order values and interests. This ideal middle-class woman wished to be educated with the same books used by men and to have access to the same professions – at least if she did not decide to marry, for Wollstonecraft endorses essentially conventional ideals of female domesticity in the family:

> I have . . . viewed with pleasure a woman nursing her children, and discharging the duties of her station with, perhaps, merely a servant maid to take off her hands the servile part of the household business. I have seen her prepare herself and children, with only the luxury of cleanliness, to receive her husband, who returning weary home in the evening found smiling babes and a clean hearth. My heart has loitered in the midst of the group, and has even throbbed with sympathetic emotion, when the scraping of the well known foot has raised a pleasing tumult.[99]

That her defense of the "woman's" right to rational education is actually meant for women of the middle orders, and not for lower-order women like the "servant maid," is made clear at key points in the *Vindication*. In the very few places in the *Vindication* where Wollstonecraft even mentions the situation of lower-rank women, her prose gains the condescending tone we hear in so many middle-class tracts of the 1790s:

> To render the poor virtuous they must be employed, and women in the middle rank of life, did they not ape the fashions of the nobility, without catching their ease, might employ them, whilst they themselves managed their families, instructed their children, and exercised their own minds. Gardening, experimental philosophy, and literature, would afford them subject to think of and matter for conversation, that in some degree could exercise their understandings.[100]

A scrutiny of this and other passages in the *Vindication* discloses a clear division of labor. If a great element of progress in women's "rights" in the eighteenth century meant that the middle rank could spend more time cultivating their "understanding," the labor they used to perform in a smaller economy, within a more prescribed "domestic" space, was increasingly shifted onto the shoulders of working-class women and men. No woman inveighed, for instance, more bitterly against the male "suppression" of female intelligence than Mary Hays in her caustic *Appeal to the Men of Great-Britain* (1798). Yet here is what Hays says about "the art of cookery" which has been "totally abandoned in the higher ranks" (meaning not just noble women, but also the upper-middle orders):[101] "I therefore with submission, think, that women of a certain rank or fortune, are fully justified in leaving both the theory and practice of this delectable and elegant art, to those whom it is their duty to employ for that purpose."[102]

Hence, writers as diverse as Wollstonecraft and More were creating an entity called "woman" whose rights and privileges were measured *not* against those of working-class men (who in fact could not vote, and had very limited access to education and other privileges) but against the rights and privileges of middle-class gentlemen. As shown in recent excellent scholarship on Victorian womanhood, it was increasingly the case that middle-class femininity became "naturalized" into the very embodiment of what was truly "woman." Hence, Sarah Stickney Elllis could claim, amazingly, that middle-class women "might be more specifically denominated *women*" than females either above or below their rank, for they "enjoy the privilege of liberal education, with exemption from the pecuniary necessity of labour."[103] Such a naturalization of middle-class femininity served as an important instrument of class-power within the household, where the Victorian matron reigned over the staff, male and female, "downstairs." By the 1830s and 1840s, as Elizabeth Langland observes in *Nobody's Angels: Middle-Class Women and Domestic Ideology in Victorian Culture*, "middle-class women controlled significant discursive practices," for they governed "the dissemination of certain knowledges and thus helped to ensure a middle-class hegemony in mid-Victorian England."[104] By these "discursive practices" Langland means the female authority over the nation's morals that was widely bestowed on women by both conservative and radical authors of the eighteenth century. It was a power exercised, for the most part, through the neglected medium of oral culture (the scolding of a servant in the parlor, the shunning of immoral women and men, the charitable advice dispensed in the home of a local poor family). But its literary manifestations include Victorian novels that, in sharp contrast with the Richardsonian model a century before, largely abandoned the fantasy of union between upper-class men and lower-order women, celebrating instead the decorous and appropriate consolidation of middle-rank identity.

To a much greater degree than is often conceded, in short, the construction of gender has been tied closely to the broader work of constructing class: from the beginning of the century, the wives and daughters of "gentlemen" played an important role in defining the boundaries and creating the values of the social stratum that, by the 1790s, had come to think of itself as the "middle-class." That not only men but also women of this era regarded Johnson's writing and words as a trove of wisdom should not, then, surprise us: just as he helped to shape an image of solid middle-class masculinity, so his promotion of learning, rationality, and virtue among women belonged to a much larger project of middle-rank consolidation – a project that, to a surprising degree, feminists like Wollstonecraft and Hays *carried on* from both male and female essayists and conduct-book authors during the previous century. Like both male and female contemporaries, and even like many suffragettes of the nineteenth century,[105] Johnson believed that the situation for women had not deteriorated but vastly improved since the seventeenth century: in the middle ranks, at least, women had more access to learning and circulated with men with a freedom they never had before. In the way Johnson and his contemporaries understood these terms, the lives of women had become *less* "domestic" and *more* "public." Women, they believed, exercised unprecedented power over society, for women were the acknowledged guardians of the nation's moral welfare, the judges of "taste," the "tamers" of men. If we now insist that the "public" must also include access to the professions or the world of politics, this is not because we are essentially overturning the principles of Johnson and his Georgian milieu. It is because we have continued to promote the founding values and strategies of middle-rank hegemony, including the greater participation of women in the work of protecting and promoting middle-class power, towards their logical outcomes.

CHAPTER 3

From "Broad-bottom" to "party": the rise of modern English politics

JOHNSON AS "REVOLUTION TORY"

In the evolution of English politics, as in the development of ideologies of class and gender, Johnson's life spanned a crucial era, and may even be said to mirror the development of a recognizably modern political praxis and philosophy. This evolution was marked by England's transformation from a society rancorously divided over questions of dynastic succession to a nation preoccupied with questions of political privilege and liberties, especially as connected with the varying rights and economic relations of its social ranks. These are the issues that increasingly pitted conservatives against radicals, a new kind of "Tory" against a new kind of "Whig." To maintain that Johnson would come even to embody the outlooks of eighteenth-century conservatism, therefore, is not to imply that he remained entrenched in the attitudes of a past era or a defunct political ideology. His "Toryism" transformed during his life in relation to a broader restructuring of English political alignments. In tracing this development in his political thought and allegiances, we can gain important insights into the early growth of the English party politics that would coalesce fully in the nineteenth century and continue to shape British politics to the present day.

This claim for Johnson's political modernity will be controversial for a number of reasons. Until recently, there has been wide consensus among historians that party, like social class, was a phenomenon only of the last decade of the eighteenth century or even later.[1] This opinion stems from the influential work of Sir Lewis Namier, who convinced most scholars that the distinction between "Whigs" and "Tories" became politically irrelevant during the age after 1714 when Whigs monopolized power. Thereafter, the only relevant division was between "Court" and "Country" – between, that is, those predominantly aristocratic Whigs who circulated through the King's cabinet and those who waited outside, usually adopting aggressive but ultimately self-interested postures of Opposition. In this portrait of

Georgian politics there is little room for ideology or political conviction, only the appetite for power among a few favored circles linked by family or patronage. Namier's picture has nonetheless been challenged, particularly by historians who have revived the Victorian assumption that Tories constituted a genuine "party" at least until their proscription from government ended with the accession of George III in 1760. Linda Colley has attempted to demonstrate a large degree of coherence and party organization among Tories even in the 1730s and 40s; J.C.D. Clark and Eveline Cruikshanks have attempted to ascribe this coherence to a hard-dying loyalty among Tories to the exiled Stuart family and the doctrine of divine right.[2]

Both the "Namierite" and "revisionist" schools have influenced scholarship on Johnson, often with clamorous results. On the side of Namier, Donald Greene fiercely challenged the old Victorian truism that Johnson was an ardent Tory by insisting that this label signified, at most, an Opposition rump of country gentlemen. Johnson may have identified with these gentlemen, but he was friendly with Whigs and in most respects close to them ideologically.[3] Greene has in turn been assailed with equal ferocity by J.C.D. Clark and Howard Erskine-Hill, who have attempted to restore the very old, even pre-Victorian, image of Johnson as a Jacobite. The battle between these groups has been heated to the point of acrimony, for no issue apparently inspires Johnson scholars with polemical passion like the issue of eighteenth-century party politics.

As in discussions of many areas of Johnson's life and thought, scholars have not often taken fully into account that his attitudes were unfolding in conjunction with the changing circumstances and ideologies of his era. In other words, Johnson's expressions in 1739, or even in 1758, must be understood as drawing from a much different political and social atmosphere than his expressions in 1770 or 1784. As a newcomer to London in the late 1730s, Johnson entered a tempestuous political climate where "party" remained a more or less dirty word. The proclaimed goal of the Opposition to Sir Robert Walpole's administration, which was allegedly founded on insular loyalty to "party" (understood as a self-serving association of patrons and cronies), was the elimination of these groups and the creation of what must now strike us as a naively optimistic goal – a political union founded solely on common loyalty to the national good (perhaps as embodied by a "Patriot King"). Hence the mission of the self-styled "Broad-bottom" politicians to draw members of all political leanings into a new "patriotic" coalition. Interestingly, Johnson appears to have been closely linked with the Broad-bottom Opposition in the decade following his move to London: I will even go so far as to suggest that he owed many of his early literary opportunities to the favor of patrons and politicians (Chesterfield, Dodsley, Lyttelton, Fielding, and others) closely linked with the Broad-bottom circle. It is also significant, however, that Johnson assertively maintained his identity as a Tory throughout his life. This label did not automatically imply that he remained loyal to the exiled Stuarts, even early in his career. In pamphlets of the 1730s and 1740s setting out a "constitution" or "revolution" Tory outlook, this term came to stand instead for belief that principle rather than expediency, conviction rather than interest, should guide political behavior. An examination of Johnson's own writings during his early years as a pamphleteer and journalist, including his vividly imagined dramatizations of parliamentary debates, suggests that he favored the Tories in this *updated* sense, an identity that suggests an important degree of modernity in his views. Consistent with the evolving idea of party, Johnson became convinced of the need for *principled* political action, while also concluding that no globalized Broad-bottom consensus could be finally achieved. Allegiance to "party," he thought, was both inevitable and commendable so far as it was founded on conviction.

To make this case for Johnson's political modernity, however, we must first cross through the scholarly battle-zone that has erupted around his views on Britain's dynastic heritage. The case for Johnson's Jacobitism leans heavily on two assumptions. The first is that, as J.C.D. Clark contends, "a real ideological divide" separated Tories and Whigs throughout the first half of the century, and that this rift opened at the question of the legitimacy of the Hanoverian succession. The word "Tory," that is, carried clear connotations of Jacobitism until at least 1745.[4] A second and associated assumption is that hostility towards the Hanoverian monarchs is a good indication of desire for a Stuart restoration, at least among those who were not violently republican Whigs. In the words of Howard Erskine-Hill, while it was "commonplace . . . to attack Walpole as the corrupt manager of a corrupt system," it was clearly quite another matter "to attack the king on the throne."[5] This inference is of particular significance to the case for Johnson's alleged Jacobitism, for the great majority of the evidence for his loyalty of the Stuarts is negative. On the one hand, he affirmed that the Glorious Revolution that dethroned James II was necessary and right; he denied that he believed in the divine right of kings; he ardently supported George III. But from early writings like "London" and *Marmor Norfolciense* to later statements to Boswell, he sometimes sounds bitterly irreverent towards the King and the Hanoverian family.

Both these contentions for Johnson's Jacobitism nonetheless confront considerable obstacles in the historical context of his work. It should pique our suspicion, first, that leaping on hearsay evidence that Johnson supported the Pretender, or construing his statements as crypto-Jacobite codes, rehearses the repeated and fairly crude maneuver of Whig polemicists and Johnson's own worst enemies. There can be no doubt that a portion of professed Tories were Jacobite or, at least, as Linda Colley has proposed, resorted to the Stuart option when their own political prospects seemed forever blocked under the Hanoverians.[6] Clearly documented negotiations between prominent Tories and the Pretender took place from Atterbury in 1722 to the Tory leaders Sir Watkin Williams Wynn and Sir John Hynde Cotton in 1743. Not surprisingly, supporters of the administration took advantage of such waverings to tar all Tories, and even most so-called Whig opponents, as a gang of crypto-Jacobites. In his long and furious attack on the Opposition, *Faction Detected by the Evidence of Facts* (1743), John Perceval, Earl of Egmont, declared that the distinction between "Whigs" and "Tories" was actually a "Delusion of Names" covering up a more sinister reality. Although, generally speaking, the administration's enemies were men of "*no Principle*" who sought only personal advancement, the Tories included covert enemies of the Hanoverian succession who only *pretended* to espouse Whig principles of loyalty to the Revolution and the Protestant religion: "the most inveterate Jacobite Faction, to carry its View, will profess to act upon Whig Principle, when that becomes the favorite Principle, as it is at this time."[7] This charge would be repeated many times in the decade following the publication of this frequently reprinted pamphlet. In 1744, a Court supporter writing under the pseudonym "Petronius" charged that the campaign against the ministry was orchestrated by "*French Jesuits* and *Popish Emisaries*."[8] As late as 1753, a pamphleteer alleged that the Tory party "is generally composed of secret *Papists*, *Jacobites*, *Non-jurors*, and such *bigoted Churchmen*."[9]

Such piling-up of political demons has the brimstone smell of a witch-hunt. And there are surely good reasons to doubt claims coming from pro-government writers with a strong vested interest in discrediting the Tories. Perceval's accusations, for example, were widely rejected even by politicians who had no reason to flatter this group. No less a convinced Whig than Horace Walpole, for instance, declared in 1748 that the Tories had "wiped off" the imputation of secret Jacobitism "by the Zeal of their whole Party for his Majesty in the Time of the Rebellion." Some historians would now claim that Walpole's assertion that "Jacobitism was extinguish'd in *England*"[10] was too hasty. But his conviction that Toryism should not be confused with Jacobitism was shared by his long-time opponent among the Patriot Whigs, George Lyttelton. As Lyttelton argued in *A Letter to the*

Tories (1747), "All Jacobites are Tories, tho' all Tories are not Jacobites . . . A Jacobite is a Tory and something more, as a Dissenter is a Whig and something more."[11]

Thesc Whig authors had come to believe protestations expressed for years by Tories that the accusation of Jacobitism was state propaganda, and that they no longer supported the Stuarts any more than the other doctrines traditionally associated with them, such as "non-resistance" to the throne and opposition to all toleration for dissenters. This was the case advanced, for example, by the anonymous author of *The Loyal or Revolutionary Tory* (1733), who insisted that Tories were no more uniformly Jacobite than all Whigs were republicans, an equally strident wing of that political grouping: "amongst the *Tories* a proper Distinction may be made, between those who are tainted with the detestable Principles of *Jacobitism*, and those *Tories*, who are as heartily attach'd to the present Establishment, as the most rigid *Whigs* in the Kingdom."[12] A later author appealed with some force to the evidence of the parliamentary behavior of the Tories, their opposition to the Excise Act, the Riot Act, the Black Act and other measures designed to put more power into the hands of parliament as evidence that Tories were the true defenders of "Revolution" principles: "From the Industry of designing Men," this author complained, ". . . the Public was inclined to think, that *Whiggism* imply'd *Resistance*, and *Toryism*, *Non-resistance*, to all Encroachments by either the *Regal* or *Ministerial* Power: But upon what Truth this *Belief* was founded, will best appear from the Conduct of the two different *Parties*, that join'd in the *Opposition* to the late *Minister*, both before and after his *Resignation*."[13]

The typical retort of "revisionist" historians like Clark or Erskine-Hill is to insist that such statements are a smoke-screen in a crypto-Jacobite strategy to infiltrate the towers of the Hanoverian elite. Yet this argument bears a disturbing resemblance to the flip of a double-headed coin. On the one hand, direct statements dismissing the identification of Tories with Jacobites are dismissed as camouflage for covert operations; on the other hand, Whig assertions that all Tories are secret conspirators for a Stuart Restoration are weighed seriously not as propaganda but as sound historical evidence. Clark's case for Johnson's Jacobitism rests heavily on charges against him by notorious Whigs such as Joseph Towers (1737–99) and John Scott (1730–83), who were still boys in 1745, and could hardly be called either objective or knowledgeable about this cause.[14] Elsewhere, he cites the polemic of another vehement Whig, Henry Brooke, as evidence that Oxford University was filled with Jacobites; yet Johnson's diatribe against the suppression of Brooke's Opposition play *Gustavus Vasa* (1738) is later cited as evidence of Johnson's Jacobitism, as if Clark had not previously deployed Brooke as a representative Whig.[15]

Nor is it accurate to infer Jacobitism from open antagonism towards the King or the House of Hanover. Not only professed Tories, but a large body of Opposition Whigs, were deeply discomforted by the image of a German princeling from a minor state exercising authority over a rising European power, concerns that sharpened into anger when it seemed that the interests of Britain were being sacrificed to those of Hanover. Such was the widespread complaint when Britain entered the War of Austrian Succession in 1742 to fulfil treaty obligations between Hanover and Vienna. The main opposition journal *Old England* reacted with patriotic fury when George II rode into the Battle of Dettington wearing the yellow sash of Hanover rather than the red sash of England. "The tawdry, worthless YELLOW was prefer'd to, and triumphed over the, till then, victorious RED,"[16] protested "Jeffrey Broadbottom," the putative author of *Old England.* The paper followed three weeks later with what might seem the amazing assertion that the coronation oath, like marriage vows, could lead in extreme cases to "a Divorce."[17] Yet even the administration knew that it was futile to brand the Broadbottom Opposition as uniformly or even largely Jacobite: while including some notorious Tories like William King, its major leaders were men of virtually uncontested Whig credentials – Lords Lyttelton and Chesterfield, William Pitt, James Ralph, Henry Fielding.[18] In 1744 Fielding wrote *A Natural History of the Hanover Rat*, sounding deceptively like his Jacobite Squire Western a few years later. Chesterfield collaborated with Ralph and Edmund Waller in pamphlets condemning English involvement on the continent, warning that "an avowed Jacobite" could not hope for a more happy opportunity to discredit "the present Royal Family."[19] These Opposition Whigs accused "*Hanoverians*" of being "Mercenaries." "We must be bled and suck'd by Foreign Troops,"[20] they declared, recalling (as we will see) Johnson's imagery in *Marmor Norfolciense* a few years before. These works suggest that English nationalism was sparked as much by hostility to the "*germanized*" accent of early Hanoverian politics as by hatred of the French.[21]

Contrary to what has been claimed, in short, "to attack the king on the throne" was neither all that unusual in the years before 1745 nor a reliable symptom of Jacobite loyalties. It is an indication of the essentially opportunistic nature of such complaints that the main Opposition authors quickly changed their tune when George II bowed to pressure to appoint Chesterfield (whom he personally despised) and some of his allies to cabinet and important government posts in 1744. *Old England* immediately declared George II a "PEOPLE'S KING"[22] and during the Jacobite invasion of the winter and spring of 1745/6, the King's old Broad-bottom opponents mobilized strongly to his side. Fielding changed his anti-Hanoverian tune, producing the boisterously pro-Hanoverian *True Patriot* (1745–6). Nonetheless, the charge that Britain was being "suck'd" of its money and soldiers by Hanover continued to be the mainstay of Opposition polemics during the 1750s. The Opposition included professed Tories, still proscribed from government, and some of these Tories identified bitterness concerning England's Continental involvements (rather than hopes for a Stuart restoration) as the very essence of their political identity. This was the claim, for example, of *The Honest Grief of a Tory* (1759), where the author denied being a Jacobite, but complained that "the greater Part of the immense Debt we labour under, was contracted by the Ministers of England, to please a Stadtholder of Holland, and two Electors of Hanover."[23] The most vociferous Tory of the 1750s, John Shebbeare, was finally condemned to stand in the stocks for denouncing, in a series of *Letters to the English People*, "the malignant Star of the *Hanoverian* Politics" which had "neglect[ed] *England*, for *Germany* and *Holland*."[24] Yet even Shebbeare celebrated "the Love of Liberty" that had driven James II from the throne,[25] and his hostility to English support for Hanover was echoed by many undisputed Whigs. None other than John Perceval, whom we just met as the author of the virulently Whig *Faction Detected*, joined in the anti-Hanoverian chorus when he was pushed from power in 1758, maintaining like Shebbeare that England's decline would persist "till all our Germanism is happily eradicated out of our politics."[26] And the most popular political pamphlet of the mid-century, *Consideration on the Present German War* (1760) by the dissenting minister and Whig author Israel Mauduit, seized the nation's attention by asking a rudely anti-Hanoverian question: "Why have we been spending twelve millions in Germany, to defend, only from insult, that, which cannot be of so much worth to us?"[27]

In short, what John B. Owen called "revulsion" concerning the financial and military burden of Hanover constituted one of the main sources of consensus among *both* Tories and Whigs in Opposition.[28] Unlike opposition Whigs, however, avowed Tories were conveniently vulnerable to the charge that their criticisms implied a treasonous preference for the heirs of James II. Hence, when Johnson accepted a pension from the new King George III in 1762, Wilkes hinted broadly at his supposed Jacobite sympathies in the pages of the *North Briton.* "I hope . . . that he is become a friend to this constitution and the family on the throne," mocked Wilkes, "now he is thus nobly provided for: but I know he has much to *unwrite*, more to *unsay*, before he will be forgiven by the true friends of the present illustrious family, for what he has been *writing* and *saying* for many years."[29] The fact that Johnson followed other Tories such as Shebbeare in supporting the new King suggests, nonetheless, that his previous hostility had less to do with loyalty to the Stuarts than with resentment about the defense of Hanover, a policy that George III quickly and strongly renounced. And when we look back to what Johnson had in fact "been *writing* and *saying* for many years," we find that his notorious hostility to George II seemed consistently connected with this complaint. In *The Vanity of Human Wishes* (1749), he reflects bleakly on the War of Austrian Succession, remarking that "bribes" had led "Britons" to "stain with blood the Danube or the Rhine" (ll. 179, 181–2, 6:100). Years later, in *Observations on the Russian and Hessian Treaties* (1756), he closely echoed the widespread Opposition attacks of this time on the government's Hanover policy:

> The King of Great-Briton has indeed a territory on the continent, of which the natives of this island scarcely knew the name till the present family was call'd to the throne, and yet know little more than that our king visits it from time to time. Yet for the defence of this country are these subsidies apparently paid, and these troops evidently levied. The riches of our nation are sent into distant countries, and the strength which should be employed in our own quarrel consequently impaired, for the sake of dominions the interest of which has no connection with ours, and which by the act of succession we took care to keep separate from the British kingdoms. (10:181)

This statement could hardly be construed as touting the cause of the Stuarts: whatever his fairly conventional dislike of George II, against whom he "roared with prodigious violence" in Boswell's *Life*,[30] he acknowledged that monarch as "our king" in the above passage and referred with apparent approval to the Act of Succession. This statement is certainly less caustic than the attacks that landed Shebbeare in the stocks, a disgrace that, much to Boswell's surprise, Johnson *defended*.[31] Nor is there much in Johnson's earlier and more notoriously "Jacobite" statements that differs significantly from the above passage. In *The North Briton*, Wilkes mentions only "London" (1738) as an example of Johnson's allegedly Jacobite writing, yet here Johnson only echoes the very general Opposition attack that George II spent too much time in Hanover (l. 247). Similarly, Johnson's most notoriously disaffected political effusion, *Marmor Norfolciense*, reaches its allegedly Jacobite climax when the learnedly inane narrator, musing on a prophecy inscribed by a "British king" on a marble tablet, reacts with alarm to the inscription's apparent allusion to the Hanoverian "horse" sucking dry the blood of the British "lyon" (10:41–2). We will recall that the same imagery of

Hanover "sucking" the wealth and strength of England was often repeated by undoubted Whigs in the Opposition such as Chesterfield and Fielding. Furthermore, as we will consider in the later chapter on English nationalism, this pamphlet might very well be interpreted as *anti*-Jacobite in its strong implication that there had been no "legitimate" royal succession since the Roman conquest of the Britons, the supposed nationality of the tablet's inscriber (see 10:27): as historians widely then conceded, England's throne had been occupied by a series of German invaders – the Saxons and even the Normans, who were also derived originally from Germany. What, Johnson seems to imply beneath his narrator, is the big fuss about the *current* German invader?[32]

Given that Johnson's disgruntlement with George II's devotion to Hanoverian interests aligns him merely with the wide and piebald gambit of Opposition opinion, we seem to have whittled down the evidence of Johnson's Jacobitism to a fairly thin stick. Clark and others allude with telling insistence to Sir John Hawkins's assurance that Johnson was a Jacobite. Yet as Hawkins neglected to produce a single statement from Johnson confirming this opinion, and was himself the kind of ardent pro-ministry Whig who dispensed politically expedient paranoias, we should probably regard his testimony as equivocal.[33] If we look instead at Johnson's political writing before 1760, we find, in fact, that it closely echoes the many pamphlets that were attempting to delineate quite a different ideal of Toryism that declared itself essentially loyal to the Hanoverian Succession. A particularly clear example of this reconstruction is a pamphlet already mentioned, *The Loyal or Revolutionary Tory* (1733). Like other authors of the time, such as David Hume in "The Parties of Great Britain" (1742), this writer insisted that the difference between a modern Tory and a Whig had become only one of "degrees."[34] While not denying the existence of a Jacobite fringe in the Tory party (just as the Whig party had a fringe of dissenters and republicans), this author insisted that "loyal" or "constitutional" Tories wished above all to preserve "a *National Establish'd Church*," which "will ever be the grand Safeguard of our Liberty and Property."[35] Notable here is the effort to distance loyalty to the church from the high-church fanaticism of figures like Henry Sacheverell. In the mind of this author, the established church was crucial for the preservation of the secular interests that had become the main priority of both Whigs and Tories. Tories defended the faith because they were the true defenders of the "constitution," that "assemblage of laws, institutions, and customs,"[36] as Bolingbroke defined it, that it was the main concern of government to uphold and preserve. In other pamphlets of the 1730s and 1740s, Tories attempted to justify the conduct of their party since the Revolution. "For half a Century past, or more," wrote the author of *Opposition more Necessary than Ever* (1742), "the *Tories* in general have been the warmest Assertors of the People's *Liberties* in every Shape; and the *Whigs* in general, on the contrary, the boldest Invaders of the People's *Liberties* and *Properties*, in every Reign, and every Instance."[37]

Johnson's early statements strongly recall these defences of a "revolution" Toryism purged of this party's old associations with non-resistence and a *jure divino* idea of monarchy. His definition of "Tory" in the *Dictionary*, for example, "One who adheres to the antient constitution of the state, and the apostolical hierarchy of the church of England," echoes the argument we have just considered that the Tories were the *true* upholders of the "constitution" and its ecclesiastical bulwark, the Church of England. The curt and highly ironic definition of "Whig," "A faction," clinches the impression that he was directly responding to Whigs in the contemporary debate. In defiance of Lord Egmont, who had claimed notoriously that "Tory" was a mere "Name" if it did not mean "Jacobite," Johnson answered by reducing "*Whig*" to a mere name, the empty label for an insignificant "faction."

Johnson's effort to present an updated version of the Tories is similarly evident in his "Debates in the Senate of Lilliput," the disguised accounts of debates in parliament and the House of Lords that he wrote for *The Gentleman's Magazine*. Consider, for example, this key moment in the parliamentary debates, the failed Patriot motion of February 1741 requesting the King to remove Sir Robert Walpole from his councils for ever. The Patriots, led by Pulteney and Sandys, found themselves abandoned by a large block of Tories led by Robert Harley's descendant Edward, the third Lord Oxford, who left the chamber rather than vote on a motion they considered unjust and devious. In the aftermath of this desertion, Whigs mocked Harley's followers as "Sneakers" who had betrayed their Patriot allies and proved their flaccid adherence to "non-resistance." The Tories and their allies, in response, set out to defend this action as consistent with their defense of English law and justice. In *The Sentiments of a Tory* (1741), an important work for understanding Johnson's political views at this time, the author points out that the Tories had repeatedly opposed Walpole on a series of substantive issues such as the Excise Act, the hire of foreign troops, and several penal laws (such as the Riot Act and the Black Act) that attacked public liberty. Unlike their Patriot colleagues, however, the Tories would not suspend the accused's right of defense even in order to rid the nation of Walpole. Walpole's actions and character, they maintained, were being denigrated without rules of evidence; the Patriots even attempted to exclude him from the chamber during debate, a clear violation of an Englishman's right to hear his accusers. In short, the Tories "have not been afraid to express their Sentiments very freely, from Principles of Affection to their Country, though others have unjustly imputed it to Affection for another Cause."[38] The present Tories were not Jacobites or believers in non-resistance, but the true defenders of the church and constitution: "they are for the Church, that they may secure Peace hereafter, and for the Constitution that they may enjoy it here."[39]

In short, the pamphlet maintains that the Tories refused to bring down Walpole from an adherence to legal and constitutional *principle*, and not because they wished to protect the Prime Minister. Indeed, Johnson ends his version of the debate by citing the arguments of *Sentiments of a Tory* with great enthusiasm. To this apology for "the *High-heel'd* Party," he concludes, significantly, "no Reply was attempted."[40] It is important to note as well that when this debate was published in 1743, readers looked back on the events of February 1741 with a sharpened sense of irony: the suspicion raised by both Walpole's allies and the Tories that the Patriots were motivated solely by personal ambition had been since confirmed when Pulteney and Carteret accepted noble titles from Walpole's successor and close ally, Henry Pelham. The Tories, by contrast, looked better than ever, the men of unswerving principle that they claimed to be. The highpoint in Johnson's dramatization is not, as Donald Greene and others have maintained, Walpole's highly equivocal self-defense,[41] but rather Edward Harley's passionate speech explaining his actions. Walpole had played a large role in sending Harley's uncle, the famous Tory minister Robert Harley, to the Tower after the Hanoverian Succession. In a grand gesture of magnanimity, however, Edward Harley refuses to subject the Prime Minister to the same injustice: "I am now, Sir, glad of this Opportunity to return Good for Evil, and do that Hon. Gentleman and his Family that Justice which he denyed to Mine."[42]

Johnson obviously looked back to Walpole's persecution of Robert Harley as an episode of particular iniquity. Many years later, in his *Life of Prior*, Johnson would again refer to this episode with obvious bitterness.[43] This suggests that Donald Greene was wrong to read Johnson's account of this debate as an indication of his change of heart about Walpole's political virtues (and therefore revealing his sympathy for Whigs). Rather, Johnson was reacting to the events of February 1741 like a true Tory, understood *not* as a supporter of the Pretender, but as a member of the party that stood up for moral and constitutional "principle" against the unscrupulous and self-interested conduct of the Whigs, both Court and Patriot. Elsewhere in his "Debates in the Senate of Lilliput," this was the image of the Tories that Johnson diligently fostered. In his version of a Commons debate on the hire of Hanoverian troops, for example, the prominent Tory MP William Shippen pronounces this classic statement of his party's commitment to balanced and independent judgment:

> Sir, as I have always endeavoured to act upon conviction of my duty, to examine opinions before I admit them, and to speak what I have thought the truth, I do not easily change my conduct, or retract my assertions; nor am I deterred from repeating my arguments when I have a right to speak, by the remembrance that they have formerly been unsuccessful.[44]

The Tories portrayed in Johnson's debates frequently affirm their rejection of any narrow interest, pandering to public sentiment or blind loyalty to "party." As Edward Harley says in the same debate: "when our decisions are not agreeable to the opinion or expectations of the people, we should at least show them that they are not the effects of blind compliance with the demands of the ministry, or of an implicit resignation to the direction of a party."[45]

These speeches are particularly noteworthy because they are largely of Johnson's invention. It is unlikely that he personally attended parliament more than once or twice, relying instead on often scanty information supplied by Edward Cave's spies in the chamber.[46] The impression he leaves that Tories are men of principle, determined to rise above the cynicism and self-interest of politics to defend the laws and constitution of the land, therefore constitutes strong evidence of what Johnson *himself* believed being a Tory meant. Later in the century, however, this meaning of Toryism was largely lost. When Tories came to support George III, their opponents rewrote history in convenient ways to suggest that Tories had *always* been on the side of royal prerogative and against "liberty."[47] Hence, younger interpreters of Johnson's politics such as Boswell misunderstood what he meant not because they had agenda to make him seem more Tory than he was, but because they had only a vague and inaccurate idea of the political situation and terminology used by an older generation. Boswell liked to call himself a "warm Tory" on the grounds that he steadily favoured the "increase" of "the power of the Crown."[48] Predictably, he tended to assume that Johnson was similarly unyielding in his support of strong "government" in all situations. The result is a curious disparity, often felt in the *Life*, between Boswell's expectations and Johnson's reactions to various events.[49]

In terms of the evolution of "party" in the eighteenth century, Johnson's politics of "principle" are significant because he belonged to a movement that was attempting to redefine Toryism in ways consistent with the realities of Hanoverian England. This was a definition that replaced loyalty to the Stuarts with loyalty to the constitution and the church. Its differences with the Whigs were real, because it opposed the oligarchic Whig politics of patronage and self-interest. To the great frustration of many Whigs, the Tories refused to play the usual political games of gaining and keeping power. Instead, they displayed the obstinate habit of butting against the doors of eighteenth-century oligarchal politics as described by Namier, one major reason why they lingered so long in the cold of the political doorstep. From Johnson's point of view, however, Whiggery was the "*negation of all principle*,"[50] a cynical and self-interested support of "faction" over what was good and right for the nation. Surprisingly, this was a judgment he leveled even at his friend Burke,[51] a man who has come, for us, to embody an emotional loyalty to the constitution and the inherited institutions of the nation – the very essence of what we now consider the Burkean heritage of conservative and later Tory politics. Yet the older Burke had, at least in this limited sense, come around to positions that Johnson had defended since the 1740s. Certainly, the Burke of the *Reflections on the Revolution in France* (1790) showed far more affection for the aristocracy than was typical of Johnson. Yet the *Reflections* also implicitly rejects the cynicism of patronage politics, along with the dynastic questions that previously divided the nation, in favour of a politics self-consciously devoted to an ideological vision of the national good.

In other words, Johnson may well be seen as one the progenitors of a typically *modern* conservatism – of a "new" Toryism that we must carefully distinguish from a cause of Jacobitism that was, in fact, dying long before the tellingly fizzled "Rebellion" of 1745.[52] (There was, of course, no English "Rebellion" at all, but only a futile invasion.) But does Johnson's Toryism mean that he also adhered to an essentially party-based understanding of politics, a conclusion that would problematize the assessments of Namier and Greene? It must be admitted that our modern conception of party (that is, as a formally organized ideological movement) had not yet been articulated. During Johnson's early career, "party" was a distinctly negative term, usually signifying nothing more than a faction of political allies who agreed to machinate together for personal interest. Hatred of "party," moreover, would become the particular cause of the Broad-bottom politicians who helped Johnson early in his career and whose attitudes he was often expressing. As we have seen, however, the Tories were perhaps closer to the modern idea of party than anyone else, not only because they were more organized (marching out *en bloc* for example to protest against the

Patriot persecution of Walpole) but because they self-consciously adhered to principle over political convenience. In sticking doggedly to his Tory identity, therefore, Johnson's views would become more rather than less pertinent as the century wore on.

JOHNSON AND THE CULTURE OF BROAD-BOTTOM POLITICS

Understood as the self-conscious politics of *principle*, Johnson's Toryism remained an important part of his social and political outlooks throughout his life. Yet there is no evidence that Johnson moved primarily in Tory circles. His early works after his arrival in London in 1737 make clear his close association with a broad movement of writers and politicians, including both Tories and Whigs, who had in common their opposition to the ministry of Sir Robert Walpole and the Pelham administrations that immediately followed Walpole's fall in 1742. A key figure connecting Johnson to the Opposition was Robert Dodsley, the footman turned bookseller who published a number of his early works, including "London," *The Vanity of Human Wishes*, and *Vision of Theodore*. It was Dodsley who won Johnson his contract with the consortium of book-sellers who financed the *Dictionary;* it was also at Dodsley's urging that Johnson sought the patronage of one of the most powerful political figures of the 1740s, Lord Chesterfield.[53] Chesterfield, who had aided Dodsley when he was imprisoned for publishing Opposition literature in 1738 (including Johnson's "London"), was the leading parliamentary figure in a group of writers and politicians who became known as the "Broad-bottom," particularly after the defection of Pulteney and Carteret to the court in 1742.

Johnson's association with the Broad-bottom is not altogether surprising: while dominated by powerful men of Whig pedigree, such as Chesterfield, Lyttelton, and Dodington, this group set out actively to heal party divisions and to champion the end of government proscription against Tories. In 1743, while still in Opposition, they established a shadow ministry that included three prominent Tories – Gower, Cotton, and Wynn.[54] For Johnson scholars, Lord Gower is particularly notable in this group, for this Lichfield politician supported Johnson's attempts to gain a honorary degree from the University of Dublin in 1739.[55] Johnson had some connection with Chesterfield, who had personal links to Staffordshire and employed Johnson's uncle Cornelius Ford as his chaplain.[56] As a talented man with little access to preferment or favor, Johnson was the kind of writer often helped by rich and influential men like Chesterfield and Dodington. Instigated by their hatred of Walpole's system of patronage, these figures championed the ideal of raising men of "merit," including, most obviously, the low-born Dodsley, but also James Thomson, Mark Akenside, William Warburton, James Hammond, Paul Whitehead, and others of modest origins. In *The Lives of the Poets* much of Johnson's most detailed and original information concerns the personal lives of the men at the center of this group: only someone in the circle of social gossip, for example, could have known the intimate details of the painful and changing relations between Pope, Bolingbroke, and Warburton, as narrated in *Life of Pope*. He also expressed strong and revealingly personal opinions about Lyttelton, Akenside, and Fielding – whom he surprised Boswell by calling a "blockhead" and "a barren rescal."[57]

It is quite obvious that Johnson did not blend in completely with these men and their culture of attitudes and values: the famous letter he wrote to Chesterfield in 1754 bristles with the hurt pride of a man who feels that he was neglected because of his low origins and inelegant manners. For all their alleged defense of "merit," it seems, Chesterfield and his friends had slighted the most worthy man of all. Nevertheless, Johnson's works of the 1740s all seem to be responding to the main themes that preoccupy the political and literary productions of the men connected with the Broad-bottom circle – the disruptive effects of "party," the national shame of neglected merit, the need for peace, and a basically distrustful attitude toward the pursuit of money and the British commercial elite. In these general respects, that is, the young Johnson displays a Broad-bottom attitude to English politics. As we have already considered, however, it is also significant that Johnson never surrendered his identity as a Tory, for he was determined to maintain the politics of "principle" flourished by self-styled "loyal" or "revolution" Tories. Nor was this proud advocate of the middle orders comfortable with the aristocratic paternalism that reigned over this group.

As suggested by its label, the most distinctive Broad-bottom values were the hatred of "party," the belief that the redemption of England depended on the elimination of party difference and, most provocatively, the ending of proscription against Tories. Sir Robert Walpole's government Whigs hated Tories with virulent and unrelieved passion. "Ware Tory!" Walpole advised Henry Pelham from retirement, while his successor meditated on negotiations with the Broad-bottom Opposition.[58] The Broad-bottom inclusion of professed Tories took inspiration from the idiosyncratic and erratic genius of Lord Bolingbroke, himself a professed Tory under Queen Anne, but a figure who could easily be mistaken for a Whig in his pronouncements in the 1730s. Contrary to the impression left by Isaac Kramnick, who imposed a conveniently Marxist clarity on Bolingbroke's career, portraying him as feudal dinosaur pining for a passing age of landed gentlemen and loyal peasants, this shifty politician finally endorsed an essentially Whig reading of the Revolution and many characteristically Whig values such as the supreme constitutional importance of "liberty" and the inherently commercial character of the English people.[59] Referring to the supposed Tory principle of non-resistance, for example, he wrote that "The Tories stopped short in the pursuit of a bad principle. The Whigs reformed the abuse of a good one."[60] His *History of England* virtually epitomized, as we will see later, what J.G.A. Pocock presents as a neo-Harrington classical republican view of English history.[61] Significantly, he was recalled most fondly mostly by radicals like Wilkes, who brandished Bolingbroke as a spokesman for liberty in his sneering *Letter to Samuel Johnson, L.L.D.* (1770).[62] For all his belated Whiggishness, however, Bolingbroke set out not to underline but undermine party difference, maintaining that England must grasp its destiny as a culture with a common interest and unified values centered on the importance of "liberty." As he wrote in his *Dissertation upon Parties* (1733–4), "the new division of the nation into Whigs and Tories brought us into extreme danger."[63] In his later work, Bolingbroke focused idealistically on a "Patriot King," a living incarnation of the "voice" of the people, a figure who expressed the communal will: the Patriot King would "distinguish the voice of his people from the character of a faction, and will harken to it."[64]

Bolingbroke's insistence on the evil of party became one of the political mantras of the Opposition era, "a Kind of Methodism in Politics," as one writer quipped in 1741.[65] "Sure it is high time," wrote another pamphleteer in 1739, "for us to throw aside all Party Names. Let us banish them [from] our Language, and expunge them from our Dictionaries, and for ever forget the injurious Thoughts of one another that have accompanied them."[66] The idea of the Patriot King had a less obvious impact on English politics: Bolingbroke wrote his *Idea of the Patriot King* in 1738, but he chose to circulate the work privately among his friends in the circle of Frederick, Prince of Wales, and it was not published until 1749. Nonetheless, his ideal of a king whose voice was indistinguishable from the unified will of the people filtered into political commentary of the 1740s.

Johnson's positive response to these political attitudes early in his career might be gauged by a rather obscure but significant piece he wrote in 1742, a review for *The Gentleman's Magazine* of the autobiographical *Account of the Conduct of the Duchess of Marlborough from Her First Coming to Court till the Year 1710*. This was the Duchess's self-defense against attacks on her character by prominent Court Whigs, for she had become an inveterate enemy of Walpole and his ministry. Not surprisingly, therefore, she was much courted by the Opposition, particularly those at the center of the Broad-bottom. When she died in 1744, she bequeathed an amazing 20,000 pounds and a diamond ring on Chesterfield, as well as 10,000 pounds on William Pitt. The close relations between the Broad-bottom and the Duchess are further evidenced by their efforts to defend her reputation from attack. Probably at Chesterfield's request, Fielding wrote *A Full Vindication of the Dutchess Dowager of Marlborough* (1742).[67] Most interesting in this pamphlet is Fielding's indifference to the supposedly scandalous accusation that the Duke and Duchess of Marlborough were "the *two staunchest Tories in the Kingdom.*" "We have seen Whigs and Tories, in later days, unite and agree in Place very well together," Fielding responded placidly, a remark that reflects the effort of Broad-bottom allies to downplay party division and solicit the support of Tories.[68]

Johnson's less partisan but warm review of the Duchess's apology must therefore have been pleasing to the Broad-bottom group. Praising the work as instructive and well written (in fact, it was probably ghost-written by Nathaniel Hooke), Johnson also mused on the Duchess's balanced presentations of Charles II and William III, monarchs closely associated with the Tories and Whigs respectively. Johnson's idealistic vision of a monarch who combined the virtues of the two kings might even be seen as an emblem of the Broad-bottom coalition that was just then taking shape in the wake of Walpole's resignation in February 1742:

> Charles the second, by his affability and politeness, made himself the idol of the nation, which he betrayed and sold. William the third was, for his insolence and brutality, hated by the people, which he protected and enriched: – had the best part of these two characters been united in one prince, the house of Bourbon had fallen before him.[69]

Even in later years, Johnson often declaimed against "The rage of faction" (14:246), as he wrote in a sermon commemorating the death of Charles I. It is of course significant that he wrote this and his other sermons for a professed Whig, John Taylor, for Johnson was expert at finding a peaceable middle-ground of shared values and interests between Whigs and Tories. His periodical essays, which censured those who "falsely think it virtue to promote" differing interests in government (*Rambler* No. 99, 4:166), are indeed distinctive for their lack of overt political bias in an age when this rivalry generally dominated the press. The *Dictionary* is also generally Broad-bottom. Despite what we noted about Johnson's partisan definitions of "Tory" and "Whig" in the *Dictionary*, the passages he used to illustrate these definitions strongly emphasize the need to placate party division. Under "Whig," for example, he cites Swift: "Whoever has a true value for church and state, should avoid the extremes of *whig* for the sake of the former, and the extremes of tory on the account of the latter." Elsewhere, as under "Moderation," he quotes Pope's scorn for party labels: "In *moderation* placing all my glory, / While tories call me whig, and whigs a tory." Moreover, as has been emphasized by Robert DeMaria, Johnson draws from the works of such notorious Whigs as Locke and Addison as frequently as from Tories such as Swift, Dryden, or Clarendon.[70]

Johnson was also willing to endorse an idea of kingship that differed little from Bolingbroke's ideal of the "Patriot King." His compliment to George III in *The False Alarm*, for example, is virtually a citation from *The Patriot King*, which the young King himself is known to have admired and emulated. Bolingbroke had urged that "The true image of a free people" was "a patriarchal family, where the head and all the members are united by one common interest."[71] In a similarly patriarchal vein, Johnson urged Tories in 1770 to realize that "they have at last a king who knows not the name of party, and who wishes to be the common father of all his people" (10:344). That Johnson was willing to invoke the spirit of Bolingbroke may surprise us, since he is well known to have despised this aristocrat's deistic religion and his affectedly gallicized prose-style.[72] Like others, however, Johnson discerned that great talents lurked beneath the dross of Bolingbroke's egotism and instability: in *Life of Prior*, he portrays Bolingbroke as a skillful diplomat instrumental in securing the Peace of Utrecht. And while infidelity or heterodoxy usually disqualified authors from the *Dictionary*, Bolingbroke's political works are cited several times.[73]

Johnson's views on the leading parliamentary figure in the Broad-bottom movement, Chesterfield, are marked by the same kind of ambivalence. There can be little doubt, on the one hand, that Johnson shared the opinion even of some of Chesterfield's allies, such as Bolingbroke, that he was a dandified lightweight, incapable of deep insight or political leadership. Chesterfield's flatterers praised his witty and facetious oratory, a style that Johnson well captures in his depiction of this politician in "The Debates in the Senate of Lilliput." One of these speeches, on legislation concerning Spirituous Liquors, is little more than a stream of sarcasm.[74] Many years later, Johnson was amused to find this and another of these speeches reprinted in Chesterfield's *Works*, one praised as written "in the strong nervous style of Demosthenes" and the other "in the witty, ironical manner of Tully."[75] Given his heralded penchant for witty satire, Chesterfield would not have been pleased to learn that Johnson named him only once in the revised fourth edition of the *Dictionary* – under "ridiculer": "The *ridiculer* shall make only himself ridiculous. *Earl of Chesterfield.*"

It is a surprising and significant fact, however, that Chesterfield and Johnson shared a great deal of common ground politically, and this was likely one reason why Johnson was initially willing to accept Chesterfield as a suitable patron. If we look at the two speeches reprinted in Chesterfield's *Works*, we find that they indeed express principles coherent with Johnson's own political views. Chesterfield argues against repeal of the Gin Act, which had been instrumental in slowing the epidemic of drunkenness among the common people. In his dark observations on the corruption of contemporary society, he recalls Johnson's own "London": "the nation is sunk into the lowest state of corruption, the people are not only vitious, but insolent beyond example." Frankly patriarchal, Chesterfield stresses that the role of the government was to uphold public virtue, condemning the ministry's cynical plan to exploit popular vice to raise tax money: "Publick credit, my lords, is, indeed, of very great importance, but publick credit can never be long supported without publick virtue; nor indeed if the government could mortgage the morals and health of the people, would it be just or rational to confirm the bargain."[76] These speeches suggest why it is misleading to think of Chesterfield, and indeed of most in the Broad-bottom movement, merely as Opposition Patriots in the same mold as Pulteney or Carteret. Unlike the Patriots, Chesterfield was prone neither to side with the merchant classes, whom he thought vulgar,[77] nor to expound the virtues of "commerce" or "liberty." He embodied the generally genteel and paternalistic tone of much Broad-bottom literature, from the pages of *Old England* to Fielding's novelistic vision of fatherly rich men caring for the needs and morals of the poor. When Chesterfield did take a stand for "liberty," it was in those cases that also attracted the support of Johnson. It was Chesterfield, notably, who led the charge against Walpole's Theatrical Licensing Act (1737), and his name, as Horace Walpole later acknowledged, became closely associated with the cause of liberty of the press: "When the Bill for Subjecting the Stage to the Power of a Court Officer was brought into Parliament, every Body must remember, to his Immortal Honour, with what Eloquence, what Force of Arguments, and Power of Wit, the honest Earl of *Chesterfield* combated so dangerous an Innovation."[78] Chesterfield energetically defended Dodsley when he was arrested for printing Paul Whitehead's *Manners* (1738), giving this printer the use of his carriage during the legal proceedings.[79] In the journal that Chesterfield financed and helped to write, *Old England*, liberty of the press is loudly proclaimed as "the SHEET ANCHOR of the COMMON-WEALTH."[80] Similarly, in striking contrast with the bellicose rhetoric of Opposition writing in the late 1730s, Chesterfield also became the leader to the Opposition attack on the war on the Continent, joining the ministry as Secretary of State for the North in October 1746 specifically on condition that the administration pursue peace with France. When the war dragged on and he resigned in 1748, a pamphleteer stressed that he had "accepted of this new Office on the same Principle that he concluded the *Broad-bottom* Negociation; for the Sake of delivering his poor Country out of the Hands of the Destroyer, and of expediting a safe and honourable Peace."[81]

Johnson's sympathy for both these causes, liberty of the press and opposition to war, suggests again that his association with Chesterfield had some basis in their shared political outlooks.[82] His satire against Walpole's Theatrical Licensing Act, *A Compleat Vindication of the Licensers of the Stage* (1738), is evidence of his early links not only with "Patriots" in general but with that group of figures – Chesterfield, Dodsley, Fielding – most directly implicated in the battle over freedom of the press and of the stage. Similarly, Johnson echoed the anti-war rhetoric of the Broad-bottom throughout the decade, comparing the War of Austrian Succession to the fireworks mounted to celebrate its conclusion – a lot of meaningless fire and smoke at enormous expense.[83] This rhetoric, we should note, became increasingly gloomy as the decade rolled on and political writers reflected morosely on the record of increasing national debt and two failed wars. Indeed, England seemed to emblematize the vanity of the bounding wishes that opened the decade, a darkly "Johnsonian" touch characteristic of many pamphlets of this period:

> How mistaken are Mortals, sometimes, in their Pursuits to that which they set their Hearts most on! How visibly does this Weakness appear in the Conduct of my Countrymen for more than Half an Age! They precipitated their Country into two bloody and burthensome Wars to rescue their Liberties and enlarge their Trade; but is not the latter visibly impair'd and the former render'd more precarious by Pursuit of those very Measures which were then judged conducive to those Ends?[84]

The gloom of this 1747 pamphlet seems, in retrospect, unnecessary: in fact, Britain was entering a period of imperial expansion, and social historians confirm that the economy had strongly recovered from its recent doldrums by the end of the 1740s.[85] But the pessimism that spread over much political writing of the late 1740s, particularly in the camp patronized by Chesterfield and his friends, could not be more different from the stridently martial tone of most Opposition writing a decade before. In the words of

James Ralph, Chesterfield's supporter and writer of the *Remembrancer*, the pro-Chesterfield weekly that replaced *Old England*, "that our Constitution is most wretched, nobody denies: It is severely felt in every Family, and it has been again and again acknowledged in the most public Manner."[86] To think of Johnson's *Vanity of Human Wishes* in this context is to realize that it captured the tone of a particular moment and a particular ideological grouping. In later versions, Johnson cleaned out some contemporary references to "blasted patriots" and the "annual tax . . . rais'd by annual wars."[87] But he retained an allusion to Continental war, the lament for "Britons" who "stain with Blood the Danube or the Rhine" (ll.180–1, 6:100), which, as we noted before, remained highly topical in political debate right into the 1760s. While such a self-consciously universal poem as *Vanity of Human Wishes* cannot, admittedly, be confined to a political occasion or to a specifically Broad-bottom outlook, it is difficult to imagine a time either before or after the late 1740s when it would have been so reflective of the national mood.

There can be little doubt, then, that the culture of Broad-bottom politics exercised a formative influence on Johnson's thought, and is particularly evident in his writings of the 1740s and early 1750s. Nonetheless, the independence of his character is evident in his disdain for the flattery of the Broad-bottom chiefs (a habit he no doubt despised in that talented "blockhead," Henry Fielding), and his repeated tendency to qualify or contest important positions typical of this group. In his review of the Duchess of Marlborough's *Account of Her Conduct*, for example, he flies Tory colours both in his criticism of Queen Anne's indulgence of Whig "schemes" and in his closing complaint about the Duchess's portrayal of Robert Harley: "all the deformities are heightened, and the beauties, for beauties of mind he certainly had, are entirely omitted."[88] We are reminded both of Johnson's highly sympathetic portraits of Harley's heir Edward in the "Debates in the Senate of Lilliput," as well as his role during the 1740s in the cataloguing of the Harleian library – more than publisher's hackwork, but a celebration of a politician who, for Johnson, embodied the best of the Tory intellectual tradition. Johnson's writing in connection with the Harleian library offers only qualified support for the Broad-bottom themes being just at that time trumpeted in the pages of *Old England*. In an essay on "The Origin and Importance of Small Tracts and Fugitive Pieces," he praises "the right of inquiring" that exists under "the form of our government." But he goes on to offer sobering reflections of the "labyrinth" of speculations that often engulf pamphlet writers who are not qualified to treat particular subjects, and who stir up disruptive political controversies.[89] Johnson commented brusquely in *Life of Savage* (1744) that his contemporaries, including Bolingbroke's admirer Pope, vehemently supported "the uncontrouled freedom of the press" only so long as they themselves were not the objects of scandal or criticism.[90]

Johnson's very willingness to acknowledge himself a Tory suggests, moreover, that he did not entirely agree with the definitive tenet of Broad-bottom ideology, the evil of "party." In the pamphlet that Johnson seems to have admired as a statement of "*High-heeled*" principles, *The Sentiments of a Tory*, the author concludes that Bolingbroke's campaign to abolish party was quixotic:

> That it would be really a very happy Thing, if there were no Parties, no Distinctions, no Separation of Interests among us, is, I presume, what no Man in his Wits would dispute; but that ever we shall be in this State, that Patriotism will perform more than Religion ever could, that is, make us all of one *Mind*, is, I likewise presume, what no Man in his Senses will believe. In short, in Judgment, a Coalition of Parties is as chimerical a Notion, as the Kingdom of Saints, or the fifth Monarchy.[91]

The realism of this Tory pamphlet anticipated a growing and significant trend in eighteenth-century politics. As early as 1742, Hume described the existence of a band of political opinion stretching from monarchism at one end to republicanism at the other. Tories and Whigs represented leanings in these directions, a situation that was inflammatory or destructive only under certain circumstances, such as occurred in the Civil Wars.[92] This was a view echoed later in the century in a sophisticated pamphlet, *Characters of Parties in British Government* (1782), written by an advocate of William Pitt. This author traced the evolution of party difference through a two-part process: first the inevitable disagreement of people concerning the relative priority of the sovereign and the people, second the raising of this "prejudice" to the level of a "doctrine." "The republican and monarchial parties," he concluded, "exist in every country, in which the people have a share in the sovereignty, for they have their foundations in the feelings of men."[93] Near the end of the century, the moderate Whig Thomas Bigge reflected similarly on the intractable existence of republican and monarchial parties, whose balanced forces were crucial to political stability.[94]

The importance of these statements is theoretical as well practical: as the century drew on, authors increasingly rejected Bolingbroke's idea of national consensus transmitted through the voice of a "Patriot King." That all could be of "one *Mind*," as *The Sentiments of a Tory* protested, was unrealistic and contrary to the nature of political society with even minimal freedom, for such societies, by their very nature, were implacably pluralistic. This was a realization most forcefully captured by Burke, whose *Thoughts on the Cause of the Present Discontents* (1770) defends the natural tendency of men to form alliances with others who share their political aims and beliefs.[95]

Johnson's conviction in the inherently *pluralistic* nature of societies seems to animate his whole personality, especially in his later writing and conversation. As portrayed for us by Boswell and others, Johnson's "spirit of contradiction" constantly re-enforces the oppositional nature of human relations. And that Johnson was a proud "party man" was notorious among all his later companions, including his friend Hester Lynch Piozzi:

> No man . . . was more zealously attached to his party; he not only loved a tory himself, but he loved a man the better if he heard he hated a whig. "Dear Bathurst (said he to me one day) was to my very heart's content: he hated a fool, and he hated a rogue, and he hated a *whig*; he was a very good *hater*."[96]

Given such testimony, it is not surprising that his writings stress that "The great community of mankind is . . . necessarily broken into smaller independent societies" (*Rambler* No. 99, 4:166). "The extinction of parties," he indicates, is a desideratum of narrow-minded "zealots of liberty" (*Rambler* No. 95, 4:146). In the *Lives of the English Poets*, he reveals his admiration for the likes of the Tory Lord Lansdowne, who "was in times of contest and turbulence steady to his party."[97] And his needling of "vile Whigs" often seems less significant as an expression of political difference than as an indication of his desire to make room for civilized, if voluble, human difference in the overlapping contexts of national, professional, and Christian unity. His well-known dictation to Boswell on the nature of the Whigs and Tories in 1781 suggests his willingness late in life to reaffirm the sentiment of *The Loyal or Revolutionary Tory* almost half a century before. Note particularly that Johnson regarded Tories and Whigs as differing by "degrees" over questions of *principle* rather than the defunct issues of dynastic succession:

> The prejudice of the Tory is for establishment; the prejudice of the Whig is for innovation. The Tory does not wish to give more real power to Government; but the Government should have more reverence. Then they differ as to the Church. The Tory is not for giving more legal power to the Clergy, but wishes they should have a considerable influence, founded on the opinion of mankind; the Whig is for limiting and watching them with a narrow jealousy.[98]

Nevertheless, Johnson's acceptance of party difference does not mean that he wholly embraced Burke's vision of unified ideological groups entering and leaving office *en bloc*. Such submission to the political interests of a group betrayed his characteristically Tory belief in the need for individuals to consult conscience and the national interest rather than strategies for gaining power. Burke's apparent assumption that "a member of parliament should go along with his party right or wrong" struck Johnson as a recipe for deceit: "It is maintaining that you may lie to the publick; for you lie when you call that right which you think wrong, or the reverse."[99] Clearly, Johnson was the idealist, Burke the politician. Yet Johnson's description of the Tory – a supporter of "establishment" rather than innovation, of "reverence" for the state and the church – is very close to Burke's definitive expression of conservative thought in the *Reflections*. In contrast with some political groups, and with the King himself, Johnson anticipated the increasingly common belief in the 1790s that equally "loyal" groups might well diverge in the direction of the throne or the people, continuity or change. By the end of his life, attempts to create Broad-bottom coalitions, such as between followers of North and Fox in 1783, were being condemned as unrealistic and even politically unhealthy.[100]

In other words, Bolingbroke's old dream of a non-partisan national consensus, expressed through the voice of a "Patriot King," crashed on the rocks of a political reality divided by groupings opposed ideologically, though agreed on a declared commitment to the "constitution" (however defined) and the Hanoverian monarchy. "Who now reads Bolingbroke?" asked Burke in the *Reflections*, "Who ever read him through?"[101] And this was a disillusionment reflected by Johnson's own drift from his early involvement in the Broad-bottom branch of the Opposition to his later and energetic participation in openly partisan party politics. In other respects, as well, Johnson mirrors wider political developments in his day. Never fully satisfied, perhaps, with the classical republican vision of politics as the enterprise of maintaining national "virtue," Johnson's vision of politics, even at a fairly early stage, tended to stress instead the political exigencies of national order and stability. As we will now see, this alternative idea of political action can be detected in his highly skeptical responses to that prized Opposition ideal of making "merit" the prime criterion of political advancement.

"MERIT," CLASSICAL VIRTUE, AND THE LIFE OF SAVAGE

In one of the most compelling alternatives to a reading of eighteenth-century political history founded on the categories of "class" or "party," J.G.A. Pocock has described the evolution from an early classical republican or neo-Harrington "language" of political action to the emerging "New Whig" ideology centered on a language, conduct, and philosophy of commerce. The earlier phase stressed the protection of reason and virtue against the incursion of political and commercial corruption as the very end of politics, a dogma that inspired the Opposition in the battle against the alleged immorality of Walpole. Even within Opposition circles, however, the protection of "virtue" seemed increasingly less the objective of politics than the promotion of commercial prosperity. Moreover, this transformation, exemplified by the "New Whig" legacy of Walpole's heirs in the inner circles of power, replaced the demand for public virtue with the promotion of "manners," the codes of behavior and language that imagined the public sphere not as the interaction of civic-minded and self-reliant individuals, but as a field of commercial and social exchange. As Pocock himself stresses, this change was neither sudden nor absolute. In late-century political writers as far apart ideologically as Junius and Burke, the old civic humanist call for public virtue resonated throughout the era. But virtue had become much less the end of action and language in *public* life, and far more the hearth-bound concern of the private man and woman.[102]

The early Opposition's ancestry in neo-Harrington republicanism is exemplified by its preoccupation with the supposed neglect of "merit" by Walpole's government and the Great Man's corresponding favor for "slaves" and panderers to his lust for power and money. As charged by the *Champion*, "Consanguinity, Servility, Venality, Prostitution of all Sorts" had become "the only Qualifications for Titles of Honour and Places of Trust and Profit."[103] The *Champion* was co-edited and largely written by Chesterfield's protégés Fielding and Ralph, both of whom owed their careers to the patronage of the powerful and well-connected men who presided over the Broad-bottom group. Chesterfield was particularly devoted to the idea that rich and titled men like himself should cultivate the talents of men of modest beginnings and meager connections. His greatest find, Fielding, honored Chesterfield with glowing tributes. "I could name a Peer no less elevated by Nature and by Fortune," he wrote in *Joseph Andrews*, "who whilst he wears the noblest Ensigns of Honour on his Person, bears the truest Stamp of Dignity on his Mind."[104] Chesterfield was later the hero of two different poems entitled "Merit," the first published anonymously in Dublin in 1746 and the second, by Henry Jones, published by Dodsley in 1753. In the first poem, Chesterfield is portrayed as embodying the ideal combination of high rank and lofty merit. He is an elegant and discerning benefactor, "encouraging, rewarding unconfin'd / Desert impartially in all mankind."[105] The second poem exalts Chesterfield as the "aweful Censor both of Books and Men," a moral and scholarly paragon in silk "Whose Life's as faultless as his learned Pen."[106]

The Opposition theme of neglected merit was powerfully articulated by Johnson in "London," with its resounding *cri de coeur*, "SLOW RISES WORTH, BY POVERTY OPPRESSED" (l. 177). This was the young Johnson's allotted role, the ragged and talented man, cast adrift in the dark world of Walpole's London. Like others, he was to be rescued by Chesterfield, so not surprisingly, when Dodsley puffed Johnson's *Plan of a English Dictionary* (1747) in the *Museum*, he gave prominent attention to Johnson's patron:

> The great Importance and general Usefulness of such a Body of Language, appeared so clearly to the noble Person to whom the Plan is addressed, that he signified a Willingness of becoming its Patron, from that unaffected Flow of public Spirit, which has ever animated his Conduct.[107]

Johnson himself was, indeed, meant to follow in the footsteps of his friend Dodsley. Dodsley had risen from even lower on the social ladder than the school-master Johnson: he had started in London as a footman, and first attracted attention with *A Muse in Livery, or, the Footman's Miscellany* (1732). This work bears the frontispiece of a figure chained by "poverty" and unable to ascend to "Happiness, Virtue, Knowledge." The obvious message is driven home in a poem: "In vain, in vain, I stretch my CHAIN; / In vain I strive to rise."[108] Later in the same miscellany, Dodsley includes an essay on that theme close to Johnson's heart, "The Contempt which Poverty brings Men into."[109] Near the end of the decade, Dodsley developed the same theme in a highly popular short play, *The King and the Miller of Mansfield* (1737), which portrays an honest and good-hearted miller, John Cockle, who humanely helps Henry II, who is lost in the woods, despite his poverty and the persecution of a wicked Walpole-like courtier. Dodsley became a prized object of the beneficent patronage of Chesterfield and Pope. Pope set up Dodsley in the highly lucrative business of selling Opposition literature, and Chesterfield loyally defended him when this work landed him in prison.

Fielding, as well, was surely honoring Dodsley with his character Joseph Andrews, the worthy and good-hearted footman ultimately raised to his deserved rank as gentleman. Joseph and Fielding's later hero Tom Jones embody the Broad-bottom myth of talent and good nature waiting to be discovered beneath the trappings of low birth. Indeed, *Tom Jones* can be read almost as an allegory of recent English politics, as seen through the lens of Patriot and particularly Broad-bottom ideology: the self-interested hypocrite Blifil has, like the false Patriots Pulteney and Carteret, stolen the favor of the King, Mr. Allworthy, usurping the place of the real man of merit, Tom. Tom exemplifies what Paul Whitehead maintained many years before in his notorious *Manners*: "Crowns and Mitres are mere Raree-show" without "Honesty of Heart."[110] The sentimentality of Whitehead's message was indeed typical of the Opposition writers allied with Chesterfield and Bolingbroke. Thomson's "Liberty" (1735) associates patriotic spirit with "an active flood of universal love."[111] And Fielding declared in *The True Patriot* that "the Man who is known to love a Guinea better than his Friend, or even his own Soul, can never deserve the Name of *Patriot.*"[112]

Beneath all their gushing over neglected "merit," however, Chesterfield and his admirers clearly remained deeply elitist – and it is this hypocritical elitism that Johnson brought forcefully to Chesterfield's attention in his letter of 1755. As a "retired and uncourtly Scholar,"[113] Johnson could not hope to emulate the graceful manners and self-conscious gentility that, in fact, remained an integral feature of what this group considered meritorious. "I am a Gentleman," announced Fielding in the opening number of his periodical *The True Patriot*, and he went to list all his friends in the Broad-bottom circle – Chesterfield, Bolingbroke, Lyttelton, Hoadly, Thomson – as exemplifying the ideal combination of learning and genteel manners.[114] (Thomson is listed last, suggesting perhaps his questionable claims to this gentility.) Johnson's feeling of alienation from this group is clear in his cold and often scornful remarks on Lyttelton, Bolingbroke, and Akenside (another associate of Dodsley) in *The Lives of the Poets. Life of Prior* similarly suggests Johnson's acute sensitivity to the elitism of English politics early in the century. Prior had been the subject of an earlier experiment in Broad-bottom politics. Though derived from "an obscure original" in a Whig family, he was brought into government by the (then) Tory Bolingbroke for his diplomatic and literary gifts, becoming a major negotiator of the Peace of Utrecht. Johnson dwells painfully on Prior's humiliation as a man used for his talents yet shunned for his modest origins by, for example, the Duke of Shrewsbury, who refused "to associate with a man so meanly born."[115] Interestingly, Prior was persecuted after the Hanoverian Succession by a Whig committee that included Walpole and was co-chaired by Chesterfield's kinsman, Lord Stanhope.

But none of Johnson's writings comments so forcefully and characteristically on the Broad-bottom ideal of "merit" as his literary masterpiece of the 1740s, *Life of Savage* (1744). This biography may be seen, indeed, as a vigorous critique of the myth of lowly merit embodied by Dodsley and celebrated by Fielding in *Joseph Andrews* and *Tom Jones*. Savage is, superficially, similar to the type of obscure but meritorious individual being idealized in much Broad-bottom writing of this decade. Despite his ragged coat and constant penury, Savage was talented and good-natured, a specimen of "natural Gentility," as Fielding called it,[116] whose genteel manners and noble serenity in distress evinced his proclaimed aristocratic heritage. Politically, as well, he was an ally of Broad-bottom ideology, avowing a "neutrality with regard to party" as well as deep admiration for Lord Bolingbroke.[117] Savage was devoted to the ideal that only *merit* deserved respect or praise, even at the cost of his own interests: he "was always ready to repress that insolence which superiority of fortune incited, and to trample on that reputation which rose upon any other basis than that of merit."[118]

Yet the multiple and complex tragedies of Savage's life testify to the profound inadequacy of the ideals expounded by the Broad-bottom. Charity or patronage was squandered on a man who, despite his talents, seemed incapable of sustained labour or self-discipline. His good nature was in fact selfish and over-bearing, for he was interested only in companions who followed his dissolute whims. His pretended gentility was a corrosive obsession that excused him from self-support and encouraged his arrogant and self-destructive contempt even of those who, like the merchants of Bristol, tried to help him. Even his indifference to party reveals an indifference to moral principle: Savage flitted from party to party, one year soliciting patronage from Walpole, whom he personally despised, and the next year trying to flatter and inveigle his way into the Opposition circle attached to Frederick, Prince of Wales. "Neutrality to party," in the figure of Savage, stands for little more than political irresponsibility and an unprincipled devotion to self-interest. He anticipates later, negative portraits in Johnson's work such as the prudent Sophron in *Idler* No. 57, who "In the state . . . is of no party; but hears and speaks of publick affairs with the same coldness as of the administration of some ancient republick" (2:179). In short, Savage is a searing parody of Broad-bottom ideals, the tragic antitype of the man of obscure merit skillfully played by Dodsley in the 1730s and later given fictional expression by Fielding.

In political terms, the *Life of Savage* signals the decline of the neo-Harrington republican ideal of reconfiguring society on the basis of "virtue." This significance is borne out by Johnson's frequent and critical comments on the ideal of meritocracy in his later writings and conversation. As in *Life of Savage*, his tendency was to insist on the virtually unfathomable complexities surrounding the judgment of merit. Merit, as he argued in *Rambler* No. 99, was a highly subjective standard, often dependent on the varying criteria used by different groups and professions, and often colored by agonistic motives and anxieties. "Every man loves merit of the same kind with his own," he wrote, "when it is not likely to hinder his advancement or reputation" (4:168). Convinced of the essential self-interest of human conduct, and of the frequent superficiality of our judgments, he seems consistently resigned to the importance of merely outward and fortuitous advantages in securing the *reputation* for merit. As he observed in *Rambler* No. 193, "unless some accidental advantage co-operates with merit, neither perseverance nor adventure attract attention, and learning and bravery sink into the grave, without honour or remembrance" (5:244).

Such "accidental advantages" certainly included *manners*, understood in the modern way as utterly distinct from either virtue or merit. Drawing from a wealth of conduct-book literature on this subject, Johnson frequently wrote about the nature of "giving pleasure" in social gatherings, inevitably reaching the conclusion, fraught with irony and bitterness, that this skill had nothing to do with (his own) more substantial qualities. As he wrote in *Rambler* No. 188, "the pleasure which men are able to give in conversation, holds no stated proportion to their knowledge or their virtue" (5:220).[119] Manners were, like commerce, a praxis of *exchange,* a capitalistic and democratizing concept of social relations rooted firmly in the experience of the emergent middle class. In contrast with a genteel notion of manners as a code of elegant conduct designed to display one's belonging in an elite social milieu, the idea of manners favored in the commercial culture of the eighteenth century stressed instead that social interaction relied on each individual giving pleasure to receive pleasure. In the words of the radical author James Burgh, writing in *The Dignity of Human Nature* (1754), "if you send others away from you well-pleased with themselves, you need not fear but that they will be well enough pleased with you."[120] Johnson teaches the same lesson in his essays: "It is well known that the most certain way to give any pleasure, is to persuade him that you receive pleasure from him, to encourage him to freedom and confidence, and to avoid any such appearance of superiority as may overbear and depress him" (*Rambler* No. 72, 4:14).

Johnson's observations on manners are therefore closely interconnected with the transformation of social rank in the England of his day. Codes of conduct nurtured in a declining culture founded on differences of birth and heredity were increasingly yielding to a new idea of the "gentleman" grounded in rules of exchange more congenial to an England stoked with the fuel of trade and commerce. Undeniably, this transformation left Johnson with deeply ambivalent feelings. On the one hand, the concept of manners as the exchange of pleasure smoothed the way for people of modest birth, such as Johnson himself, to participate as virtual equals in the social world of the elite: this new praxis was, indeed, even designed to remove markers of hereditary rank and *unpleasing* questions about social origin. On the other hand, it is impossible to ignore the note of disdain and even distress that always sours Johnson's remarks on a society where true merit and virtue are outweighed by the respect earned by pleasing manners and wealth. This discomfort colors Johnson's withering irony when he comments on the impotence of merit in modern culture: "In civilized society, personal merit will not serve you so much as money will. Sir, you may make the experiment. Go into the street, and give one man a lecture on morality, and another a shilling, and see which one will respect you most."[121]

As on the issue of social rank, however, Johnson insisted on the necessity and even the importance of accepting the new order founded on the power of money. To claim that society could be rebuilt as the kind of meritocracy imagined by the Broad-bottom Opposition was deluded or disingenuous: Johnson dismissed Fielding's masterful fable of wronged merit, *Tom Jones*, as a simplistic falsification of real life. Moreover, as the reputed "respectable Hottentot" famously spurned by his erstwhile "patron" Lord Chesterfield,[122] Johnson knew that this celebrated exemplar of highly-placed merit actually valued people for their elegant manners and elevated rank, *not* for their worth. The quest for a society based on merit was indeed socially disruptive. This was partly because of the infinite complications of determining merit dramatized in *Life of Savage*, showing, as he later told Boswell, that we could never decide on a fixed standard for evaluating merit: "we should soon quarrel about the degrees of it."[123] Given the inherent self-interest of human conduct, moreover, everyone believes that his or her own merit is superior to others, a conviction with dire consequences for social stability. This is a lesson preached in one of the sermons he wrote for his friend John Taylor:

> He that sets too high a value upon his own merits, will of course think them ill rewarded with his present condition. He will endeavour to exalt his fortune, and his rank above others, in proportion as his deserts are superior to theirs. He will conceive his virtues obscured by his fortune, lament that his great abilities lie useless and unobserved for want of a sphere of action, in which he might exert them in their full extent. Once fired with these notions, he will attempt to encrease his fortune and enlarge his sphere; and how few there are that prosecute such attempts with innocence, a very transient observation will sufficiently inform us. (14:68–9)

Johnson's response to this potential for disruption was a conservative re-enforcement of traditional forms of hierarchy: his notoriously vociferous insistence on the need to maintain "subordination," his diligent promotion of a professedly "Tory" reverence for government and the established church, all these famous aspects of Johnson's "conservatism" reflect his concern that commercial civilization had destroyed traditional measures of dignity and social elevation, leaving society at the mercy of self-interest and humanity's inevitably superficial and erroneous judgments of merit. Johnson's "conservatism," that is, belongs to a fundamentally skeptical tradition of conservatism that essentially distrusts the capacity of human beings to reach secure judgments or make disinterested decisions. He leaned on traditional institutions and hierarchies as an irenic force to stabilize the energies released by the material enrichment of society. To repeat the essential point – Johnson was not merely a backward-looking and intransigent conservative who clung vainly to old values, old learning, and old politics in the face of change or progress. His political outlooks represent, rather, the conjunction of a clear-sighted recognition of the social-economic *transformation* that had gripped his society with the conviction that the emergent order provided nothing to fill the vacuum of tradition.

It is in this sense that Johnson should be regarded as formulating a "new" conservatism or Toryism that was every bit as attuned to social change as the less cautious and more confident strategies of liberals and Whigs. In the terms used by J.G.A. Pocock, the modernity of Johnson is signaled by his separation of virtue or learning from the sphere of politics. His mature political statements consistently stressed that politics and public life are not likely to be terribly virtuous or meritorious in the sense assumed by Bolingbroke and his followers. Correspondingly, Johnson's moral writings have remained resistant to political analysis because he so determinedly distanced moral, religious and aesthetic discourse from the language of politics, dwelling consistently on the realm of private life. As he wrote in *Rambler* No. 68, "It is, indeed, at home that every man must be known by those who make a just estimate either of his virtue or felicity" (3:360). It was in private that people, men and women equally, seem to become merely "human" rather than actors on the public stage. For the public in Johnson's thought is a distinct sphere with its own rules and priorities, a belief widely shared in an era that was creating this idea, the "public," along with its belief in the responsibility of the state to the people and the supreme virtue of "public spirit."

CHAPTER 4

"The voice of the nation": the evolution of the "public"

PUBLIC SPIRIT AND PRIVATE INTEREST IN A COMMERCIAL NATION

A leitmotif crossing through much that we have discussed so far has been the concept of the "public." As we have seen, eighteenth-century debates surrounding the emergent middle class concerned, above all, the unprecedented access of middling-order people to the public spaces and public activities that had previously signalized the social privilege and seclusion of the aristocracy and upper gentry. If in a previous time, for example, gardens embellished with musicians and delicacies had existed only behind the great homes of the aristocracy, now the public gardens of Vauxhall, Ranelagh, and Marylebone emulated precisely this style, screening out only those who could not pay the moderate but still respectable admission charge. Similar financial barriers were set up at the doors of coffee-houses, which began as little more than courtyards that admitted patrons for a penny, but gradually became more self-consciously "genteel," barring the riffraff and priding themselves on a specialized "elite" clientele.[1] And although these caffeine-fueled zones of middle-rank discourse were widely regarded, it seems, as places of refuge from middle-rank wives, a new literate order of ladies had never before experienced such exposure to the public, had never been allotted such authority on issues of public taste and spending, and had never exercised such a liberty to express themselves publicly, even if the range of that expression was curtailed along lines that we notice because, for the first time, they existed at all. In other words, the proclaimed confinement of women to the "domestic" sphere may strike us as a particularly late-century phenomenon precisely because women's new visibility in English society made it necessary to determine how "public" they should be.

In particular, this incursion of women into public zones made it necessary to articulate that only men could act in the professional and political roles. Yet how much authority did even most middle-rank men wield in the privileged areas of social management? If we consider only the rawest evidence, we find that a greater percentage of men could vote at the beginning of the century than at the end – or even, strikingly, after the 1832 Reform Bill. In other words, the waist-coated pundit of the coffee-house, *pace* Jürgen Habermas, had little more power than his wife to influence the course of events through actual participation in political institutions. As in the case with women, however, we must enlarge our idea of the "public" if we are to understand the changing dimensions of male middle-rank authority in the eighteenth century. The argument can be made – and has been made with intimidating erudition by J.C.D. Clark – that England of this era was little less monarchial and aristocratic than France: "neither the public nor the press was admitted by the professional politicians, whether commoners or peers, to be arbiters of what was honourable in their betters' conduct."[2] In scanning those who sat at the cabinet table or moved in upper government circles, significantly, we find mostly a coterie of well-connected and usually titled men holding the doors of power open just ajar for their friends and family. As other historians have pointed out, however, parliament or cabinet do not represent the only sources of power and influence even in a relatively oligarchic political structure. A large number of historians including John Brewer, H.T. Dickinson, and Nicholas Rogers have focused on ways the public exerted a major impact on the course of affairs in eighteenth-century England through other levels of administration (particularly the City of London and other municipal governments) and, even more important, through the influence of an expanding popular press.[3]

As a major "public" figure of the eighteenth century, Samuel Johnson looms with his usual girth. Nevertheless, as usual, his shadow casts more paradoxes than certitudes. The Johnson of English political legend (a legend that has its basis in certain important truths) fulminated with sometimes hilarious cynicism, as in *The False Alarm* (1770), at the bumptious inebriation of quasi-"democratic" decision-making, best represented in the eighteenth century by its increasingly popular technique of the petition: "One man signs because he hates the papists; another because he vowed destruction to the turnpikes; one because it will vex the parson; another because he is poor; one to shew that he is not afraid, and another to shew that he can write" (10: 338). What elitism. Yet what man of the eighteenth century do we take more seriously as a barometer of eighteenth-century political attitudes than the famously anti-democratic Johnson – a man who not only never held political office, but who may never have voted? Even

J.C.D. Clark wrote a political life of this untitled son of a failed book-seller, as if his conservatism mattered.

To seize on the importance of Johnson as a public and political figure of the eighteenth century is indeed to realize the paradox not only of this major literary personality but of eighteenth-century England as a whole – a society that was not yet "democratic" in institutional terms, but which was beginning to take itself very seriously as a political community. An indication of this rising consciousness of communal duty was a term that echoed through eighteenth-century political discourse like a magic formula, "public spirit." Closely connected with the coalescing virtue of patriotism, "public spirit" denoted what every politician was supposed to treasure, and what every individual was supposed emulate on the model of Pope's Man of Ross, Fielding's Mr. Allworthy, Mackenzie's Mr. Harley – or Boswell's Doctor Johnson. Boswell portrays Johnson not only as a man with obsessive opinions on public issues but as an exemplary citizen whose big pockets bulged with pennies of commitment to even the street-bound detritus of London society. As usual, however, Johnson seems most significant as a figure crossing from one era into the next. We have already considered that the Opposition advocated by Johnson in his very earliest writings shines with the classical-republican ideals of public virtue. Walpole's crime was against public spirit, the supposedly highest virtue of all concerned with public life. The notion of a political "public," or the "people," would indeed continue to be the mainstay of radical and populist discourse throughout the century. Johnson's conservatism, on the other hand, may almost be measured by his early and deepening skepticism with this concept. From an early stage, Johnson doubted that true public spirit was possible and that a public could cohere in the corporate sense implied by late-century radicals. At least in political and social matters, the late Johnson tended to see society as a compact of distinct and self-interested *individuals*, an outlook that is basically consistent with what we have already considered concerning his belief in the inevitability of ideological divisions in society, the source of "party" in its modern form.

How do we account for these changes, and for the continuing paradoxes in Johnson's views (for he never ceased to be a proponent of public spirit in certain forms)? To resolve these contradictions cannot, indeed, be our aim – for Johnson incarnates contradictions that haunted, and continue to haunt, the mansions of English culture. The crux of the paradox is formed by two coincident forces in the making of modern England, economics and nationalism. We have seen that Johnson's economics were essentially "capitalist," to the extent that he rose self-consciously on the wave of the market-place, refusing to share the cassandric despair of many contemporaries about the scourge of luxury. In the following pages, however, we will see Johnson's devotion to ideals of English nationalism and even imperialism, a disposition that represents a readjustment and deepening of the Patriot ideals he imbibed as a feisty Broad-bottom Tory in the 1740s. Economic individualism and national identity represent forces that – while meshing at certain convenient intersections – also strike with sparks of illuminating contradiction and uncertainty in the thought of Samuel Johnson.

Let us absorb, first, Opposition discourse of the early century, where the virtue of public spirit is vaunted as a total commitment to the interests of the nation rather than oneself. This virtue was therefore extremely similar to Christian virtues such as self-abnegation and universal love. Its prominence in political discourse of this era exemplifies the deeply religious and moral tenor of early eighteenth-century politics. "Public spirit" denoted a total package of moral virtues where the promotion of national goals, such as promotion of British colonial interests abroad, could not be separated from domestic virtues such as benevolence, compassion for the poor or chivalry towards women. The sea-captain Thomas Coram (1668–1751), for example, was eulogized as an exemplar of "Publick Spirit" because of two activities curiously, for us, associated in the mind of his anonymous admirer: promoting the colonization of Nova Scotia and establishing the Foundling Hospital in 1739.[4] Similarly, according to an article published in 1746 in Dodsley's journal *The Museum*, love of country was the supreme virtue, embracing all other moral relations:

> There is hardly any moral Duty of more unexceptionable Obligation than *the Love of our Country*. The Reason is plain; for almost all our moral Relations are included in our Country, and consequently, all particular Duties which are subordinate to the Duty that we owe the Public. A Father, a Son, a Friend, a Husband, are all indebted, for their respective Enjoyments, to the Protection of that Civil Society under which they live; therefore the Relation in which they stand to that Society, is more important than that in which they stand to any of its Members; they therefore owe it a more indispensable Duty.[5]

This commitment to the interests of the commonweal or public seemed to most eighteenth-century people absolutely necessary to the prosperity and even the survival of the nation. In the words of John Dennis, "publick Spirit" constitutes the very "soul" of the social body, without which the nation, like a body deprived of its soul, will disintegrate into its original elements.[6] For those devoted to Bolingbroke's ideal of a nation without party, the great enemy of public spirit was "faction," a narrow devotion to a particular ideology or group of men rather than the interests of the whole nation. In an Opposition pamphlet published in 1736, *The Present Necessity of Distinguishing Publick Spirit from Party*, the anonymous author urges the necessity "of dropping Party-views of all Kinds, and uniting in the true publick Spirit."[7] As opposed to the party-man, motived by "a Spirit of Ambition and Revenge,"[8] the public-spirited man "looks abroad for the Motive, and within for the Reward of his Actions; knows no View but publick Good, Benevolence, and Virtue."[9]

The evil of Walpole's corrupt and venal regime was allegedly that it betrayed the responsibility of those in power to act in this spirit of disinterested patriotism and benevolence. Walpole's reputed maxim that "every man has his price" epitomized the self-interested spirit corrupting the nation. Even two years after the Great Man's fall, *Old England* was reviling the "absurd" and "knavish" maxim that "*every man has his Price.*"[10] And in the City periodical that set the tone for radical journalism from the 1750s onwards, *The Monitor*, Walpole is still recalled as "the grand corrupter-general."[11] "Every man has his price" is denounced as "a detestable maxim; a vile libel upon human nature."[12] In later decades, public spirit and its closely related virtue, patriotism, remained closely connected with a pious disdain for private emolument and a devotion to the welfare of others. In Wilkes's *The North Briton*, the Great Commoner William Pitt is lauded over and over for his high-minded virtue and disinterested service to the country, qualities contrasted with the vilified Lord Bute, charged with being "wholly engrossed by private views, the qualities of his head as yet doubtful, and those of his heart too plain."[13] In a pamphlet published in 1780, *Unity and Public Spirit*, this virtue is again associated with a generally benign and disinterested moral character. This author proposed the following signs to detect "a man regardless of the interest of his country": "Examine his character, and you will generally find him coiled up in selfishness," a Blifil-like serpent, "morose, avaricious and unsocial."[14] The ideal man of public spirit, on the contrary, combined moral benevolence and a vigorous and even militaristic devotion to national interests. As in the case of Captain Coram thirty years before, the navy supplied the exemplary model of patriotic character. *Unity and Public Spirit* concludes with a eulogy for the seventeenth-century naval hero Admiral Blake, who is praised for "a zeal and veneration for the English name and character, rising almost to enthusiasm."[15]

Johnson himself had written a *Life of Blake* for *The Gentleman's Magazine* in 1740, similarly praising this admiral for his "intrepidity, honesty, contempt of wealth, and love of his country."[16] Especially in the early years of his career, Johnson endorsed a conventional ideal of public spirit that linked love of country with a more general rectitude and generosity of character. As with others, moreover, it was the British navy that seemed to supply the loftiest exemplars of this ideal. In the same year as he wrote *Life of Blake*, he also produced a *Life of Drake*, where that great hero of the Opposition is portrayed as a devout patriot, selfless leader, and pious Christian. The obvious political goal of these works was to embarrass Walpole's administration for its reluctance to strike heroically, in the manner of Blake and Drake, against the perfidious Spanish in the Caribbean. And the public spirit of these heroes contrasted with the avaricious, self-serving, and corrupt motives of the Prime Minister and his cronies. In Johnson's early Swiftian satire on Walpole's Theatrical Licensing Act, *A Compleat Vindication of the Licensers of the Stage* (1739), the putative author – a Gulliver-like toady of the administration – applauds his political masters for driving "out of the world the old prejudices of patriotism and publick spirit" (10:73). Walpole and his allies, we are told, have relied on the cynical assumption that "publick spirit is generally too weak to combat with private passions" (10:65). Even more than a decade later, in *Rambler* No. 27, Johnson recalled the corruption and self-interest embodied for his generation by Walpole. In this essay, a young writer is driven, after repeated rebuffs from patrons, to pander his literary virtues to the corrupt statesman "Eutyches." With interesting and typical complication, however, Johnson gives a new twist to the old cliché about Walpole, for it is not the young author, but the statesman, who is "bought": the author finds that "there was a certain price at which [his favour] might be bought," and that price is the author's dignity and "virtue" (3:150). In Johnson's presentation of the old Walpole myth, it is the shameful prostitution of literary talent, not the sleazy demands of corrupt politicians, that absorbs our attention.

It would nonetheless be wrong to conclude from this shift of focus that Johnson became more sympathetic to Walpole after his fall in 1742, as Donald Greene and others have claimed.[17] Indeed, given Greene's case for Johnson's essential liberalism (his allegedly strident individualism, his resentment of authority and so forth), this was a strange case to maintain, for it was Walpole, and certainly not Toryism, that was most responsible for the autocratic and anti-populist traditions of eighteenth-century politics that, in Greene's view, Johnson disdained. Even in later years, as a supporter of strong government against radical insurgence, Johnson was not merely surrendering to Walpoleian *Realpolitik*, that ideology's cynical prescription that strong and stable government was oiled by the greasy palms of dependants and insiders. In later years, Johnson's utter contempt for government hacks like David Mallet (who offered his pen to help execute Admiral Byng) is palpable.[18] In his speech for Henry Thrale, *The Patriot* (1774), Johnson rehearses the old ideal of true public spirit as a genuine challenge to those who took this quality lightly: "A *Patriot* is he whose public conduct is regulated by one single motive, the love of his country, who, as an agent in Parliament, has for himself neither hope nor fear, neither kindness nor resentment, but refers every thing to the common interest" (10:390). Similarly, his bitter complaint against the American revolutionaries in *Taxation No Tyranny* (1775) was that they had failed to see the need for commitment to the public over merely private interest: "By this principle it is, that states are founded and consolidated. Every man is taught to consider his own happiness as combined with the publick prosperity, and to think himself great or powerful in proportion to the greatness or power of his governors" (10:420).

These passages suggest Johnson's continuing willingness to appeal to the ideals of public spirit which inspired Patriot attacks on Walpole's administration and which continued to resonate throughout the political discourse of the era, particularly among late-century radicals. Nonetheless, it seems undeniable that Johnson felt increasing unease with the ideals of his time concerning a disinterested devotion to the common good. Behind this skepticism was his usual acute awareness of the transformation of English society by capitalism. As we have seen, the commercialization of England was not a transformation that he liked or welcomed in all ways. Nonetheless, he was deeply sensible of the inconsistency between the virtues of frugal public spirit and an economy increasingly dominated by the self-interest encouraged by trade and commerce.

This was an inconsistency brought brazenly to the attention of the public by the satires of Bernard Mandeville. Mandeville's *Fable of the Bees*, which metamorphosed between 1714 and 1723 from a doggerel poem into a quasi-philosophical tract, takes unambivalent aim at the conventional view that, as Dennis wrote, "publick Spirit" is the very "soul" of the social body, without which the nation, like a body deprived of its soul, will disintegrate into original elements.[19] Mandeville retorted that public spirit was no more than a myth contrived by self-interested politicians who wished to make the public more tractable, "It being the Interest . . . of the very worst of them, more than any, to preach up Publick-spiritedness, that they might reap the Fruits of the Labour and Self-denial of others."[20] What really held society together was not public spirit at all, for people are essentially and, from an economic point of view, *beneficially* self-interested and acquisitive. What contained the agitation of individual self-interest within the compass of relative order and civility was not public spirit but law and government. Consider carefully the opening sentence to the complete *Fable of the Bees*, where Mandeville deploys a materialist metaphor of the body-politic to counter the conventional dualism of public spirit and the social body: "Laws and Government are to the Political Bodies and Civil Societies, what the Vital Spirits and Life it self are to the Natural Bodies of Animated Creatures."[21]

Whatever its popularity among the skeptical *lumières* of the French Enlightenment, or among disciples of free-market liberalism in our time, Mandeville's effusions disturbed and upset without really changing the direction of English debate, at least in ways that are immediately recognizable. Not only was *Fable of the Bees* widely attacked, as by John Dennis, but the conventional language of Opposition continued to exalt the virtues of disinterested public spirit, condemning the supposed self-interest, corruption, and luxury of successive administrations. To the Opposition, Sir Robert Walpole seemed, indeed, the very Frankenstein monster of Mandeville's cynical and materialist laboratory. Nevertheless, Johnson was among the many who were impressed by Mandeville's apparently demystifying analysis. As he famously said to Boswell, Mandeville "opened my views into real life very much."[22] What he shared with Mandeville was, in part, a deep skepticism with the ideals of disinterested virtue that, particularly as disseminated through the work of Lord Shaftesbury, strongly influenced ideals of public spirit. Among members of the Broad-bottom group, such as Henry Fielding, these ideals are closely linked to a conviction in the possibility of selfless moral action. Fielding's definition of patriotism in the *True Patriot* will remind us strongly of the selflessly benevolent heroes of his novels (who indeed are meant as exemplars of public spirit): "The Man who is known to love a Guinea better than his Friend, or even his own Soul, can never deserve the Name of *Patriot*."[23] Johnson, on the contrary, belongs to what I have elsewhere called the "Christian Epicurean" tradition of British ethics that accepts the inevitably selfish nature of human motivation: "Every man is conscious, that he neither performs, nor forbears any thing upon any other motive than the prospect, either of an immediate gratification, or a distant reward" (14:149).[24]

Significantly, this sentence comes from one of Johnson's sermons, for even in his Christian teaching (where he is usually quite demanding on human nature) he is soberly realistic about the difficulty, even the impossibility, of inherently public-spirited action. In Sermon 23, a politically charged homily on the January 30 anniversary of Charles I's execution, he observed that people join in "perpetual confederacy" (14:238) for protection against the uncertainties of life in the state of nature. Society served the material self-interest of its members, and this position led to the following detailed and carefully reasoned refutation of the whole ideal of the citizen selflessly devoted to the common good:

> As it is not possible for a being, necessitous and insufficient as man, to act wholly without regard to this interest, so it is difficult for him to place his interest at such a distance from him, as to act, with constant and uniform diligence, in hopes only of happiness flowing back upon him in its circulation through a whole community, to seek his own good, only by seeking the good of all others, of many whom he cannot know, and of many whom he cannot love. Such a diffusion of interest, such sublimation of self-love is to all difficult, because it places the end at a great distance from the endeavour; it is to many impossible, because to many the end, thus removed, will be out of sight. (14:238–9)

This skepticism concerning the possibility of truly public-spirited action has considerable significance for understanding Johnson's philosophy of society. Society, he believed, could not function in a peaceful and orderly way merely through promotion of communal generosity, as imagined by so many writers from John Dennis to the writer of *Unity and Public Spirit*. As we will see, he did imagine the possibility of mass consciousness and social mobilization, but he usually associated this phenomenon with the popular madness instigated by the radical press. Taken to excess, even public spirit could become a social evil. In *False Alarm* (1770), Johnson's deeply conservative response to the Middlesex election controversy, he decries the spread of public spirit to common people who should confine their concerns to their private affairs: "The sphere of anxiety is now enlarged; he that hitherto cared only for himself, now cares for the public; for he has learned that the happiness of individuals is comprised in the prosperity of the whole, and that his country never suffers but he suffers with it, however it happens that he feels no pain" (10:335).

The Middlesex election represented one of the historical moments mentioned in Sermon 7 when "all regard for private interest has been absorbed and lost, in the concern for the welfare of the publick, to which virtue itself has been made a sacrifice" (14:75). Yet his intention was clearly not merely to suggest the worthlessness of a principled commitment to public welfare. He also recognized the dangers of excessive individualism and self-interest, particularly as promoted by a capitalist economy. In balance with these warnings against overly zealous concern for the public, he noted that at other times in history "every heart has been engrossed by low views, and every sentiment of the mind has been contracted into the narrow compass of self-love" (14:75). Such, Johnson believed, was the root of discontent in

America, a nation of "Whigs" and merchants where "low views" and narrow, mercantile selfishness had overwhelmed the commitment that Johnson assumed they should still feel for the British community. "A merchant's desire," he observed, "is not of glory, but of gain; not of publick wealth, but of private emolument" (10:415). The Americans confirmed that "There will always be part, and always be a very large part of every community that have no care but for themselves, and whose care for themselves reaches little farther than impatience of immediate pain, and eagerness for the nearest good" (10:415). This utter lack of any "extensive views," to echo Johnson's resonant opening to *Vanity of Human Wishes*, led inevitably to the "strife and confusion" of competing individual interests, the disintegration of all social bonds, described in Sermon 23.

In short, Johnson's understanding of national community harbours an important paradox regarding the competing claims of public and private interest. On the one hand, he insisted on the self-interested basis of human conduct, and certainly believed that this self-interest could be beneficially harnessed in a capitalist economy; on the other hand, the very individualism encouraged by capitalism threatened to dissolve social unity and order into the "strife and confusion" described in Sermon 23. To resolve this paradox, Johnson, like Mandeville, looked to "laws and government." As disinterested commitment to the community was ultimately unreliable – and even disruptive when the masses became inflamed with concern for supposed public good – only popular submission to the immediate interest of obeying the law and the state could provide consistent order and stability:

> As all government is power exerted by few upon many, it is apparent that nations cannot be governed by their own consent. The first duty therefore of subjects is obedience to the laws, such obedience as is the effect, not of compulsion, but of reverence; such as arises from a conviction of the instability of human virtue, and of the necessity of some coercive power, which may restrain the exorbitancies of passion, and check the career of natural desires. (Sermon 24, 14:258–9)

This passage is comparable to Mandeville in its investment in coercive power over selfless community. Like Mandeville, Johnson held an essentially materialist understanding of society: he rejected the "dualistic" model of society found in the works of John Dennis and others who imagined public spirit as the "soul" animating the social body. Rather, Johnson and Mandeville argued that communities are essentially individualistic and reliant on the levers of pleasure and pain to maintain unity and stability. Given the impossibility, that is, of a truly bonding "soul" of public spirit, diffused throughout the entire body-politic, Johnson concluded in principle that public order relied on strong government and laws.

Yet even this generally valid assessment conceals important ambiguities and complications. In ways that are not immediately obvious, Johnson felt a real pride in the supposed "liberty" of England, a quality that he would not sacrifice even for the admittedly greater efficiency of an autocratic government. This greater efficiency, he admitted, was obvious in a time of war. During the mounting hostilities between France and Britain in 1756, for example, Johnson explained the remarkable success of the former French Chief Minister Colbert in making his kingdom a major imperial power: "it must be considered, that Colbert had means of acting, which our government does not allow. He could inforce all his orders by the power of an absolute monarch; he could compel individuals to sacrifice their private profit for the general good" (10:140–1). This advantage in mobilizing a nation's military and financial might was lacking in a mercantile nation like Britain, with its traditions of untrammeled private interest: "No mercantile man, or mercantile nation, has any friendship but for money, and alliance between them will last no longer than their common safety or common profit is endangered" (10:143–4).[25] Despite genuine feelings of discomfort with the merchant class, however, Johnson was certainly *not* suggesting that Britain would be better off as despotic monarchy like her enemy across the channel. In this ultimately patriotic warning against the power of the French, his point was rather that public spirit, touted as the very "soul" of the nation in so much political discourse, was in fact less binding and forceful than his compatriots seemed, at their peril, to believe.

Comparing Johnson's statements with those in pamphlets and newspapers of the same years – the highly patriotic years that began the Seven Years' War – one is struck by the degree to which he was in direct dialogue with other authors and journals. Just a few months earlier, for instance, the militant City journal *The Monitor* had similarly applauded Colbert for his far-sighted foreign policy: "He saw with concern, that while other nations were establishing colonies at both ends of the world, France alone had neglected the sea." But *The Monitor* went on to claim that, after Colbert's death, these advantages had been squandered by the arbitrary power of France: Louis XIV, "deluded by his mistress and confessor, deserted the true interest of his people."[26] This journal, which was subtitled "the Freeholder" and boisterously championed the interests of merchants and traders, counted on the public spirit of noble men of commerce to lead the nation in a victorious campaign against "the perfidious French." The response of Johnson, as we have seen, was that one could certainly *not* depend on merchants to sacrifice self-interest for the common cause. Especially as mercantile capitalism maximized the essential self-interest of human beings, a commercial people like the English could not hope to emulate the unity of purpose of an absolute monarchy like France.

Hence, while in sympathy with Mandeville's insistence on the importance of "law and government" as the only truly binding powers in a capitalist society, Johnson's full philosophy is much more nuanced and paradoxical. Oddly, given Mandeville's present reputation as a precursor of free-market liberalism, Johnson implies that the Mandevillian thesis, if applied to the real nature of societies, would require absolute monarchy to work efficiently. Mandeville assumed that public-spiritedness represented a kind of grand national delusion. "Cunning politicians," he argues, persuaded people to surrender their self-interest to the supposed "virtue" of serving public good in order, in fact, to facilitate the selfish ambitions of their masters. Although Johnson was concerned by the power of the press as a means to manipulate public opinion, as we will consider, he was very far from accepting this fantasy of national indoctrination. In Johnson's thought, the bond of society is not delusion but popular *knowledge*. The worst political evil, in Johnson's view, was the necessity of ruling the people not by their consent but by force. This was the danger that he saw looming with the increase of popular agitation during the 1760s. As he wrote in a pamphlet of 1766, "Consideration on Corn," the "miseries of the poor" had driven the government towards "one of the greatest of political evils, – the necessity of ruling by immediate force" (10:306).

In other words, it was finally enlightened *consent*, not merely the force of legislative power, that Johnson relied on as the source of social order. He did not believe that public spirit, in the sense of a selfless concern for the welfare of all, was efficacious enough to be the basis of national unity and harmony, but he did believe that most individuals could come to understand and accept the need for traditional forms of hierarchy and authority. For this reason, as we shall go on to examine, he was a great promoter of public education and public enlightenment, though he had little patience with idealized appeals to "the voice of the nation."

EXPANDING THE "PUBLIC SPHERE": FREEDOM OF THE PRESS AND KILLING ADMIRAL BYNG

We have considered that consciousness of a public strongly informs political and social debate in the eighteenth century. As stressed in modern scholarship, this consciousness reflects above all the sense of a common identity and a common purpose created by a widening network of communication – the expanding literary market-place and the popular press, along with the clubs and coffee-houses where news and events were discussed. Together, these routes of communication constitute what Jürgen Habermas has called "the bourgeois public sphere," a restructuring of social discourse that, allegedly, mobilized the middle class to demand a new role and new powers in public affairs. According to this argument, a knowledgeable and public-spirited middle class, armed with tools of "rational political discourse" honed in coffee-house controversy, increasingly refused to give their consent to the arbitrary and unjustified measures of the state, which was ultimately forced to relinquish large areas of its authority to the fora of public debate and democratic ratification.[27]

As even Habermas's admirers have admitted, however, this thesis presents a rather idealized picture of what happened in the eighteenth century.[28] First, as we have considered, the middling ranks remained a highly inchoate and heterogeneous body throughout most of the century, deeply divided between the often conflicting interests of the City, the untitled gentry and the literary/professional community represented by Johnson. We cannot really speak coherently of a middle class (much less a French-style bourgeoisie) until very late in the century, when authors like Gisborne, Malthus, and Wollstonecraft began to define a set of political and economic priorities distinct from both the upper class and the lower class. For most of the century, it is difficult to detect the class-unity implied by the "bourgeois public sphere." As studies of the eighteenth-century coffee-house show, this was an institution devoted to promoting the clubbish diversity of (largely) male culture. There were coffee-houses catering to lawyers (Nands's or the Grecian, near the Temple), merchants (pre-eminently Jonathan's, the first "stock-exchange," but also Garaway's), clergymen and university types (Truby's or Child's), slave-traders (the Virginian or the Jamaican), Whigs (St. James or Smyrna), Tories (the Cocoa-Tree or Ozinda's), Scots (Forrest's or the British), Frenchmen (Giles's or Old Slaughter's), and so on through a widening fan of diverse cultural and ideological leanings.[29] *What* coffee-house you frequented became a politically significant detail, reflecting and consolidating political divisions that scholars have not even begun to explore in any detail. Second, *contra* Habermas, it was a major anxiety in the eighteenth century that the press was certainly not encouraging "rational political discourse." At a much earlier stage than we are apt to imagine, eighteenth-century people became concerned that the press was being used to manipulate popular prejudice for the political ends of particular factions or even, as the Opposition complained, on behalf of the government.

Coffee-house politics, ran a common complaint, were shallow, distorting, and essentially emotional. Scenes of mass protest and violence in the streets intensified the feeling that the press was being used as a tool to ignite anarchic passions rather than to inform rational debate on matters of national importance.[30]

Hence, the battle in the eighteenth century over the control and appropriate use of the press. With the lapsing of the Licensing Act in 1695, England was left with no formal legislation to control the press. An Act of 1707 made support for the cause of the Pretender a capital crime, legislation that sent one John Matthews to the gallows in 1719;[31] Walpole's Theatrical Licensing Act in 1737 provided an avenue for direct government control of the stage. Otherwise, however, administrations that wished to suppress dissident opinions were forced to pursue their enemies through the courts on the criminal charge of seditious libel, a notoriously slippery and ill-defined area of the law. There was quasi-official consensus among all sides in English politics that liberty of press was an indefeasible right. Even when Walpole's administration was actively exploring ways to silence the Opposition, the government organ, *The Daily Gazetteer*, acknowledged that "The Liberty of the Press is an undoubted Right we ought ever to regard, so far as it relates to the propagating [*sic*] Sound Learning, Good Morality, True Virtue, and Knowledge of Arts and Sciences in general."[32] Similarly, a pro-government pamphlet in 1756 called liberty of the press "a Privilege dear as Life." As this author went on to declare, however, "all *Liberty* has its proper Bounds,"[33] and debate swirled around precisely this question of where the "bounds" of liberty should be set.

The insistent complaint under Walpole was that the Opposition was using the press irresponsibly and libelously to inflame popular sentiment against the government. In Johnson's version of the parliamentary debates, for example, Horace Walpole attacks "the mercenary scribblers of disaffection" who were "the oracles only of the lowest of the people."[34] The Prime Minister's own "scribblers," meanwhile, fulminated that Opposition attacks threatened civil order by diminishing "reverence" for both the King and his administration. "I appeal to any on the plainest Understanding," wrote Francis Squire, "(who has the least Notion of Authority or Government) whether any Subject (either National or Domestick) will continue to pay an outward *Obedience* without an inward *Reverence*."[35] If the Opposition wished to bring an accusation against the government, they should expect to "PROVE IT" rather than simply relying on libelous insinuations and ungrounded suspicions.[36] Characteristic of pro-Walpole literature is its skeptical and sometimes even contemptuous portrayal of the public as irrational and ignorant, unable to understand much less direct the affairs of the state. The *Daily Gazetteer* commented scornfully that "the Affairs of Administration (by means of Weekly Scandalous Papers) are canvassed even in every common Alehouse, and by all Ranks of People."[37] Johnson's parliamentary debates portray Sir Robert Walpole contemptuously rejecting a petition from London merchants as failing to show "the reverence due to this assembly;"[38] elsewhere, the Prime Minister condemns attacks on his government by the Opposition press as attempts to "obstruct" the administration.[39] Popular outcry against the former Patriots who joined the administration after 1742 provoked the similar defense that, as John Perceval argued bitterly in *Faction Detected* (1743), the public was "prejudiced" and badly informed, led astray by the half-truths and rabble-rousing rhetoric of the Opposition.[40] A common charge against the English public was that it would support no one in government, but was naturally and automatically insolent against all forms of authority. [41]

The cause of the free press, on the other hand, was championed during the Walpole era by Opposition journals, particularly Bolingbroke's *The Craftsman*. Yet, as government writers were eager to point out, Bolingbroke himself had aggressively suppressed Opposition opinion during his four years in power under Queen Anne.[42] Indeed, it is quite arguable that the elite figures who commanded the Opposition throughout the 1730s and 40s liked to declaim on the theory of a free press but, in reality, had a very qualified commitment to protecting "the voice of the people." One does not have to scratch Opposition propaganda very deeply to find a patrician contempt for the ignorance and violence of the "illiterate Rabble" comparable in every way to the more overt anti-populism of Walpole and his supporters.[43] When Fielding, under the name "Pasquin," defended himself against the Theatrical Licensing Act in the pages of *Common-Sense*, he identified very closely with the attitudes of the educated elite. "However the very Name of Power may frighten the Vulgar," he wrote, "it will never be honoured by the Philosopher, or the Man of Sense, unless accompanied with Dignity." Fielding went on to assure his enemies that he counted "the greatest Wits, and the finest Gentlemen" among his friends.[44] Even *The Craftsman*, which had become boldly Whig (and anti-Tory) by the later 1730s, conceded to Walpole that he had the right to purge certain irregularities from the stage, particularly "those *wretched low Tricks* and *mobbish Entertainments*, which the MANAGERS have lately introduc'd upon it."[45]

It is hardly surprising, as Horace Walpole pointed out, that Patriot leaders like Chesterfield and Lyttelton seemed to lose their enthusiasm for liberty of the press once they themselves had achieved places in the administration.[46]

And in later years, there was a growing consensus in the governing classes that excessive liberty of the press undermined public order. On the one hand, for example, the pro-Pitt weekly *The Con-test* made conventional claims to stand front-and-shoulder with a free press: "Heaven forbid! That we should call ourselves *Britons*, and attack the *liberty of the Press*." Yet it then went on to recommend quite draconian controls on the press, even denying that "any INDIVIDUAL, has a right to *censure* the arts of government, or the members of the administration." All criticism of government, it maintained, should be done through the parliamentary representatives or by means of the petition, an outlet that even most conservatives conceded as a legitimate channel of organized protest.[47]

Johnson's early support for the Opposition's defense of the free press is shown by his *Compleat Vindication of the Licensers of the Stage* (1739), his satire on Walpole's 1737 Theatrical Licensing Act. Seen in context, Johnson's pamphlet is very close in tone and message to the attacks on Walpole by the members of the Bolingbroke-Chesterfield circle. Indeed, Johnson joins in the ritual of scattering laurels in the direction of the main Opposition figures, including Lyttelton, Pitt, and even Pulteney (see 10:56–7 and 72). After Bolingbroke's departure in 1736 from *The Craftsman*, which subsequently became virulently pro-Whig and anti-Tory, the vehicle of the Broad-bottom Opposition was *Common-Sense*, co-edited by Chesterfield and Lyttleton, with the help of an arch-Tory, William King. The publisher of *Common-Sense*, John Brett, published Johnson's Opposition satire *Marmor Norfolciense* (1738).[48] Just a month before the publication of Johnson's *Compleat Vindication* in May 1739, *Common-Sense* printed a very similar satire which, as in Johnson's work, adopted the voice of a supposed supporter of the government. The rationale of this ironic technique, as explained in a previous number, was that Walpole's attempt to silence the press had left his opponents with no options except "Burlesque, or Buffonery, to express what they think."[49] These weapons were put into action on April 21, 1737, when a toadying flatterer of the ministry declares that "it is fit a great M____ should be strengthen'd with Power enough to crush whom he pleases; for great Men must be made easy." The narrator applauds "the Example of our great Man's Integrity and Modesty," and expresses confidence that the Act has prohibited some "very wicked Plays," though he confesses that he has not actually read them.[50] Much the same method is used in Johnson's satire, where an unabashedly venal narrator condemns the Patriots for showing "irreverence" to great men in authority, kindling the destructive flames of public spirit, and spreading the seditious doctrine that virtue and merit are more important than dependency and bribes.

Like other Opposition writing of this period, the *Compleat Vindication* sounds almost democratic in its bold and unqualified support for "liberty of the press, which is the darling of the common people" (10:73). Even at this stage, however, Johnson's attitudes were less radical than might appear. The *Compleat Vindication* does not, in fact, criticize the original rationale for the Theatrical Licensing Act – the suppression of obscenity on the stage, a problem that even Walpole's opponents admitted was real. The main irony exposed by Johnson's satire was rather that Walpole's government, despite its own extremely dubious virtue, was using this legislation to ban even such a dourly virtuous play as Henry Brooke's *Gustavus Vasa*. After Walpole's fall, one notices a certain reticence and lack of emotion in Johnson's comments on freedom of the press. In his little treatise on the "Origin and Importance of Small Tracts and Fugitive Pieces," which he wrote as part of his work cataloguing the Harleian Miscellany, Johnson remarks that "The form of our government . . . gives every man, that has leisure, or curiosity, or vanity, the right of inquiring into the propriety of publick measures." Johnson commends this liberty for spurring industry and creativity, but he also comments on the inconvenience of "political or religious controversies," recounting at some length how "the mind . . . suffered to operate without restraint, necessarily deviates into peculiar opinions, and wanders in new tracks, where she is, indeed, sometimes lost in a labyrinth, from which . . . she cannot return, and scarce knows how to proceed."[51] This is hardly enthusiastic praise for liberty of the press, and it even verges on the typical government complaint that the press gave a public voice to people who were simply unqualified to treat the difficult subjects they broached.

Johnson's concerns about the abuse of the press increased during the popular furor that surrounded the beginning of the Seven Years' War. This was a time, as we have noted, of belligerent drum-beating in the popular press, no doubt reminding people of Johnson's generation of their own bellicose rhetoric during the War of Jenkins' Ear twenty years before. That war, promoted with much patriotic fury by the Opposition press, had failed to yield its promised harvest of military glory, and Johnson seems to have learned his lesson. "Among the calamities of war," he wrote in the *Idler* No. 30 (November 11, 1758), "may be justly numbered the diminution of the love of truth, by the falsehoods which interest dictates and credulity encourages" (2:95). Johnson did, in fact, agree that French aggression needed to be checked, and he later remembered this successful war as a time of considerable national glory.[52] But he strongly criticized the shallowness and bias of the news-reporting, which seemed designed for a "nation . . . eager to hear something good of themselves and ill of the enemy" (2:94). *Idler*

No. 8 opens with a patriotic-sounding call for public spirit in a time of national crisis: "In time of publick danger, it is every man's duty to withdraw his thoughts in some measure from his private interest, and employ part of his time for the general welfare" (2:26). Given Johnson's usually ambivalent feelings about the value of public spirit, especially among the "vulgar," we might catch an undertone of irony in this statement. And indeed the essay becomes increasingly mocking and ludicrous, as Johnson recommends that British soldiers be trained like hungry mastiffs to associate the enemy with hunks of beef and pots of beer.

These essays are satires on the popular press, with its attempts to whet the national appetite for war with blood-thirsty jingoism and rage against the French. But they also reveal a more general concern that the "news" could be used to misinform and manipulate the public. This new consciousness of the press as a tool of propaganda reflects a more general concern among the ruling elite of the nation. Even those who had championed the cause of the free press in the 1730s and 1740s began to worry about the power of the press to distort and mislead the public, often with frighteningly disruptive results. These concerns were brought into focus by public reaction to the trial of Admiral Byng in the winter of 1756. The unfortunate Byng was accused of and finally shot for cowardice during his failed attempt to lead a fleet against the French at Minorca. Even before Byng arrived back in England to face court-martial, the government had spread reports that accused Byng of shirking engagement with the French. Byng's private letter explaining his failure to open fire on the French was published by the ministry edited of all self-justifying evidence. The scent of cowardice was quickly sniffed by the public, which had been schooled to think that their nation, birthplace of Drake and Blake, should always triumph on the seas. By the time Byng finally landed back on shore, he found himself the most reviled man in England. Everywhere his effigy was burned by angry mobs; everywhere broadsheets and ballads breathed revenge against Byng for humiliating the country. As some suspected, however, Byng was at most only partly responsible for the disaster at Minorca. Supplied with a badly inadequate fleet, the commander had merely chosen survival over suicidal valor.[53]

These events were significant and unprecedented, for they marked the first time in England that a government had wielded the old weapon of Opposition, public anger, to justify its own measures or inadequacies. The public, in turn, had been obligingly stupid and vengeful. As Pitt's advocate *The Con-test* put it, the Newcastle ministry had "succeeded in a manner, which does more honour to the public spirit, than the humanity of our countrymen."[54] The Opposition press responded with revealing confusion, for their main source of legitimacy, the "people," failed to confirm its own reading of events. A good example of this confusion is John Shebbeare. This furious anti-Hanoverian had previously assailed the ministry with a series of *Letters to the People of England* that leaned on the assumption that the "people" were wise and virtuous. In face of government subterfuge, therefore, he now published *An Appeal to the People*, reprinting Byng's letter with the expurgated sections restored. "To you I appeal," wrote Shebbeare, "be *Englishmen*, and I fear no Injustice to him who is thus unjustifiably pursued."[55] Unfortunately, the public failed to divert its anger against the government, which responded by hiring David Mallet to write a pamphlet that appealed similarly to "the justice of the nation" to lay the entire blame on "ONE MAN."[56] Shebbeare responded, uncharacteristically, with a "letter" addressed not the "people" but to the ministry, whom he accused of "mean Artifices" to "skreen themselves, and satisfy the Nation; whose Anger they had so artfully contrived to be kept alive against him."[57] Shebbeare's reply concludes with a tellingly beleaguered testimonial to his lonely mission for "Truth" and "the Service of my Country."[58]

Shebbeare and Johnson shared much in common, as revealed by their very similar pro-government and anti-populist writing after 1760, when both became pensioners of the new court. As Boswell commented, "Johnson and Shebbeare were frequently named together, as having in former reigns had no predilection for the family of *Hanover*." The pun on Shebbeare's name, plus their similarly ursine approaches to political affairs, led to their being linked as "*He*-bear" and "*She*-bear."[59] Yet, revealingly, Johnson did not express any strong objections when Shebbeare was condemned to the pillory for his anti-Hanoverian writing in 1758: Boswell, who liked to flaunt his vaunted Toryism around Johnson, asserted that Shebbeare was *not* "dishonored" by his time in the pillory. (Shebbeare, in fact, had been allowed to sit *on* the pillory to great acclamation.) But Johnson disagreed, suggesting that no respectable person would dine with a disgraced writer like Shebbeare.[60] Unlike "She-bear," Johnson had never made an "appeal to the people." His reaction to the Byng affair stressed, above all, the utterly irrational and unjustified reaction of the public to the accusations against this victim of the ministry's propaganda. In a review partly devoted to *Appeal to the People*, Johnson endorsed Shebbeare's attack on the ministry. Indeed, he went beyond what even the turbulent Shebbeare had declared by inferring that the ministry had *deliberately* lost Minorca and then shifted the blame onto Byng (see 10:231–2). Nevertheless, he made clear that he placed absolutely no trust in the justice of the people: "Such is the plea of the persecuted Byng, on which, though we do not suppose that the public will pay much regard to our determination, we shall give our opinion with the freedom of men uninfluenced by dependence or expectation" (10:239).

It is revealing of our democratic age, perhaps, that Johnson's utter dismissal of the public's "justice" here seems arrogant and elitist. Yet nowhere will we find Johnson being so profoundly committed to "new Toryism" in his insistence on the rule of law over the mere force of public pressure. What enraged Johnson most about the Byng affair was that the admiral was tried by the press and public rather than by the law and its institutions:

To hear both parties, and to condemn no man without a trial are the unalterable laws of justice. The man who lately commanded the English fleet in the Mediterranean; after having had his effigies burnt in a hundred places, and his name disgraced by innumerable lampoons; after having suffered all that the malice of wit or folly could inflict on his reputation, now stands forth, and demands an audience from those who have almost universally condemned him, but condemned in his own opinion without justice, and certainly without any calm or candid examination. (10:219)

Johnson was hardly alone in making this complaint: he was in fact echoing one of the pamphlets he was reviewing, *A Letter to a Member of Parliament in the Country, from his Friend in London, relative to the Case of Admiral Byng*, by his former Broad-bottom ally Paul Whitehead.[61] But Johnson's concern to protect the rule of justice against mere public opinion represents one of the most consistent features of his political and social outlooks, recalling, for example, his typically Tory opposition to the attempt of Patriots to suspend the rule of justice in the prosecution of Walpole. Nevertheless, it is also notable that at no point does Johnson actually call for the restriction of the free press. In recorded conversations with Boswell, he did suggest that "liberty of the press" was less important than many pretended. "Suppose you and I and two hundred more were restrained from printing our thoughts:" he said in 1768, "what then? What proportion would that restraint upon us bear to the private happiness of the nation?"[62] But he also acknowledged that the nation had generally benefitted from the diffusion of information, even through a medium, newspapers, that he ridiculed for its shallowness: "The mass of every people must be barbarous where there is no printing, and consequently knowledge is not generally diffused. Knowledge is diffused among our people by the news-papers."[63]

Hence, faced with the rabble-rousing "patriotism" of Wilkite radicals in the 1760s and 70s, Johnson's reaction was not, like some other conservatives, to demand tougher restrictions but rather to fight fire with fire. His reputation among some readers throughout history as a particularly prejudiced and blustery Tory derives in large part from political pamphlets he wrote from 1770 to 1775 that attempt to match radical discourse in their aggression and flamboyant rhetoric. It is a strange but real possibility that one of his inspirations for this new conservative rhetoric was the radical author Junius who, between 1769 and 1772, produced a series of hotly insolent letters on political events, galvanizing the nation. Johnson admitted some admiration for this virulent voice on the side of radicalism. In a pamphlet on the Falkland Islands conflict in 1771, written largely in response to a bellicose letter by Junius in the *Public Advertiser*,[64] Johnson declared Junius "one of the few writers of his despicable faction whose name does not disgrace the page of an opponent" (10:369). He even thought that Junius was actually Burke, about as high a compliment as Johnson could give.[65] Yet Johnson also charged Junius with the same kind of self-serving, ephemeral, and distorting use of the press charged against the ministry during the Byng affair. As described by Johnson, Junius's letters bore no similarity to the "rational discourse" described by Habermas as the hallmark of the "bourgeois public sphere." Junius appealed to the basest emotions of an uneducated and prejudiced public, courting "the sympathetick favour of plebeian malignity." He profited from the "rage of defamation and the audacity of falsehood," "the contempt of order, and violence of outrage" (10:377). Junius's immense popularity, alleged Johnson, did not reflect the quality of his arguments, but rather his reliance on the most facile tricks of surprise and novelty, drawing "the rabble after him as a monster makes a show" (10:376–7).

At no point, however, did Johnson hint that the ministry should have Junius stopped. As the preceding quotes reveal, his method was rather to match his radical opponent blow by blow with a rhetoric equally charged with provocative overstatement, impassioned exclamations, and novel, even bizarre, turns of imagery. At a climactic moment in his pamphlet on the Falkland Islands, for example, he dramatically dismisses Junius as "only a meteor formed by the vapours of putrefying democracy, and kindled into flame by the effervescence of interest struggling with conviction" (10:378). Junius was not the only one who "makes a show," for Johnson attempts to overwhelm his audience with writing characterized not by careful reasoning but by strokes of rhetoric designed, no less than the rhetoric of Junius, to dazzle and inflame. Taken together, Johnson's reflections on the press suggest that he accepted the essentially populist and performative nature of public political discourse. As we have seen, he had no high opinion of newspapers, which he considered vapid, repetitive, and often deeply prejudiced. He also agreed with his conservative cohorts that radical discourse was undermining "reverence" for government, with potentially disruptive consequences for social order. As he wrote in Sermon 24, "he that encourages irreverence, in himself, or others, to publick institutions, weakens all the human securities of peace, and all the corroborations of virtue" (14:259). On purely political matters, however, he evidently supported no strengthening of the libel laws to protect the dignity of the state. As he once told Boswell, "Sir it is of . . . much more consequence that truth should be told, than that individuals should not be made uneasy . . . A minister may be notoriously known to take bribes, and yet you may not be able to prove it."[66] This reference to the bribe-taking "minister" may well remind us of Walpole. Unlike some of his former allies in the Opposition, we find, Johnson did not merely abandon his old Patriot principles, for he continued to regard even harsh criticism of government as a legitimate part of the political process.

If Johnson supported the need for a free press, however, he had also lost what faith he ever had in the stability and rectitude of the public voice on political affairs. Allowing the dissemination of opinions was one question; guiding the state by "majority" opinion was, clearly, another matter entirely. Indeed, his writing after the late 1750s strongly recalls the pro-Walpole press in his sharply pronounced contempt for the ignorance and irrationality of the "rabble." It is remarkable, for example, how Johnson's *Thoughts on . . . Falkland's Islands* or *The Patriot* sounds like Perceval's anti-Patriot tract *Faction Detected* (1742), with its lament that "Treason, was become a publick Topic of Discourse" and "all Decency, Order, and Subordination, was in a manner destroyed."[67] Yet here again we encounter an apparent inconsistency in Johnson's work. For on *non-political* issues, Johnson seems to have held quite different ideas about press freedom and the authority of the public. As I have discussed elsewhere, Johnson held rigid views on the right of the magistrate to repress religious opinions that dissented significantly from the official doctrines of the Church of England: on such questions, he believed, the possibility that doctrinal controversy would ignite public disorder was too urgent to be tolerated, as proven by the outbreak of the Civil Wars.[68] On *literary* judgments, however, Johnson's insistence that the "public" constituted the only legitimate court-of-appeal was virtually unqualified. Compare, for example, Johnson's extremely hostile remarks on the public in his later political writings with the following statement in *Rambler* 23 (June 5, 1750) on literary merit: "there always lies an appeal from domestick criticism to a higher judicature, and the publick, which is never corrupted, nor often deceived, is to pass the last sentence upon literary claims" (3:128). Even on literary matters, this assertion that the public is "never corrupted" must surely be regarded as a rhetorical exaggeration. (Indeed, in the 1756 fourth collected edition of the *Rambler* Johnson showed signs of second thoughts, changing "can never be corrupted" to the somewhat more judicious "never is corrupted.") Elsewhere, as in *Adventurer* No. 138 (March 2, 1754), Johnson acknowledged that the dominance of a few critics could cause the "perversion of publick judgment." Here again, however, he insisted that the public's judgment constituted the "final justification of self esteem" (2:496). And this confidence in public opinion, at least as proven over time, remained the premise of Johnson's argument in the Preface to his edition of Shakespeare (1765), which was written amidst the tumultuous fracas over the suppression of Wilkes's radical journalism. In this cogent analysis of literary judgment, Johnson maintains that the public's historical approval of Shakespeare's plays is the only reliable indicator that he is indeed "the poet of nature" (7:62).

Why should Johnson have taken such different views of the reliability of the public in making political, religious, and literary judgments? The core of this matter seems to lie in the differing influence of self-interest on the ways that people think and judge. As we have considered, Johnson distrusted his contemporaries' promotion of public spirit because he believed in the essentially self-interested nature of human motivation with regard to social and political activity. Religion, which concerned prospects of eternal welfare, intensified this preoccupation with the self to volatile and potentially violent levels. But the ideal *aesthetic* judgment was, for Johnson, a disinterested judgment. The durability of Shakespeare's appeal to the public proved that his original popularity did not rely on merely social and political prejudices that had long since expired: "The effects of favour and competition are at an end; the tradition of his friendships and his enemies has perished; his works support no opinion with arguments, nor supply any faction with invectives" (7:61). One feels here, of course, the influence of recent political controversies on Johnson's presentation of Shakespeare's greatness: unlike the elder Pitt and (later) Junius, both of whom Johnson calls the "meteors" of temporary public favor,[69] Shakespeare has endured, a sign that his fame is based on some virtue more real than the vicissitudes of political fashion and temporary self-interest. Politics, Johnson believed, lay outside the realm of "nature," the universal and enduring values of human life. But as these are the intrinsic values of literature, Johnson could appeal with confidence to the public response on literary questions upon which all people, as equal participants in life, are equally qualified to judge.

In considering Johnson's attitudes to the "public," therefore, we must finally take into account the differing forms of public discourse. Johnson despised the idea that traders and artisans, clamorously debating in a coffee-house, should decide the direction of public affairs which, in his view, they knew virtually nothing about. This hostility to public opinion was even more intense with regard to religious affairs, which in fact he had good historical reasons to consider socially disruptive. Johnson also believed that literature could diffuse socially harmful messages: *Rambler* No. 4 criticizes the realistic novel for mirroring the confusion of good and evil in the real world, muddling the already confused impressions of the young, and we now wonder at his religiously upright, though critically perverse, opinion that Nahum Tate did right in changing the end of *King Lear* to save both Cordelia and the ideal correspondence of virtue and happiness.[70] Nevertheless, he ultimately trusted the "common reader," his repeated term in *Lives of the English Poets*, to make more reliable judgments about literature than the professional critic, whose assessments were tainted by the political world we all know in professional academics. In his unphilosophical way, Johnson was approaching a definition of the disinterested "aesthetic" being developed during his life by Baumgarten and Kant, who, in turn, tended to underrate the extent to which art and life, politics and aesthetics, tend to interpenetrate in the world of human affairs.

At the edge of much that we have discussed regarding the "public" is another concept, "the nation." The two concepts can indeed hardly be separated in eighteenth-century discourse: to devote oneself to the public is to be a "patriot," a lover of one's nation. At the same time, eighteenth-century people lacked a fully developed notion of cultural specificity, or of one nation representing not humanity in general but a specific set of national values. To sacrifice oneself for the nation or the public was, in an important sense, to embody eternal *human* values – an attitude captured with evidently resonant force by Addison's *Cato* (1713). Cato falls placidly on the sword of public interest, a gesture interlocked with his conviction of having a "Roman soul." But "Roman soul" apparently denoted a disposition that was more than skin-deep, as implied when the Numedian (that is, African) Jura is credited by embattled Cato with precisely this hidden jewel (even in doubting that his daughter should marry a black man). In this version of patriotism, that is, devotion to country means devotion to an ideal that supposedly exceeds local and cultural divisions, becoming an attitude where being "Roman" equates with the universal human condition of "liberty."

In his *Life of Addison* Johnson called Cato "unquestionably the noblest production of Addison's genius,"[71] and there is a good case to be made for Johnson's continued, maybe wistful, attachment to the toga of early-century classicism. Johnson's "Englishness" seems often associated with the conviction that to be "English" is simply to be human at a more advanced level, an attitude that he would carry into the Scottish Highlands in 1773, abrading the sore spirit of a nation undergoing a self-conscious conversion to "modernity." And this was also an abiding notion of Johnson's Victorian successors, who liked to believe that they were not imposing an English identity on the world, but rather endowing "less-advanced" people with a treasure-box of eternal truth wrapped in a Union Jack. At the same time, the trek of an unhealthy sixty-four-year-old English writer across the Highlands is itself extraordinary testimony of a desire to test the dimensions of Englishness and to reflect on the nature of the "Britain" which had emerged in Johnson's lifetime. The significance of this journey, and of the writing and experience of the older Johnson, was indeed to intensify this "Englishness," to make him more of a figure who, unlike Addison's Cato, truly embodied a *particular* cultural outlook rather than being nobly "human" in a universal sense. What angered many of Johnson's Scots hosts is that he seemed to present himself as both eternal moralist and English conqueror, Cato and John Bull, and here perhaps we locate the essence of a potent mixture behind Johnson's nationalistic allure.

CHAPTER 5

The construction of English nationhood

ENGLAND AND THE FULFILMENT OF NATIONAL DESTINY

"Many will start," writes Boswell, upon reading Johnson's famous statement in 1775: "Patriotism is the last refuge of a scoundrel." He goes on to defend Johnson against the suspicion that he merely dismissed the worth of loving one's country: "let it be considered, that he did not mean a real and generous love of our country, but that pretended patriotism which so many, in all ages and countries, have made a cloak for self-interest."[1] Johnson's apparent dismissal of "patriotism" nonetheless remains among his most notorious statements. It apparently confirms that the study of his life and thought should not be confined to a narrowly "English" context, for he was skeptical of English contemporaries prejudiced in favor of their homeland, taking an admirably "extensive view" (l. 1, 6:91), as he wrote in "The Vanity of Human Wishes," of human affairs. According to one influential argument, as articulated by Robert DeMaria and others, Johnson is best seen as a figure attached as much to the intellectual world of the European Continent, with its deep roots in Renaissance humanism, as to the world of contemporary or ancient England.[2] We are nonetheless faced with the complication that Johnson did become a virtually iconic Englishman for the Victorians, a tradition that still endures in his popular reputation and at the houses devoted to his memory in London and Lichfield. Nor did any author of his time contribute so much to building what Benedict Anderson called an "imagined community," a self-reflexive image of nationhood constructed above all in dictionaries, editions of canonical authors, histories, works of fiction, and all the publicly disseminated products of "print-culture."[3]

As Johnson demonstrates, however, "nationalism" is not the same as "patriotism," at least in the context of eighteenth-century England. Ever since the prominent Patriots Pulteney and Carteret were seduced to the plush benches of the House of Lords in 1742, professions of patriotism had become deeply suspect. As the Broad-bottom ally James Ralph wrote in his journal *The Remembrancer* in 1748, "The infamous Behaviour of *Patriots* transformed to *Courtiers*, have [*sic*] drawn the very Name of *Patriotism* into Detestation."[4] And Johnson's own fulminations against patriotism, as Boswell understood, drew from the same bitter experience of betrayal. He later echoed his former associates' widespread contempt for Pulteney, whom he called "as paltry a fellow as could be," adding facetiously, "He was a Whig who pretended to be honest; and you know it is ridiculous for a Whig to pretend to be honest."[5] By the time Johnson made this judgment in 1773, moreover, elite and upper-middle-order perceptions of patriotism were marred by the additional stigma of class prejudice. While Wilkes and his radical allies fanned the flames of patriotism among the lower-middling orders, the ruling order and old "Patriots" like Johnson worked vigorously to rein back national sentiment towards officially sanctioned symbols and institutions. The speech that Johnson wrote for his friend Henry Thrale in October 1774, *The Patriot*, rehearses with historic eloquence the widespread view of that time that patriotism should be recast as an essentially conservative disposition, an acquiescence to reigning social structures. "That man . . . is *not a Patriot*." he writes, "who denies his governours their due praise, and who conceals from the people the benefits which they receive" (10:398). "Fired with the fever of epidemic patriotism," he worried a few years earlier in *The False Alarm*, "the taylor slips his thimble, the drapier drops his yard, and the blacksmith lays down his hammer" (10:335).

In other words, the apparent mildness of the mature Johnson's own patriotism, his reluctance to indulge in the kind of chest-thumping jingoism we associate with the late Victorians, must be understood within the context of the political and social experience that marked his lifetime. Nor are his attitudes entirely without a legacy even in our time: educated English opinion about football hooligans, skinheads, or the National Front both recalls Johnson's hatred of plebeian patriotism and contrasts with the more boisterous and ubiquitous patriotism still prevalent in the United States, with that nation's abiding cultural ancestry in English radicalism of the seventeenth and eighteenth centuries. Nevertheless, if Johnson finally disliked the idea of being a patriot, he remains a central figure of English nationalism. And here we must turn to the interesting body of scholarship concerned with what being "English" meant to people of the eighteenth century.

The few scholars who have grappled with the task of saying what kind of England emerged from the eighteenth century – a time indeed of crucial self-assertion and international ascendance – have generally fallen back on suspiciously monotone generalities: the Georgian English prided themselves on being a commercial nation, England united behind the cause of Protestantism, the English hated the French.[6] As we have seen in previous chapters, however, the commercial world of the City was regarded with considerable distrust, not only in the genteel and courtly precincts of Westminster but also among professionals and writers. As for England's or Britain's distinctive Protestantism, Murray G.A. Pittock rightly points out that a large minority of English people who did not belong to the Established church, about one in five, could have found only ambivalent grounds for national loyalty on religious principles.[7] Similarly, the negative national identity implied by francophobia might seem, superficially, to supply a key to understanding the eighteenth-century English, who spent much of this period lobbing cannon-balls into French forts and ships. Yet the manners of the ruling class, as embodied for example by the suave francophilia of Lords Bolingbroke and Chesterfield, cultivated Gallic fluency and *politesse* as the ideal posture of Patriot manners. Even such a personally inelegant populist as John Brown bemoaned the loss of traditional "manly" principles displayed admirably by the courtly French.

Let us then view this problem rather differently. English nationalism in the eighteenth century might appear elusive or merely negative because, in part, it lacked certain features that we associate with strong national identities. These salient identities have tended on the whole to belong to small nations with a powerful sense of the past and a continuous heritage – the nationalism, for example, of the Scots, Irish, and Welsh in the eighteenth century. The Scots claimed a 2,000-year-old heritage of unmixed and unsubdued independence; the Irish and Welsh, while pushed to the peripheries by barbarian invaders, had the dignity of being indigenous peoples with an ancient legacy of language and community. The English, on the other hand, lacked precisely this sense of a continuous and distinct heritage, for England was a nation of Saxon invaders who had, in turn, been conquered, its customs and ethnic identity mixed with the culture and blood of foreigners. Hence, in contrast to the historically oriented nationalism of their Celtic neighbours, English national identity tended to focus early in the eighteenth century not on what England *had been* but what it would *become*. And in this powerful emphasis on fulfilling some "destiny" of greatness, England exemplifies a nationalism of a very modern kind, comparable to that of many subsequent and powerful nationalisms that have either lacked a coherent past, or have emerged from a sense of national catastrophe or failure – post-Revolutionary France, post-Tsarist Russia, or even the United States, where patriotism has repeatedly thrived in the hot-house of national "challenge" or catastrophe. That all these modern forms of nationalism have also become the energizing force of empires or expansionist mentalities is significant as well, for this phenomenon suggests that the attempt to *create* nationhood is a more muscular patriotism than a passive confidence in a fixed national ancestry.

For the English of the early eighteenth century, this ancestry provided, put mildly, a very uncertain foundation for national pride. The British Isles had been overrun by a series of invaders: the Britons had been conquered by the Romans and then, with the receding of the empire, by the Saxons, who in turn were occupied by the Danes and then totally subjected by the Normans. The English people that emerged from these convolutions was, as Defoe wrote in "The True-Born Englishman" (1700), an "Amphibious ill-born Mob." An unflattering message – yet Defoe's aesthetically maladroit poem flowed through fifty editions by mid-century:

> By sev'ral Crowds of wand'ring *Thieves* o'er run
> Often unpeopled, and as oft undone;
> While ev'ry Nation that her Powers reduc'd,
> Their Languages and Manners introduc'd.[8]

In this "mongrel" nature, England contrasted with the supposedly pure and continuous heritage of other peoples, including, naggingly, the Scots. According to the tradition of national myth-making passed down from the Scottish humanist scholars Hector Boece (*c.* 1465–1536) and George Buchanan (1506–82), the Scots had possessed a continuous royal line since Fergus I, three centuries before the birth of Christ. In the words of the historian Patrick Abercromby in *The Martial Atchievements of the Scots Nation* (1711), Scotland was "by far the most Antient of all *European* States," the pure and unconquered "Sanctuary" of an aboriginal North British people which had never mixed with any others and still retained its immemorial customs.[9] The achievements of this people were many: they had possessed an advanced literary culture while the Saxons still lolled in barbarity, and they were responsible for founding the Universities of Padua and Paris, restoring European letters and reconverting the heathen to Christianity.[10] Above all, the Scots had retained their independence and proved their greatness with the sword, resisting or overwhelming all the various invaders that had humbled their abject neighbors to the south.

To this claim of a proudly continuous Scottish history, the English had a famous counterpoint – the ancient constitution. The importance of this model in the Anglo-American memory has been proved with considerable force by J.G.A. Pocock.[11] Yet the ancient constitution lacked the unifying influence of Scots history, for it splayed in various political directions. The Whig form of the ancient constitution stretched in the direction of celebrating this history as the continuous triumph of English bravery over oppression, the dogged persistence of British and later Saxon freedoms even under the yoke of foreign domination. This was the history of, for example, the Whig William Petyt (1636–1707), who maintained in 1680 that even the ancient Britons were democratic and that the Saxons made their parliament an essential component of government, developing a code of rights and freedoms that remained largely intact even under William the Conqueror.[12] Similarly, *The General History of England* (1697–1704) by James Tyrrell, an intimate friend of John Locke, absolutely rejected the notion that the ancient British kings were "Absolute or Despotick," for "we find that Government unsuitable to the Temper of the *British* Nation, both then, and in succeeding times."[13] It is interesting that this was the version of the "ancient constitution" carried into the years of Johnson's early career principally by that erratic Tory Patriot Lord Bolingbroke. In *Remarks on the History of England* (written *c.* 1735; published 1752) Bolingbroke orated with his usual melodramatic *gravitas* about "the spirit of our ancestors" which endured even through all the catastrophes of conquests and oppressions:

> This was the present constitution of our government forming itself for about two centuries and a half, a rough building raised out of the demolitions which the Normans had made and upon the solid foundations laid by the Saxons. The whole fabric was cemented by the blood of our fathers; for the British liberties are not the grants of princes. They are original rights, conditions of original contracts, coaequal with prerogative and coeval with our government.[14]

It is hardly fortuitous, surely, that Bolingbroke sounds a great deal like Addison's Cato, prone as that tragic hero is to similarly sententious proclamations about the ancient constitution:

> Remember, O my friends, the laws, the rights,
> The generous plan of power delivered down,
> From age to age, by your renowned forefathers
> (So dearly bought, the price of so much blood).[15]

From such Roman soil would spring the radical language of Wilkes, Junius, Catherine Macaulay, and others, though these writers often gave classical republican discourse a plebeian raciness entirely absent from the marble purity of Cato.[16] None other than John Wilkes, that saucy veteran of the Hell-Fire Club, was willing to quote Bolingbroke at admiring length in his reply to Johnson's *The False Alarm*.[17] By the same token, Burke's open contempt for Bolingbroke in *Reflections on the Revolution in France* reflects the discomfort of late-century conservatives with the "ancient constitution," at least as inflected in the radical key. In qualification of J.G.A. Pocock (who has famously linked Burke with this tradition),[18] the "ancient constitution" does not serve us well as a model of eighteenth-century political "language" unless we keep fully in mind that the same language, in different mouths and in different contexts, could have very different meanings.

The language of the "ancient constitution" had indeed a Tory or conservative dialect, characterized by its stress on slow and organic change rather than continuous blood-letting in the name of "freedom." Robert Brady (1627–1700), Tory court physician for the last two Stuart kings, replied to William Petyt with *An Introduction to the Old English History* (1684) by denying the originally democratic nature of the Britons and the importance of the parliament among the Saxons (whom he portrayed as illiterate barbarians). While accepting that some weakened version of the old Saxon constitution survived the Norman conquest, Brady upbraided Petyt for being "mightily possessed of the *Lenity* of *William* the *Conqueror*."[19] The Conqueror, he insisted, had made an indelible impression on the heritage of English laws and rights. The Glorious Revolution brought new historical problems for Tories, as evidenced by William Temple's *An Introduction to the History of England* (1695), which Johnson knew and cited. Perhaps best known to us now as an early patron of Jonathan Swift, Temple had been a leading diplomat under James II, who finally alienated this irenic Protestant by receiving Roman Catholics into the inner chambers of power. Having maintained an awkward silence during the Revolution, Temple worked hard to reconcile himself with William III, composing a history that performed a strangely contorted political gesture: he attempted to turn William's namesake, the Conqueror, into a hero. According to Temple, William I had reconciled himself to the Saxons, preserving their constitution and earning their loyalty, though he, like William III, was a foreigner. Temple even attempted to make William the Conqueror's most notorious disgrace – he was the illegitimate son of Prince Robert of Normandy – into a virtue: recalling Dryden's indulgent portrait of Charles II's illegitimate son the Duke of Monmouth in "Absolom and Achitophel," Temple suggested that William was begot with abnormal "Force and Vigour" after his royal father became inflamed by a voluptuous Norman farm-girl.[20]

More commonly, however, "William the Bastard's" illegitimacy served as a bitter metaphor for England's own consciousness of "bastardy," as in Defoe's defense of William III's accession, "The True-Born Englishman." The image of bastardy became, indeed, strangely recurrent in English literature of the first half of the eighteenth century, from Richard Savage's poem "The Bastard" (1728) to Johnson's *Life of Savage* (1744) to Fielding's *Tom Jones* (1748). In the massive *General History of England* (1747–55) by the Jacobite Thomas Carte (1685–1754), William the Conqueror presents a serious historical obstacle to the defense of "divine right" and legitimate succession. On the one hand, William seemed no less a foreign "usurper" than William of Orange or George of Hanover – though Carte, like David Hume later on, makes some effort to maintain that the Normans were not truly French but themselves Gauls like the Saxons and the Danes, assuring some sort of ethnic continuity between the conquered and the conquerors. On the other hand, the Conqueror had established the royal line that, at least in Jacobite eyes, had passed down in legitimate fashion until the last Stuart. In the face of this dilemma, Carte portrayed William in an ambiguous crisscross of light and shadow. He highlights William's cavalier-like gallantry and courtly demeanor, as well as his supposedly devout Christianity. The defeat of the Saxons, Carte suggests, resulted from their drift away from the true religion, an impiety that he contrasts with William's ardent prayers before the Battle of Hastings, and his subsequent revival of the Saxon custom of anointing the King's head at his coronation.[21] Unlike Temple, however, Carte does not attempt to gloss over William's remarkable cruelty in suppressing Saxon dissent against his reign. And the dark legacy of William's militarism and ambition, he claims, had been six centuries of foreign wars and intestine conflict.

For scholars who wish to build a case for Johnson's supposed Jacobitism, it may seem of considerable interest that he recommended this history to an acquaintance, the Reverend Daniel Astle of Ashbourne, in a course of study reproduced by Boswell.[22] Johnson certainly admired Carte's voluminous learning; it was with this historian in mind that he said, famously, "a man will turn over half a library to make one book."[23] Yet Johnson himself approached ancient British history and the "ancient constitution" in a way that, while affirming a broadly conservative tradition, must be distinguished from the pious royalism of Carte. From about 1766 to 1770, Johnson helped his friend Sir Robert Chambers draft *A Course of Lectures on the English Law* (1767–73) in fulfilment of Chambers's duties as Vinerian Professor of Law at Oxford University. While the extent of this collaboration cannot be known for certain, it may well have been extensive (there are strong marks of Johnson's lofty prose style throughout the lectures) and this work must at least accord largely with Johnson's outlook. What we find here is a legal history that portrays the ancient Britons and Saxons as essentially barbaric and illiterate, incapable of the democratic sophistication ascribed to them by Whig historians such as Petyt and Tyrrell, as well as by Bolingbroke in his Patriot history of England. Like the Tory Sir William Blackstone, the first Vinerian professor,[24] Chambers and Johnson uphold a rather weakened form of the "ancient constitution," which they trace back to the Saxons and, particularly, Alfred the Great. Here, indeed, Chambers and Johnson do find common ground with Carte, with whom they shared a deep veneration for the king whom Carte called "the most perfect character that is known in history."[25] Boswell was told by William Adams that Johnson himself had planned to embark on a life of Alfred the Great before his fortunes were turned in a different direction by the contract to write an English dictionary.[26] According to Chambers and Johnson, however, the constitution inaugurated by Alfred was neither an assertion of royal paternalism, as imaged by Carte, nor a declaration of the people's rights and liberties, the great myth of Whig, Patriot, and radical histories. Rather, Alfred had upheld the *balance* of powers between the King, the people, and nobility.[27] Moreover, while certain essential laws and customs had survived the Conquest, Chambers and Johnson make clear that this event profoundly changed the course of English history.[28] While far from romanticizing the Conqueror, whom they describe as equally barbaric as his contemporaries, they stress the gradual evolution and refinement of the ancient constitution from Alfred, through the Conquest, and to the present day, an organic progression motivated less by conscious principles of "freedom" or "justice" than by a long series of compromises between vying interests.

In short, the *A Course of Lectures on the English Law* presents an essentially progressive vision of English history as proceeding from "barbarity" to "civilization," all the while retaining respect for Anglo-Saxon heritage. In this context, we might recall Johnson's statement in the preface to Shakespeare (1765) that, even in the late sixteenth century, England was "yet struggling to emerge from barbarity" (7:81). Johnson considered himself as participating in the *first* properly "civilized" time in English history, a view that might remind us of the so-called Whig history of Thomas Babington Macaulay. Author of the most influential history of England in the nineteenth century, Macaulay celebrated the progressive course of English history, focusing on the century just before as an age of spectacular advancement. By the time Chambers and Johnson were working on the Vinerian lectures, however, this progressive view of England was neither especially Whig nor Tory nor radical, much less "Jacobite." It represented the gathering and unifying consciousness of English nationhood at the moment of its imperial ascendence in the mid- and late eighteenth century. In contrast with the romantic "pastness" of Scottish nationalism, the English increasingly imagined themselves as a people just emerging into greatness, a nation whose pride lay in the present and future rather than the past.

The road to this pride was long and arduous, beginning only as a dream of future greatness in the work of early eighteenth-century authors like Daniel Defoe. Defoe was at the forefront of English efforts in 1706 and 1707 to persuade Scotland to merge into a new political Union, a project that Defoe justified on purely practical and commercial grounds. If together England and Scotland would cease their useless conflicts with each other, he argued, their combined power could crush France and seize the markets of the world: "these two Twin Nations may become one United *English* Empire, resolved into one Form of Government, one Interest, one Body Politick, under one Head, one Administration, one Representative, and Strengthened by one United Body of Power."[29] When finally Defoe's beloved Union was achieved (though over the backs of so many Scots unwilling to sacrifice cultural nostalgia for gold) an anonymous author – probably not Defoe himself but an admirer of "The True-Born Englishman" – toasted the event with *The True-Born Britain* (*sic*) (1707), a prophetic vision of the glorious new "British" identity which lay on a horizon of fish-filled oceans and fruitful tropics:

> No more shall those Distinctions be of *Scot*
> And Englishman; it is our happy Lot
> To assume the Name of thrice *Great Britains* all,
> A Name which soon will make *French* Scepters fall.[30]

For all the bravado of this vision, however, it disguised a discomfort, even an embarrassment, with the English past. As we have seen, Defoe aggressively satirized claims to English ethnic purity in "The True-Born Englishman." In his propaganda in favour of the Union with Scotland, similarly, he obviously regarded the Scots' pride in their supposed historical continuity and lineal heritage as an obstacle to his political objectives. This form of patriotism had to be neutralized, and Defoe contended at length that the Scots, too, were more "mongrel" than they liked to admit – a view that would later be echoed by pro-British Scots like Hume and Robertson.[31]

Patriotic language of the early eighteenth century generally confirmed Defoe's determination to stay focused on the future, avoiding the gnawing self-consciousness of military defeat and foreign domination in the past. Even the heroic visions of the early century tend to be about nobility in the face of defeat rather than the glory of overcoming and subduing the enemy: what else is Addison's *Cato,* so admired by two generations of theatre-goers, than the myth of a steely-jawed and incorruptible loser who prefers to kill himself than surrender to the triumphant Caesar? Similarly, the most apparently triumphal nationalistic rhetoric of the 1730s and 1740s simmers with subdued anger and bitterness that the historical humiliations of the past threatened to be repeated in the present: England had always suffered, and resisted, enslavement; England had endured abuse from Romans, Danes, and Normans. Now English (actually Welsh) captains like Jenkins were being handed their left ear by Spaniards, all with the approval of a government that seemed willing to appease their supposed enemies in France and Spain. The claim of Patriots that Sir Robert Walpole's regime had "enslaved" England carried such resonance because it seemed, historically, so much *the same auld sang*. For reasons of self-enrichment and entrenched power, Walpole seemed prepared to dash English hopes for a proud future blown into reality from the bows of battle-ships. The great patriotic hymn of the 1740s, James Thomson's "Rule, Britannia!" (1740), actually taps a mood of dreadful insecurity, implying insistently that while the English "*will* not be slaves," they have been in the past. The English have been subdued but never, never "tamed":

> Thee haughty tyrants ne'er shall tame;
> All their attempts to bend thee down
> Will but arouse thy generous flame,
> But work their woe and thy renown.[32]

It must surely rank as one of the great ironies of eighteenth-century patriotism that these lyrics, roared out by English theatre-goers of the 1740s, were actually penned by an immigrant Scot, James Thomson, who knew just how to prod the discomfort of his hosts in order to elicit the maximum patriotic charge. And this irony intensifies when we realize that "Rule, Britannia!" was originally the culminating chorus of a masque, *Alfred* (1740), written by two immigrant Scots, Thomson and David Mallet, that similarly rubs the English nose in its own historical failures. Drawing on that resonant leitmotif in English national consciousness, the "darkest hour," Thomson and Mallet present the Saxon king so admired by Johnson and others gripped by literally suicidal despair in the face of Danish invaders:

> All, all is lost – And *Alfred* lives to tell it!
> His cities laid in dust! his subjects slaughter'd!
> Or into shameful slaves debas'd! The murderous foe
> Proud and exulting in the general shame![33]

For English audiences of the 1740s, the contemporary relevance of Alfred's despair was palpable: while the British Isles had not actually been invaded by foreigners, British ships were being boarded in the Caribbean, British rights were being violated and degraded, British government was in thrall to "foreign" interests harbored by the "slave-master" Sir Robert Walpole. Jenkins's ear continued to burn like an unrequited cuff on English pride. But *Alfred* also showed its audience a shining beam of prophetic light: Thomson and Mallet introduce a hermit to encourage Alfred with uplifting visions of England's future greatness. The wondering Alfred watches as the hermit conjures up Elizabeth capsizing the Spanish Armada, William III subduing French aggression on the Continent and (with notably less enthusiasm) the glorious reign of George II, for whom this masque was first performed. The hermit's final speech, intoned right after "Rule, Britannia!", delivers an ecstatic prophesy of England's emerging commercial empire:

> I see thy commerce, *Britain*, grasp the world:
> All nations serve thee; every foreign flood,
> Subjected, pays its tribute to the *Thames*.
> Thither the golden South obedient pours
> His many treasures . . .
>   This new world
> Shook to its centre, trembles at her name:
> And these, her sons, with aim exalted, sow
> The seeds of rising empire, arts, and arms.[34]

The prophetic tone of this passage should remind us of much else in the previous 100 years, from the millenarianism of the Civil War era to the closing hundred lines of Pope's "Windsor Forest" (1711). Pope's paean to the Peace of Utrecht, an important step towards the creation of the British Empire, begins similarly with a dark allegory of the past, "a dreary desert, and a gloomy waste," but ends with Father Thames's picture of "Augusta's glitt'ring spires" rising gloriously over a world gratefully obedient to English interests and ideals.[35]

These were lines enjoyed by the English readers of the nineteenth century, and it is of the greatest importance to understanding the Victorians' lusty jingoism that Father Thames's prophesies had, in effect, been fulfilled. What more energizing joy can there be to nations as to individuals than the awareness of having triumphed over uncertainty, to have finally realized the greatness that had previously seemed only a shining dream? For a certain brilliant yet struggling ex-teacher arriving in London in 1737, however, this glory was still far in the future. In "London" (1738), Johnson does find inspiring moments in the past, but they are scattered and transient, serving mostly to highlight the disgraces of the present. Greenwich, the birthplace of Elizabeth I, reminds Johnson's speaker of the queen whose association with the defeat of the Spanish Armada contrasts with Walpole's anti-heroic appeasement of Spain. Near the end of the poem, Johnson evokes the legendary justice of Alfred the Great, throwing into sharp relief the dingy crime and decadence of the present:

> A single jail, in Alfred's golden reign,
> Could half the nation's criminals contain;
> Fair justice then, without constraint ador'd,
> Held high the steady scale, but drop'd the sword.
> (ll. 248–53, 6:60)

In other works of his early career, Johnson showed the same gloominess about England's past that we find in Defoe's "True-Born Englishman" or in the early paragraphs of Pope's "Windsor Forest." His satire *Marmor Norfolciense* (1738) is particularly intriguing in this regard because it pretends to be a work of English antiquarianism, a subject for which Johnson much later developed a nationalistic interest, as we will see. Echoing the prophetic strain of much early eighteenth-century literature, this tract also concerns a prophesy, though the vision here is of a distinctly negative kind: the supposed writer of the inscription on the marble tablet, found in the earth of Walpole's native Norfolk, predicts a future of violence, conquest, and oppression, a world over which "Discord [shall] stretch her wings, / Kings change their laws, and kingdoms change their kings" (10:25). This sounds a great deal like English history since the Roman conquest. And, indeed, the putative antiquarian concludes that the tablet was inscribed by an ancient Briton rather than a Roman or Saxon:

> An argument in favour of the Britons [rather than Saxon authorship], may indeed be drawn from the tenderness, with which the author seems to lament his country, and the compassion he shows for its approaching calamities. I, who am a descendant from the Saxons, and therefore unwilling to say any thing derogatory from the reputation of my forefathers, must yet allow this argument its full force: for it has been rarely, very rarely, known that foreigners however well treated, caressed, enriched, flatter'd or exalted, have regarded this country with the least gratitude or affection, till the race has by long continuance, after many generations, been naturaliz'd and assimilated. (10:27)

Scholars of Johnson have usually assumed that the prophesy in *Marmor Norfolciense* refers to the supposed oppressions of Walpole, or even, if we believe that the young Johnson was a Jacobite, to the Hanoverian Succession.[36] As an ancient Briton, however, the writer of the inscription could be referring to *every* conquest and oppression from the invasion of the Saxons onward. (As the inscription was supposedly written in Latin, we are meant to understand that it was composed during the Roman occupation, which most historians agreed was relatively benign.) As told to every English boy and girl with access to education, the Britons had invited the Saxons to England after they were abandoned by the retreating Romans and invaded by the Scots. The barbarous Saxons had then driven Britain's original inhabitants into the mountains of Wales and the extremities of Cornwall, a betrayal also recalled in "London," where Thales's voluntary exile to "Cambria" will "Give to St. David one true Briton more" (ll. 7–8, 6:48).

This depiction of Wales as the refuge of "true Britons" might bring to our minds the Victorian romance where ancient Welshness is evoked, in particular, by King Arthur, who gallops with patriotic majesty through the poetry of Tennyson and his contemporaries. But that was a later era. The Tudor cult of Arthur, as Murray Pittock has observed, fell into abeyance in the England ruled by Stuarts and Hanoverians.[37] When Sir Richard Blackmore attempted to build a British epic around the young Arthur in 1695, the critic John Dennis complained about the irrelevance of such a heroic version to a nation derived not from the Britons but the *Saxons*.[38] Similarly, Johnson consistently identified himself and the English language with the Saxons, portraying the Britons as the vanquished precursors to the genuine "English." In his Preface to Shakespeare, he would dismiss Malory's "*The Death of Arthur*" as appealing to a former age of "childish credulity . . . unenlightened by learning" (7:82). Given Johnson's own failure to identify with the ancient Britons, it is revealing that the putative author of *Marmor Norfolciense* admits to being Saxon. And this identification not with the original inhabitants but with the *conquerors* of England should make us rethink Johnson's political intentions in this pamphlet. The supposedly "Jacobite" climax of *Marmor Norfolciense* comes when the narrator displays flustered alarm at the very thought that the "horse," portrayed in the inscription as draining the life-blood of the English "lyon,"could possibly mean the armorial white horse of the Hanover family then inhabiting St James's Palace. In the context of the pamphlet, however, this "Briton's" prophesy could refer to any of the blood-sucking invasions of England since the Saxon conquest, the resonantly Germanic forerunner of the Hanoverian Succession. The strong implication of this pamphlet is that the Hanoverian Succession represented nothing new, but was simply another invasion from the Teutonic regions of the Continent. So far from showing that Johnson was a "Jacobite," *Marmor Norfolciense* seems in fact to undermine Jacobite forms of nationalism, for this satire implicitly, yet clearly, acknowledges that English royalty and national identity had been shaped by repeated eruptions of Continental betrayal and pillage.

This picture of the English past seems bleaker than most Patriot works of the same years, which tended to echo Bolingbroke's glorification of

England's historically dogged resistance to tyranny and its devotion to "liberty." Moreover, nothing in *Marmor Norfolciense* looks forward to the heroic military future so enthusiastically imagined in Defoe's "True-born Englishman," *Alfred*, and other Patriot works, though Johnson would join the drum-beat of Patriot militarism in his *Lives* of Blake and Drake, both written for *The Gentleman's Magazine* in 1740. At this early stage, Johnson seems to have taken a dim view even of England's progress from barbarity to civilization, the major source of the nation's pride later in the century. In "London," he wonders why anyone would choose the "Strand" over the "rocks of Scotland" (l. 10, 6:48), for English civilization had over-ripened into decadence and corruption, becoming a nation of fops, pimps, and flatterers where "falling houses thunder on your head, / And here a female atheist talks you dead" (ll. 17–18, 6:48). Nevertheless, a public change in Johnson's attitudes was just around the corner. In his *Plan of an English Dictionary* (1746), addressed to Lord Chesterfield, Johnson portrays himself as Caesar come to civilize the barbarous Britons:

> When I survey the Plan which I have laid before you, I cannot, my Lord, but confess, that I am frighted at its extent, and, like the soldiers of Caesar, look on Britain as a new world, which it is almost madness to invade. But I hope, that though I should not complete the conquest, I shall, at least, discover the coast, civilize part of the inhabitants, and make it easy for some other adventurer to proceed further, to reduce them wholly to subjection, and settle them under laws.[39]

This lexicographic metaphor of civilizing the barbarians is continued into the preface of the completed *Dictionary* in 1755, where he describes the original Saxon tongue as a "wild and barbarous jargon" and laments the "spots of barbarity impressed so deep in the English language, that criticism can never wash them away."[40] In the preface to the edition of Shakespeare, as we have noted, Johnson portrayed England as just emerging from "barbarity" in the sixteenth century. And the law lectures he wrote with Sir Robert Chambers describe even the celebrated framers of Magna Carta as illiterate barbarians in "an age of tyranny darkness [*sic*] and violence."[41]

Especially towards the middle part of his career, in short, Johnson increasingly prized the *modernity* of England, delving into history mostly with the view of tracing the progress of England towards its current state of civility and intellectual achievement. Indeed, at times in his work of the 1750s and 1760s, Johnson seems to have lost all interest whatsoever in the "ancient constitution"and England's historical legacy of laws and customs. In his *Introduction to the Political State of Great-Britain*, for example, he writes that "The present system of English politics" could be dated no further back than "the reign of Queen Elizabeth" (10:130). These were his attitudes when he left on his historic trip to the Scottish Highlands in 1773, a journey from the Strand to "the rocks of Scotland" prefigured in "London," but now reimagined as a trip back in time to a treeless hinterland just emerging into the light of knowledge and progress. In this influential formulation of British nationalism, the "Britain" then absorbing northern Scotland was virtually synonymous with "civilization," an ostensibly culturally neutral condition that represented the ideal destiny of all "barbarous" peoples in every corner of the globe.

By 1773, however, we also cross into another phase in the evolution of Johnson's nationalism. For at this late stage in his career, we also hear, for the first time, an underlying strain in the full symphony of triumphant British patriotism, a whimsical harkening back to the romantic past still audible, though barely, in the Highlands.

THE JOURNEY TO SCOTLAND, CIVILIZATION AND THE ROMANCE OF THE PAST

The significance of Johnson's *Journey to the Western Islands of Scotland* (1775) for understanding the historic eighteenth-century debate concerning Scottish nationalism, and indeed concerning nationalism in general, has been recently pronounced by Katie Trumpener, who nonetheless portrays Johnson as the prejudiced and anti-nationalist spokesman for English "imperialism":

> Johnson faults the Scottish Enlightenment for its fatal complicity with the work of nationalist revivalist mythmakers: in Scotland, all nostalgia clinging to ruins, to dubious past glories, impedes the productive potential of the present. The *Journey* attempts to establish the primacy of a cosmopolitan and imperial vision of Enlightenment activity, over what it sees as Scotland's nationalist Enlightenment, of the forces of linguistic normalization over those of vernacular revival, and of a London-centered, print-based model of literary history over a nationalist, bardic model based on oral tradition.[42]

Trumpener's antagonistic reading of Johnson's *Journey* carries on a long tradition of critical commentary. In the decades after its publication, Johnson was accused of going to Scotland with the conscious design of giving "a distorted representation of every thing he saw on the north side of Tweed," and of having "brought a deluge of falsehood and abuse upon us."[43] This outrage has been sustained even into modern times. "What is to be done in the face of such dogmatic close-mindedness and racial bigotry (for that is what it is)?" asks Howard Gaskill, a rebuke echoed in Richard Sher's condemnation of "Johnsonian prejudices against Ossian and the Scots."[44] Johnson's disbelief in the authenticity of James Macpherson's supposed "translations" of the "epics" of Ossian has stirred particularly sharp antagonism, even though Johnson's skepticism would be later confirmed by both English and Scots scholars.

In this tradition of criticism, Johnson has clearly become more than one famously plain-spoken and opinionated author. He exemplifies "the usual extravagance of *English* prejudice,"[45] embodying a whole cultural attitude, a dark historical force much larger than himself. The allegedly self-satisfied English imperialist, sneering at the lowly natives in a newly conquered land, Johnson abraded the feelings of a nation that, in the words of a recent scholar, had been "subjected to ruthless and unrelenting oppression" after the defeat of the Jacobite army in the spring of 1746.[46] One wonders, however, if even Scots of that time would have agreed that they were "oppressed." In fact, the greatest offense caused by the *Journey* concerned Johnson's assumption that the Highlands had been "conquered" or overwhelmed at all. Johnson's Scots critics, who were unanimously pro-Union, portrayed themselves as neither the victims nor the benefactors of the English, but as at least their cultural equals and even their superiors. These replies make clear that Johnson insulted not the sensitivities of a "conquered" or colonized people but rather an understanding of Scots history and national identity that was in the process of painful transformation – what Colin Kidd has even called a "crisis."[47]

This critical transformation reflects, with important Gaelic variants, the pattern of English nationalism that we have just traced. As we have seen, this national consciousness was both shaped and troubled by a number of interconnected factors. First, English history had furnished meager nourishment for English national pride: to understand the attitudes reflected in *Journey to the Western Islands of Scotland*, we need to keep in mind that Johnson considered *himself* to be a member of a "conquered" and "colonized" people that had just emerged from "barbarity," even as recently as the age of Shakespeare. Even the main alternative to pride in the past, celebration of English progress and modernity, was itself disturbed by fears of the supposedly effeminizing influence of luxury. A similar constellation of national sentiments and anxieties was forming in Scotland when Johnson visited there in the autumn of 1773. Scotland's own historical pride had been threatened by Culloden and its aftermath, for this event undermined the intense traditional pride of Scots in their military invincibility. Certainly, not all Scots were willing to surrender their historical claim to military prowess: Johnson's most furious antagonists, including Donald M'Nicol and James Macpherson himself, continued to promote the historical myth of Scotland as a great and ancient civilization that had resisted wave after wave of invaders, in contrast to the historically feeble and bastardized English. Nevertheless, particularly among Lowlands intellectuals, Culloden seemed to demand a new orientation for Scotland's historical identity. It was not Johnson or any English writer, but Scottish historians Hume and Robertson who began reimagining Scotland as a nation just emerging from "barbarity" into the light of modern commerce and a political stability pioneered by the English. At the same time, some Scots intellectuals, prominently Adam Ferguson, harbored deep anxieties, comparable to the fears of Englishmen like John Brown, concerning the effeminizing effects of luxury. These fears of emasculation seem indeed especially intense in Scotland, entirely stripped of its weapons after Culloden, and even denied the right to a militia in 1757. This exclusion, as shown so well by Richard Sher, became a burning issue in the parlors of mid-century Edinburgh, where pro-Union, conservative Scots intellectuals were fashioning a modernized Scots identity within that new national identity, "Britain."[48]

Here, indeed, is a clue to explaining an interesting conjunction described by Sher. For the same pro-Union Lowlands intellectuals who ardently promoted a Scots militia (advocated as a way of defending the Lowlands against future Jacobite invaders) also keenly encouraged James Macpherson's researches into the nostalgic and intensely militaristic poetry supposedly left by the second-century Highlands bard, Ossian. It was they who dispatched this curiously reluctant and embarrassed Highlander north to scribble down ancient ballads; it was they who, like Hugh Blair, expatiated lyrically about Macpherson's construction of Ossian, whom they compared in all seriousness with Homer. Yet there is important evidence that the Edinburgh literati and Macpherson were not, in fact, waving Scottish national flags of precisely the same colour. The "Dissertations" that Macpherson appended to both the Ossianic epics, *Fingal* (1762) and *Temora* (1763), reinforce the impression that this author wished not only to preserve a tradition of ancient Scots legend, but moreover to prove the myth of Scots military invincibility and ancient civilization. This was the myth that Hume, Robertson, and other members of the Scottish Enlightenment had recently done much to discredit, siding as they did, in an often anxious way, with the notion of modern, progressive nationalism widely embraced to the south. The evidence of work by Hugh Blair and Adam Ferguson suggests that the Edinburgh intelligentsia did not want Ossian to be taken as a historical account, but rather as the inspiring artifact of an admittedly "barbaric" age. They valued the Ossian poems as contributions to a national *literary* heritage, and as a corrective to the ambivalent influence of civilization, with its effeminizing wealth and self-indulgence. They accepted and even encouraged this modernity, but they also counted on poetry to stand in for history, and to stiffen a national culture allegedly grown feminine under the influence of luxury. They wanted Ossian for reasons comparable to their rationale for ardently promoting a Scots militia.

We have of course heard a version of this story before, an English version. Not only did the emergent English middle class widely distrust the effeminizing effects of luxury, but it also widely followed Johnson in promoting the education and political power of an old aristocratic regime. Art gained its modern foothold as a palliative to the vulgarizing influence of wealth and trade. This is not to claim that Scotland and England followed precisely the same path of national development. Scotland had lost a heroic vision of itself that England never possessed with the same conviction. Scotland learned to lament its past poetically with an intense nostalgia that still seems curiously unEnglish – in the way that Sir Walter Scott could never be mistaken for an English author. On the other hand, Scotland, Wales and Ireland may be responsible for nudging England towards a revival of its historical roots that, in the glow of its success, gained a deeply Romantic redolence. And here again Johnson is absolutely typical. Only the most blinkered reading of Johnson's *Journey* could lead to the claim that he had no interest or appreciation for Scots antiquities and its romantic past. Something drove this aging, overweight, and asthmatic author across the Highlands, and it was not merely the desire to assert English hegemony. This work is filled with passages of romantic nostalgia for the customs and lore of the past, moments when the scenes and personalities of northern Scotland filled Johnson, as Boswell observed, with "the old Highland spirit."[49] This spirit reflects Johnson's enthusiastic interest in English and Celtic antiquities during the last two decades of his life. And it was precisely this combination of progressive "modern" nationalism with a romantic nostalgia for the past which is dramatized in the travel accounts of both Johnson and Boswell. This nationalism is significant because it constitutes the mortar of a quintessentially *British* nationalism blending (in sometimes unstable quantities) nostalgia for the past with pride in progress and modernity.

As we briefly suggested before, the old humanist form of Scots nationalism was far more substantial than the "bardic" romance of kilts, thistles and folk-songs that began to emerge in the time of James Macpherson.

The tradition of Scots scholarship from Boece and Buchanan to the era of the Union contended for the *literal* historical existence of a dynasty and developed Scots civilization dating back to Fergus I, three centuries before Christ. Songs and sporrans had little to do with this legacy, which instead glorified, above all, a history of Scots military prowess. As argued for two folio volumes in Patrick Abercromby's *The Martial Atchievements of the Scots Nation* (1711), the Scots were the last remaining undefeated country on earth. They had resisted and even defeated the mighty Romans; they had stood unshaken against the sword of William the Conqueror. After the Union with England in 1707 – which ordinary Scots massively detested as an ignominious sell-out to their richer southern neighbours – the martial grandeur of Scotland's lost independence was lamented with great passion. The anti-Union speech of the Scots parliamentarian Lord Belhaven was even turned into a popular poem:

> Our *Stewarts*, unto peaceful *James*, *Gordons*, *Kers*, *Campbells*,
> *Murrays*, *Grahams*,
> Hero's, from Tyber known to *Thames*,
> For Freedom stood;
> And dy'd the Fields, in purple Streams
> Of hostile Blood.[50]

Such claims had the inevitable, and perhaps expected, effect of enraging the English, burdened as they were with an embarrassing history of repeated capitulation to foreign invaders and repeated interruptions to their royal line. The contrast between the supposed gloriousness of the Scottish past and ignominy of English history became a taunting refrain in anti-Unionist literature such as William Wright's *The Comical History of the Marriage-Union betwixt Fergusia and Heptarchus* (1706). In deviation from the aggressively masculine presentation of Scotland in histories of its military glory, Wright portrays "Fergusia" as a "Lady of venerable Antiquity, of a competent Estate and Fortune, and a Sovereign over a bold and hardy People."[51] This feminization of Scotland sets up the comical allegory of Fergusia's courtship by "Heptarchus," whose name refers to the "Heptarchy" of seven kingdoms in early Saxon England. Wright's personification of England is a vulgar *nouveau riche* with a bastardized pedigree of ignominious defeats and mixed blood:

> This Gentleman is young and lusty, very opulent and rich, and upon that Account, a great Contemner of his Neighbours. He was of Old, very much oppress'd, and intirely subdu'd first by the *Caesarians*; then upon their Declension, by the

Fergusians, against whom he call'd in, to help him, a barbarous Pagan People out of *Alemania*, who, of Servants and Confederates, made themselves his Masters. He was afterwards oppress'd by the then fam'd nation of *Lochlans* [i.e. the Danes]: And at last, by a bravading *French* Bastard, he was hector'd into an entire Submission, in so far, that he kept nothing of himself, but the old Name: So that this Gentleman has all the Blood of these annex'd People in his Veins.[52]

South of the Tweed, such ridicule was often countered with appeals to the chief source of English pride and, indeed, the only argument for Union likely to persuade the proud Scots: whatever its failures in the past, England was richer than Scotland in the present. Over and over again in the eighteenth century, the well-fed body of John Bull would be juxtaposed with the gaunt and ragged figure of Sawny the Scot, a reminder of the economically depressed state of Scotland in the decades immediately before and after the Union.[53] (Johnson's own greedy act of "feeding," as ridiculed by at least one Scots antagonist and often detailed by Boswell, symbolized the spectacle of England's well-padded and self-indulgent identity.)[54] But English scholars also seemed intent on silencing Scotland's vaunting pride in its history. Building on previous arguments by the English historian William Camden (1551–1623), two prominent Anglican churchmen, William Lloyd and William Stillingfleet, attacked Scottish claims to a 2,000-year old royalty as fabulous. Lloyd, the Bishop of Asaph and later Bishop of Lichfield, accused the Scots of "giving too easie a belief to those Fictions which I am now about to disprove."[55] Lloyd's disproof leaned heavily on the same historical conviction that would much later inform Samuel Johnson's rejection of the authenticity of James Macpherson's *Ossian* poems: the Scots lacked writing for many centuries after the time they claimed to begin their history, and unwritten history is no history at all: "We have much reason to doubt whether those unlettered Nations had any desire to convey any knowledge of themselves to Posterity. But if they had the Will, they wanted the means to do it: and therefore we cannot wonder that we know so little of them or their condition, either in, or before the *Roman* times."[56]

The replies of Scots to this criticism also foreshadowed the showdown between Johnson and Macpherson. In *A Defence of the Antiquity of Scotland* (1685), a reply to Lloyd, Sir George Mackenzie affirmed the long-standing literacy of the Scots, but he also rejected the belief that only written documents provided a foundation for a genuine national history. Mackenzie's position was that oral tradition should be regarded as probable where supported by documentary evidence and general consistency with exterior evidence:

> The surest Foundation then of all Histories, is the common belief and consent of the Natives: For Strangers cannot know but from them, and this consent and belief may be founded upon credible Tradition, Manuscripts, Domestick Witnesses, but especially when these are fortifi'd, by the concurring Testimonies of foreign Authours, probable Reasons, and the acquiescence of Mankind.[57]

This statement exemplifies a historiographic outlook virtually extinct in England by the later seventeenth century. The reasons behind the differing practices of Scots and English historians at this point are complex. Scottish claims to possessing a glorious kingdom even before the Roman invasion really did lack irrefragable written evidence. The English, on the other hand, had little to lose in insisting on documentary sources for their much less glamorous history, and indeed made their very honesty about their past failures into a national virtue. Whatever their sources, England and Scotland possessed strikingly different forms of national identity at the time of the Union in 1707. Scottish national consciousness remained entranced by its self-image as an ancient and independent kingdom that had been culturally in advance of England for over 2,000 years. In the eyes of many Scots, the Union was shameful: England, unable to conquer the Scots militarily, had finally stolen away its independence with bribes to a small coterie of greedy Scots politicians who acted for personal emolument rather than for the welfare of the people. Even when Johnson visited Edinburgh in 1773, Sir James Kerr, Keeper of Records at Parliament, was still lamenting that "Half our nation was bribed for English money."[58] As we have seen, however, the golden spell of history had little effect in England. Johnson's England might, on the contrary, be called the first characteristically "modern" nation in its heavy investment in economic and intellectual progress, not history, as the bulwark of national identity.

As the century wore on, however, it became more difficult for Scots to draw uncritically on the old vision of themselves as an ancient, invulnerable and ethnically pure civilization. One factor inducing this shift of attitude was that the Union had brought economic benefits and political stability in the eyes of many patriotic Scots. Even James Macpherson admitted in his *History of Great Britain* (1775) that Scotland had been so corrupt and depressed at the time of the Union that "no expedient could be deemed unfortunate that put an end to their own government."[59] And while Scots remained widely reluctant to concede that even the crushing of the Jacobite army at Culloden marked a military defeat for "Scotland" (most Scots, it was said, had themselves opposed a rebel army consisting only of "Catholics, the poor, the profligate, and the desperate")[60] the subsequent disarming of the Highlanders, and the banning of plaid associated with Scotland's military identity, made the long arm of London's political power unmistakable. Such indeed was precisely the demoralizing cultural intention of Westminster's denying the Scots even a loyal militia. And such were the *Realpolitik* anxieties that inspired "Butcher" Cumberland's infamously savage "mopping-up" after Culloden, when wounded stragglers were cut down, and barns full of clansmen set alight. The message was clear: Scotland's legacy of military prowess should never be revived, except, as we shall see, within the safe confines of British regiments, theatre walls, and the covers of modern novels.

As far as "real" history went, the time had evidently come for a new history of Scotland more in line with the scrupulously archival and "progressive" kind of history that had been predominant in England since the seventeenth century. As shown so well by Colin Kidd, the "debunking" of the old Scots history was not executed by English writers, and certainly not in the pages of Johnson's *Journey*, but by the work of Scottish Enlightenment historians, particularly David Hume and William Robertson.[61] Ironically, given his Scottish nationality, Hume's *History of England* (1754–62) stands as the century's most accomplished example of the unromantic, anti-feudal and factually scrupulous historical writing pioneered in England. It was certainly not recent English historical practice that Hume admonished when he charged that "Poets . . . disfigure the most certain history by their fictions." Rather, he had in mind "the fabulous annals, which are obtruded on us by the Scottish historians."[62] As for Scotland, which remains at the geographical and thematic outskirts of the *History*, Hume makes clear that his homeland was the most barbarous outpost on an island overrun for centuries by barbarians. It was this opinion that finally led him, like Johnson, to deny the authenticity of the Ossian poems. According to Hume, these compositions could never have been conceived and transmitted "through ages totally ignorant of letters, by the rudest, perhaps, of all the European nations; the most necessitous, the most turbulent, the most ferocious, and the most unsettled."[63]

It was nonetheless not Hume, but William Robertson, who turned the full force of English realist history against the old Scottish myths and legends. In *The History of Scotland* (1759), this central figure among the Edinburgh literati declared his determination to trust only "well-attested annals," avoiding "fictions and absurdities."[64] He harshly criticized former Scots historians for "Relying upon uncertain legends, and the traditions of their ancient bards," hence reckoning "a series of kings several ages before the birth of Christ."[65] Dismissing Boece and Buchanan as "credulous,"[66] Robertson presented a distinctly sobering image of ancient Scotland as not a glorious civilization of gallant warriors defending the independence of their homeland, but rather as a disordered hive of feuding barbarians impatient with justice, antagonistic to neighbouring clans, and hostile to the distant kings of Edinburgh, very many of whom fell victim to assassins. Again and again, "The offended baron assembled his vassals, and wasted the lands, or shed the blood of his enemy. To forgive an injury was mean; to forbear revenge, infamous or cowardly."[67] This chaos remained basically the state of Scotland until the Union, which Robertson portrayed as a great blessing. The Union had not only rescued Scotland from its dreadful poverty, but had bestowed on a fractious and unstable kingdom the rights and liberties that the English "had purchased with so much blood."[68]

Significantly, nothing in Johnson's *Journey* deviates substantially from what these Scots historians had already written. He considered Highland Scots before the Union to be "barbaric" and "addicted to quarrels," too far from the distant court in Edinburgh to be controlled by law (9:46). He stressed the importance of English commerce in the Highlands, which had made the people more civilized, industrious, and peaceable (see, e.g., 9:58). He doubted mere fables and unwritten histories, insisting that the Ossian poems should not be counted on as an accurate historical record: "If we know little of the ancient Highlanders, let us not fill the vacuity with Ossian" (9:119). Why then should Johnson's remarks in the *Journey* have come under such fierce attack? The obvious response is that Johnson not only embodied English literary society and political power (especially through his recent and strident writing on behalf of the administration) but disdained the kind of genteel *politesse* that might have smoothed the raw feelings of his Highlands hosts. In other words, it was less the message than the nationality and rudeness of the messenger that Scots resented. A comparison between Johnson's *Journey* and the work of a contemporary visitor to the Highlands, Thomas Pennant, is instructive. In his uncontroversial *A Tour of Scotland. MDCCLXIX* (1771), Pennant ventured many of the same observations that soon after made Johnson the target of literary claymores: he credited the influence of Cromwell and the defeat of the Jacobites for enriching and civilizing Scotland, thought Highlanders were lazy and superstitious, and complained about deforestation.[69] But this itinerant zoologist also identified himself as a Welshman ("an ancient *Briton*"),[70] was more disposed than Johnson to admire rugged vistas, and dwelled enthusiastically on ducks and castles rather than prickly questions of politics and sociology.

Moreover, replies to Johnson also reveal simmering divisions between Scots themselves, for the angriest attacks leaned heavily on the old form of Scots history that the Edinburgh literati had set about to debunk. In his *Remarks on Dr. Samuel Johnson's Journey to the Hebrides*, for example, Donald M'Nicol fulminates that Johnson shows "an amazing ignorance of the history of Europe" in not knowing that Scotland "has never been conquered" and had repulsed all the invaders who had made an "easy" conquest of England, that Scotland had been exchanging goods and arts with France when the English were still sunk in barbarity, that Scotland had been ruled peaceably by a court in the days of Fingal, and that this court had spread "refinement" across the Highlands.[71] In a later polemic, John Clark portrayed a very similar image of the ancient Highlands as so highly organized that there were "academies" for bards, who were fully literate.[72] In part, that is, Johnson had become a displaced target for tensions *within* Scotland during a time of important transformation in its national self-image. And Johnson's own reactions and statements reflect in turn his own unromantic understanding of English history.

The sparks ignited by Johnson's *Journey* sprang, in short, from the friction between two transforming national identities, the English and the Scottish. And nowhere was this friction so complicated or intense as in the debate over Macpherson's pretended "translations" of the Highland Bard Ossian. While modern scholarship has focused squarely on Johnson's denial that the Ossian poems were "authentic," much more was at stake. Johnson believed that the poems of Ossian were being allowed to stand in for the "vacuity" of *history*, representing for their contemporaries a factually accurate picture of a semi-civilized, even "polite," ancient world. This was *not*, as we will see, the view of the Edinburgh literati who encouraged Macpherson to find and translate Highland poems. Rather, they admired and patronized these poems as fabulous artifacts of an admittedly "barbarous" age that nonetheless corrected the luxurious and "effeminate" spell of commercial modernity. As for Macpherson, however, there are reasons to believe that Johnson was right in suspecting that he was attempting to smuggle in the old story of Scotland's antique grandeur through the backdoor of poetic "translations."

The poems themselves promote the old historical outlook only in subtle and indirect ways. Like other Scots literature of the time, such as John Home's popular tragedy *Douglas* (1755) – which portrays tragically fractious but heroic Scots setting out to defeat the same Danes who had such significant success in King Alfred's England – *Fingal*, *Temora*, and the other Ossianic fragments give poetic expression to the old myths of Scots military glamor. These were the myths which, as Hume observed, Macpherson contemplated with such joy: "He would have all the Nation divided into

Clans, and these clans to be allways fighting."[73] With thudding repetition, Macpherson's heroes slash and dismember each other for no apparent reason besides glory.[74] Nonetheless, as Adam Potkay has shown so well, these gruesome encounters are rendered fit for ladies in the drawing room, unfortunate heroes crashing to the heath without the discharge of brains and entrails common in the traditional epics.[75] In the Scottish epic, moreover, beautiful ladies, with white arms and heaving bosoms, regularly distract the heroes from their gory routine. If this is a militaristic world, it is also strangely civilized and chivalric, full of the sentiments that Enlightened Scots considered the mark of advanced culture.[76] Where Macpherson really crosses into the territory of fraud, however, is in his copious prefatory "Dissertations" on the age of Ossian. He even begins the "Dissertation" opening *Fingal* with a claim to historical skepticism and assiduity reminiscent of Hume and Robertson:

> Inquiries into the antiquities of nations afford more pleasure than any real advantage to mankind. The ingenious may form systems of history on probabilities and a few facts; but at a great distance of time, their accounts must be vague and uncertain . . . The arts of polished life, by which alone facts can be preserved with certainty, are the production of a well-formed community. It is then historians begin to write, and public transactions to be worthy remembrance.[77]

What followed in this dissertation is an outrageous parody of the careful historical methods exemplified by Hume and Robertson: Macpherson wonders aloud about the possibility of "fraud" in Ossian's allusions to the Romans.[78] He fusses scrupulously over the question of whether the "Caledonians" derived originally from "Celtic Germany" or "Gaul,"[79] not mentioning that virtually every Scots and English historian denied the very existence of a people called the "Caledonians," distinguishing ordinarily between the "Scots," the "Picts," and (as in Hume's case) the Lowland Saxons.[80] In this first "Dissertation," he simply omits to mention the widespread claim that the Scots were originally immigrants from Ireland, though his notes cast doubt on the reliability of Irish antiquities and Irish historians,[81] whom he later dismissed angrily as "Credulous and puerile to the last degree."[82] Between these performances of historical care on imaginary or uncontroversial points, Macpherson drops startling assertions as if they were universally conceded. With regard to second-century "Caledonians," for example, he observes that "The form of their government was a mixture of aristocracy and monarchy, as it was in all countries where the Druids bore the chief sway."[83] While to modern sensibilities Macpherson's Druids may seem elegantly antique, these were not the Druids ordinarily identified in eighteenth-century histories with human sacrifice and a ghastly hegemony over a superstitious population. And the notion that Macpherson's poems exhibited a second-century Highland society with a regular form of "government" centered in the power of a generally recognized monarch flew in the face of all that Hume and Robertson had detailed about the fractiousness and barbarity of ancient Britain, *especially* in the Highlands.

This observation raises the question of why the Edinburgh literati not only encouraged Macpherson's researches, but continued to support his credibility for decades after, though with increasing indecision and embarrassment. The nonsense of the prefactory "Dissertations" did not go entirely unnoticed. An English historian who was learned to the point of pedantry, John Whitaker, went through Macpherson's "evidence" citation by citation, showing the author repeatedly misquoting or mistranslating his sources in ways that should have been obvious to anyone even modestly literate in Latin.[84] Macpherson's learned patrons in Edinburgh must have noticed these inaccuracies as well, yet they showed little attention to his historical claims, which were so clearly at odds with their own. In *A Critical Dissertation on the Poems of Ossian, the Son of Fingal* (1763), the longest and best-known argument for the genuine antiquity of these works, Hugh Blair does not mention Macpherson's "Dissertations." Blair's few references to the historical context of the poems are awkwardly indecisive and ambivalent. Whereas Macpherson, for example, had insisted that Scots had populated Ireland, Blair observes at one point that "the scene of Temora, as of Fingal, is laid in Ireland," later relocating the scene of the poems to Scotland, and still later insisting that it did not matter whether the poems were set in Ireland or Scotland, for the populations freely "migrated" – though he does not make clear whether the migration was from Ireland to Scotland or in the other direction.[85] Elsewhere Blair contradicts Macpherson: whereas Macpherson deemed it "ridiculous" to witness people "branding their ancestors, with the despicable appellation of barbarians,"[86] Blair left no doubt that the ancient Scots were a "barbarous" people comparable in many respects to the native people of North America.[87] Indeed, his "internal" evidence for the authenticity of the poems relies on the assumption, a very debatable one, that the manners of the characters are so simple and illiterate that their origins had to lie in an ancient society, though Blair avoids confirming Macpherson's specious dating of the poems in the second century CE. Beyond these broad allusions to the historical setting of the Ossian poems, however, Blair makes very clear that they are totally unreliable as sources of information about a real society. "The beginnings of society, in every country, are involved in fabulous confusion," he writes, echoing the usual disclaimer of the new Enlightenment historians.[88] "In so rude an age," he goes on, "when no written records were known, when tradition was loose, and accuracy of any kind little attended to, what was great and heroic in one age, easily ripened into the marvellous in the next."[89]

Hence for Blair, as for the other members of the Edinburgh "cabal," the importance of the Ossian poems did not lie in their supposed evidence of a great and purely "Caledonian" civilization in the ancient Highlands. Rather, Blair's *Critical Dissertation* is preoccupied by the aesthetic qualities of the poems: his interest in Macpherson's productions reflects a shift, a very marked shift in later Scots writing, from insistence on the historical greatness of Scotland to a willingness to value that past as a literary or mythopoeic construction. In the tradition that flowed from the age of Hume and Robertson, Scots historians authors reached a virtual consensus that the heaths of ancient Caledonia were home to plundering gangs of lawless and skin-clad savages. This rather grim picture of the distant past, comparable to the long-standing English view of their own barbarous Saxon ancestors, can be found for example in *The History of Scotland from the Union of the Crowns* (1800) by Malcolm Laing, whose edition of *The Poems of Ossian* lambasted belief in their authenticity as ancient compositions.[90] During the same period, however, the romantic legend of the Highlands not only endured, but blossomed in all its enduring pageantry. Sir Walter Scott, who concocted such compelling national tales of Highlands romance, fully subscribed to Johnson's allegedly "racist" view that the Highlanders remained a "primitive"people even at the time of the Jacobite uprising. This historical observations by no means undermined his (and his readers') ability to relish the "romance" of the Jacobite invasion of England in distinctly literary terms:

> Looking at the whole in a general point of view, there can be no doubt that it presents a dazzling picture to the imagination, being a romance in real life equal in splendour and interest to any which could be devised by fiction. A primitive people residing in a remote quarter of the empire . . . fearlessly attempted to place the British Crown on the head of the last scion of those ancient kings, whose descent was traced to their own mountains.[91]

Scott's patriotism, that is, was not the patriotism of Sir George Mackenzie or even of James Macpherson: his depiction of the pre-1745 Highlanders as "primitive" inhabitants of an obscure corner of the "empire" hints that his understanding of history had been strongly informed by the English practice extended to Scotland by Hume, Robertson and others. As he quickly goes on to clarify, "In a work founded on history, we must look more closely into the circumstances of the rebellion, and deprive it of some part of the show which pleases the fancy, in order to judge it by the sound rules of reason."[92]

Scott drew a line that was not clearly recognized in Macpherson's supposed "translations" of Ossian. In these poems, history and literature flow into each other in ways that aggravated Johnson, with his fixedly English modern style of historical thinking. On the other hand, Macpherson himself felt at home in England, and represents an important movement towards the more self-conscious division of history and literature found in Scott. The nostalgic melancholy that hangs like a heavy Highlands mist over the Ossian poems arose from the painful conflict in Macpherson's own soul between the past and the present, his Highlands heritage and his belief in the advantages of Union with England. It is the same tension that we find in the work of philosophers like Adam Ferguson, another of Macpherson's early supporters. Ferguson clearly advocated the new thinking in Scotland about the unreliability of oral or traditional legends. Moreover, his painting of ancient Scotland is stripped of Fergusian gilding of pre-Christian elegance: as he observes in *An Essay on the History of Civil Society* (1767), "the inhabitants of Britain, at the time of the first Roman invasions, resembled, in many things, the present natives of North America: They were ignorant of agriculture; they painted their bodies; and used for cloathing, the skins of beasts."[93] Like English authors over the previous few decades, however, Ferguson also worried that the march of civilization, while bringing welcomed peace and prosperity, also carried dangers. While the lives of ancient people were nasty and fractious, they were not brutish. They possessed a sense of community and a military fibre subsequently weakened by the leisure and ease spread particularly by commerce. Hence Ferguson's ardent faith in the stiffening tonic of a national militia. And hence his conviction that even the *legend* of past vigor and militarism contributed a crucial palliative to the effeminizing spell of modern civilization and wealth:

> When traditionary fables are rehearsed by the vulgar, they bear the marks of a national character; and though mixed with absurdities, often raise the imagination, and move the heart: when made the materials of poetry, and adorned by the skill and the eloquence of an ardent and superior mind, they instruct the understanding, as well as engage the passions. It is only in the management of mere antiquaries, or stript of the ornaments which the laws of history forbid them to wear, that they become even unfit to amuse the fancy, or to serve any purpose whatsoever.[94]

Ferguson's point in this fascinating passage is that factual history cannot replace national myth. "National character" (a term that he, along with

Hume,[95] may even have created in its modern form) relies not merely on "truth," but on the stories that a culture tells about itself. Ferguson feared particularly that a society without stories of its own military valour would become weak and disunified.

All this rehearses, in a characteristically Scottish key, a melody of national consciousness that had already become familiar in England. The differences are important: the nostalgic mood of loss could never be felt so deeply in England as in Scotland, where the Enlightenment had dispelled a romantic story of national greatness that had never crystalized so sharply in England. On the other hand, the parallels are intriguing: both England and Enlightenment Scotland confronted what Johnson called the "vacuity" of reliable history. Both north and south of the Tweed, this vacuity was being filled with literature – by Ossian and Scottish literary culture, but also by Johnson's own effort to enrich England, recently emerged from "barbarity," with the recently minted gold of Shakespeare and the *Lives of the English Poets*. In historically significant ways, Johnson's trip to the Highlands, so far from being an imperial progress across a conquered land, constituted an exploration of Johnson's own identity as an Englishman.

In insisting on the recent "barbarity" of the Scots, Johnson was not suggesting that the historical evolution of Scotland was any different from the history of England. As we have seen, he himself acknowledged that England was "just emerging from barbarity" even in the time of Shakespeare. Even his notion of the "useful violence"(9:27) imposed on the Highlanders by Oliver Cromwell and later by the Hanoverian forces at the "conquest" echoed a familiar theme in the historical consciousness of the English, who had long been accustomed to admitting that the Romans and even the Normans had helped to lift them from barbarity. Such admissions represented no disgrace to national pride in a country that, almost by force of its inglorious history, had come to value itself for what it had *become*, not for what it had been. Moreover, what Johnson believed he witnessed in the Highlands was not the imperial extension of "English" manners over a foreign people (however we might now believe that this was exactly the case). Rather, Johnson thought that the Highlanders were merely emerging from a "barbarous" to a "civilized" state that represented the common and ideal destiny of all humanity. According to such a conception of history, a distinct "national character" represented a condition belonging mostly to pre-civilized peoples. As he suggests at several points in the *Journey*, in becoming more "civilized," the Highlanders were losing their national character. "Such are the effects of habitation among mountains," he observed, "and such were the qualities of the Highlanders, while their rocks secluded them from the rest of mankind, and kept them an unaltered and discriminated race. They are now losing their distinction, and hastening to mingle with the general community" (9:47).

On the other hand, Johnson did seem keenly conscious and often appreciative of the "national character" of the Highlanders. "Civility seems part of the national character of Highlanders," he noted at one point. "Every chieftain is a monarch, and politeness, the national product of royal government, is diffused from the laird through the whole clan" (9:29–30). As this passage intimates, *pace* Johnson's modern critics, the history and traditions of the Highlands did often cast their romantic spell over the visiting Englishman. "This is truly the patriarchal life:" he said to Boswell one morning "in fine spirits," "this is what we came to find."[96] Elsewhere in Boswell's *Tour to the Hebrides*, Johnson even took his friend's side when, in a wonted fit of feudal enthusiasm, the young Scot "warmly" criticized Lady McLeod for wanting to abandon her historic home in Dunvegan for something more modern and comfortable.[97] Although Boswell's strong desire to wrap up Johnson in the tartan of his own romantically feudal nationalism might well make us suspicious, his reports on Johnson's shared enthusiasm are strongly corroborated by *A Journey to the Western Islands of Scotland.* Of the two accounts, indeed, Johnson's is far more alive to the physical and social ambience of the Highlands. (Boswell was so preoccupied with "dining" on Johnson's conversation, as he puts it, that much of the *Tour* could have occurred in the parlors of London rather than the castles of northern Scotland.) Admitting that he came to the Highlands "to hear old traditions, and see antiquated manners" (9:128), Johnson often expresses chagrin at evidence of a modern commercial world destroying the feudal virtues of the past. "I saw with grief," he notes at one point, "the chief of a very ancient clan, whose island was condemned by law to be sold for the satisfaction of his creditors" (9:85). He could even savor the militaristic spirit of old Scotland, indulging "a generous and manly pleasure" at the thought of armed clansmen assembling loyally behind their chief: "This was, in the beginning of the present century, the state of the Highlands. Every man was a soldier, who partook of national confidence and interested himself in national honour. To lose this spirit, is to lose what no small advantage will compensate" (9:91). Consistent with the militia issue preoccupying the Edinburgh literati, Johnson even seemed uncertain about the virtues of the laws disarming the Highlanders and suppressing their wearing of tartan. He wonders aloud whether by "disarming a people thus broken into several tribes, and thus remote from the seat of power, more good than evil has been produced" (9:90). And while denying that "the heavy hand of a vindictive conqueror" had been "cruel" in stripping the Highlanders of their tartan, he acknowledged that this measure had created "much discontent" by making "every eye bear witness to subjection" (9:89).

Such passages reveal a significant tension in Johnson's outlook concerning the passing of a world which, while he called it "barbaric," also possessed chivalrous virtues and an antique glamor for which he felt strong attraction, especially as an older man. Indeed, Johnson and Boswell evidently felt much alike on the condition of modern Scotland, despite their different nationalities. While Boswell swells with pride in his Scottish heritage throughout the *Tour*, this patriotism is always of a distinctly nostalgic and romantic kind. His greatest source of pride during this journey was clearly the presence of England's most famous writer, an ambassador of the very "civilized" world that was allegedly relegating ancient Scotland to the pages of romance. Johnson's devotion to the values of "civilization" are made abruptly, even rudely, evident in both his *Journey* and Boswell's *Tour*, his repeated themes being the poverty, brutality, inconvenience, and "savagery" of the Highlands before the Union and "conquest." On the other hand, now fading and deprived of any real political significance, this old world could be appreciated by Johnson at a safe distance, embraced in a purely emotional or spiritual way, and even missed for its unskeptical loyalties and faith. It is evidently the comfort of safe distance, for example, that allows Johnson to breathe deeply from the sentimental atmosphere of the ruins of Iona in an often quoted passage:

> Far from me and from my friends, be such frigid philosophy as may conduct us indifferent and unmoved over any ground which has been dignified by wisdom, bravery, or virtue. That man is little to be envied, whose patriotism would not gain force upon the plain of Marathon, or whose piety would not grow warmer among the ruins of Iona? (9:148)[98]

Here, we might well say, is "bardic nationalism" – though the bard in this case is Samuel Johnson. Nor is this nostalgic celebration of the British past exclusive to his trip to Scotland. His later writing and conversation are dotted with remarks and passages suggesting his movement towards a more "romantic" understanding of national heritage. Less than a year after his trip to the Highlands, Johnson was once again in search of Celtic antiquities, this time with the Thrales in northern Wales. On the whole, Wales disappointed Johnson; it was too *modern*.[99] As recorded in his private journal, however, he did enjoy the remnants of the chivalric past at Beaumaris Castle on Anglesey Island in northwest Wales: "The castle corresponds with all the representations of romancing narratives. Here is not wanting the private passage, the dark cavity, the deep dungeon or the lofty tower. We did not discover the well. This is [the] most complete view that I have yet had of an old castle. It had a moat. The towers" (1:202–3). The "gothic" and the "sublime" are not, of course, modes that we usually associate with Johnson. Yet at points in his journal of Wales, the author of "London" could almost be mistaken for Ann Radcliffe or Horace Walpole:

> We saw Hakeston, the seat of Sir Rowland Hill, and were conducted by Miss Hill over a large tract of rocks and woods, a region abounding with striking scenes and terrifick grandeur . . . Though it wants water it excells Dovedale, by the extent of its prospects, the awfulness of its shades, the horrors of its precipices, the verdure of its hollows and the loftiness of its rocks. The Ideas which it forces upon the mind, are the sublime, the dreadful, and the vast. (1:174–5)

Corresponding with this heightened, even proto-Romantic openness to the antique and the sublime was Johnson's deepening interest in antiquarian scholarship, which had become, indeed, a marked trend in late eighteenth-century British culture. In the field of language, he became one of the century's most energetic supporters of projects to preserve and protect ancient British tongues. He urged Boswell to collect a whole "folio" of "north-country" words, encouraged William Drummond's Erse translation of the Bible, and supported William Shaw's Erse grammar; while in Wales, he showed an active concern for the promotion of Welsh, urging the republication of David ap Rhees's Welsh Grammar, and offering a "scheme" to his hosts for preserving Welsh (see 1:190–1); he wrote twice to the Irish antiquarian O'Connor, commending his studies of the Gaelic tongue, and lauding Ireland as "the school of the West."[100] Significantly, this growing interest in antiquities extended also to the history of England. He warmly commended studies of the Saxons begun by Thomas Astle, Keeper of Records at the Tower of London and an outstanding antiquarian. "To see a Man so skilful in the Antiquities of my country," he wrote to Astle, "is an opportunity of improvement not willingly to be missed." From Astle, he wished to know particularly if "the Saxons had any gold coin," reflecting the supposed connection between civilization and the introduction of money that also interested him in Scotland.[101] With Thomas Percy, the author of *Reliques of Ancient English Poetry* (1765), Johnson continued a long friendship, despite Percy's habit of crossing his opinions and needling his foibles with a fearlessness virtually unmatched in Boswell's *Life*. (At one comically memorable point, for example, Percy leaves Johnson "puffing hard with passion struggling for a vent" by informing his "good friend" that he was too "short-sighted" to see Scotland properly.)[102] Johnson's willingness to endure this friction was encouraged, as he wrote to Boswell, by his great respect for this scholar: "It is sure that he vexes me sometimes, but I am afraid it is by making me feel my own ignorance. So much extension of mind, and so much minute accuracy of enquiry, if you survey your whole circle of acquaintance, you will find so scarce, if you find it all, that you will value Percy by comparison."[103] It is hardly surprising then, as Percy admitted, that the dedication to his *Reliques of Ancient English Poetry* "owed its finest strokes to the superior pen of Dr. Johnson"[104] – and, on the evidence of the dedication's loftily Johnsonian tone, it might well have owed much more to him than a few "strokes." Johnson's contribution to this dedication to Lady Northumberland is suggestive, for it advances a strong defense of explorations into the English past: "No active or comprehensive mind can forbear some attention to the reliques of antiquity: It is prompted by natural curiosity to survey the progress of life and manners, and to inquire by what gradations barbarity was civilized, grossness refined, and ignorance instructed."[105]

In considering Johnson's maturing nationalism, then, we must keep these passages and these sentiments in mind alongside his more famous pride in English "civilization" and "progress." That his genuine fascination with ancient Britain (enough of a fascination that it impelled his ailing and aging body across the rugged terrain of northern Scotland) flowered only late in his life is itself revealing: after about 1760, the English had begun to think of themselves as having fulfilled the most optimistic prophesies of darker days in the 1730s and 1740s. In effect, the concluding vision of the Hermit in *Alfred* of England had been marvelously realized in Britain's string of victories over the French in the summer and autumn of 1759. After that year, it could be felt indeed that England had come to "grasp the world"[106] from Quebec to India, from Jamaica to the Grand Banks. The public consciousness of England as a triumphant "civilization," which coalesced during the first decade of George III's reign, gave a different significance to the past. No longer was history merely a register of English failure (as in *Marmor Norfolciense*) or, at best, dogged English resistance to tyranny (as in Patriot or Whig accounts). Rather, it could be examined with interest and even exaltation as a measure of how greatly England's "barbaric" system of government had gradually evolved into a splendid balance of powers. This satisfaction with English progress characterizes much that the older Johnson has to say about his national history, sentiments widely shared by contemporaries across the political spectrum. In the words of Thomas Warton, another antiquarian with whom Johnson shared an intellectually harmonious though personally rocky friendship, "That these speculations should become the favourite pursuits, and the fashionable topics, of such a period [of refinement], is extremely natural. We look back to our ancestors with the triumph of superiority; we are pleased to mark the steps by which we have been raised from rudeness to elegance."[107]

Furthermore, a major claim of this chapter has been that the path of national development in England was followed, with important variations, in eighteenth-century Scotland. The major figures of the Scottish Enlightenment increasingly acknowledged that their country, like England, had evolved from "barbarity" to modern civilization, particularly as led by trade and commerce. Like the English, moreover, they worried about the paradoxically effeminizing influence of wealth and luxury. The anxiety of the Edinburgh literati about London's refusal to grant Scotland a militia, plus their enthusiastic encouragement of a highly martial vision of Scots history – as exemplified not only by the poems of Ossian but also by popular works like Home's *Douglas* (1755) – reflects their belief, so well articulated in Ferguson's *History of Civil Society*, that the refinement of manners in a commercial society also had the paradoxically negative effect of undermining national virtue. Ferguson was no primitivist; there could be no return to the past. But national fables of military glory, along with a belief in the Stoic simplicity of the past, offered some palliative to the enervating influence of wealth, mediating between past and present. Here again we might think of Johnson. As we have seen, he did not share the intense fear of luxury found in the jeremiads of John Brown and others; his confidence in the benefits of commerce – and even luxury in a tempered form – is highly comparable to the equanimity of Scottish economists like James Steuart and Adam Smith on this subject. Nevertheless, we will also recall Johnson's commitment to the "liberal" education of gentlemen, grounded in the classics and morality, as an antidote to the growing narrowness and immorality of commercial society. And his *Journey to the Western Islands of Scotland* evinces a deepening interest in the British past and his capacity to share the nostalgia for the lost virtues of a time committed to personal loyalty, not money.

This is not to suggest that Scots and English nationalism are the same: the hand-wringing sense of loss that absorbs the heroes of Scottish literature from Ossian to Scott, from Henry Mackenzie to Hogg, contrasts with the relative equanimity of poets and novelists in England, who evidently could not recall a historical past worth preserving, except in the amber of literary expression and museums. It might even be said that Scotland, very much like England of the early eighteenth century, remained, and perhaps remains, stuck on the upward curve of that familiar cycle of modern nationalism – from failure to victory, conquest to independence, promise to fulfilment. In the late Georgian period, however, the reduction of Scottish nationalism to a romantic or "bardic" form provided one necessary element in the matrix of a *British* nationalism.[108] Increasingly, the English could take pleasure in kilt-flashing dance or a phalanx of droning bagpipes, as well as in legends of the Welsh King Arthur and in colorful Irish *raconteurs*. Some historians such as Tom Nairn (whose views are continued by Katie Trumpener) have portrayed this theatrical Celticism as the essence of national consciousness, even a kind of proud riposte of suppressed people against their imperial masters.[109] Yet it should be recognized that this kind of wistful nationalism played an important role in keeping the bits of the British Empire glued together, becoming part as well of a renewed English sense of its own romantic history. In the words of Murray Pittock, "Nostalgia was an aesthetic keynote in Victoria's reign in England as well as in Scotland. Not only was there a recrudescence in medievalism, and such connected ideas of a unified British past. England was not immune from the fairy-dress school of history largely pioneered in Scotland."[110] In so far as this nostalgia took the form of middle-class Victorians donning armor and jousting on the weekends, it represented a harmless and even vital ingredient in national consciousness. In the triumphant imperial atmosphere of Victorian England, however, this backward gaze could take the more sinister form of Anglo-Saxon racialism and the aggressive confidence of innumerable lecturers and pamphleteers that the Saxons were God's "chosen people" always destined to extend their reign over the whole globe. In the words of one anonymous pamphleteer ("Antiquary") in 1873, the Anglo-Saxons were the "race now occupying the strongest and most defensible positions on the surface of the globe, from which they issue forth conquering and to conquer with their free institutions, their open Bible, and the most beautiful liturgy in existence."[111]

Significantly, these were the same generations that seemed so attuned to the works and life of Samuel Johnson, particularly as he was portrayed and celebrated by that great aficionado of whisky-flavored nationalism, James Boswell. This enthusiasm seized in part on Boswell's portrait of Johnson as a devout and conservative Anglican, his "open Bible" on his table, his heart and mind committed to "the most beautiful liturgy in the world." But Johnson's very life, as so dramatically evoked by Boswell, seemed to symbolize the noble ascent of his homeland. Johnson's life was, to cite again Pittock's description of Celtic nationalism, "a narrative of crises,"[112] the story of a young man of disgraceful heritage who harnessed his great potential to overcome every obstacle, and through a series of great nation-shaping triumphs (the *Dictionary*, the edition of Shakespeare, *Lives of the*

English Poets) became the "literary dictator" of taste and "common sense" not only in England, but in Scotland, where Boswell carried him like a hero, and wherever the English language was taken around the world. In this lasting and popular image, Johnson was surely, as Boswell painted him, "at bottom much of a *John Bull*; much of a blunt *true born Englishman*."[113] Note, for example, how much the following description of the typical Englishman ("John Bull") by the late nineteenth-century phrenologist Lorenzo Fowler not only resembles Boswell's characterization of Johnson, but may even, one suspects, have taken its inspiration partly from that portrait:

> The English are generally rotund in form, full-blooded, have an ample degree of Vitality, capacity to enjoy life, and naturally have good digestive powers . . . They are remarkable for their sociability, friendliness, love of home and family, for their hospitality and philanthropy, their practical talent, their knowledge of the world, their interest in general affairs, their love of experiments, and their capacity to entertain persons with the knowledge they possess . . . They are often very blunt in speech, and can say plain things in a very plain way, without stopping to put on the polish, like a Frenchman . . . But with all their bluntness, they have a kind heart, are generous to a fault . . .[114]

This portrait of "John Bull" differs sharply from the famous depiction of typical Englishness by John Arbuthnot at the beginning of the eighteenth century: Arbuthnot's "John Bull," in keeping with the self-doubt and paranoia of that era, is a good-natured but fatuous ninny, fooled and manipulated by all around him, the victim of his own bad judgment and ungoverned temper.[115] In the intervening era of national victory and ascendance, however, Johnson became the appropriate model for a "John Bull" characterized by dogged determination in the face overwhelming obstacles – a victor against all odds.

The rich and profitable field that gave life to a fully-blossomed English nationalism was, of course, the British Empire. Even in darker days, "patriots" had envisioned Britannia ruling the waves and all the land around them, and by the end of century these prophesies seemed to be approaching fulfilment. The impact of the Empire on the nation's self-image might be gauged by the following passage from John Lingard's *History of England* (1819–30) which imagines the first arrival of Caesar's fleet on the shores inhabited by ancient Britons:

> The natives carefully followed the motions of the fleet, urging their horses into the waves and, by their gestures and shouts, bidding defiance to the invaders . . . after a short pause, the standard-bearer of the tenth legion, calling on his comrades to

follow him, leaped with his eagle into the sea; detachments instantly poured from the nearest boats; the beach, after a short struggle was gained; and the untaught valour of the natives yielded to the arms and the discipline of their enemies.[116]

This passage bears the marks of the unsentimental and "demythologized" history that became standard in England and later Scotland during the eighteenth century. Lingard's Britons are clearly savage and primitive, and Lingard's ancient "Caledonians" are even further back on the scale of civilization. The noble Scots of Ossian are here downgraded to "hordes of savages" who shelter "almost naked" under rocks and engage in the "strange and disgusting practice" of painting their bodies blue, thus making themselves look like "Ethiopians."[117] Indeed, the identification solicited by the above description is not between modern Britons and the ancient "tribes" who inhabited their island but rather between modern Britons and the Roman invaders. The scene strongly evokes the familiar scene of well-organized British troops landing on savage coastlines. Lingard links modern British imperialism with the Roman invasion of Britain, implicitly relaying a number of judgments about the goodness of that invasion in subduing and "civilizing" the Britons (who albeit are credited with "untaught valour") and of the civilizing influence of Englishmen, the new Romans, around the world. If a hundred years before the English had struggled in various ways with the consciousness of being historical losers, Lingard finds no difficulty in identifying his nation with history's winners and conquerors.

Lingard's *History of England* was a product of its own historical moment. The modern imperial state had become a reality, and Britain now identified its national character with recent success, progress, and its mission to change the world in its own image. This change, like so many others, was a product of Johnson's own lifetime. What then was the reaction of this most "typical" Englishman? If he contributed so significantly to articulating and representing English nationalism, was he not also influential in promoting the imperial spirit that became so central to England's national consciousness over the next century? This bare proposition will be not be easily conceded even by scholars who know Johnson's work well, for he has long had the reputation of nobly opposing his nation's imperial expansion. A more careful examination of this issue, however, may well reveal that Johnson's ideological stance was essentially consistent with imperialism, and that this attitude grew in confidence and firmness in his later life.

CHAPTER 6

The material and ideological development of the British Empire

"UNIVERSAL MONARCHY" VERSUS THE "EMPIRE OF GOODS": DEBATES ABOUT EMPIRE 1690–1760

Johnson may have been born into a nation that considered itself a medium power, a factionalized outpost on the watery margins of imperial grandeur on the Continent, but he died in a nation that wielded a sceptre over large swaths of the world. It was his age that gave the world the British Empire – a process that was gradual and closely interconnected with the other social, political, and economic developments that we have examined in previous chapters. Particularly in more fashionable branches of literary and post-colonial studies, however, it often seems that "imperialism" sprang, like Milton's Sin, from a contriving brain instilled with the fully formed "project" to appropriate the globe. It is merely "curious," writes Edward W. Said, that the Victorian defender of British imperialism J.R. Seeley should have thought that "some of Europe's overseas empires were originally acquired absentmindedly." The British Empire, from the beginning, must have been intended: "the enterprise of empire depends upon the *idea of having an empire.*" "We must not forget that there was very little domestic resistance to these empires," Said tells us, for "*imperium*" implies "a protracted, almost metaphysical obligation to subordinate inferior, or less advanced people."[1] The thesis that British imperialism, from the outset, represented a conscious, aim-driven, and nationally sanctioned drive to absorb the world and its lesser peoples has remained the virtually unchallenged premise of post-colonial scholarship. The ideology of imperialism, writes Laura Brown, was "hegemonic" even in the early eighteenth century, opposed only by a few scattered voices unable to consolidate into an effective opposition.[2] Disclaimers of imperial ambition among authors in pre-Hanoverian England, another scholar has recently insisted, must be regarded as "factitious," a view that endorses Said's thesis concerning the full-blown imperial intentions of the nation even during the Restoration.[3]

In Johnson scholarship, it is similarly taken for granted that he belonged to a society where the quest for empire was already an established national creed, though he himself stood bravely, a lonely rock of liberal enlightenment, against this ideological tide. "If there is one aspect of Johnson's political thinking that is clearly defined and that does not vary from his earliest to his latest writings," wrote Donald Greene, "it is his distrust of the foreign invaders of a land and his sympathy with those who originally occupied it."[4] Similarly, Thomas Curley observes that "Johnson had little patience for the kind of imperialistic program of commercial expansionism spearheaded by the elder and younger Pitts."[5] Clement Hawes has more recently applauded Johnson's "anti-imperialism," his "systematic and lifelong loathing of empire."[6] The central claims of the following chapter, on the contrary, can be stated quite succinctly. First, whatever his other sins, J.R. Seeley was essentially *correct* to maintain that British imperialism emerged in a piecemeal, half-conscious way, the product of mercantile adventures of various kinds, only gradually backed by the state, and then mostly in the effort to appease the wealthy merchant class and combat the much feared aggression of other European powers. The "hegemonic" status of imperial ambitions in eighteenth-century England is indeed very doubtful. The very word "imperialism" was not coined in English until the mid-nineteenth century, first to condemn the aggressive policies of Napoleon III, and later transformed into a term of political *abuse* in attacks by Gladstone's Liberals against the foreign policies of Disraeli's government.[7] It follows from this understanding of the slow and confused evolution of imperialist ideology that Johnson cannot be called "anti-imperialist" in any comfortable way, for "imperialism" had not yet coalesced into the hegemonic and self-conscious policy that we associate today with Lord Curzon or Rudyard Kipling.

Nonetheless, it cannot be denied that Johnson lived through a time when England was becoming cognizant of its new and unfamiliar status as an imperial power, giving rise finally to a national debate, confused and often acrimonious, about what the British Empire meant and how this imperial status could be justified and preserved.[8] In this chapter, I will begin by setting out the argument that early in the century England's activities abroad were merely commercial, and had nothing in common with the grasping imperial ambitions of ancient Rome or modern nations like France and Spain, who were widely accused of aspiring to "universal monarchy." England's colonial possession were, as T.H. Breen put it, an "Empire of Goods," or, to use the favored formulation in the early eighteenth century, an "Empire of the Sea," meaning that England intended only to protect its "right" to free trade between its harbors and plantations around the globe.[9] The War of Jenkins' Ear (1738–40), with all its noisy displays of self-righteous fervor, was fought on this principle. Yet as the century wore on, it became more difficult to distinguish British colonialism from allegedly "bad" empires, past and present. The Seven Years' War was clearly about ruling large tracts of land, not just the waves, for the French had forced the issue by building a string of forts through the middle of North America. The subsequent uprising of American colonists against British taxes, leading to the Declaration of Independence, obliged the British state to think about the rights, duties, and responsibilities of the people who lived on the lands they ruled. Finally, the trial and impeachment of the Governor-General of Bengal, Warren Hastings, raised the spectre that British rule could be as cruelly despotic as any empire in history, leading to the acceptance that governance of this empire could not be left to the trading companies and merchants who had inaugurated the "Empire of Goods." Both as a political and ideology entity, the British Empire finally became an unignorable fact – a fact that the Age of Victoria made glorious.

At no point during these developments were Johnson's views about empire unembarrassed with self-contradiction and uncertainty, waverings that register the general confusion of his culture about this issue. He certainly distrusted and often seemed to despise the avarice that motivated the earliest colonial ventures, and this hatred of immoral traders helps to explain his attacks on the exploitation of American native people, the Catholic Irish and African slaves. On the other hand, Johnson's attitudes were generally evolving in tandem with events. He supported the War of Jenkins' Ear, writing patriotic tributes to the "dominion of the sea" established by Drake and Blake; he accepted the need for war against the French in North America; he strongly upheld the right of Britain to maintain full imperial power over America; he befriended Warren Hastings and adamantly refused to condemn this self-styled imperial "despot" to the end of his life. I will also propose here that, psychologically, Johnson had been predisposed to recognize the "glory" of empire from his early life, and that a fascination for imperial glamor informs *Irene*, *The Vanity of Human Wishes*, and much of his later work. With increasing conviction, Johnson turned toward the attitude that empires could be grand and even beneficial in spreading civilization and Christianity, an outlook that in fact strongly anticipated the moralistic and grandiloquent imperialism in the Victorian era. As J.R. Seeley told his Cambridge audience in 1882, Britain possessed an empire not for any financial advantage but as a Providentially imposed *duty*: "we hold the position not merely of a ruling but of an educating and civilizing race."[10]

This, however, was the unapologetic imperialism that became respectable (though never uncontroversial) in a later era. Particularly in the early stages of the nation's imperial expansion, the very word "empire" sounded less like the triumphant blast of a trumpet than an ambivalent swell of ominous chords. It is very probable that the dark undertone of this word derived from the uncomfortable consciousness that England had itself been the victim of repeated conquest, and that England had enlisted only belatedly in the stakes of world domination, being the largely inert witness to Spanish *conquistas* in the sixteenth century, and to Dutch and finally French expansionism in the seventeenth century. In the late seventeenth century, it was still possible for a supporter of English colonialism like Charles Davenant, a moderate and intelligent Whig often cited in later writing, to inveigh emotionally against what he called "universal monarchy," the lust for territorial consumption that he believed he witnessed particularly in his foreign contemporaries:

> Private Persons would not be unhappy, tho with less Possessions of Land or Money, and Civil Life would not be so obnoxious to Law, Contentions, Fraud, Perjury, and Oppression, if Men would set some Bounds to their desire of Having. Commonwealths, well founded, would be Eternal, if they would contain themselves within a reasonable Extent of Territory, and Princes would make their own and the Condition of their People much more happy, if, instead of leading them out to Foreign Conquests, they would endeavour to Rule 'em at home in Pease, with wholesome Laws, Piety, and Justice.[11]

Davenant certainly recognized the evils of expansion motivated not by the hunger for political domination but for personal enrichment, what he denounced as "the Rapacious Temper of some of our Men of Business."[12] His attack on the self-serving attitudes of the East India Company suggests, in particular, that concerns about the capacity of the merchants to run the empire they were acquiring, as effectively argued much later by Adam Smith and Edmund Burke, belonged to a long-term unease in professional and intellectual circles of British society with the vulgar upstarts in the City. On the other hand, the City worried Davenant much less than the Sun King's France, which clearly aspired to "Great and perhaps Universal Empire," and the Spanish, whose gold-sucking greed for dominion reminded him of Alexander the Great and the fanning legions of ancient Rome.[13] These were state-sanctioned expansions, brutal expressions of the desire of certain monarchs to tyrannize over stretches of the globe. And the terror that others, particularly the French, were engaged in a "long concerted design of swallowing up the whole,"[14] would continue to drive English foreign policy throughout the century. Even that most objective commentator on the imperial struggles of Europe, David Hume, worried in 1742 that France had its sights set on "universal monarchy" – though he came finally to believe that Britain was excessively preoccupied with checking the progress of its supposed rivals for trade, exhausting itself in continuous and unnecessary wars as the result.[15]

From a very early stage, therefore, the English conceived of themselves not as an expanding or ambitious power, but as the nation allotted the arduous task of maintaining "The Balance of Power." In his essay with that title, Davenant complained that his compatriots "take little thought of what becomes of the ballance of *Europe*," looking with unconcern on "the Growth and Power of *France*, and the dangers that threaten *England*."[16] Political commentators throughout the eighteenth century were obsessed with strategies for ensuring that one of England's mighty neighbors did not succeed in engulfing the whole world. Perhaps, as Defoe argued in 1711, England should side loyally with Spain against the French, for of these two inveterate rivals, Spain would always be the weaker.[17] But a policy of this kind seemed to lead to the Spanish depredations in the Caribbean during the 1730s, spurring charges that England had become too complacent with the ambitions of Madrid and finally leading to the War of Jenkins' Ear. Similarly, the Seven Years' War, which would win Britain glorious imperial trophies from Canada to Bengal, was understood not as a battle to gain an "empire" but as a struggle to halt the aggressive "encroachments" of the French, who had laid claim to stretches of the American interior as far east as Ohio and had forged a frightening alliance with various First Nations against the British colonies on the Atlantic. Quite a few commentators admitted that the British had no more right to control these "Indian" territories than did the French, yet this made no difference to the fact that the French had to be stopped.[18] In a 1755 number of the proto-radical journal *The Monitor*, credited by some historians with exerting crucial pressure on the King to bring Pitt into the war cabinet,[19] claims of imperial ambition on England's part are hotly rejected. Imperial expansion, "Mr. Freeholder" asserted, was the defunct ambition of barbaric princes in a former age; this war was rather about freedom of *trade*:

> our present quarrel with France is not . . . for extent of territory, dominion, glory, religion, or any of those worn-out motives, that formerly possessed the heads of princes, and kindled so many unmeaning bloody wars among them; [it is] *for extent of trade* . . . France is never disposed to quit her encroachments without force; and if it be lawful to scrutinize the councils of this nation, and to infer from the necessity of raising of large supplies; there is no appearance of our sheathing

the sword of justice, till our fleets have blown up their navigation; and our armies have reduced the French colonies to their pristine narrow bounds.[20]

Even the great gains of North American territory that Britain made in the war that followed were justified as elements of a policy to neutralize the French ambition "of swallowing up the whole." It should perhaps not surprise us, then, that not a single book or pamphlet published during the Seven Years' War (according to the English Short-Title Catalogue) contained the term "British Empire" in its title.

This expression "British Empire," or more often "English Empire," had occasionally been used to denominate the New World colonies, as in John Oldmixon's survey *The British Empire in America* (1708). Oldmixon was extending, in an unusual way, a term more often applied to the union of England, Scotland, Wales, and, sometimes, Ireland – which, as we consider later, became an important prototype for the more genuinely "imperial" outlook of Britain later in the century. Even for Oldmixon, however, the "British Empire" was above all a trading unit rather than a body of land ruled by the British monarch, the creature of merchants rather than kings or politicians. Oldmixon's rather dull compendium, dedicated to the merchant John Bromley, consists almost entirely of delighted inventories of the various goods passing through English ports from Savannah to Boston. Similarly, it was the fundamentally economic nature and purpose of the British colonial network, according to Sir William Keith, writing on behalf of the Opposition pushing Walpole towards war with Spain in 1738, that distinguished modern English possessions from the veritable empires of the ancient world. The "State Policy" of the Romans, Keith observed, "chiefly consisted in gratifying the immoderate Desire of Power and Conquest." Among them, "Trade was no otherwise regarded, than as it became subservient to their ambitious Designs." But the pursuit of trade represented the finest expression of the civilized desire for mutual harmony and mutual benefit: "the Law of Nations . . . has made but one Society of all the Free States of the World . . . particularly in protecting every Country and State in the Enjoyment of those Profits, which may be acquired by carrying on a National and Fair Trade."[21] It followed from this logic that the expansion of British trading interests, as well as the aggressive protection of "free trade" from the imperial ambitions of the French and Spanish, constituted a highly positive and moral force – a force indeed not of subjugation but of the liberation of peaceful and prosperous swaths of humanity. "Trade is the Child of Liberty,"[22] affirmed Keith. The benevolence of English trade, implicitly contrasted with destructive empires of the past, is lauded by the aptly named character Trueman in one of the most popular plays of the early eighteenth century, George Lillo's *The London Merchant* (1731):

> I have observed those countries where trade is promoted and encouraged do not make discoveries to destroy but to improve mankind – by love and friendship to tame the fierce and polish the most savage; to teach them the advantages of honest traffic by taking from them, with their own consent, their useless superfluities, and giving them in return what, from their ignorance in manual arts, their situation, or some other accident, they stand in need of.[23]

The innocence, and even rightness, of England's global meanderings seemed confirmed by its vaunted control not over land but water. The liquid nature of the "English Empire" became a major theme in writing of the mid-seventeenth century, particularly after Cromwell deployed Admiral Blake to enforce English interests on the seas against the Dutch and the Spanish. Cromwell even ordered a translation of John Selden's *Mare clausum, seu de Dominio* (1618), first written for James I but now prefaced with a poem spoken by "Neptune to the Common-wealth of England" along with a grovelling dedication to the Lord Protector. The frontispiece of this book contains the first depiction of Britannia, seated with her famous shield against a sea-scape, from which emerges a subservient Neptune, paying homage. The book itself consists of an exhaustive and legalistic argument for England's "*Dominion* or *Ownership* of the *Sea*, incompassing the Isle of *Great Britain*, as belonging to the Empire of the same."[24] The curious feature of an "empire" over the sea was, of course, that it hardly seemed an "empire" at all, at least in the sense of the ancient dominions of Greece or Rome or the modern drive for "universal monarchy" ascribed to the perfidious French and Spanish. In Drake's celebrated destruction of the Spanish Armada in 1588, Blake's attacks on Spanish and Dutch ships during the Interregnum, or Admiral Vernon's broadsides against Spanish ports and ships in 1738–40, the English were presumably simply protecting their "right" to free trade and unhindered navigation. English colonies, always bordering on the sea, seemed only an extension of that right to navigation. The economist Sir Josiah Child, for example, strictly distinguished between Spanish "Conquest" and English "Planting," the one being the brutal and greedy oppression of foreign populations, the other being the sea-washed enterprise of coastal visitors (the annoying acknowledgement being that the root word in Latin, *colonia*, actually meant "plantation").[25] Indeed, until France built a spine of forts right up the middle of North America, writers like Johnson had only a vague conception of North America as a mass of land that could be mapped, and that bore a discomforting resemblance to the supposedly abhorred empires of the past and present.

Thomson's resonant chorus that "Britannia rules the waves" thus contained the hidden justification that, unlike *Doña España*, Dame Britannia had avoided ruling the land. During the War of Jenkins' Ear which inspired this patriotic song, British ambitions seemed as free as a merchant's sail flapping in the breeze of the North Atlantic, as suggested in the concluding section of Paul Whitehead's *Manners: A Satire*, the poem that landed Johnson's friend the publisher Robert Dodsley in gaol:

> Wrapp'd into Thought, *Lo*! I *Britannia* see
> Rising superior o're the subject Sea;
> View her gay Pendants spread silken Wings
> Big with the Fate of Empires and of Kings . . .
> On Fancy, on; still stretch the pleasing Scene,
> And bring fair *Freedom* with her golden Reign;
> Chear'd by whose Beams ev'n meagre Want can smile,
> And the poor Peasant whistles midst his Toil.[26]

The beneficent nature of English colonial expansion was further confirmed by England's treatment of the "savage" people in other regions, particularly as contrasted with their immoral and aggressive neighbours. One of the lugubriously self-justifying leitmotifs of British economic literature of the Restoration and eighteenth century is the cruelty of avaricious Spaniards in the New World, their bloody oppression of Mexicans and Incas. The merchant Sir Dalby Thomas, writing in 1690, strongly condemned the complacency of the English monarchs before Elizabeth for allowing the Spanish to "Rifle" and "Plunder" the New World, partly for losing the advantage of expanded trade, but also because they could have stood nobly in the path of the *conquistadores* before they committed "Unpresidented [*sic*] Cruelties, Exorbitancies and Barbarities . . . on a Poor Naked and Innocent People."[27] These Hispanic evils against the people of the New World became a particularly self-satisfied theme during the hostilities with Spain in the late 1730s. The Spanish, wrote Richard Copithorne in *The English Cotejo* (1738), were "but too justly stigmatized with the Character of being the most cruel Nation in *Christendom*: which is confirmed by the Account given us of their Barbarity towards the poor, ignorant *Indians*, by an Author of their own."[28] "The Author of their own" was Bartolemé de Las Casas, whose widely translated *Historia de las Indias* had the paradoxical influence of both increasing awareness of European violence against American peoples and providing a justification for England's supposedly more benign colonialism. According to the early Opposition journal *The Craftsman*, for example, the "Musquito" people of modern Belize and Guatemala hated the Spanish "for their Inhumanity and Cruelty in destroying many Millions of their Neighbours." As the result, "The *Musquitos* have a very great Affection for the *English* Nation; and are so fond of every Thing, which belongs to Us, that They are never easy till They have obtain'd an *English* Name, which they go by ever afterwards, and will not be call'd by any Other." The lesson for English colonial policy was to cultivate good relations with all "savage" peoples they encountered, all of whom would "most readily put Themselves under our Protection" in exchange for humane treatment.[29]

English satisfaction at its own humanity with relation to the aboriginal peoples of the Americas became, nonetheless, more difficult to sustain in the decades that followed. The Spanish had enforced their rule with blunderbusses and attack dogs, but the North American French took a much different approach: as detailed in a series of books, beginning with *The History of the Five Indian Nations of Canada* by the Governor of New York, Cadwallader Colden, first published in 1727 and then repeatedly republished and expanded for over thirty years, the French had carefully cultivated good relations with the indigenous peoples of eastern Canada and America, adhering to a severe honesty in commercial and land dealings, deploying bible-laden Jesuits into the heart of indigenous communities, and even encouraging inter-marriage between French settlers and native women (the origin of Canada's modern *Métis*). As French ambitions in North America became evident in the early 1750s, these good relations became increasingly worrisome, and the British began to reflect more critically on their own less harmonious history of affairs with native people. In 1751 another colonial official in New York, Archibald Kennedy, complained particularly about the dishonest dealings with First Nations among merchants and traders. This "Tribe of Harpies or Handlers, their Relations, and Understrappers," wrote Kennedy, "have so abused, defrauded, and deceived those poor, innocent, and well meaning People, that . . . at present we have very few *Indians* left that are sincerely in our Interest, or that can be depended upon."[30] Like a lot of American colonists, Kennedy's concerns about the disaffection of the aboriginals were mostly political rather than humanitarian: the Indians had to be secured to British interests to waylay the encroachments of the French. Writing in 1755, the Boston doctor William Clarke came as close to a genuinely "racist" outlook as was possible before the invention of race science, maintaining that the white settlers should "scour" the land of "Tawnies" just as they had made the world brighter by "scouring" the land of trees. Yet even Clarke worried that "the French are continually making Use of every Art Policy can suggest . . . to reduce *Indians* in alliance with the *English*, and draw them over to their Interest."[31] From the distance of the Atlantic, British authors found it easier to idealize the First Nations into Noble Savages, and to blame the American colonists directly for the mistreatment of the natives. The anonymous English author of *The State of the British and French Colonies in North America* (1755), relying solely on second-hand accounts, contrasted the "luxurious, dishonest and effeminate" Europeans with the Indians, who "rightly place the happiness and dignity of man, in living according to the simplicity of nature."[32] If the colonists found that the First Nations were against them, they had only themselves to blame, for "all the considerable wars or slaughters made by the *Indians* in the Colonies, have been owing to the provocation given them, either by seizing their lands or mal-treating them in trade or otherwise."[33]

Yet, significantly, even this idealistic author, who harbored inherent doubts about the whole project of colonizing North America, urgently recommended strong action against the incursions of the French. Sentimental regrets about the treatment of indigenes, that is, made little difference to the exigencies of modern politics, as they were perceived: the balance of power had to be maintained; the grasping designs of the imperialistic enemy had to be checked. That the British were in fact in the process of consolidating and increasingly their *own* empire seemed very far from the thoughts of the polemicists and news-writers of in the early years of the Seven Years' War. It was only in the aftermath of Britain's great victories in this conflict, and particularly in the face of the American colonies' increasing discontent and questioning of the mother-country's imperial rights, that authors began to muse widely and openly about the nature of the "British Empire." At this point, the "empire" had become more than dominion of the sea, and more than the protection of free trade and the curtailing of foreign aggressors. It became a question of reflecting on the history and policies that had incurred Britain a massive national debt to maintain territories where, to everyone's apparent surprise, colonists now questioned their own "Englishness" and their need for imperial support.

This process, which would lay the foundation for British imperial ideology in the nineteenth century, nonetheless belongs to a phase after the (supposedly defensive) victories of the "French-Indian Wars." In turning to Johnson's career before this time, therefore, we should not be surprised if his views on colonization and empire waver along the inchoate and evolving lines of his culture and generation. If he seems at times to be superficially "anti-imperialist," we must keep in mind that most of his contemporaries were "anti-imperialist" in the sense that they opposed the grasping designs of Britain's European enemies. The "English Empire," which was conventionally contrasted with the territorial conquests of antiquity, allegedly represented something different and better – the mere globalization of trade, the spreading of liberty, the civilization of backward people.

Especially in his writing between the War of Jenkins' Ear and the Seven Years' War, Johnson seemed willing enough to rehearse the conventional distinction of his time between the evils of foreign empire and the benignity of England's "dominion of the sea." In "London," England's aquatic majesty is feted with the flair of a loyal comrade. The act of bidding farewell to Thales at Greenwich, the birthplace of Elizabeth, summons "Britannia's glories back to view; / Behold her cross triumphant on the main, / The guard of commerce, and the dread of Spain" (ll. 26–8). But Johnson's most stridently Patriotic work is *Life of Blake*, published in *The Gentleman's Magazine* in 1740, where he plunges with relish into the task of stirring his readers into martial fury against England's current enemies: "At a time when a nation is engaged in a war with an enemy, whose insults, ravages, and barbarities have long called for vengeance, an account of such English commanders as have merited the acknowledgements of posterity, by extending the powers, and raising the honour of their country, seems to be no improper entertainment for our readers."[34] Whereas Johnson declaims in imperialistic tones about "extending the powers" of England, he is thinking mostly of the "dominion of the sea,"[35] the subject as well of his *Life of Drake*, also written in 1740. Johnson's Drake is, above all, a peripatetic of the seven seas, checking Spanish encroachments on every shore, and repeatedly encountering the savage victims of Spanish cruelty. After Drake and his crew are attacked by the natives of the Caribbean island "Mucho," for example, Johnson comments:

> No reason could be assigned for which the Indians should attack them with so furious a spirit of malignity, but that they mistook them for Spaniards, whose cruelties might very reasonably incite them to revenge, whom they had driven by incessant persecution from their country, wasting immense tracts of land by massacre and devastation.[36]

In contrast with the brutal treatment of savages by the Spanish, Drake maintains a high-minded and Christian patience, seeking trade but never conquest. The one time that he actually "takes possession" of a native territory "in the name of queen Elizabeth" is when the savages, overawed by the English, *voluntarily* give themselves up to his sovereignty. Drake "thought it not prudent to refuse," but regrets that "this acquisition might have been of use to his native country, and that so mild and innocent a people might have been united to the church of Christ."[37]

This does not sound precisely like anti-imperialism, and indeed Johnson was pointing even at this stage to a proper and "English" kind of colonialism based on trade, civilization, and religion. In a 1738 segment of his "Debates in the Senate of Magna Lilliput," written for *The Gentleman's Magazine*, he again contrasts Spanish ("Iberian") greed and cruelty with the practice of England ("Lilliput"), whose "Art of civilizing their remote Dominions" had benefited the inhabitants of America ("Columbia"). This attitude reflects the Patriot sentiments of its time, for Johnson echoes the Opposition complaints against Walpole's apparent unwillingness to check Spanish designs of "Universal Monarchy":

> The *Lilliputians*, contrary to the ancient Genius of that martial People, make very liberal Concessions such as rather drew upon them the Imputation of Cowardice than the Praise of Moderation; but the *Iberians*, insatiable in their Ambition, resolved to insist on nothing less than the absolute uninterrupted Possession of that whole Quarter of the World.[38]

Other doubts about the justice of empire in this tract seemed, similarly, aimed mostly at the quest for territorial expansion rather than the spread of trade. He notes for example the futility of "possessing vast Tracts of Land, which are too spacious to be constantly garrison'd, and too remote to be occassionally and duly supply'd."[39] This was the same point made by Montesquieu in *Considérations sur les causes de la grandeur des Romains*, first translated into English four years before as *Reflections on the Grandeur and Declension of the Romans* (1734). "The unbounded Extent of the *Roman* Empire," wrote Montesquieu, "prov'd the Ruin of the Republic."[40] And the same warnings about the dangers of overexpansion would be echoed thoughout the century, most famously by Gibbon in *The Decline and Fall*.[41] Hence, Johnson was not slaughtering any sacred cows when, for example, he has Cali Bassa in *Irene* warn Mahomet (and echo, interestingly, Donne) that "Extended empire, like expanded gold, / Exchanges solid strength for feeble splendor" (I, v, ll. 37–8, 6:132).

We will see that concerns about the overstretch of British colonial possessions would increase during the course of century, particularly in the wake of the loss of America. The Scottish philosopher Francis Hutcheson had warned in his *System of Moral Philosophy* (1734–7) that even trading colonies would eventually gain the desire for independence,[42] and the American struggle for independence seemed to fulfil that prophecy. In the meantime, however, Johnson forcefully articulated the orthodox view that Britain must take all necessary measures to protect its trade and plantations from the aggression of its competitors. Looking over the history of

England's trading policies in *An Introduction to the Political State of Great-Britain* (April 1756), published just before the outbreak of war against France, Johnson blamed past monarchs like James I for idly watching the Spanish, Dutch and French grasp large shares of world trade. Recalling his old Patriot themes, he also strongly denounced the Whig administrations after the Peace of Utrecht for their lack of vigilance against the French and Spanish, whom he portrayed as England's natural enemies:

> Instead therefore of opposing, as we had hitherto professed to do, the boundless ambition of the house of Bourbon, we became on a sudden solicitous for its exaltation, and studious of its interest. We assisted the schemes of France and Spain with our fleets, and endeavoured to make these our friends by servility, whom nothing but power will keep quiet, and who must always be our enemies while they are endeavouring to grow greater, and we determine to remain free. (10:146)

One could hardly find a more comprehensive statement of the attitudes towards foreign competition and colonialism that prevailed during the first sixty years of the eighteenth century. Britain must maintain the balance of power against enemies bent on world-wide domination; it must above all vigilantly uphold its "empire of the sea" (10:143). Unusually for him, Johnson even gestures approvingly toward that militant Whig sentiment that wars against the French and Spanish enemy were necessary if "we determine to remain free." None of these conventional sentiments constitute a plan of British imperialism, and there seems no reason to doubt that Johnson and most English people *did* regard themselves as standing up for "freedom" against the encroaching darkness of Gallic or Hispanic domination.

As we have remarked, this myth of British benevolence was undermined during the 1750s by the militarily worrisome alliance between the French and most American aboriginals, who had clearly met with fairer treatment and a warmer embrace *chez les Canadiens* than among British-American colonists. While basically echoing the sentiments of other commentators like Cadwallader Colden, Archibald Kennedy, and Lewis Evans, Johnson cut, with singular force and clarity, right to the heart of this problem. *Neither* the French nor the English had any more right to the land they disputed than two highwaymen had rights to the booty of a stage-coach. "The American dispute between the French and us" was, in fact, "only the quarrel of two robbers for the spoils of a passenger" (10:188). On the other hand, everything that Johnson wrote about the battle for North America indicates that he, like even his most enlightened contemporaries, considered the legal right of Europeans to this region to be an academic question. In the world of *Realpolitik* this issue had ceased to be soluble. The French encroachments had to be resisted, and their alliance with the First Nations, however deserved morally, constituted a strategic problem for the British that was best met by imitating the French techniques of fair-dealing, appeasement, and cultural absorption:

> Their great security is the friendship of the natives, and to this advantage they have certainly an indubitable right; because it is the consequence of their virtue. It is ridiculous to imagine, that the friendship of nations, whether civil or barbarous, can be gained and kept but by kind treatment; and surely they who intrude, uncalled, upon the country of a distant people, might consider the natives as worthy of common kindness, and content themselves to rob without insulting them. (10:150)

Whatever the origins, goodness or usefulness of these possessions, that is, they represented an irreversible reality of the modern political situation. Indeed, the suggestion of some of Johnson's work in this era is that English and European empires revealed a *providential* mandate. In *Rasselas* (1759), published at the height of the war for control of North America, Imlac recalls his first encounter as a trader with "the nations which are now in possession of all power and all knowledge; whose armies are irresistible, and whose fleets command the remotest parts of the globe" (16:46). When the naive Rasselas wonders in response why Europeans "can so easily visit Asia and Africa for trade or conquest," while Asians and Africans have planted no colonies in Europe, Imlac's answer is resigned: the Europeans have prevailed so widely "because they are wiser; knowledge will always predominate over ignorance." But why the Europeans are so much wiser than other peoples cannot be known, for it has been ordained by "the unsearchable will of the Supreme Being" (16:47).

There seems no great gap between Imlac's sentiment here and that of the English apologist for the British Empire in India, J.R. Seeley, who pleaded that "we are in the hands of a Providence which is greater than all statesmanship."[43] For Seeley and other Victorians, the "Providential" nature of their empire seemed confirmed by the fact they remained firmly unpersuaded that this sprawling administration was especially profitable in financial terms: "We draw no tribute from it; it is not to us a profitable investment."[44] The empire in India and elsewhere was created "blindly" through the various ventures of merchants and trading companies, sanctioned yet by no means instigated by the British government.[45] Such statements may seem merely disingenuous, a justification of British profiteering.

Yet we have been too easily persuaded that power in Britain during its colonial conquests was centralized in the hands of the state, and that merchants always acted with full public approval and as agents of a national "hegemony." In reality, as we have considered near the beginning of this book, attitudes among the gentry and professional classes towards merchants were deeply conflicted and even hostile. Nor was there any consensus that colonies contributed to the material good of the nation, even if England, having obtained its empire, was "Providentially" bound to uphold and defend it.

MERCANTILISM AND THE RISE OF BRITISH IMPERIAL CONSCIOUSNESS: 1760–80

Was empire generally understood by people of Georgian England to be highly profitable? It may seem obtuse even to raise this question. Yet even such a pre-eminently clear-headed economist as Adam Smith noted in *The Wealth of Nations* (1776) that this utility "is not altogether so clear and evident." "It was not understood at their first establishment," he went on, "and was not the motive either of that establishment or of the discoveries which gave occasion to it, and the nature, extent, and limits of that utility are not, perhaps, well understood at this day."[46] Smith's mixed feelings about the economic virtues of imperialism – the possession of an empire was rather "a relative than an absolute advantage," it tended to enrich individual merchants more than the nation as a whole[47] – have indeed been weighed by historians of economics right up to the present day. Could England have become a great industrial power without an empire? (Yes, but more slowly.) Did the ballooning national debt incurred by protecting the colonies outweigh the advantage of widening markets for English goods? (In the long term, probably; in the short term, probably not.) These questions are still alive among scholars with a seriously statistical approach to eighteenth-century economics.[48]

Hence, we should perhaps relax our skepticism about the sincerity of doubts about the economic virtues of colonialism that were commonplace from the beginning of the eighteenth century. In the conventional terms of that time, the prosperity of a nation was directly proportionate to the number of its inhabitants, a principle that Davenant drew from Machiavelli: "whosoever would make any City Great and apt for Dominion, must with all Industry endeavor to throng it with Inhabitants."[49] As John Oldmixon observed in his pro-colonial *The British Empire in America* (1708), "The main Objection made by the Enemies of our *Colonies* against them, is, That by draining *England* of her People, they weaken us at Home, and consequently are more harmful than beneficial."[50] The weight of this objection seemed to be proved by the case of Spain, which, according to a Patriot myth, had been stripped both of trees to build boats and of people to sail in them.[51] Among the supporters of colonization, who were largely the merchants who benefitted directly from this practice, the challenge had to be neutralized in order to maintain the official support they needed. In *An Historical Account of the Rise and Growth of the West-India Collonies* (1690), the merchant Sir Dalby Thomas made a rather provocative distinction between "Laborious and Industrious People," who consisted of merchants and farmers, and "unemploy'd" people, who included not only beggars and criminals, but all "Gentry, Clergy, Lawyers" and other professionals.[52] In other words, the wealth of a nation was proportionate not to its sheer quantity of souls, but to the number of hard-working merchants and farmers. And between the "venturing merchant" and the farmer, the former was by far the most productive, for he produced new wealth rather than just recycling it back into the soil. Thomas followed with grandiose claims for the profitability of the plantations, maintaining that "this Nation saves and gains by the People Employ'd in those Collonies 400 000 000l. Sterling *per An.*"[53] The state should do everything in its power, he concluded, to ensure that mercantile ventures were supported.

Yet Thomas's optimism about colonization, while certainly welcomed by minions of the merchant community like Oldmixon, failed to convince all or even most Britons. Even much later in the eighteenth century, Oliver Goldsmith worried that colonization drew away "the brave and enterprizing,"[54] and wrote a poem, *The Deserted Village* (1770), to lament the supposed exodus from the English countryside to "distant climes" (l. 341). Johnson, who contributed the doleful final four lines of Goldsmith's poem, spent his trip to the Highlands a few years later bemoaning the "epidemick desire of wandering" (9:96) that had infected Scotland, the source not only of impoverishment but disaffection with the mother-country. "Undutiful subjects," he grumbled, ". . . will not much mend their principles by American conversation" (9:97). Even among most writers on trade and commerce, who before the Scottish Enlightenment tended to be merchants, the hazards of colonization were openly acknowledged. Those afraid that "his *Majestie's Plantations* abroad, very much prejudiced this *Kingdom* by draining us of our People," admitted Sir Josiah Child in his *Discourse about Trade* (1689), included "some *Gentlemen* of no mean Capacites."[55] But what was to be done? If England did not want her colonies somebody else certainly did, and the only solution was to make the colonies as profitable as possible, despite their inherent disadvantages. Above all, Child urged vigorous interference by the state in the economic affairs of the colonies, especially through the strict imposition of laws to ensure that *only* the mother-country gleaned their profits. "All Colonies and foreign Plantations do endamage their Mother Kingdoms," he asserted, "whereof the Trades of such Plantations are not confined to their said Mother Kingdoms, by good Laws and severe execution of those Laws."[56]

Here is the sentiment that spurred Britain's mercantilist policies throughout most of the eighteenth century. As the quote from Child's book indicates, its basis was fear – the fear that colonization, a process initiated by merchants rather than the state, had to be carefully regulated by the state in order to be made profitable. These anxieties came to a head with Joshua Gee's *The Trade and Navigation of Great-Britain Considered* (1729), which Hume later identified as a key work in the promotion of the mercantilist policies that the himself had come to distrust. "The writings of Mr. Gee," wrote Hume in 1742, "struck the nation with an universal panic, when they saw it plainly demonstrated, by a detail of particulars, that the balance was against them for so considerable a sum as must leave them without a single shilling in five or six years."[57] With more accuracy than scholars have generally assumed, Gee complained that support for colonial ventures, so far from being "hegemonic," remained very low. "I hope the Time is drawing near," he remarked, "when those Colonies will be more valued, and a greater Care taken to improve and preserve them."[58] His prayer was soon answered in a very dramatic form by the War of Jenkins' Ear. While supposedly only a battle for free trade against the perfidious and imperialistic Spanish, this conflict and its surrounding patriotic furor signaled a new fixation in the public with the welfare of the nation's colonial traffic. This fixation had been stirred by the conviction, as Gee writes at the end of his book, that the colonies were draining the nation not only of its people but of its riches: "I am afraid the present Circumstance of our Colonies carries out more Riches than it brings home."[59] This anxiety became all the more urgent over the following decades as Britain's successive conflicts with Spain, France, and the American colonies fattened the national debt to astronomical proportions. According to the late-century historian John Knox, the Seven Years' War added £71 million to the Debt, which ballooned to £146 million by 1763, and then *doubled* during the American War.[60]

Mercantilistic anxiety, in short, became something of a self-fulfilling prophesy. Convinced that the colonies would only be profitable through vigorous military action against all competitors, successive British administrations ended up virtually bankrupting the nation. But this was only one of mercantilism's explosive ironies. While technically only a doctrine about liberty of trade, which the English liked to tout as their only ambition, mercantilism dictated harsh economic and political control of colonies. Writing near the outset of the war against Spain in 1738, for example, Sir William Keith made much of the liberty, prosperity, peace, harmony, and so forth that English trade was spreading around the globe. Yet, following the advice of Child and Gee, Keith also vigorously proclaimed both the right and the economic necessity for Britain to rule over its colonies with an iron hand, permitting neither dissent nor challenge to its supreme authority:

> Care has been taken not only to preserve the Sovereignty and Allegiance due to the Crown of *Britain*, but likewise to restrain the People of the respective Colonies, from enacting amongst themselves any By-Laws or Ordinances whatsoever, repugnant to, or any ways inconsistent with, the Fundamental Laws and Constitution of the Mother-State to whose Legislative and Supreme Authority they most certainly are, and ought always to be subjected.[61]

Hence, while denying that British colonialism had anything to do with "the universal monarchy" allegedly desired by the French and Spanish, the British felt obliged to behave very much like a despotic imperial power. The great prototype for this policy was Ireland, which, being separated from England by a narrow body of water, seemed to reflect the colonization of America in miniature. When the Irish Whig William Molyneux argued in 1698 that the Irish parliament had supreme authority over Ireland – a position that he argued on the Lockian principle that Ireland had not been conquered, "justly" or otherwise, and so had never given up that legislative power – he was denounced in a small flood of pamphlets for sounding "*Sheba*'s Trumpet of Rebellion."[62] Of course Britain had "conquered" Ireland: "the *Crown* and *Kingdom* of *England*" had made "an absolute acquisition of the Land of *Ireland*."[63] These were the words of William Atwood, who later wrote pamphlets declaring that Scotland too had been seized by English conquest – pamphlets duly incinerated by the public hangman in Edinburgh. Atwood also became Chief Justice of New York, and his unusually blunt admission that the British colonies belonged to a real "empire," and should be governed with the imperious authority of a conquering power, became an increasingly orthodox view of America as well, especially after the Seven Years' War. This war, as we have considered, made the empire in America seem "real" in English minds, giving it Appalachian depth, dispelling the myth that the colonies consisted merely of a necklace of ports along the Atlantic. And the financial hangover left by this war made the exercise of Britain's imperial "rights" in America a compelling option. Reasoning that Americans should help foot the bill for a war to protect their property, the government imposed the Stamp Act in 1764, and the wheels leading to the American Declaration of Independence spun into motion.

What transpired during these years between 1764 and 1776 was the century's central debate concerning the nature of the "British Empire." While this term was only rarely used before 1760, it became quite normal by the time of the American Revolution. Johnson himself began to deploy the expression in a modern sense, writing about "the whole system of European empire" (10:350) in his pamphlet on the Falkland's Islands incident in 1771, and maintaining in *Taxation No Tyranny* (1775) that "of every empire all the subordinate communities are liable to taxation" (10:418). But nascent imperial consciousness in England did not create unity or even a "hegemony" even at this point. The American conflict exposed, on the contrary, deep fissures in the whole ideology of colonization that had been slowly gestating throughout the century. On the one hand, the American slogan, "no taxation without representation," found receptive ears among English Whigs because it echoed their own creed of the "ancient constitution" as a tradition of rights preserved through a long history of unwavering resistance to imperial subjection. Even the Irish, as Molyneux had argued years before, were not taxed without representation, and this exchange was considered both a national inheritance and a "natural right" in a Lockian sense. Sympathy for the American cause was by no means anti-imperialistic. Indeed, it is one of the revealing ironies of this whole controversy that the most forceful advocate for the American cause in England was undoubtedly the politician who had done most to secure the "British Empire" in North America, William Pitt. So far from embodying a particularly original or "modern" viewpoint, Pitt was carrying on many of the central themes and attitudes characteristic of the Patriot tradition thirty years before. He believed profoundly in the mission of England to spread "liberty" to every corner of the globe and defended British colonialism as merely an exercise in trade. The French and the Spanish, in his dichotomized vision, represented an evil axis of imperialism. Oblivious to the view urged by Johnson during the Falklands dispute, Pitt saw no reason to notice that these competitors might have legitimate concerns about *English* designs of world domination.

While Pitt was not original, others were, and this period gave rise to some brilliant speculations on the nature of international economies and politics. Hume and Smith both poured scorn on the whole logic of mercantilism, with its obsessive control of trade and fear of losing ground to international competitors.[64] Josiah Tucker presented the American drive for independence as a natural upshot of imperial expansion, a view that elaborated usefully on an older pessimism about empire found, for example, in Goldsmith's *Citizen of the World* (1760).[65] And the American revolution became the crucible which formed the outstanding intelligence of Edmund Burke, who urged his contemporaries to consider the Americans as a *different* culture, founded to be sure by Englishmen whose furious commitment to "liberty" blew them across the Atlantic long before, but who had now matured into a people with distinct values and priorities. This cultural identity, Burke pleaded, had to be respected if the Union Jack was to continue to fly over Philadelphia.[66]

For better or worse, this advice was ignored. The general cast of legislation, pamphleteering and speechifying during this period suggests that the mercantile logic seminal to the "British Empire" continued to constitute the main thrust of English cultural attitudes. In conservative discourse, the charges became routine: Americans had done little for the country they had left for personal profit and with the understanding that their interests would be protected as *Englishmen*, not as members of some useless foreign appendage that contributed nothing to the welfare of the whole. Even without the conviction that colonialism was useful in the first place, England had lived up to its side of the bargain by defending the colonies against the French, whom the colonists allegedly feared because Frenchmen hate "liberty." Now London wanted a little recompense for contracting the largest national debt in world history. But Philadelphia, with the monumental ingratitude of a bad child (a major motif in this whole debate), defied the whole logic of mercantilist policy by claiming that *they* should decide on imperial policy, regardless of the interests of the mother-country or its recently acknowledged "empire." These were the views articulated by Lord Grenville in a speech to parliament in 1766:

> When [the American colonists] want the protection of this kingdom, they are always very ready to ask it. That protection has always been afforded them in the most full and ample manner. The nation has run itself into an immense debt to give them their protection; and now they are called upon to contribute a small share towards the public expence [*sic*], an expense arising from themselves, they renounce your authority, insult your officials, and break out, I almost say, into open rebellion . . . Ungrateful people of America![67]

Granville's accusation of "ingratitude" became a plaintive refrain in conservative reactions to the American disturbance. Even Josiah Tucker and Adam Smith, who both advised against open conflict with the colonists, sounded piqued by the unblinking self-righteousness of British settlers who seemed so deeply in Britain's debt.[68] Not yet rehabilitated by Burke's philosophizing about the evolution of cultural difference, Americans remained, in most British minds, *British.* This was the argument of Johnson's erstwhile nemesis, now strange bedfellow, James Macpherson, who stormed against "THESE MEN" who "assume the name of Patriots, yet lay the honour, dignity, and reputation of their Country under the feet of her rebellious subjects."[69] But conservative reaction to America drew from a philosophical reservoir as well as a reservoir of resentment. Above all, supporters of the government's intransigent policy on colonial dissidence rejected American claims to representation founded on either the Whiggish version of the "ancient constitution" or Lockian norms of "natural right." On the supposedly *inherited* right to representation, James Macpherson was one of many who pointed out that "scarce one in twenty-five of the people of Great Britain is represented."[70] It had never been the case that the massive majority of ordinary farmers or tradesmen – and the Americans were essentially farmers and tradesmen in England's Wild West – had a vote in England. On "natural rights," conservatives insisted that rights and privileges belonged to a national inheritance, and were not bestowed by "nature." Colonists had always cleared the land and hoed the soil of America under an English charter – activities that had theoretically cost much and gained little for the mother-country – and this charter, like any "constitution," could not be declared invalid merely because it seemed inconvenient right now. As John Wesley preached to the colonists in *A Calm Address to our American Colonies* (1775), "You are no longer in a state of nature."[71] The quite considerable freedoms of the Americans had been bestowed solely by the charter that had legitimized their first possession of America: "They do inherit all the privileges which their ancestors had: but they can inherit no more."[72]

Important here is that these authors, left and right, were actually debating the nature of empire. "Let us consider," proposed Wesley, "the nature of our Colonies."[73] And so they did, laying the foundations of imperial ideology during precisely the event, ironically, when the most valued chunk of that empire was breaking away. The most thunderous canon of the whole anti-American campaign mobilized by Lord North's administration was Johnson's *Taxation No Tyranny* (1775), which attracted a flock of pro-American replies, and continues to be an embarrassing document for those who want to see Johnson as an open-hearted, anti-imperialist liberal of a modern kind. For no document summarized so forcefully the conservative case against America. And by extension, no work highlights so well a certain powerful strain in the evolution of British imperial ideology.

As we have considered, the young Johnson virtually enlisted in the Patriot movement and echoed many of its central themes: he denounced the alleged imperialism of the Spanish, toasted England's "empire of the sea," and urged the need for war to protect trade, a position that he strongly reiterated at the outset of the Seven Years' War. But he also shared the widespread concerns about the ultimate commercial worth of colonial expansion. Like Charles Davenant, who maintained that "the right Strength of this Kingdom depends upon the Land, which is infinitely Superior and ought much more to be regarded than our Commerce in Trade,"[74] Johnson argued in *Further Thoughts on Agriculture* (1756) that "trade and manufactures, however profitable, must yield to the cultivation of lands in usefulness and dignity" (10:122). If trade and colonization were to be made profitable, he believed, they had to be strictly controlled to serve the national interest. This was the mercantilist position behind his rebuttal to Americans in *Taxation No Tyranny*: "That our commerce with America is profitable, however less than ostentatious or deceitful estimates have made it, and that is our interest to preserve it, has never been denied; but surely it will most effectually be preserved, by being kept always in our own power" (10:415). Note that Johnson refers to *commerce* with America, rather than imperial control, though mercantilist logic in fact dictated a system that might well strike us as essentially imperialistic. Central to this position was his insistence, despite his friend Burke's urgent appeals to the contrary, that the Americans were *not* a distinct nation or culture. Like James Macpherson and other conservative commentators, he made clear that he considered the colonists to be *British*, a position that he expressed sarcastically near the beginning of the essay:

> To love their country has been considered as virtue in men, whose love could not be otherwise than blind, because their preference was made without a comparison; but it has never been my fortune to find, either in ancient or modern writers, any honourable mention of those, who have with equal blindness hated their country. (10:412)

He rejected the arguments of Pitt, Burke, and others that the colonists would be willing to be behave like loyal Britons if they were treated fairly, for the colonists had proved themselves not only seditious but ungrateful: "With what kindness they repay benefits, they are now shewing us, who, as soon as we have delivered them from France, are defying and proscribing us" (10:450). With respect to the demand for representation, Johnson articulated the view of the administration and its supporters. First, representation formed no part of the inherent and perennial rights of the English:

"though power has been diffused with the most even hand, yet very small part of the people are either primarily or secondarily consulted in legislation" (10:427). As only about one in five Englishmen could vote,[75] the demand for such a "right" by men who had abandoned the country struck Johnson, like others, as distinctly *contrary* to the "ancient constitution." Second, with regard to "natural" rights, Johnson gave strong expression to the conservative insistence that the Americans could not speak as "the naked sons of Nature" (10:428). If the colonists of America had "rights" at all to the land they occupied, it was because of "charters" that, until very recently, their ancestors had wielded to justify their right to this land: "Without their charter there would be no power among them, by which any law could be made, or duties enjoined, any debt recovered, or criminal punished" (10:424).

Johnson thus took a strong stand against a fundamentally ahistorical and therefore (according to Johnson) arbitrary appeal to a realm of transcendental rights, insisting instead that the Americans owed all their rights and privileges to the sanction of British law and tradition. As in so much debate concerning the American situation, Ireland seemed to push forward as the colonial prototype. The Americans and their British advocates pointed to Ireland (along with Wales, Scotland, and even Chester and Durham) as precedents for the "natural right" of representation in exchange for taxation, following the Lockian principles applied to Ireland by William Molyneux.[76] Johnson actually cited this late seventeenth-century debate in *Taxation No Tyranny*. But he took the side of Atwood, Davenant, and others that Ireland, like America, was indeed a "colony" and therefore under the full powers of the mother-country. If Ireland, Chester, Durham, Wales, and other places possessed privileges of representation, it was because England had seen fit to grant those privileges (see 10:433–4). We will recall that debate between Molyneux and his respondents turned on the question of rights of conquest, Molyneux holding the Lockian position that only "just" conquest bestowed rights of dominion – and then only over those who had actively resisted the "just" conqueror – and his opponents maintaining that "many Nations have been subdued for their own good, and whoever hath been an Invader that way, hath done them Right and not Wrong."[77] Johnson's position on right of conquest, or at least the position he advocated in his later career, is made clear in the Vinerian law lectures that he wrote during the years 1766 to 1770 with Sir Robert Chambers (who, it is worth noting at this point, soon after became a judge in Britain's relatively new conquest in India). That Ireland processed a parliament, wrote the authors of these lectures, must be considered not a right but a "honourary distinction conferred on it by the English Parliament," a privilege that by no means endowed Ireland with any "degree of independence and can hardly be said to have any legal effect."[78] Over Ireland, England possessed the right of conquest – a right that Chambers and Johnson, somewhat surprisingly, extended to the American colonies:

> all the provinces in America have been either conquered or colonized by Englishmen, authorized protected and sustained by the crown of England. Conquered countries are absolutely under the dominion of the conquerors – naturally and justly where justice is on the side of the victors, and in all cases by the laws and practice of nations, because in all cases the conquerors either believe or pretend that their cause is just, and whether it is or no can only be decided by the sword.[79]

This statement represents a direct rebuttal to Locke's analysis of conquest: contrary to Locke, Johnson and Chambers denied in particular that any meaningful distinction could be made between "just" and "unjust" conquest, for conquerors could always find some justification, however specious, for their aggressions. (As Johnson had written in 1756 of Frederick the Great's Continental campaigns, "Princes have this remaining of humanity, that they think themselves obliged not to make war without a reason. Their reasons are, indeed, not always very satisfactory."[80]) Bereft of Locke's apparent ability to distinguish with certainty between "just" and "unjust" conquest, people in the real world are thrown back on the "law and practice of nations," the option that seems least likely to invite recourse to the "sword" to enforce disputed "rights." It seems probable that Johnson took this reasoning with him in 1773 to Scotland, where he so offended his hosts by referring repeatedly to England's "conquest" of the Highlands. And in the face of American claims to "the rights of nature" two years later, Johnson seemed perfectly willing to endorse military action against the rebellious colonies in order to restore "the order of life, and the peace of nations."[81]

Such sentiments sound like those of an "imperialist" of the nineteenth-century mould – and indeed Johnson belonged to the era that was shaping that mould. As we have seen, however, he and his contemporaries arrived at this self-consciously imperialistic outlook only through a lengthy and complex ideological journey. The beginning of this journey did not lie in some national or kingly aspiration to take over the world, but rather in increasing anxieties about the costs of colonization and the need to check the imperial designs of competitors. Given the allegedly world-devouring tendencies of the French and Spanish in particular, Johnson's growing concern was not merely to protect British imperial claims but also to maintain "the peace of nations" in a world where the jarring claims of competing empires had become an irreversible reality. It was, in part, a question of international law that compelled Johnson to advocate war against the French in 1756: by building a string of forts through the interior of America, the French had challenged what Johnson took as the tacit and customary agreement among nations that they who settled the coast also had rights to the interior: "When therefore we planted the coast of North-America we supposed the possession of the inland region to an indefinite extent, and every nation that settled in that part of the world, seems, by the permission of every other nation, to have made the same supposition in its own favour" (10:190). The interesting implication of this statement is that America had ceased to be some appendage to England's vaunted "empire of the sea;" it had gained real depth, becoming a territory rather than a series of ports up the north Atlantic coast. A few months later, in the autumn of 1756, Johnson published a review of Lewis Evans's *Analysis of a General Map of the Middle British Colonies in America.* The word "Middle" in this title implies something important, for, as Johnson himself remarks, the hostilities with the French had encouraged a new vision of America as a huge landmass extending inland:

> the war now kindled in America, has incited us to survey and delineate the immense wastes of the western continent by stronger motives than mere science or curiosity could ever have supplied, and enabled the imagination to wander over the lakes and mountains of that region, which many learned men have marked as the seat destined by Providence for the fifth empire. (10:200)

"Fifth empire" is an allusion to the interpretation of Nebuchadnezzar's dream in the Book of Daniel 2:36–45, where Daniel prophesies a final kingdom "that shall stand forever." Implicitly, Johnson was conceding that England indeed had an "empire" of virtually biblical significance. And having made this crucial acknowledgment, Johnson could negotiate the mental leap of considering territorial possession from both sides of the question. It seemed less strange that the French and English "charge *each other* with aspiring to universal monarchy" (10:188, my italics). If such a recognition did not make him more peaceable during the Seven Years' War, it was because he believed that the French had indeed transgressed a fundamental principle of international relations by occupying the interior of North America, and thus undermining the customary principles (not the *rights*) ensuring "the peace of nations."

In other situations, indeed, Johnson's goal of promoting international peace is more obvious. The dispute with Spain over the Falkland Islands in

1771 provides an intriguing prelude to the controversy about America four years later because it pitted the parties in that debate on reversed sides. The American crisis might leave the impression that Johnson was the proto-imperialist, while Pitt and his allies seem the friends of peace and freedom. Nevertheless, when the Spanish Governor of Buenos Aires sailed a large fleet to the Falkland Islands in June 1770, formally expelling the recently arrived English as invaders of the King of Spain's possessions, it was Pitt who led the charge to plunge England into an imperial war. From the point of view of Pitt, Junius, and other Whig observers, this was clearly a question of England's "natural rights" being violated. England had occupied islands that, while claimed by Spain as a natural appendage to their undisputed Continental possessions, contained no Spaniards. For Pitt and his allies, this was besides a question of national "honour," that old rabble-rousing refrain of '38. Junius, for instance, did not even discuss the question of "right" over the islands, taking as self-evident that "the Spaniards had no claim of right." For him, it was a question of national "honour," for the King of England had been slapped across the face not just by the King of Spain but, more disgracefully, by "his Catholic Majesty's" *servant.* When Lord North's negotiators accepted a mere withdrawal of the Spanish from the Falklands, rather than a formal ceding of all claims to these islands, Junius chastised George III for not resenting the "insult" like a gentleman, writing that the King should confess humbly to a nation mortally aggrieved by its own disgrace: "I have received a blow, – and had not the spirit to resent it. I demanded satisfaction, and have accepted a declaration, in which the right to strike me again is asserted and confirmed."[82] The echoes of Patriot attacks on Walpole's former pliability with Spanish "depredations" were loud and clear. And Junius's usual haughty language of offended gentility – which he expected to be shared by his constituency of lower-middle-rank radicals – suggested the extent to which international relations had become entangled with domestic struggles over rank and social class. By speaking as an offended gentleman on behalf of the lower-middle ranks, that is, he implicitly empowered them to think themselves the equals of gentlemen and even the King. As Junius asserted in the guise of "Philo-Junius" in a subsequent letter, he made "no distinction between the real honour of the crown and the real interest of the people."[83]

From the early years of the Seven Years' War, with its beer-fueled spectacles of public patriotism, Johnson had been acutely discomforted by this effort among radicals to use international disputes as petrol to feed the flames of lower-middling-rank resentment and agitation. In his long and careful reply in defense of the administration's approach to the Falklands dispute, he insisted that the nation's "honour" had been safeguarded by the Spanish withdrawal. But he also insisted on the need to abstract this controversy from raw emotion and to consider, in a rational way, the problems of international law and custom that the crisis had raised. The confrontation had brought into dispute "the whole system of European empire" (10:350), for this system relied absolutely on certain acknowledged rules about when territory could be claimed:

> We have now for more than two centuries ruled large tracts of the American continent, by a claim which perhaps is valid only upon this consideration, that no power can produce a better; by the right of discovery and prior settlement. And by such titles almost all the dominions of the earth are holden . . . Should we allow this plea to be annulled, the whole fabrick of our empire shakes at the foundation. (10:368)

The Falklands dispute hence called into question the basis of Britain's own empire, which Johnson now clearly acknowledged to be a massive territorial entity rather than a metaphor for free trade on the sea. The Spanish claimed these islands because they adjoined a continent that, by papal mandate and long-term settlement, had been relinquished to Madrid's control; the English claimed that they may have first seen and named the islands in the 1590s, and that they were now the first to settle them. Who was right? Before the British let loose the dogs of war, the answer to this question should be settled: "The right of discovery indeed has already appeared to be probable, but the right which priority of settlement confers I know not whether we yet can establish" (10:359).

This problem of the "general system of empire" raised during the Falklands crisis continued to be pertinent with relation to America because Johnson considered the colonists to be "infringing the system of dominion" (10:433), and hence undermining "the peace of nations," by dictating to the mother-country the terms of obedience. According to Johnson, in short, the Americans were trying to change the rules that governed imperial possession all over the world. Late in his pamphlet, Johnson recalled that Great Britain itself was a conquered island, imagining a Cornish separatist inveighing against the illegal Saxon conquest of his nation. Such a diatribe, he indicated, would be more rationally justifiable than American declarations of independence. (The Cornish were indigenous Britons overwhelmed by a foreign invader, whereas the Americans had freely left Britain under certain agreed terms and conditions.) Yet who would not consider such fulminations addressed to the "Congress of Truro" as "written in jest, or written by a madman" (10:448)? Hence, if we consider *Taxation No*

Tyranny as a strong defense of the terms and nature of imperial authority – and there are good reasons to assert that this self-proclaimed inquiry into "how a colony is constituted" (10:419) should be regarded in precisely this way – then it was inspired by Johnson's broader concern to secure international peace by recognizing that imperial control was an irreversible reality founded on tacitly agreed principles and procedures. Indeed, there was no returning to "nature" anywhere, for all the world, including Great Britain and all of Europe, was "post-colonial."

The older Johnson certainly believed that empires could be better or worse in moral terms, affirming that mother-countries possessed duties as well as rights. This belief is most evident in his reactions to the financial and religious subjugation of the Irish. We have seen that Johnson upheld England's authority over Ireland, both in the Vinerian lectures he wrote with Sir Robert Chambers and by extension in his defense of British authority in North America. Nevertheless, Boswell's *Life of Johnson* provides consistent evidence that the severe financial disabilities suffered by Ireland aroused Johnson's legendary ire as much as any issue whatsoever. By one of his many close Irish friends, Rev. Dr. William Maxwell, Johnson is reported as exclaiming,

> Let the authority of the English government perish, rather than be maintained by iniquity. Better would it be to restrain the turbulence of the natives by the authority of the sword, and to make them amenable to law and justice by an effectual and vigorous police, than to grind them to powder by all manner of disabilities and incapacities. Better (said he,) to hang or drown people at once, than by an unrelenting persecution to beggar and starve them.[84]

In Johnson's mind, however, such clearly was not an injustice faced by the Americans. Indeed, one of the slow-burning fuses of resentment running through *Taxation No Tyranny* is that the Americans had done rather well for themselves in the colonies, accumulating riches and lands not usually available to political dissidents, transported convicts, and small tradesmen in England, and all with the military support of the mother-country. Indeed, like Burke, Johnson recognized that this was not really a question about "taxation" at all, but rather about the rights and relations of colonies and mother-nations. Johnson agreed with contemporaries like Josiah Tucker that Ireland had been ground down in unconscionable ways by English traders (with the support of government), but such was surely not the case in America.[85] The whole problem of America was not about money – Johnson agreed with the majority of the English intelligentsia that America was profitable financially only through strict control – but about "higher" issues of imperial competition, rights of representation, the nature of colonies, the rights and moral welfare of indigenous peoples, and so forth. Increasingly, as members of the intelligentsia and professions such as Johnson, Smith, Hume, and Tucker took over this whole debate from merchants like Sir Josiah Child and Joshua Gee, imperialism became as much a moral as a commercial question. Johnson's observation that "A merchant's desire is not of glory, but of gain; not of publick wealth, but of private emolument" (10:415) raised angry defenses of the merchant community in replies to *Taxation No Tyranny*. But it reflected a widely held view that the British Empire had to be founded on something more solid than the private profit of traders. Even Adam Smith, who wanted to withdraw the state from the regulation of trade, was *not* essentially "pro-merchant." In fact, he complained about "the meanness of mercantile prejudice," meaning that while merchants could not be restrained from pursuing individual profit, it was not they whose interests and values (as insisted by Joshua Gee) should be ensconced as the main principle of colonial government.[86]

In a developed modern empire, therefore, what should be the principles governing the mother-country's political relationship with its colonies? This was the problem that increasingly preoccupied Britons of the late eighteenth century, and they were increasingly prepared even to concede, to quote *Taxation No Tyranny* again, that "glory" was a better motive than "private emolument." Is not the "glory" of a conqueror better than the mean interest of a trader who cheated Indians, a tax-hating American rebel, a corrupt East India official in Bengal? Here we approach, of course, a certain self-righteous Victorian perspective on empire, and it is one that we might find worked out, in its fundamentals, in Johnson's early writing.

JOHNSON AND THE CULTURE OF IMPERIAL GLORY

As the six volumes of Gibbon's *Decline and Fall of the Roman Empire* rolled from the presses between 1776 and 1788, America slipped from England's grasp, the decline and fall it seemed of its own imperial grandeur. It appeared to many of this time that they were witnessing "The decline of National importance."[87] Nonetheless, we can see in retrospect that the "British Empire" was actually taking conceptual and physical form during just this era. The expression itself became a normal part of the cultural and political vocabulary, and the whole nation began to reflect seriously on the questions raised by Johnson in *Taxation No Tyranny* – "how a colony is constituted, what are the terms of migration as dictated by Nature, or settled by compact, and what social or political rights the man loses, or acquires, that leaves his country to establish himself in a distant plantation" (10:419). What then did Johnson come to think of the British Empire that first rose into view, like the rock of Quebec, in the decades following the Seven Years' War? The answer to this question is perhaps rather surprising, for there is evidence that Johnson increasingly abandoned the conventional pride in England's grandly "free" trading empire and began to lean towards an attitude that we usually associate with a later era. Whatever its mercantile roots, the British Empire could not be understood as primarily an *economic* empire, for it truly constituted a Providential responsibility, a mission of civilization and Christianity, and a glorious though arduous task to be embraced as essential part of England's national identity.

To understand the development of this mentality, we need to go back, even to the beginnings of Johnson's career. From a young age, in fact, Johnson had been drawn imaginatively towards the idea of imperial grandeur. The play he worked on throughout the 1730s, and which he brought with him to London in 1738, explored precisely that theme in searching detail. The story of *Irene* derives from a book that Johnson would portray in *Rambler* No. 122 as the greatest historical narrative in English history – Richard Knolles's *The Turkish History, from the Original of that Nation to the Growth of the Ottoman Empire* (1603). "None of our writers," wrote Johnson, " . . . justly contest the superiority of Knolles, who in his history of the Turks, has displayed all the excellencies that narrative can admit" (4:290). What aroused Johnson's enthusiasm for this book, which other readers, like Horace Walpole, found pedantic? In turning to that massive folio, we find that Knolles shared his culture's general fear and loathing of the Turks, whom he regards as embodying the "ardent and infinite Desire of Sovereignty," a lust for "the Monarchy of the whole World."[88] For Knolles, indeed, the Turks constituted the evil empire *par excellence*, a force of fanatic Islamic superstition and violence pushing at the borders of Christian Europe. Yet in its very vastness and malignant energy, the Ottoman Empire gains, in Knolles's account, a gloomy awesomeness, as suggested in the history's preface:

> at this present if you consider the beginning, progress and perpetual felicity of this the *Othaman* Empire, there is in this World nothing more admirable and strange; if the greatness and lustre thereof, nothing more magnificent and glorious; if the Power and Strength thereof, nothing more Dreadful and Dangerous: Which wondering at nothing but the Beauty of it self, and drunk with the pleasant Wine of perpetual felicity, holdeth all the rest of the World in Scorn, thundering out nothing still but Bloud and War with a full persuasion in time to Rule over all, prefixing unto it self no other limits than the uttermost bounds of the Earth, from the rising of the Sun unto the going down of the same.[89]

Here indeed it is easy to imagine Johnson's young mind racing as he, perhaps, turned the pages of Knolles's history in his father's bookshop. For the book presents itself as not just as a portrait of evil triumphant, decked out in all the exotic spoils of oriental despotism, but as a moral and Christian lesson concerning the vanity of human wishes, as must have appealed to Johnson's visceral religiosity. The Turks are painted at their haughty meridian, but "the uncertainty of Worldly things, which is subject to perpetual Change, cannot long stay in one State, but as the Sea with the Wind, so are they in like sort tossed up and down with the continual Surges of Waves of alternation and change." As "Time" had triumphed over "the greatest Monarchies that ever yet were upon the Earth," so the Turkish empire would in time come to an end as well.[90] This connection between empire and the mutability of human fortune would indeed become one of the great leitmotifs of eighteenth-century history, and particularly as Britain became aware of its imperial status. During the Seven Years' War, interestingly, there were new editions of Nicholas Tindal's translation of Demetrius Cantemir's *The History of the Growth and Decay of the Othman Empire* and Montesquieu's *Reflections on Causes of the Grandeur and Declension of the Romans.* And this genre would, of course, achieve its zenith with Gibbon's *Decline and Fall.*

From Knolles's *History* Johnson took the story of the conquest of Byzantine Constantinople in the fifteenth century by Mahomet II. In *Irene,* Mahomet and his regime exemplify that mixture of horror and awe in the presence of the Orient which characterizes Knolles's book, and which evidently continued to color Johnson's views on India even near the end of his life. On the one hand, Johnson portrays the Turkish conqueror as a proto-Gothic villain much given to the bleak joys of stretching out torture as long as possible. Indeed, there is something nefarious about all the Muslims in this play, even the Turks who conspire with the conquered Greeks against the Sultan. The discontented Cali Bassa strikes an alliance with the noble Christian Greek Demetrius, but plots to murder him after he ceases to be useful; the tempestuous Abdalla also secretly plans to murder his Greek ally, thirsting to wreak his lust on Aspasia, the betrothed of Demetrius. Yet this play is certainly also about the seductive attractions of worldly dominion, as illustrated especially by the eponymous Irene, the beautiful Greek woman who is seduced by the doting Mahomet to "Grasp at command, and tow'r in quest of empire" (III, viii, l. 114, 6:167). "Empire" is the ruling metaphor of the play, capturing the essence of a world that Johnson imagines incessantly in terms of power and submission, control and manipulation. Irene exercises her "empire" over the heart of Mahomet;

virtue struggles for "empire" over Irene's repentant mind late in the play; Demetrius and Aspasia plan to escape to "Tuscan courts" where "despotick Eloquence" will "resume / Her ancient empire o'er the yielding heart" (IV, i, ll. 116, 120–1, 6:177). There is no question of avoiding power in Johnson's play, only of ensuring that power is correctly placed.

This fact of Johnson's vision – which indeed seems basic to virtually everything that he ever wrote or said – suggests that the attitudes towards empire implied in *Irene* are more complicated than might first appear. In key ways *Irene* seems to brood over the possibility that there are "good" and "bad" empires, that favourite distinction of his contemporaries. The play opens with Demetrius and his friend Leontius reflecting on the downfall of their own Byzantine empire in ways that must have been meant to worry Johnson's English audience. Leontius wants to blame the military superiority of the Turks, but Demetrius blames the effeminizing influence of wealth and luxury: " 'Twas vice that shook our nerves, 'twas vice, Leontius" (I, i, l. 56, 6:115). The young Johnson imagined a good Christian empire falling pray to its own cancerous luxury and a Turkish lust for empire shared, given the political context, by the French and Spanish. Nevertheless, the play's most prominently virtuous character, Aspasia, makes clear that we are not to condemn empire itself, but the abuse of a power properly bestowed by Providence rather than actively sought. Accused by Irene of being deficient in imperial ambition, Aspasia answers indigently in one of the key speeches of the play:

> On me, should Providence, without a crime,
> The weighty charge of royalty confer,
> Call me to civilize the Russian wilds,
> Or bid soft science polish Briton's heroes:
> Soon shouldst thou see, how false they weak reproach.
> My bosom feels, enkindled from the sky,
> The lambent flames of mild benevolence,
> Untouch'd by fierce ambition's raging fires.
>
> (III, viii, 103–10, 6:166–7)

That "Briton's heroes" needed any polishing from Romans was at that time a controversial position, as Whig historians had generally preferred to read English history as the story of noble indigenes resisting tyrannical invaders, preserving the "ancient constitution" against all foreign dilution. But one implication of this play was not controversial: neither Aspasia, nor Johnson, meant to condemn empires so much as the barbarous tide of infidel imperialism. "Providence," as Aspasia indicates, might decide to bestow an empire on a particularly worthy people, a refrain that would continue to orient British imperialism a century later.

The imperialist implications of this play might indeed be expressed as follows: the love of empire might be inherently self-defeating and immoral, but it is an intensely "natural" and human drive, the most perfect expression of the self-destructive yet exquisitely human ambition to overreach the geographic boundaries of the imagination. Understood in this way, *The Vanity of Human Wishes* (1749) is one of the most forceful expressions of the nascent English imperial mentality of the mid-century. Right at the middle of this poem, the portrait of the Swedish conqueror Charles XII rehearses the story of the inevitable decline and fall of imperial ambition, the theme pronounced at the beginning of Knolles's *History of the Turks*: indeed, it is interesting that Charles, a kind of male Irene, met his downfall by forming an unholy alliance with the Ottoman Empire against the Russians. Nevertheless, Johnson encourages the reader to sense the glamor of Charles's questing imagination and conquering prowess. Endowed with "A frame of adamant, a soul of fire, / No dangers fright him, and no labours tire" (ll. 193–4, 6:101), Charles's fate to dwindle pathetically into the object of satiric reflection, a mere name "To point a moral, or adorn a tale" (l. 222, 6:102), has the curious effect of making Johnson's own role as tale-telling moralist the demeaning antithesis of Charles's splendidly imperial aspirations. That said, few works could be so well described as displaying "an imperial gaze" as *The Vanity of Human Wishes*, which opens with a globalizing "extensive view . . . from China to Peru" (ll. 1–2, 6:91) and seems to aspire to its own apotheosis as a sweeping compendium of humanity's thwarted dreams in all parts of the globe and choices of life. Above all, the poem indicates that the desire for conquest is as natural and "resistless" as any other of those painfully futile drives of human existence:

> The festal blazes, the triumphal show,
> The ravish'd standard, and the captive foe,
> The senate's thanks, the gazette's pompous tale,
> With force resistless o'er the brave prevail.
> Such bribes the rapid Greek o'er Asia whirled,
> For such the steady Romans shook the world;
> For such in distant lands the Britons shine,
> And stain with blood the Danube or the Rhine.
> (ll. 175–82, 6:101)

In alluding to the blood-stained waters of "the Danube or the Rhine," Johnson echoed his countrymen's widespread discouragement with the

Continental war that ended with the anti-climactic Treaty of Aix-la-Chapelle in 1748, and which seemed to show that the English warrior, like some red-tuniced aquatic animal, was out of his element on land. Yet Johnson could hardly have expected his readers to have resisted a sense of pride for Britons who "shine" alongside those other territorial warriors "the rapid Greek" and the "the steady Romans."

Undoubtedly, while fascinated from a young age with the spectacle of imperial ambition, Johnson seldom reflected on these sentiments without moral discomfort. A good example of this tension between sentiment and reason is *Adventurer* No. 99 (October 16, 1753), where Johnson reflects in his wonted way on the hunger of the imagination and the inevitable sag of human ambition. The opening example of "ideas of greatness" (2:430) is, significantly, again imperial conquest, and Johnson flips through a school-boy's picture-book of conquering heroes – Caesar, Cataline, Xerxes, Alexander, Swedish Charles, Peter the Great, and (strikingly) Columbus – to illustrate that "rapidity of imagination and vastness of design" that "raise such envy in their fellow mortals, that every eye watches for their fall" (2:430). There follows a paragraph disclaiming his sympathy for these "projectors." Yet one might well feel that Johnson has caught himself revealing an attraction to imperial conquest that, according to the official values of his time, he was not supposed to experience:

> I am far from intending to vindicate the sanguinary projects of heroes and conquerors, and would wish rather to diminish the reputation of their success, than the infamy of their miscarriages: for I cannot conceive, why he that has burnt cities, and wasted nations, and filled the world with horror and desolation, should be more kindly regarded by mankind, than he that died in the rudiments of wickedness; why he that accomplished mischief should be glorious, and he that only endeavoured it should be criminal: I would wish Caesar and Catiline, Xerxes and Alexander, Charles and Peter, huddled together in obscurity or detestation. (2: 433)

Ironically, Johnson's own essay itself contradicts this worthy intention of consigning imperialists to "obscurity or detestation," particularly when he goes on to preach a doctrine of courage and ambition: "Those who have attempted much, have seldom failed to perform more than those who never deviate from the customary roads of action" (2:435).

This and other works by Johnson are intriguing because they connect his own all-consuming capacity for work and accomplishment with imperial ambition. One recalls again his metaphor in his proposal for a new English dictionary, where, addressing Lord Chesterfield, he compares himself "to the soldiers of Caesar" landing on the shores of Britain. "I hope, that though

I should not complete the conquest," he proclaims, "I shall, at least, discover the coast, civilize part of the inhabitants, and make it easy for some other adventurer to proceed further, to reduce them wholly to subjection, and settle them under laws."[91] Particularly striking in this attraction to images and tales of imperial conquest is Johnson's lack of enthusiasm, especially after 1740, for the *commercial* motivation of empire. As we have remarked, he urged the necessity of war against the French in order to protect British trading interests; he also wrote an introduction to Richard Rolt's *A New Dictionary of Trade and Commerce* (1757), where he lauds England as "a maritime nation" and counsels that "The state of our colonies is always to be diligently surveyed."[92] While these statements are not insincere – Johnson, son of a tradesman, was no "enemy" to trade – they are the sort of things that one must say at the beginning of a *Dictionary of Trade and Commerce*. He admitted to Boswell that he had not even looked at Rolt's book: "I knew very well what such a Dictionary should be, and I wrote a Preface accordingly."[93] And where he does specifically address the quest for conquest in the name of commerce, his views tend to be strongly, even uniquely, negative.

If, for example, Johnson invites the reader to feel the glamour of Charles XII's questing ambition in *The Vanity of Human Wishes*, there is no such enticement – none of what W.J. Bate famously called "satire manqué," a final softening of Juvenal's unforgiving satire with a sigh of compassion[94] – when he comes to "the gen'ral massacre of gold," the "Wide-wasting pest! That rages unconfin'd" (ll. 22–3, 6:92). He opens the poem with the lust for gold because this drive apparently embodies human dreams at their most debased and groveling nadir, so that we rise *up* to the glorious empire-building of Charles XII, with his "soul of fire." These flashes of scorn for mercantile expansion had a fascinating impact on his reactions to the war against the French in the late 1750s, the most prolific period in Johnson's authorial career. In his *Observations on the Present State of Affairs* (May 1756), the second installment of his reflections on the looming war with France in the *Literary Magazine*, he made the provocatively unpatriotic observation that the French and English "charge each other with aspiring to universal monarchy" (10:188), unsettling enough for the majority who perceived this war as a historic confrontation between liberty-loving Englishmen and tyrannical Frenchmen. But Johnson went even further in commenting that the French entered the war with the military, and perhaps also the *moral*, advantage of placing the desire for wealth in second place behind love of empire in their designs on North America: "They have more martial than mercantile ambition, and seldom suffer their military schemes to be entangled with collateral projects of gain: they have no wish but for conquest, of which they justly consider riches as the consequence" (10:195). For the French that is, the primary object of conquest was martial glory rather than gold – and this statement should be read in the context of Johnson's very strong criticisms of the way English traders had "defrauded" the American natives, in contrast with the benign, Christian and paternalistic policy of the French.

While openly in support of the need to confront the French, that is, Johnson was needling his contemporaries about the motivation and purposes of this conflict. Even in the wake of magnificent victories in the autumn of 1759, Johnson's *The Bravery of the English Soldier* (1760) debunks the notion that English Peter was any more committed to "liberty" than the French Pierre he so successfully slaughtered:

> There are some, perhaps, who would imagine that every Englishman fights better than the subjects of absolute government, because he has more to defend. But what has the English more than the French soldier? Property they are both commonly without. Liberty is, to the lowest rank of every nation, little more than the choice of working or starving; and this choice is, I suppose, equally allowed in every country. (10:283)

But Johnson had stridden most boldly into controversy two years before, a time when English victory seemed still to hang in precarious balance. An important stone had been added to the advantage of the English side of this balance by the capture of the Cape Breton port of Louisbourg in July 1758. This was a recapture of considerable moral and military value, moral because it had been seized in 1745 by an American-led force but then ceded to the French in the disappointing Treaty of Aix-la-Chapelle, and military because Louisbourg had become the hub of the French naval expedition in the North Atlantic. From both a nationalistic and pragmatic viewpoint, therefore, this was certainly an appropriate occasion to march Louisbourg's captured *fleurs-de-lis* into St. Paul's Cathedral, as was done. Yet Johnson's lonely determination to rain on this parade struck some contemporaries, as it may still strike us now, as strangely bloody-minded. While acknowledging that the French "value [Louisbourg] as a port of security for their ships, as the place where their American forces may safely assemble" (10:270), he complained that the enemy flags proudly displayed to the public "were not torn down from the walls of Paris or Toulon" (2:273), and bore no comparison to Marlborough's victories against the French at Blenheim or even the more recent taking of Cherbourg, the port in northern France. When a correspondent to the *Universal Chronicle* replied scornfully that

Louisbourg was "of ten times more importance to the welfare of Great Britain" than either Paris or Toulon (10:274), for this was a war for the control of North American colonies, *not* an imperial siege of mainland France, Johnson stuck to his guns. "Nothing but strong drink," he answered, "will ever persuade [the public] to believe, that Louisbourg and Paris are to be named together" (10:276). Most striking about Johnson's response is his clear implication that the war in America, with all its surrounding atmosphere of patriotic fanfare, remained petty and debased compared with the great territorial battles of the past, such as the actual seizing of Paris by Edward III and Henry V. We might recall Johnson's remark many years before in "London" that he "Was early taught a Briton's right to prize, / And lisp the tale of Henry's victories" (ll. 119–20, 6:54).

During the very time that Johnson was writing these skeptical remarks for the *Universal Chronicle*, he troubled again over Louisbourg in *Idler* No. 22 (August 26, 1758), an essay that reinforces the impression that he was comparing the British war of trade unfavorably with the French war of imperial glory. In this essay, Johnson wonders how the fall of Louisbourg would be reported differently by future English and French historians. He begins by imagining the future English account, which is filled with patriotic bombast about the intrepidity of the Britons and the cowardice of the French enemies. The future French historian, on the contrary, is imagined remarking scornfully on the English lack of reverence for any goals but wealth and self-interest: "An Englishman has no ardour for honour, nor zeal for duty; he neither values glory nor loves his king" (2:65). "The only motive for their settlement is avarice," he observes, and for that reason the English are universally distrusted and hated by the Indians, for "A trader always makes war with the cruelty of a pirate" (2:64–5). The French, on the contrary, valued "virtue" and had drawn the Indians into alliance through "humanity." The fact that the French account comes second, ending the essay without further comment by Johnson, itself creates a strong impression about the direction of his sympathies. The essay implies that those who fight for higher values than lucre are capable of retaining their virtue and humanity even in the midst of defeat.

During these final years of the 1750s, that is, Johnson's stand was less against "empire" *tout court* than against the avarice and viciousness of those who colonized and conquered only for wealth. This sharpening antagonism to the unprincipled greed of "traders" in distant climes (connected no doubt with his anxieties about the increasing militancy of "traders" at home in the streets of London) is reflected again in his introduction to a collection of travel accounts, *The World Displayed*, published in that same pivotal year of England's imperial fortunes, 1759. This introduction expresses, with admirable passion and conviction, Johnson's outrage at the brutalization of West African people by the Portuguese who first landed in that region in the late fifteenth century. The Portuguese, like the Spanish, had long been the conventional targets of English recrimination for their violent oppression of indigenous populations. But in the midst of a war that raised serious concerns about Britain's own record with regard to North American peoples (if only for military reasons), Johnson's use of the term "European" implied an indiscriminate condemnation of colonial attitudes in general: "The Europeans have scarcely visited any coast, but to gratify avarice, and extend corruption; to arrogate dominion without right, and practice cruelty without incentive."[95] The primary culprit is not the drive for "universal monarchy," that old ideological whipping-boy of the English, but the more modern quest for riches: "When a fort is built, and a factory established, there remains no other care than to grow rich."[96] In short, this introduction draws from Johnson's profound and growing disillusionment with the old distinction between the innocent activities of merchants and traders and the supposedly evil and outdated quest for glory through conquest. Conquerors for glory (like Charles XII or even the modern French in America) seemed at least susceptible to notions of "honour" and responsibility towards those they conquered; mean-minded traders eyed colonized peoples merely as tools for profit.

These are the attitudes that Johnson carried with him into *Taxation No Tyranny*, where he observed that "A merchant's desire is not of glory, but of gain; not of publick wealth, but of private emolument" (10:415). Yet Johnson's intention here was not to undermine but to uphold direct imperial control of the American colonies by the British throne. Like contemporaries such as Smith and Burke, Johnson came to believe that only governments would consult "the general interest of the empire" (10:433), appealing as well to the higher motives of religion, virtue, and the welfare of colonized people. Too much of a realist to believe that empire could be merely undone, Johnson became convinced that the imperial dominion originally gained by the venturesome greed of traders could be turned towards moral and Christian ends. This theme is spelled out clearly in his introduction to *The World Displayed*. "There is reason to hope," he declared there, "that out of so much evil, good may sometimes be produced; and that the light of the gospel will at last illuminate the sands of Africa, and the deserts of America."[97] Most dismaying for Johnson was the failure of European powers to use their imperial influence as an instrument for the conversion of nations: "What may . . . raise higher the indignation of a

Christian mind, this purpose of propagating truth appears never to have been seriously pursued by any European nation; no means, whether lawful or unlawful, have been practised with diligence and perseverance for the conversion of savages."[98] During the same year, indeed, Johnson suggested that the Europeans had neglected this duty to enlighten and uplift "savages" to their own peril. In the wake of James Wolfe's stunning victory at Quebec in the autumn of 1759, a conquest of a seemingly impregnable rock that destroyed the morale and military fortunes of the French, Johnson responded in his now usual role as self-appointed fire-extinguisher of patriotic fervor. In *Idler* No. 81, he portrays "one of the petty chiefs of the inland" watching the British take charge of the Plains of Abraham, and remarking with vengeful anger that the Europeans had shared neither their knowledge nor their religion:

> Their power they have never exerted in our defence, and their arts they have studiously concealed from us. Their treaties are only to deceive, and their traffick only to defraud us. They have a written law among them, of which they boast as derived from him who made the earth and sea, and by which they profess to believe that man will be made happy when life shall foresake him. Why is not this law communicated to us? (2:253)

This speech conveys both a threat and a vision of something better – the threat that the British should gird themselves for conflict with the First Nations people they had defrauded and neglected, and the vision of a better colonial relationship, both morally and practically, where the Indians were allowed to reap the benefits of occupation by a civilized, Christian people. Whether or not we agree with Donald Greene that this outlook reveals Johnson's "far-sightedness and humanity," all the evidence of this period in Johnson's career does, indeed, indicate that he advocated the "ideal of a colonizing population conciliating and assimilating the aborigines instead of destroying and exploiting them."[99]

But does such an outlook make Johnson less or *more* of an "imperialist" in a modern sense? The British would indeed go about following Johnson's advice, diligently Christianizing and "civilizing" native Canadians right into the twentieth century – and leaving a bitter legacy of cultural devastation and law-suits. In fact, the crucial switch in Georgian attitudes exemplified by Johnson's ideological development, the transition from an economic justification of colonial policy to a belief in England's "Providential" duty as bringer of light and salvation, prefigures closely the so-called "New Imperialism" that reared up, in all its mustachioed vanity, under Disraeli's administration in the 1870s and 1880s. This was an ideology that had ceased to make any claim to an "economic" justification of colonization, as advocated by Gladstone's "free-trading" liberals, and instead insisted on England's God-given and moral duty to make the world English. According to the unrepentantly imperialist editor of the *Observer*, Edward Dicey, writing in September 1877, Britain had "substituted law and order for anarchy and oppression in Canada and Australia." It had "instilled the rudimentary ideas of individual liberty, equality before the law, and public duty" among "lower" people like the inhabitants of India. In performing these beneficent acts, the British had not pursued personal profit but instead, laden with the frankincense and myrrh of Western truth, had only followed "our star, fulfilled our destiny." In an age that was consciously rehabilitating the whole vision of ancient imperial expansion, it seemed no longer a sin to declare that England had been given "a mission like that of ancient Rome" to shoulder the white-man's burden in the wastelands of barbarity.[100]

To argue that the road between Johnson and this "imperialism" is not very twisty or indirect, but rather fairly direct and narrow, is not necessarily to imply that he is "guilty" of some original sin. That Johnson was a moralist who believed that he was *correcting* the evils of a commercially driven colonialism only proves, at worst, that the best intentions can pave many different roads to Hell. As we have already seen, moreover, Johnson's values could lead to conclusions that modern liberal values teach us to condemn in one form but commend in another. Hence, in *Taxation No Tyranny*, a tract that even his warmest advocates have found difficult to defend, Johnson skewered American hypocrisy on the evils of African slavery with a famous rapier-jab: "how is it that we hear the loudest yelps for liberty among the drivers of negroes?" (10:454). As I argued at length elsewhere, however, there is absolutely no inconsistency between Johnson's conservative views on American democracy and his opposition to slavery. In fact, *most* of the opponents to slavery in his time were not Whigs or radicals, who often had deep financial stakes in the slave-trade and plantations, but rather morally oriented Anglicans like Johnson, Granville Sharpe, Thomas Clarkson, James Ramsay, Beilby Porteus, William Paley, Edmund Burke, and John Wesley (whose pamphlet on America agrees with Johnson's point by point). The great parliamentary advocate against the slave-trade, William Wilberforce, was a devout Anglican and social conservative whose successful struggles to end British slavery would be rewarded with a grandiose state funeral at Westminster Abbey. And the British Empire would spend much of the nineteenth century policing the Atlantic for slave-ships, demonstrating to all the world that it had established a dominion of Christian morality rather than amoral profiteering.

On the other hand, it would clearly be wrong to describe British imperialism as a single current of ideas, undivided by ideological tributaries. We have already seen that Pitt and his Whig allies could defend the rights of Americans while chest-pounding about the rights of British expansion into the South Atlantic. Americans themselves, so jealous of their "natural rights," felt little compunction about continuing the European wash westward across North America, ultimately creating a whole film-genre, the Western, about just this imperial expansion. For the British, no issue so deeply divided and confused the problems of imperial responsibility as the "jewel in the crown," India. Stormy debate over the East India Company's administration of Bengal would erupt over the last decade of Johnson's life, involving, on opposed sides, some of his warmest acquaintances. His own indecision and confusion in the face of the imperial issues raised by this debate reflected wider and long-lasting divisions in English culture concerning its role and responsibility as the world's pre-eminent imperial power.

BURKE, INDIA AND THE RISE OF THE SECOND EMPIRE

The years between Johnson's death in 1784 and the ascension of Queen Victoria in 1837 were marked by vigorous imperial enterprise, particularly in the Far East. Fueled by the industrial revolution, Britain overwhelmed the collapsing Dutch Empire in South India, Ceylon, Indonesia, and the Cape of Good Hope. What historians call "the Second British Empire" (the First having ended with the loss of America) coalesced around a new and self-conscious ideology and administrative strategy, the lessons learned from the disasters of the eighteenth century. An old theme in Johnson's writing, the need to ensure that strong agriculture was not sacrificed to the lure of trade, seemed all the more pertinent to authors like Arthur Young and John Knox, who led a successful campaign to convince the state that the foundation of a strong empire must be agrarian.[101] Johnson's strong criticism of Europeans for not doing more to spread Christianity from "the sands of Africa" to "the deserts of America"[102] was more widely heeded, particularly during a time when Anglican evangelicalism had become orthodoxy in the halls of power, including the office of Pitt the Younger and the Colonial Office. The French Revolution had raised distrust against Methodist and dissenting proselytizing, which seemed linked to political radicalism, yet "a style of 'providentialist' Christian evangelicalism . . . became an important component of Britain's new imperialism."[103] Finally, the anti-mercantilist contention of Adam Smith, along with others like Hume and Burke, that merchant companies and their policies should not be allowed to direct colonial policy became widely accepted.[104] Increasingly, the powers and privileges of companies were curtailed, and a new official class of colonial bureaucrats was installed around the Empire, carefully separated from the lures of commerce and dangerous fraternizing with the native peoples.

This last policy was forged during the heated investigation and trial of Warren Hastings, a campaign spearheaded by that admired member of Johnson's literary circle, Edmund Burke. While Burke is rightly admired by some post-colonial scholars for his impassioned humanity and open-minded approach to ethnic difference, he might well be regarded as one important architect of the new colonial policy that would emerge after the loss of America.[105] His target was not the Empire itself, which he supported, even glorified, but rather a man and an administration who appeared in his eyes to embody all the evils of an unregulated, avaricious, and mercantilist system of colonial control. Though he bore the title of Governor, and later Governor-General, of Bengal, Hastings was essentially a creature of the East India Company. He inherited the legacy of Robert Clive, who had seized control of Bengal from the French in 1757, an event of literally world-shaping significance that passed almost unnoticed against the more visible backdrop of the North American conflict. Clive and his successors regarded their job not as providing good government for Indians but as securing maximum profits for the Company, a task that Hastings pursued with a ruthless efficiency worthy of Machiavelli. Hastings followed Clive's policy of forming alliances with amenable Nawabs against obstreperous Nawabs, throwing British money and troops against the Rohillas, and lavishing gifts on murderous megalomaniacs, while never forgetting that his primary personal objective was to fill his own spacious coat-pockets. As Indians starved, and the country plunged into virtually constant civil war, Hastings reneged on agreements and broke his own laws when they became inconvenient, took bribes, corrupted justice, and eliminated people, white and brown, who got in his way. The most notorious of these manipulations was the execution of a wealthy Calcutta businessman and prominent administrator named Maharaja Nandakumar, who had charged Hastings with taking bribes, some proffered by Nandakumar himself. Hastings spun the tables of justice, using his leverage with Bengal's chief justice and old school chum Sir Elijah Impey (the boss of Johnson's friend Robert Chambers), to bring charges of forgery against Nandakumar and members of the colonial governing council, including (Johnson's friends) Joseph and Francis Fowke, who had formed an opposition to Hastings's corruption. The Fowke brothers evaded the noose, but the Indian did not, and he swung as the result of a charge over which Hastings did not in fact have legal jurisdiction, as the alleged forgery concerned a fellow Indian rather than an East India Company employee.[106]

This at least is the version of the story accepted by Edmund Burke, as he pored, with rising horror, over the records of the East India Company's activities. "The Company's government," he told parliament in a speech in December 1783, "is not only full of abuse, but is one of the most corrupt and destructive tyrannies, that probably ever existed in the world."[107] Burke's concern was partly Hastings's contempt for the cultural traditions and institutions of the Indians whom he should have been protecting rather than oppressing: Hastings, thought Burke, had been utterly insensitive to traditional hierarchies and the venerated customs of the Indian people, running roughshod over their ruling class, desecrating their manners, disgracing their women. And here indeed we recognize that the older Burke, despite accusations by his critics of self-contradiction,[108] was coming to hear his political calling. He had defended America's right to self-determination within the Empire not because he believed in the "rights of man," whose legibility he denied, but because he believed that the descendants of Puritans and dissidents, separated from England by 3,000 miles of ocean for over a century, had woven a fabric of cultural outlooks that had to be respected. Signaling the crystalized imperial consciousness of Britain, he urged that any "extensive Empire" ultimately confronted the same reality, comparing the America situation, daringly, with the discrepancies faced by the Ottoman Empire: "The Turk cannot govern Aegypt, and Arabia, and Curdistan, as he governs Thrace."[109] The French Revolution repelled Burke for entirely comparable reasons, for here, he thought, was a brutal attempt to colonize the traditional customs and institutions of a culture with the offspring of abstracted Enlightenment brains, a usurpation that impelled him towards an even clearer conception of England as *itself* a distinctive culture like America or India.

In all these views, Burke sounds like an *avant la lettre* proponent of postcolonial diversity. Yet he was strangely wrong about Warren Hastings's failure to account for the cultural difference between Britain and India. In fact, Hastings believed he understood Indians very well: he was the first Governor to speak Hindi, and he cultivated an enthusiastic orientalism that appears to have enthralled his friend Johnson. But Hastings believed that the Indian soul was compelled towards murder, riot, and devastation. In his trial, he appealed repeatedly to his need to behave like a despot in a nation that respected only despots, to hit hard against people who respected only force. And here we must transfer our thoughts back to the attitudes of that aging veteran of England's early empire, Samuel Johnson, for Johnson liked and admired Hastings very much.

Johnson had met Hastings in the late 1760s as a member of the Robert Chambers circle at Oxford, which also included Robert Vansittart, brother to Henry Vansittart, Governor of Bengal from 1761 to 1764. In a letter written in March 1774 to Hastings, who had recently taken up the post of Governor, Johnson began by acknowledging that "I have had but little personal knowledge of you." Yet this little knowledge had earned Hastings a long and affectionate letter in which Johnson declared that he was "very desirous of your regard."[110] What was it that drew Johnson's affections so strongly to Hastings? Thomas M. Curley rightly points to Johnson's enthusiasm for oriental studies.[111] He had been on the point of accompanying his friend Joseph Fowke to India in the 1750s, and may even have considered going there with Henry Vansittart in 1766 – a trip that Johnson fortunately avoided, as Vansittart's ship was lost in the passage. When Johnson first met Hastings, he must have cut a romantic figure – a man of notorious charm and mental deftness still tanned, perhaps, from fourteen years in India, where he had flown on an adventurous whim at age eighteen. In his letter to Hastings in 1774, Johnson dwells hungrily on his desire for more knowledge of India:

> I have no questions to ask, not that I want curiosity after either the ancient or present state of regions in which have been seen all the power and splendour of wide-extended empire . . . I can only wish for information, and hope that a Mind comprehensive like yours will find leisure amidst the cares of your important station to enquire into many subjects of which the European world either thinks not at all, or thinks with deficient intelligence and uncertain conjecture.[112]

This letter suggests that his boyish fascination with oriental exotica had not dissipated: "the power and splendour of wide-extended empire," an allusion to both the Greek and Muslim invasions of India, still captured the imagination of this ardent enthusiast for Knolles's *History of the Turks*. Some of that imperial splendor, it would seem, had also attached itself in Johnson's mind to Warren Hastings. Increased knowledge, the expansion of intellectual horizons, had long been for Johnson one of the gifts bestowed on humanity by even bad empires. In his introduction to the *World Displayed*, Johnson acknowledged that "Much knowledge had been acquired" by the cruel and avaricious marauding of the Portuguese in Africa.[113] Stephen

Greenblatt is surely correct to remind us that intellectual awe has been one of the great motivations to modern empire.[114] But there are also many indications that Hastings and the older Johnson basically saw eye-to-eye on issues of imperial government, and that Johnson had only limited sympathy, if any at all, for Burke's prosecution of the Bengalese Governor-General.

Much of the evidence for Johnson's leanings on this issue comes from a source that we cannot trust implicitly, Boswell's *Life of Johnson*. The *Life* was published in 1791, right in the middle of the seven-year long trial of Hastings, and Boswell leaves no doubt about the direction of his own sympathies. Hastings's correspondence with Johnson is introduced by Boswell with all the feudal enthusiasm that once reduced Jean-Jacques Rousseau to fits of laughter: "While my friend is thus contemplated in the splendour derived from his last and perhaps most admirable work, I introduce him with peculiar propriety as the correspondent of WARREN HASTINGS! a man whose regard reflects dignity even upon JOHNSON; a man [Hastings], the extent of whose abilities was equal to that of his power."[115] Not surprisingly, then, Boswell loses no occasion to show Johnson weighing in on the side of Hastings during the first parliamentary indictment of the Governor-General's administration in 1783. He records Johnson saying,

> I am clear that the best plan for the government of India is a despotick governour; for if he be a good man, it is evidently the best government; and supposing him to be a bad man, it is better to have one plunderer than many. A governour whose power is checked, lets others plunder, that he himself may be allowed to plunder; but if despotick, he sees that the more he lets others plunder, the less there will be for himself, so he restrains them; and though he himself plunders, the country is the gainer, compared with being plundered by numbers.[116]

If we are to believe Boswell's account, Johnson exceeded even his Scottish friend in his excuses for colonial "plunder." In 1775, when Johnson's views must have been formed principally by those of Hastings and Robert Chambers (who had recently left to take his lucrative post as Sir Elijah Impey's subordinate in the Bengal court), Johnson is presented by Boswell as defending the right of judges in India to engage in trade: "why (he urged) should not Judges get riches, as well as those who deserve them less?" Boswell interjects that it would be better to give the Anglo-Indian judges better salaries, but Johnson will have none of this: "No Judge, Sir, can give his whole attention to his office; and it is very proper that he should employ what time he has to himself, for his own advantage, in the most profitable manner."[117] The reasoning here is consistent with Johnson's apparent complacency concerning fortune-making in India throughout the

Life. According to Boswell, he later regretted not accompanying an unnamed acquaintance, whom we now know to be Joseph Fowke, to India in what was explicitly a mission to repair a shattered fortune.[118] The incident creates the impression that the perennially impoverished Johnson was himself thinking about a form of gold rather more widely exchangeable than knowledge.

Outside the *Life*, Johnson's writing conveys a more complex but essentially consistent impression. When Chambers was whisked off by patronage to the courts of Bengal, Johnson wrote with open-hearted generosity to Boswell, "Chambers is going a Judge, with six thousand a year, to Bengal."[119] He also wrote to Chambers from the Isle of Skye, lecturing him paternally against the "opportunities of profitable wickedness," but also hoping to "see you come [back] both with fortune encreased, and Virtue grown more resolute by contest."[120] The Scottish provenance of this letter is interesting. We have noted Johnson's controversial tendency to view Highlanders as a people beneficially "conquered," even by the dissenting-devil Cromwell, who destroyed episcopal churches but taught the Scots to make shoes. That a benignly English conquest of a later time, the spreading of an Anglican-purpled commerce over backward regions, could be repeated in India seems suggested by an interesting detail – that Warren Hastings was one of the select recipients of pre-publication copies of *Journey to the Western Islands of Scotland* (1775) in December 1774. Johnson's accompanying letter to Hastings makes obvious that he regarded himself as enacting, in a less adventuresome way, a trip to the British imperial hinterlands: "I have lately visited a region less remote and less illustrious than India, which afforded some occasions for speculation. What occurred to me, I have put into the volume of which I beg your acceptance."[121] Johnson and Hastings were apparently meant to find common ground in "knowledge," as hoarded by both the determined defender of the English "conquest" in Scotland and the self-styled despot of backward India.

It might be objected that Johnson was simply not fully abreast of the supposed abuses of power occurring far away in Hastings's Bengal. As early as 1776, however, Johnson had received the full brunt of the charges against Hastings by one of his main accusers, Joseph Fowke, the same man that Johnson had once thought of accompanying to India. Having been prosecuted by Hastings for his support of Nandakumar, Fowke sent Johnson a package of papers relating to this affair and Hastings's alleged maladministration of Bengal, hoping that his influential friend would serve as an English conduit for publicizing his case. Johnson certainly looked at the papers; he wrote sympathetically to Joseph's brother Francis that he "seems to have been much injured by the prosecution and the Sentence." But he would not act as Fowke's ally, pleading that "I live in a reciprocation of civility with Mr. Hastings, and therefore cannot properly diffuse a narrative intended to bring upon him the censure of the publick."[122] Indeed, so far was Johnson from scrutinizing his own ties with Hastings – who, we should recall, had been accused of murder – that we find him writing warmly again to the Governor-General in January 1781, apologizing for interrupting the "affairs in which your great Office engages you," commending Hastings for promoting "Learning," and recommending to his good influence a young friend named John Hoole.[123] That he did not write back to the beleaguered Joseph Fowke apparently grated on Johnson's conscience: he finally wrote to Fowke in April 1783, apologizing that "To your former letters I made no answer, because I had none to make." He also made some sympathetic noises with regard to the now long-deceased Nandakumar: "Of the death of the unfortunate man, I believe Europe thinks as you think."[124] But that Johnson did not think exactly as Europe thought seems indicated by the fact that only three days before he had sent a set of the *Lives of the English Poets* to Warren Hastings, along with sets intended for Fowke and Chambers.[125]

For Johnson's inertness at this major cross-roads in England imperial ideology, many excuses can be offered. Friendship certainly trumped ideology in most of Johnson's personal relations, particularly as his health deteriorated in later years. "You and I . . . have more urgent cares, than for the East India Company," he wrote to John Taylor in November 1783, "We are old and unhealthy."[126] And there are also signs that the charges against Hastings had upset and confused him. In the same letter to Taylor, he acknowledged that "corruption and oppression are in India at an enormous height." But he seemed to struggle against the suggestion that Hastings or the East India Company was truly to blame. "It has never appeared," he urged, that this corruption was "promoted by the Directors, who, I believe seem themselves defrauded, while the country is plundred [*sic*]." His anger at Fox's ministry for "laying violent hands on the East India Company" reflects his anti-Whig predilections, and his long personal connection with this Company, which he long before promised Chambers to defend.[127] Moreover, Johnson's reasoning about the administration of India does seem to follow a coherent line. We find him again a political realist. Nandakumar's execution, he told Fowke, "was past prevention."[128] Attempts to control an administration so far away, he suggested to Taylor, would certainly fail: "I doubt whether the Government . . . will do more than give another evidence of its own imbecility."[129]

Yet this political realism was also the backbone of Hastings's own defense against the charges he faced. In short, it is difficult to avoid the final impression that he and Hastings shared more than a keenness for orientalism, and that they also spoke to each other in the same political language of strong government, the need for law and order, especially in the face of "savage" lawlessness. The need for strong government seems, indeed, to be a leitmotif in Johnson's ruminations on India. While we know virtually nothing about Johnson's private, but obviously cordial, conversations with Hastings, he writes to him like a brother-in-arms about "the agitations of an unsettled government, and the struggles of a feeble ministry."[130]

Hence, when Burke sent Johnson a copy of his sonorous philippic against Hastings, delivered in parliament on December 1, 1783, Johnson's reaction was dryly unenthusiastic. "Mr. Burke has just sent me his speech upon the affairs of India," he wrote to Taylor on January 24, 1784, "a volume of above one hundred pages closely printed. I will look into it." In the context of this letter, his willingness to sympathize with Burke's campaign against Hastings does not seem likely. He had just finished railing to Taylor that "the King and parliament have lost even titular dominion of America, and the real power of Government every where else." "Thus Empires are broken down," he went on, "when the profits of administration are so great, that ambition is satisfied with obtaining them, and he that aspires to greatness needs do nothing more than talk himself into importance. He has then all the power which danger and conquest used formerly to give."[131] Such an inactive talker was not Hastings, who, whatever else we think of him, was certainly committed to "danger and conquest."

We are left with the vision of Johnson deteriorating physically as the debate about Britain's role in India swirled around him, voices impinging on his darkening world from all sides. Even as late as September 13, 1784, shortly before his last birthday, Johnson was writing to John Hoole that he had received a mysterious "Packet" from Warren Hastings.[132] As we have seen, Johnson's responses to the Hastings affair were distracted by ill-health and his benevolent desire to act as a loyal buffer between mutual friends. Nonetheless, we need to ask whether his views during this time concerning Britain's contentious authority of India, the vaunted "jewel in the crown" of the Empire, were consistent with the ideological developments we have traced in eighteenth-century British culture and in his own attitudes.

Initially surprising about his reflections on India is that he seems to side with the merchants, the makers of money, whose largely self-interested sway over Bengal was precisely what Burke and his allies despised. Johnson, as we have seen, had himself cast opprobrium on the avarice of British merchants and traders during the Seven Years' War and later in his fulminations on America. But Hastings, while a Company man, was in no recognizable way a vulgar "cit": he was an undeniably erudite, sophisticated, and (in his Machiavellian way) able despot with a profound interest in the country he nonetheless ruled with an iron fist. He combined two virtues that might be regarded as the latent and explicit themes of Johnson's evolving reactions to the evolving Empire. The latent theme is a flair for the exotic, a taste for adventure, and a romantic perception that conquest represented a great expression of the human imagination, vain and hungry, superior to the mere groveling for profit. The explicit theme is *Realpolitik*, the irritable conviction that, at least in our imperfect world, it takes many broken eggs to make a worthwhile omelette, an omelette that could cover the world with a placenta of civilization and Christianity.

If Queen Victoria had reflected on Johnson's colonial attitudes (as she almost certainly did in its more obvious representations in Boswell's *Life* and the political tracts) would she have felt challenged, attacked, or confirmed? She almost certainly felt confirmed, on many levels. This is not to deny at all the relevance of Burke's campaign against Hastings, for Burke succeeded in giving the British Empire a kind of conscience. Hastings was exonerated, and his press in the nineteenth century, as in James Mill's multivolume *The History of British India* (1817–58), was generally sympathetic to his supposedly special challenges in controlling a "backward" population so far from Albion's civilized bosom.[133] Yet the so-called "New Imperialism" that emerged after Disraeli's election in 1874 rested heavily on the justification that English rule abroad was founded not on profit but on a purely moral duty to spread order and prosperity around the globe. In the words of a recent Indian writer on colonialism, authors from Carlyle to Ruskin to Froude believed that "colonial expansion" was "a task worthier of England than materialism and mammon-worship."[134] Kipling's famous phrase "the White Man's Burden" may well have made Burke cringe; unlike most politicians, and unlike many Victorians, Burke was not being merely rhetorical when he proclaimed that "I set out with a perfect distrust of my own abilities,"[135] a self-doubt that gave him the scope to believe that his role, and England's role, was not to save the planet. Nevertheless, Burke's demand for ethical high-mindedness in the colonies, while violated perhaps by every colonial official, became the reigning panacea of British imperial reign.

We have seen that Johnson certainly believed in the moral role of empire – an exigency made even more piquant by his discomfort, shared by many Britons, with the vulgarly avaricious motives that first engendered colonial expansion. We have also seen that he seems to have been particularly devoted to the evangelizing motive of imperialism: for all his reputation as a high-churchman, Johnson had a deeply evangelical impulse, as proven not only by his friendship with Evangelicals like John Wesley and Hannah More (who also defended Hastings), but also by the proselytizing tone of his sermons.[136] Johnson's leanings towards a more Christian trajectory for the empire were endorsed when, as Homi K. Bhabha observed, "the East India Company reintroduced a 'pious clause' into its charter for 1813."[137] But Johnson was in fact all the more obviously than Burke a precursor of "Victorian" imperial attitudes in his faith that what England exported to its colonial appendages was not merely a form of culture, but culture itself. Johnson, as we have seen, sympathized with the anger of North American indigenes as they struggled in the teeth of unscrupulous English traders in the first years of the Seven Years' War. Yet *Adventurer* No. 67 (June 26, 1753), a celebration of London's commercial vigor, casts icy water over the whole cult of the noble savage's wholesomely natural penury. "This picture of a savage life," he wrote, "if it shews how much individuals may perform, shews likewise how much society is to be desired. Though the perseverance and address of the Indian excite our admiration, they nevertheless cannot procure him the conveniences which are enjoyed by the vagrant beggar of a civilized country" (2:388). From his back-patting observations on the advent of Highland manufacture to his diatribes against Rousseau and Monboddo in Boswell's *Life*, the mature Johnson appears to have believed that, however much modernism had diluted a spirit of loyalty that warmed his heart, civilization develops along a linear course from barbaric chieftains to laws and institutions exemplified by modern English society. It is certainly true that Johnson deployed no systematic structure of racial difference – hardly surprising since "race" itself was the invention of Swedish, French, and German scientists whose influence on even the most knowledgeable Britons remained minimal until the early nineteenth century.[138] Yet even in the Victorian era, the Enlightenment ideals of progress and civilization, of the English way being the common route for *all* humanity, remained strongly entrenched in imperial ideology. It was an ideology that the Victorians were increasingly willing to enforce with the butt of a gun and the heel of a boot, which explains their general tendency to side with Hastings against Burke.

In connection with the ideology and practice of empire, therefore, as in connection with the other fields we have examined, Johnson embodies one prominent pattern in the evolving fabric of English culture. To call him "imperialist" would be wrong to the extent that "empire," both physically and ideologically, was only gradually emerging in its modern form during his lifetime, becoming a fully fledged element in the nation's political mindset only during the last twenty or so years of his life. He nonetheless played a role, even a forceful one, in the evolution of the imperial mentality: he wrote some of his most vigorous prose on imperial questions and he was friends with many of the principal actors in the physical and ideological creation of the British Empire. Much the same may be said of all the other dimensions of eighteenth-century English experience and consciousness that we have discussed. C.A. Bayly rightly notes, for instance, that "British nationalism and imperialism reached maturity at the same moment."[139] And social class, the middle-class woman, modern political parties, and the idea of the public were all products of precisely the same era. To what extent, then, do these developments constitute a single network? Do they represent mutually dependent developments and, if so, what is the nature of their connections? In stepping back for a final survey of the ample Johnsonian corpus, we will try to make some sense of the whole, as embodied by this major participant in the social, literary, and political life of Georgian England.

Conclusion

From the "Age of Johnson," England was born with features that are still recognizably modern, however the nation may now be maturing gradually into a post-modern, post-colonial, even post-British state. It was a nation with a highly subtle and contentious, yet politically decisive, structure of social class. Its female citizens, at least of the middle and upper classes, were playing a more vigorous and public role in English life, though their sphere of influence generally lay outside the parliament, the courts, and the clergy. It had a political party system divided between Tories and Whigs, later Liberals, along philosophical, social, and economic rather than dynastic lines. It had a vigorously engaged public, and a widening though volatile system of political representation. In contrast with the Swiftian bleakness of the early century, it had a proud sense of itself as a modern, powerful, and progressive nation joined politically and culturally in a common mission with the Celtic peripheries. And overseas it had a self-acknowledged empire that, while it has been relaxed into a "commonwealth" today, has left a global imprint of English-speaking people, English political institutions, English literature – including the international reputation of Samuel Johnson. The point of this book has certainly not been that Johnson made all this possible. Nevertheless, in the dialectic between material and cultural forces, we can hardly do better than Johnson as a personality, as a *text*, for understanding how modern England came about.

In writing this book, here were the questions that I wanted to answer: What were the forces that impelled all these historical developments towards the making of modern England? Are these changes interrelated and, if so, what is the nature of these relations? At the end of this process, I would identify the following motors of change, as mirrored by the life and circumstances of Johnson. In material terms, Johnson rose from obscurity to fame in a nation that was responding culturally and politically to the considerable enrichment of its upper and middle ranks. In the words of John Rule, "According to most historians, somewhere in the eighteenth century there began a transformation of production so that output per head was to rise to new heights and the economy revealed a new ability to sustain this growth throughout successive generations. England not only got richer, it stayed richer."[1] But the cultural impact of this enrichment (*pace* a certain naive economics and sociology) was not contentment and stability. First, while it is easy to see in retrospect that England was moving towards greater wealth, confidence, and power, this evolution did not seem so obvious to people of that time. The pace of economic development was gradual and uneven: according to most economic historians, growth remained slow and even stagnant until about 1740, when it began to accelerate. Even afterwards, some people benefitted more than others, a decline in agricultural production between 1740 and 1780 pushing down real incomes among working people, many of whom had been deprived of self-subsistence by enclosure. Only after 1780 did England's economic power really begin to make its muscle obvious at home and abroad. In the interim, there was no exact correspondence between what Marxists used to call the economic "base" and the ideological "superstructure" – for "ideology" was being conjured from incomplete and often inaccurate impressions of what was happening. Hence the intense mood of nervousness, anxiety, and vulnerability that seems to permeate so much eighteenth-century discourse. Indeed, one of the ironies that I have suggested at several points in this book is the following: England was driven to become the most powerful nation of the nineteenth-century world because, 100 years before, it seemed to most as so far behind its competitors and so fraught with economic, political, and social problems. The economic energy of English society was, that is, being powered by its deep cultural anxiety.

Johnson's role in this process was as an influential creator of the ideological impressions that, in turn, would inform the way people behaved in every facet of English life, from the relations of rank and gender, to the political activities behind nationhood and the emerging Empire. He was simultaneously a product and producer of social realties. On the one hand, he himself had emerged from a particular, and oddly emblematic, socio-economic background. Boswell's *Life of Johnson* appealed so strongly to Victorians, and to so many English-speaking people subsequently, because its portrait of a man struggling forcefully against economic and personal challenges, retaining both his virtue and his proud independence of mind, seemed to affirm England's national journey and its splendid results. Not only did Johnson's rise from desperate obscurity to fame apparently chart his nation's course during the same years, but he seemed to prove that England was indeed a Mecca of liberty and equality, a perception that became the ideological foundation of national pride and imperial expansion over the next century. With regard to his own writing, I remember being struck, as a student two decades ago, when I heard Walter Jackson Bate refer in a presentation to Johnson's essays as "tonic," as a kind calming medicine against anxiety. Tonics are needed by people with anxieties to qualm. While Johnson did register the angst of his time, as perhaps particularly in his caustic political pamphlets and in his numerous portraits of men and women who struggle to interpret the changing society around them, he had the talent of making specific cultural reactions and crises seem like the eternal verities of human life. In an age searching for the assurance of order in confusing and anxious times, Johnson did, indeed, deliver that philosophical "tonic."

This was a role he played most crucially during the 1750s, which, more than any other decade, might be most closely connected with his name. Between *The Vanity of Human Wishes* (1749) and the *Idler* (1758–60), Johnson produced his *Dictionary of the English Language* (1755), almost all of his periodical writing, and a significant chunk of his political writing, prefaces, and other occasional pieces. He began the decade as a self-acknowledged "drudge," but he ended the decade in line for a state pension. The 1750s was also a decade of historic change for the English nation, which began the mid-century deeply worried about the "effeminacy" created by a surge of economic growth, but ended up, nine years later, ringing the bells of victory, the pungent incense of imperial glory floating in the air. Let us reflect on this decade as a smaller image of the joint evolution of Johnson and of England.[2]

As it was the *Dictionary* that really established Johnson's "greatness," it is worth reminding ourselves about its significance as a *national* project, a work that contemporaries regarded in patriotic terms as squaring the score with the French, envied as they were as a cultural as well as political power. That Johnson wrote this work without the backing of a national academy made it all the more typically "English." And despite complaints about Johnson's Jacobite tendencies among Whig antagonists, the dictionary in fact possessed a political and ideological breadth that impressed even a radical like Joseph Priestley, the sprinkling of acidly "Tory" definitions revealing Johnson's particularly blue stripe of Englishness. In general, as I have maintained, Johnson's work of the 1750s leans in no obviously partisan direction. The *Rambler*, *Adventurer*, and *Idler* show Whigs and Tories, merchants and gentlemen, men and women, facing common human problems, usually in the setting of the English capital, which becomes almost a microcosm of human life. Johnson himself liked to imagine London as the whole "world," telling Boswell that "by seeing London, I have seen as much of life as the world can shew."[3] Even his political writings of the 1750s, most for the *Literary Magazine* in the early years of the Seven Years' War, avoid obvious partisanship, denouncing the government's handling of the Byng affair, but remaining generally supportive of Pitt's direction of the war-effort. One recalls here Johnson's early involvement in the Broad-bottom campaign against divisive party politics, and his own participation in the creation of an updated "revolution" Toryism devoted to national interest rather than self-interest.

If Johnson's orientation evolves during this decade, the change can be best described as driven by the concerns of social class rather than party. Johnson became alarmed by the increasing aggression of the lower-middle ranks, who indeed found a vehicle for their own domestic political goals in the patriotic fervor stirred up by the conflict with the French. Early in the decade, in the *Rambler* and the *Adventurer*, Johnson had quite arguably given the people of the City of London an unfamiliar level of moral respectability. In sharp contrast with the more effete West End periodicals of the same time, such as the *World* and the *Connoisseur*, the *Rambler* showed middle-rank commercial people, men and women, struggling with the same human problems as their contemporaries in the precincts of St. James, and usually with superior dignity. No wonder that this work remained such a fixture on middle-class bookshelves for more than a century. In the *Idler*, at the end of the decade, we find quite a different sociological attitude. Whereas the *Rambler* tended to portray people from the nobility, gentry, and upper merchant ranks, the characters of the *Idler* – Ned Drugget, Tim Wainscot, Betty Broom, Dick Minim, Sam Softly – are largely servants, apprentices, shop-keepers and small tradesmen. They are, that is, members of the lower-middle ranks that had during these very years seized a more visible and vocal role in the patriotic fervor stirred by the war with France. Johnson sharply criticized the ignorance and impudence of these people in his reflections on the prosecution of Admiral Byng, on the celebrations after the capture of Louisbourg, and on other events in the early years of this war. And what scholars have noted as the light and comic tone of the *Idler*, as compared to the graver *Rambler*, reflects the sardonic and distrustful perspective on the lower-middle orders also found in his political writing of the same time. His guffaws in response to social impropriety become increasingly loud when dim-witted "pedlars" try to appropriate the privileges of "gentlemen." And so the stage was set for Johnson's anti-radical and socially conservative writing of the 1760s and 1770s.

What the 1750s epitomize, therefore, is Johnson's development from a moderate advocate for social change – change that had indeed made possible his own rise to respectability – to a writer preoccupied with the need to control and structure that change. This balance characterizes his mature attitudes on virtually every question that we have considered. While he was by no means "anti-trade" (his own roots in the trading classes help to make sense of his affection for the brewer Henry Thrale), he shared the concern of many contemporaries to preserve reverence for morality, Christianity, knowledge, and the other castles of traditional ideology. Johnson never ceased to be, as he began, a man devoted to imparting the ideal erudition of "gentlemen." His tremendous value for literary art to the end of his life reflects this concern to "polish" his contemporaries, for "taste" (a term he liked less than authors influenced by sensationist philosophy) played an important role in giving the middle class its social and political identity, its unwritten right to hold itself aloof from the lower and lower-middle orders. Similarly, Johnson promoted, with even unusual energy, the right of middle-rank women to learning. But he seems to have upheld an unapologetic "double standard" when it came to women's sexual freedom compared with men, or their right to enter the clergy and other professions.

There is no reason to doubt that this poise of balance and control was valued by most men, and most women. For Johnson, so widely associated with images of weighty "common-sense" and impatience with transient "cant," functioned like a literary anchor in the rocking seas of a changing society. It was this weightiness that has made him seem a "typical" Englishman even to the present day. With regard to English nationhood, indeed, his distrust of a clamorous and irrational "patriotism," his tendency to value progress ballasted with a respect for history, his sense of England as a bastion of civilization and wise order, do seem descriptive of a broadly and typically *English* sense of cultural identity.

That I have situated Johnson quite firmly in a contemporary English context, insisting that here is where we must seek the significance of his life and work, runs against the grain of much recent scholarship that has dwelled instead on his roots in Continental forms of Renaissance humanism, or has given priority to testing his views ethically against the standards of modern (and largely North American) liberal-democratic values. My argument has not been, however, that Johnson merely shadowed forth some kind of all-embracing English *Zeitgeist.* Every era, and every nation, are woven from many multi-hued and often clashing trends and vectors: I have rummaged in this book for metaphors of unfolding tapestries, shifting constellations, many-tongued watersheds and so forth to express just this combination of diversity and unity. Johnson differed from many in his age in his tendency to stress individual motivation over public spirit, and in his promotion of public education as the ideal vehicle of social cohesion, as opposed to inflaming calls for patriotic solidarity. Hence, Johnson upheld freedom of the press, bouncing energetically into the ring of political debate, while resisting the assumption that wrestling in the public sphere was fundamentally structured or rational. He would not be caught up by popular jeremiads against the supposedly effeminizing effects of luxury, insisting instead that the craving for "excess" was an essentially healthy impulse of civilization when directed towards the right ends, such as the pursuit of knowledge. Knowledge, indeed, constitutes a major lynch-pin in his whole social and political outlook. For example, he valued knowledge as a means not just to discipline women's behavior (the running theme in conduct books) but more important to fulfil women as human beings. We rightly call this attitude admirable. But Johnson could also remain insensitive, arguably, to the colonial administration of Warren Hastings, because Hastings was a man he valued for his "knowledge." On the other hand, Johnson was ahead of his time in his realistic emphasis on the need to build traditions of international law, and in his capacity to view the world situation from the point of view of England's powerful competitors on the Continent.

In the face of such complex and discontinuous attitudes, our assessments of Johnson must be similarly complex and nuanced. He is not the bombastic Tory of a certain mythology, nor the proto-liberal campaigner of another. His life and work show that history is both distant and close. Distant because he swam, like we all do, in the ocean of his own contemporary culture; close because the waters of his cultural ocean still drive powerful currents through our own. Johnson is both typical and singular in the making of modern England. Typical because the material forces that shaped his life and our modernity still pour up and down the middle of England like the M1; singular because by reading this vastly read author, the English found *not* just a mirror image of themselves. Rather, they were drawn towards a portrait with the singular, even mythic, power of representing themselves in a compelling way. Johnson, that is, both was made by and helped to make England. For those of us still swept along by the powerful swell of eighteenth-century English culture, that, finally, is why he still needs to be read.

Notes

INTRODUCTION

1. Psychoanalytic studies of Johnson were popularized in particular by the highly influential work of W.J. Bate, particularly *The Achievement of Samuel Johnson* (New York: Oxford University Press, 1955) and his biography, *Samuel Johnson* (New York: Harcourt, Brace, Jovanovich; London: Macmillan, 1977). Deconstructions of Johnson include Steven Lynn, *Samuel Johnson after Deconstruction: Rhetoric and "The Rambler"* (Carbondale: Southern Illinois University Press, 1992) and Martin Wechselblatt, *Bad Behavior: Samuel Johnson and Modern Cultural Authority* (Lewisburg: Bucknell University Press, 1998). There has been a strong recent trend towards tracing Johnson's thought to Renaissance humanism, led especially by Robert DeMaria in *The Life of Samuel Johnson: A Critical Biography* (Oxford: Blackwell, 1993). Seventeenth-century homiletics is the main background cited by scholars of Johnson's religious thought, including Maurice J. Quinlan, *Samuel Johnson: A Layman's Religion* (Madison: University of Wisconsin Press, 1964) and James Gray, *Johnson's Sermons: A Study* (Oxford: Clarendon Press, 1972). A work more interested in developments in religious thought in Johnson's time is Chester Chapin's *The Religious Thought of Samuel Johnson* (Ann Arbor: University of Michigan Press, 1968). On the classical background to Johnson's thought, see especially Adam Potkay, *The Passion for Happiness: Samuel Johnson and David Hume* (Ithaca and London: Cornell University Press, 2000).
2. Studies that fall generally into the category of cultural history include Alvin Kernan, *Print Technology, Letters and Samuel Johnson* (Princeton: Princeton University Press, 1987); Katherine Kremmerer, *"A Neutral Being between the Sexes": Samuel Johnson's Sexual Politics* (Lewisburg: Bucknell University Press, 1998), and Kevin Hart, *Samuel Johnson and the Culture of Property* (Cambridge: Cambridge University Press, 2000). For shorter pieces that exemplify the recent tendency to present Johnson's thought as amenable to modern liberalism, much in the tradition of Donald J. Greene, see Clement Hawes, "Johnson and Imperialism," in Greg Clingham (ed.), *The Cambridge Companion to Samuel Johnson* (Cambridge: Cambridge University Press, 1997), 114–26; Clement Hawes, "Johnson's Cosmopolitan Nationalism," in Philip Smallwood (ed.), *Johnson Re-Visioned: Looking Before and After* (Lewisburg: Bucknell University Press;

London: Associated University Presses, 2001), 37–63; James G. Basker, "Samuel Johnson and the African-American Reader," *The New Rambler* (1994–5): 47–57, and "Multicultural Perspectives: Johnson, Race, and Gender," in Smallwood (ed.), *Johnson Re-Visioned*, 64–79.

3. See, e.g., John Ruskin, *Praeterita*, in *Works*, 39 vols., ed. E.T. Cook and Alexander Wedderburn (London: George Allen; New York: Longman, Green and Co., 1903–12), 35–225; Thomas Seccombe, *The Age of Johnson (1749–1798)* (London: George Bell and Sons, 1900), 2; George Saintsbury, *A Short History of English Literature* (London: Macmillan and Co., 1925), 615.
4. See Donald J. Greene, *The Politics of Samuel Johnson* (New Haven: Yale University Press, 1960).
5. The *OED* cites Croker's use of "conservative" to describe the government of Sir Robert Peel as the first example of this word employed in a specifically political sense. It derived originally from the language of science.
6. Christopher Hollis, *Dr. Johnson* (New York: Henry Holt and Company, 1929), 6. See also Sir Walter Scott's short *Memoir of Samuel Johnson*, in *The Miscellaneous Prose Works*, 6 vols. (Edinburgh, 1827), 283–96; Angus Wilson, *The Strange Ride of Rudyard Kipling* (London: Secker and Warburg, 1977), 289.
7. The case for Johnson as a Non-juror and Jacobite was made most notoriously by J.C.D. Clark in *Samuel Johnson: Literature, Religion and English Cultural Politics from the Restoration to Romanticism* (Cambridge: Cambridge University Press, 1994). Clark's book generated a furious debate in Johnson criticism, as represented in volume 7 of *The Age of Johnson* (1996), which is partly devoted to this issue.
8. Sir Leslie Stephen, *English Literature and Society in the Eighteenth Century* (London: Duckworth, 1903), 194.
9. Thomas Carlyle, *On Heroes, Hero-Worship, and the Heroic in History* (1841), ed. Michael K. Goldberg, Joel J. Brattin, and Mark Engel (Berkeley, Los Angeles, and Oxford: University of California Press, 1993), 153.
10. Seccombe, *The Age of Johnson*, 2.
11. Walter Raleigh, *Six Essays on Johnson* (Oxford: Clarendon Press, 1910), 32. See also John Bailey, *Dr. Johnson and his Circle* (London: Williams and Norgate, 1913), 9–10, 16.
12. See M.J. Daunton, *Progress and Poverty: An Economic and Social History of Britain 1700–1850* (Oxford: University Press, 1995), 135.
13. See Peter Borsay, *The English Urban Renaissance: Culture and Society in the Provincial Town 1660–1770* (Oxford: Clarendon Press, 1989), and Peter Borsay (ed.), *The Eighteenth-Century Town: A Reader in English Urban History* (London and New York: Longman, 1990). On London's population growth, see also E.A. Wrigley, "A Simple Model of London's Importance in Changing English Society and Economy, 1650–1750," *Past and Present* 37 (1967): 44–70.
14. W.A. Cole, "Factors in Demand 1700–80," in Roderick Floud and Donald McCloskey (eds.), *The Economic History of Britain Since 1700*, 2 vols. (Cambridge: Cambridge University Press, 1981), 1:39.

15. See in particular Neil McKendrick, "The Consumer Revolution of Eighteenth-Century England," in Neil McKendrick, John Brewer and J.H. Plumb, *The Birth of a Consumer Society: the Commercialization of Eighteenth-Century England* (Bloomington: Indiana University Press, 1982), 9–33. It is not agreed, however, that economic statistics bear out the thesis that middle-rank people were spending appreciably more on luxuries in the eighteenth century. See Carole Shammas, "Changes in English and Anglo-American Consumption from 1550 to 1800," in John Brewer and Roy Porter, *Consumption and the World of Goods* (London and New York: Routledge, 1993), 177–205 and Lorna Wetherill, "The Meaning of Consumer Behavior in Late Seventeenth- and Early Eighteenth-Century England," in *Consumption and the World of Goods*, 206–27. This issue will be taken up in chapters 1 and 2, below.
16. See Cole, "Factors in Demand," 57–8; Daunton, *Progress and Poverty*, 235–9.
17. Raymond Williams, *The Long Revolution* (London: Chatto & Windus, 1961).
18. On this question, Greene made Johnson sound like Margaret Thatcher: "Johnson was far too much of a Protestant, as well as a rationalist, to think of society as anything but a collection of individuals" (*Politics*, 250).
19. For more detailed discussion of Johnson's conservatism, see Nicholas Hudson, *Samuel Johnson and Eighteenth-Century Thought* (Oxford: Clarendon Press, 1988), and "The Nature of Johnson's Conservatism," *ELH* 64 (1997): 925–43.
20. James Boswell, *Life of Johnson* (1791), ed. G.B. Hill, rev. L.F. Powell, 6 vols. (Oxford: Clarendon Press, 1934–50), 2:348.
21. All parenthetical references in the text are to *The Yale Edition of the Works of Samuel Johnson*, gen. eds. A.T. Hazen and J.H. Middendorf, 14 vols. (New Haven and London: Yale University Press, 1958–).
22. See, eg. Paul Langford, *A Polite and Commercial People: England 1727–1783* (Oxford: Clarendon Press, 1989), 3–4, and *Englishness Identified* (Oxford: Clarendon Press, 2000), 77; Linda Colley, *Britons: Forging the Nation* (New Haven and London: Yale University Press, 1992), 55–100.
23. See DeMaria, *The Life of Samuel Johnson.*

CHAPTER 1

1. See E.P. Thompson, "Eighteenth-Century English Society: Class Struggle without Class?", *Social History* 3 (1978): 133–65.
2. On the late emergence of "class" as a valid category, see E.P. Thompson, *The Making of the English Working Class* (New York: Vintage Books, 1966), 11–12; Harold J. Perkin, *The Origins of Modern English Society, 1780–1880* (London: Routledge and Kegan Paul; Toronto: University of Toronto Press, 1969), 176–217; W.A. Speck, *Stability and Strife: England 1714–1760* (London: Edward Arnold, 1977), 31–2; R. J. Morris, *Class and Class Consciousness in the Industrial Revolution, 1780–1850* (London and Basingstoke: Macmillan, 1979), 12–20; J.C.D. Clark, *Revolution and Rebellion: State and Society in England in the*

Seventeenth and Eighteenth Centuries (Cambridge: Cambridge University Press, 1986), 43; Penelope J. Corfield, "Class by Name and Number in Eighteenth-Century Britain," in Penelope J. Corfield (ed.), *Language, History and Class* (Oxford: Basil Blackwell, 1991), 101–30; John Richetti, "Class Struggle without Class: Novelists and Magistrates," *The Eighteenth Century: Theory and Interpretation* 32 (1991–2): 203–18; Dror Wahrman, *Imagining the Middle Class: The Political Representation of Class in Britain c. 1780–1840* (Cambridge: Cambridge University Press, 1995); David Cannadine, *Class in Britain* (New Haven and London: Yale University Press, 1998), 24–56. For a defense of a traditionally Marxist division of "classes" in the eighteenth century, see R.S. Neale, *Class in English History* (Oxford: Basil Blackwell, 1981), 68–99.

3. Peter Laslett, *The World We Have Lost* (2nd edn, London: Methuen, 1971), 24. See also G.E. Mingay, *English Landed Society in the Eighteenth Century* (London: Routledge and Kegan Paul; Toronto: University of Toronto Press, 1963), 278–9.
4. The claim that Johnson upheld a "natural" order as assured by the Chain of Being is made by Cannadine, *Class in Britain*, 26 and 32. According to Corfield, similarly, Johnson believed that rank is "beyond human intervention" ("Class by Name and Number," 104).
5. In his much-used work on eighteenth-century social history, *English Society in the Eighteenth Century* (rev. edn, London: Penguin, 1990), Roy Porter regularly cited Johnson in his conventional persona as "an idolator of rank" (64). Similarly, John Barrell presents Johnson as an authoritarian supporter of the upper classes in *English Literature in History, 1730–80: An Equal, Wide Survey* (London: Hutchinson, 1983), 144–61. These views are generally corroborated by John Cannon in *Samuel Johnson and the Politics of Hanoverian England* (Oxford: Clarendon Press, 1994), 155–90.
6. For literary scholars, the belief that the middle class "rose" in the eighteenth century is best known from Ian Watt's *The Rise of the Novel* (Berkeley and Los Angeles: University of California Press, 1956), 35–59, where this supposed phenomenon is directly linked with another supposed "rise," that of the novel. Nevertheless, as Lawrence Stone maintains in "Social Mobility in England, 1500–1700," *Past and Present* 33 (1966): 16–55, there was relatively little movement in eighteenth-century society from the lower orders into the middle ranks, or from the middle ranks into the nobility or upper gentry: that is, the middle class, while sharing the enrichment of English society at its top layers, remained quite static rather than "rising." These observations are confirmed by Geoffrey Holmes in *Augustan England: Professions, State and Society* (London: George Allen & Unwin, 1982), 11–18.
7. My approach differs from that of previous historians of the middling orders such as Peter Earle and Margaret R. Hunt because I avoid any equation between this broad stratum and the commercial classes. As I will argue, indeed, a primary obstacle to the formation of a politically unified middle class was bridging the divergent interests of the commercial class, the untitled gentry and the professionals, a grouping that perhaps still remains a tenuous marriage of political convenience. This alliance, moreover, was even designed to keep a

large segment of the "middling sort" – the lower ranks of the artisan and shop-keeping communities – safely distant from political and social influence. For the contrary assumption that the "middling orders" can be regarded as largely equivalent with commercial and trading interests and manners, see Peter Earle, *The Making of the English Middle Class* (Berkeley and Los Angeles: University of California Press, 1989), 3–16; Margaret R. Hunt, *The Middling Sort: Commerce, Gender, and the Family in England 1680–1780* (Berkeley, Los Angeles, and London: University of California Press, 1996), 15.

8. Guy Miège, *The Present State of Great Britain and Ireland* (1707; 8th edn, revised, London, 1738), 165.
9. Henry Fielding, *Enquiry into the Causes of the Late Increase of Robbers* (1752), ed. Malvin R. Zirker (Oxford: Clarendon Press, 1988), 67.
10. Fielding, *Enquiry*, 69–70.
11. *Ibid.*, 84.
12. *Ibid.*, 77.
13. On the changing idea of the "gentleman," particularly as a background to the formation of a middle class, see Earle, *Making of the English Middle Class*, 3–6.
14. William Higford, *Institutions or Advice to his Grandson* (London, 1658), sig. A5v.
15. Richard Brathwait, *The English Gentleman* (London, 1630), 112.
16. Henry Peachum, *The Compleat Gentleman* (London, 1634), 11.
17. *Ibid.*, 12–13.
18. See John Evelyn, *A Character of England* (1659), in *The Writings of John Evelyn*, ed. Guy de la Bédoyère (Woodbridge: The Boydell Press, 1995), 85–6.
19. See William Ramsey, *The Gentleman's Companion* (London, 1672), 121–2 and 117.
20. William Darrell, *A Gentleman Instructed* (London, 1704), 155.
21. Daniel Defoe, *The Compleat Gentleman* (n.d.), ed. Karl D. Bülbring (London: David Nutt, 1890), 4.
22. *Ibid.*, 4.
23. *Ibid.*, 20.
24. *Ibid.*, 4.
25. As argued by Earle, *Making of the English Middle Class*, 5–12.
26. See Edmund Bolton, *The Cities great Concern, in this Case or Question of Honour and Arms, whether Apprenticeship Extinguisheth Gentry* (London, 1674).
27. Miège, *Present State of Great Britain and Ireland*, 170.
28. See John Constable, *The Conversation of Gentlemen* (London, 1738), 199–200.
29. See *ibid.*, 250–1.
30. Daniel Defoe comments on this phenomenon in his defence of the dignity of trade in *The Complete English Tradesman*, 2 vols. (1725–27; 2nd edn, London, 1727; facs. repr. New York: Augustus M. Kelley, 1969), 1:301–3. See also Porter, *English Society*, 51–2.
31. See Josiah Tucker, *A Brief Essay on the Advantages and Disadvantages which respectively attend France and Great Britain with regard to Trade* (1749; 2nd edn, London, 1750), 26–7. See also the very similar comparison of England and

France in John Brown's *Estimate of the Manners and Principles of the Times* (London, 1757), 205–7.

32. Tucker, *A Brief Essay*, 34–5.
33. See Josiah Tucker, *An Humble Address and Earnest Appeal to those Respectable Personages in Great Britain and Ireland who, by their Great Permanent Interest in Landed Property, their Elevated Rank and Enlarged Views, are the Ablest to Judge, and the Fittest to Decide, whether a Connection with, or a Separation from the Continental Colonies of America, be most for the National Advantage, and the Lasting Benefit of those Kingdoms* (Gloucester, 1775).
34. On the rise of non-classical schools in the eighteenth century, see Nicholas Hans, *New Trends in Education in the Eighteenth Century* (London: Routledge & Kegan Paul, 1951); Richard S. Thompson, "English and English Education in the Eighteenth Century," *Studies in Voltaire and the Eighteenth Century* 167 (1977): 65–79, and *Classics or Charity? The Dilemma of the 18th-Century Grammar School* (Manchester: Manchester University Press, 1971); Rosemary O'Day, *Education and Society 1500–1800* (London and New York: Longman, 1982), 196–216. Also on the declining reputation of grammar schools, especially in connection with their reputation for bad morals, see Hunt, *The Middling Sort*, 62–4.
35. James Barclay, *A Treatise of Education: or, an Easy Method of Acquiring Language, and Introducing Children to the Knowledge of History, Geography, Mythology, Antiquities &c.* (Edinburgh, 1743), 60. See similar statements in Francis Brokesby, *Of Education with Respect to Grammar Schools* (London, 1701), 3 and *passim*; Joseph Priestley, *An Essay on a Course of Liberal Education* (London, 1765), 22–4; Adam Smith, *An Inquiry into the Nature and Causes of the Wealth of Nations* (1776), ed. R.H. Campbell, A.S. Skinner, and E.B. Todd, 2 vols. (Oxford: Clarendon Press, 1976), bk. 5, chap. 1, part 3, art. 2, 784–7.
36. See Paul J. Korshin, "Johnson, the Essay, and *The Rambler*," in Clingham (ed.), *Cambridge Companion to Samuel Johnson*, 51–66.
37. Cannon, *Samuel Johnson and the Politics of Hanoverian England*, 170.
38. *Johnsonian Gleanings*, (ed.), Aleyn Lyell Reade, 10 vols. (New York: Octogon Books, 1968), 6:44; James Boswell, *Life of Johnson* (1791), ed. G.B. Hill, rev. L.F. Powell, 6 vols. (Oxford: Clarendon Press, 1934–50), 1:97.
39. Compare Johnson's "Scheme" in the *Life* with John Clarke's proposals in *An Essay upon the Education of Youth* (1720; 3rd edn, London, 1740). Clarke's emphasis was on translation and imitation of the best classical authors rather than mere memorization of grammatical rules, as had been generally the case previously. As Clarke wrote, "the Propriety of the *Latin* Tongue is no other way to be attain'd, than by a careful attentive Perusal of the best Authors, and Writing and Speaking as much as possible in Imitation of them" (35–6). In his "Scheme," Johnson wrote similarly, "The greatest and most necessary task still remains, to attain a habit of expression, without which knowledge is of little use. This . . . can only be acquired by a daily imitation of the best and correctest authours" (Boswell, *Life*, 1:100). In addition, Johnson began his course with Clarke's edition of the *Colloquies* by Corderius, a text designed to

lead students gently and naturally into Latin. Elsewhere, I have argued that Johnson and John Clarke also shared very similar views on the foundation of moral obligation, the subject of some excellent and unrelated works by Clarke. See Hudson, *Samuel Johnson and Eighteenth-Century Thought*, 77–85.

40. Boswell, *Life*, 2:171. See also Elphinston's poem *Education, in Four Books* (London, 1763), which sets out his goal to provide an education with reduced emphasis on the classics, and appropriate for both gentlemen and men of commerce.
41. See William Cooke, *The Life of Samuel Johnson, L.L.D.* (1785), in O. M. Brack, Jr. and Robert E. Kelley (eds.), *The Early Biographies of Samuel Johnson* (Iowa City: University of Iowa Press, 1974), 91; Anon., *The Life of Samuel Johnson*, in Brack and Kelley (eds.), *Early Biographies*, 226.
42. On the relatively high status of the book-seller compared with other trades, see for example R. Campbell, *The Complete London Tradesman* (1725–7; London, 1747; facs. repr. New York: Augustus M. Kelley, 1969), 128–34.
43. Boswell, *Life*, 1:34.
44. *Ibid.*, 2:332, n.
45. Samuel Johnson, *Works*, 12 vols. (Oxford: Talboys and Wheeler; London: W. Pickering, 1825), 6:435. This edition hereafter referred to as *Works* (1825).
46. See Sir John Hawkins, *The Life of Samuel Johnson* (London, 1787), 123. Like Boswell, Hawkins abhorred the democratization of "gentleman," though he himself was of modest origins. See *Life of Samuel Johnson*, 261.
47. On "symbolic capital" and its place in Bourdieu's sociology, see Pierre Bourdieu, *Language and Symbolic Power*, ed. John B. Thompson, trans. Gino Raymond and Matthew Adamson (Cambridge, MA: Harvard University Press, 1991), introduction, 14–15; *The Field of Cultural Production: Essays on Art and Literature*, ed. Randal Johnson (Cambridge: Polity Press, 1993), introduction, 1–25. Debate concerning the importance of "emulation" in the eighteenth century has continued since Thorstein Veblen's *The Theory of the Leisure Class: An Economic Study of Institutions* (London: George Allen & Unwin, 1925). Not all historians have accepted Veblen's suggestion that consumer behavior is driven by emulation of the upper orders. "There is no evidence," writes Lorna Wetherill, "that most people of the middle-rank wanted to be like the gentry" ("The Meaning of Consumer Behaviour," in Brewer and Porter (eds.), *Consumption and the World of Goods*, 208). In fact, there *is* considerable evidence that the gentry set the standards for "fashionable" or "polite" society, as we have now seen. Nevertheless, Wetherill and others are right to insist that the identity of the middle ranks cannot be reduced simply to imitation of the gentry. For further discussion, see the essays by Colin Campbell, Roy Porter, Jan de Vries, Joyce Appleby, Carole Shammas and Amanda Vickery in *Consumption and the World of Goods*.
48. *Works* (1825), 6:56.
49. Boswell, *Life*, 2:153.
50. James Boswell, *London Journal, 1762–1763*, ed. Frederick A. Pottle (New York, London, and Toronto: McGraw-Hill, 1950), 320.

51. For further discussion of the importance of "reverence" in Johnson's thought, see my "The Nature of Johnson's Conservatism," *ELH* 64 (1997): 925–6.
52. Vicesimus Knox, *Liberal Education: or, a Treatise on the Methods of Acquiring Useful and Polite Learning* (1781; 5th edn, London: 1783), 5. On Knox's formulations of middle-class identity, see Wahrman, *Imagining the Middle Class*, 46–52.
53. See James Beattie, "On the Utility of Classical Learning," in *Essays on the Nature and Utility of Truth* (Edinburgh, 1776; facs. repr. New York: Garland, 1971); Joseph Cornish, *An Attempt to Display the Importance of Classical Learning* (London, 1783); Percival Stockdale, *An Examination of the Important Question, Whether Education at a Great School or by Private Tuition is Preferable* (London, 1782).
54. Stockdale, *An Examination of the Important Question*, 22–3.
55. See Hans, *New Trends in Education in the Eighteenth Century*, 212; M.L. Clarke, *Classical Education in Britain 1500–1900* (Cambridge: Cambridge University Press, 1959), 70.
56. William Stevenson, *Remarks on the Very Inferior Utility of Classical Learning* (Manchester, 1796), 35.
57. Thomas Gisborne, *An Enquiry into the Duties of Men in the Higher and Middle Classes in Great Britain,* 2 vols. (1794; 2nd edn, London, 1795), 2:235
58. Edmund Burke, *Reflections on the Revolution in France*, in *The Writings and Speeches of Edmund Burke*, vol. 6., ed. L.G. Mitchell (Oxford: Clarendon Press, 1989), 85, 94.
59. Edmund Burke, *An Appeal from the Old to the New Whigs* (1791), in *Works*, 12 vols. (Boston: Little, Brown and Company, 1899), 4:190.
60. Burke, *Reflections*, in *Writings and Speeches*, 8:126.
61. *Ibid.*, 8:187.
62. Sir Frederic Morton Eden, *The State of the Poor: or, an History of the Labouring Classes in England,* 3 vols. (London, 1797), 1:2.
63. Thomas Malthus, *An Essay on the Principle of Population, as it Affects the Future Improvement of Society* (London, 1798), 207.
64. See Wahrman, *Imagining the Middle Class*, 214–20, 298–327; F.M.L. Thompson, *The Rise of Respectable Society: A Social History of Victorian Britain 1830–1900* (London: Fontana, 1988), 16–17; Anna Clark, *Struggle for the Breeches: Gender and the Making of the British Working Class* (Berkeley, Los Angeles, and London: University of California Press), 7.
65. Sarah Stickney Ellis, *The Women of England, Their Social Duties and Domestic Habits* (1839; 21st edn, London and Paris: 1847), 343–4.
66. Barrell, *English Literature in History 1730–80*, 148.
67. See especially Olivia Smith, *The Politics of Language 1791–1819* (Oxford: Clarendon Press, 1984), 14–17; Tony Crowley, *Language in History: Theories and Texts* (London and New York: Routledge, 1996), 94. Besides my "Johnson's *Dictionary* and the Politics of 'Standard English,'" *Yearbook of English Studies* 28 (1998): 77–93, which is partly reprinted in what follows, other studies relevant to the social-political orientation of the *Dictionary* include Robert

DeMaria, "The Politics of Johnson's *Dictionary*," *PMLA* 104 (1989): 64–74; Allen Reddick, *The Making of Johnson's Dictionary 1746–1773* (2nd edn, Cambridge: Cambridge University Press, 1996), 141–69; Anne McDermott, "Johnson's *Dictionary* and the Canon: Authors and Authority," *Yearbook of English Studies* 28 (1998): 44–65.

68. Preface to the *Dictionary*, in *Works* (1825), 5:27.
69. *Ibid.*, 5:23.
70. *Ibid.*, 5:44–5.
71. *The Gentleman's Magazine* 25 (April 1755): 147. Similarly, in a review of the *Dictionary* in *Journal Britannique* 17 (juillet et août 1755), Matthew Maty, a friend of Chesterfield, criticized Johnson's definitions of technical terms as "trop étendues."
72. Boswell, *Life*, 3:196–7.
73. In the *Dictionary*, Johnson correctly traced *cant* to the Latin *cantus*, referring to the sing-song solicitation used by beggars even into the eighteenth century.
74. Preface to the *Dictionary*, in *Works* (1825), 5:46–7.
75. *Ibid.*, 5:24–5. The term "illiterate writers" perhaps derives from Dryden, who is contrasting ordinary writers with those "learn'd in schools." See Robert DeMaria, *Johnson's "Dictionary" and the Language of Learning* (Chapel Hill and London: University of North Carolina, 1986), 54. It seems important to keep in mind that Johnson was not referring here to the lower classes, since they remained predominantly "illiterate" in the modern sense of not knowing how to read and write.
76. The case for Johnson's belief in the stabilizing power of print is made by Kernan in *Print Technology, Letters and Samuel Johnson*, 181–205.
77. On literacy rates in the eighteenth century, see especially Roger S. Schofield, "Dimensions of Illiteracy in England 1750–1850," in Harvey J. Graff (ed.), *Literacy and Social Development in the West: A Reader* (Cambridge: Cambridge University Press, 1981), 201–13; David Vincent, *Literacy and Popular Culture in England 1750–1914* (Cambridge: Cambridge University Press, 1989). As these studies confirm, the rate of literacy remained fairly steady throughout the eighteenth century at about fifty percent, though there were important structural changes: tradesmen and women were more likely to be literate, but the great mass of the poor, particularly the rural poor, remained overwhelmingly unlettered.
78. Boswell, *Life*, 3:136.
79. Preface to the *Dictionary*, in *Works* (1825), 5:47.
80. *Ibid.*, 5:48.
81. See Nicholas Hudson, "Samuel Johnson, Urban Culture and the Geography of Post-Fire London," *Studies in English Literature* 42.3 (2002): 577–600.
82. *The World* No. 101 (December 5, 1754): 604–7.
83. *Ibid.*, 607.
84. Johnson's offended reaction to these papers was no doubt prompted in part by Chesterfield's oblique references to his inelegance and isolation from polite circles: "I had a greater opinion of his impartiality and severity as a judge, than of his gallantry as a fine gentleman" (*The World* No. 605).

85. Samuel Johnson, *Letters*, ed. Bruce Redford, 5 vols. (Princeton: Princeton University Press, 1992–4), 1:95. Hereafter referred to as *Letters*.
86. Letter to Daniel Wray, May 23, 1755, Oxford, Bodleian Library, Bodleian MS 1012, 208.
87. Cited in James L. Clifford, *Dictionary Johnson* (New York: McGraw-Hill, 1979), 52. On the Marchioness Grey, the granddaughter of Henry Grey, Duke of Kent, see Sylvia Harcstark Myers, *The Blue-Stocking Circle: Women, Friendship and the Life of Mind in Eighteenth-Century England* (Oxford: Clarendon Press, 1990), 65–8. See also James Thomson Callender's attack on Johnson's polysyllabic terms in *A Critical Review of the Works of Johnson* (Edinburgh, 1783; repr. New York and London: Garland Press, 1974), 27–8, and the extended attack on his diction and style in Archibald Campbell's *Lexiphanes*, discussed below. Johnson's penchant for "inkhorn" terms reveals the influence of seventeenth-century science and philosophy on his thought, as shown by W.K. Wimsatt, Jr., in *Philosophical Words: A Study of the Style and Meaning in the "Rambler" and "Dictionary" of Samuel Johnson* (New Haven: Yale University Press, 1948), 1–49.
88. While often associated recently with Renaissance humanism, the attack on Johnson as a vulgar and inelegant word-monger echoes the old complaint of the humanists against the scholastics. The humanists, it is useful to recall, were dominated by teachers of rhetoric to the wealthy. See Anthony Grafton and Lisa Jardine, *From Humanism to the Humanities* (London: Duckworth, 1986), 1–28; Erika Rummel, *The Humanist-Scholastic Debate in the Renaissance and Reformation* (Cambridge, MA, and London: Harvard University Press, 1995), 58–9.
89. Archibald Campbell, *Lexiphanes: A Dialogue* (London, 1767), 3.
90. *Ibid.*, xix–xx, xxii.
91. See Callender, *Critical Review of Johnson*, 29. In a sympathetic biography written in 1785, William Shaw noted the prejudice faced by authors like Johnson whose relied on writing for their livelihood, and were not "independent of the Booksellers" in the manner of "gentleman-authors" like Hume, whose gracefully written compositions of the 1750s, according to Shaw, overshadowed Johnson's achievements of the same decade. See Brack and Kelley, eds., *Early Biographies*, 163.
92. James Greenwood, *An Essay towards a Practical English Grammar* (London, 1711), 36. For statements articulating a similar standard in later works, see John Fell, *An Essay towards an English Grammar* (London, 1784; repr. Menston: Scolar Press, 1967), 1; John Walker, *A Critical Pronouncing Dictionary* (London, 1791), vii.
93. Quintilian, *Institutio Oratorio*, trans. H.E. Butler, Loeb Classical Library, 4 vols. (Cambridge, MA: Harvard University Press; London: Heinemann, 1930), 1:113, 132–3.
94. See G.A. Padley, *Grammatical Theory in Western Europe 1500–1700*, 2 vols. (Cambridge: Cambridge University Press, 1985–8), 2:5–153; Angelo Mazzocco, *Linguistic Theories in Dante and the Humanists* (Leiden, New York, and Cologne: E.J Brill, 1993), 13–23 and *passim.*

95. See Claude Favre de Vaugelas, *Remarques sur la langue française*, 2 vols. (1647; Versailles: Cerg; Paris: Baudry, 1880), 1:43; Dominque Bouhours, *Entretiens d'Ariste et d'Eugène* (Amsterdam, 1671), 134–5.
96. On French debates pitting the standards of "usage" and "reason," see Padley, *Grammatical Theory*, 2: 390–407. The political stakes in this debate are excellently discussed by Ulrich Ricken, in *Linguistics, Anthropology and Philosophy in the French Enlightenment*, trans. Robert E. Norton (New York and London: Routledge, 1994), 5–8.
97. On the ancient debate concerning "analogy" and "anomaly" in language, see R.H. Robbins, *A Short History of Linguistics* (2nd edn, London: Longman, 1979), 20–2. For a good discussion of analogy in Varro, see Daniel J. Taylor, *Declension: A Study of the Linguistic Theory of Marcus Terentius Varro* (Amsterdam: Benjamins, 1974).
98. Michael Mattaire, *The English Grammar* (London, 1712; repr. Menston: Scholar Press, 1967), 30.
99. *Ibid.*, 1.
100. Jonathan Swift, *A Proposal for Correcting, Improving, and Ascertaining the English Tongue*, ed. Herbert Davis and Louis Landa (Oxford: Blackwell, 1957), 10.
101. *Ibid.*, 6.
102. Joseph Priestley, *Rudiments of English Grammar* (London, 1761; repr. Menston: Scholar Press, 1969), vii.
103. *Ibid.*, vi.
104. Preface to the *Dictionary*, in *Works* (1825), 5:49. See also 5:46.
105. *Plan of an English Dictionary*, in *Works* (1825), 5:19.
106. Preface to the *Dictionary*, in *Works* (1825), 5:42.
107. *Ibid.*, 5:28.
108. George Campbell, *Philosophy of Rhetoric*, ed. Lloyd F. Bitzer (Carbondale: Southern Illinois University Press, 1963), 168. For an excellent overview of polite and courtly language in the eighteenth century, see Carey McIntosh, *Common and Courtly Language: The Stylistics of Social Class in 18th-Century English Literature* (Philadelphia: University of Pennsylvania Press, 1986).
109. Hannah More, *Strictures on the Modern System of Female Education* (1799), in *Works*, 2 vols. (New York: Harper & Brothers, 1835), 1:324.
110. Jane West, *Letters to a Young Lady*, 3 vols. (1806; 4th edn, London, 1811; facs. repr. London: William Pickering, 1996), 3:33.

CHAPTER 2

1. Leonore Davidoff and Catherine Hall, *Family Fortunes: Men and Women of the English Middle-Class 1780–1850* (Chicago and London: University of Chicago Press, 1987), 275. These authors deal only sketchily with the position of women before 1780, generally relying on evidence that women lost their position in the workplace advanced in Alice Clark, *Working Life of Women in the Seventeenth Century* (London: Routledge, 1919) and Ivy Pinchbeck, *Women Workers and the Industrial Revolution, 1750–1850* (1930; London, Virago, 1981).

The analysis of Clark and Pinchbeck gained further support in Bridget Hill, *Women, Work and Sexual Politics in Eighteenth-Century England* (Oxford: Basil Blackwell, 1989).

2. Some of the more prominent studies of this kind include Nancy Armstrong, *Desire and Domestic Fiction* (New York and Oxford: Oxford University Press, 1987); Gary Kelly, *Women, Writing, and Revolution 1790–1827* (Oxford: Clarendon Press, 1993), 4 and *passim*; Michael McKeon, "Historicising Patriarchy: The Emergence of Gender Difference in England, 1660–1760," *Eighteenth-Century Studies* 28 (1995): 295–322; Anna Clark, *Struggle for the Breeches*, 2, 7, 97–9; Elizabeth Kowaleski-Wallace, *Consuming Subjects: Women, Shopping, and Business in the Eighteenth Century* (New York: Columbia University Press, 1997); Paula McDowell, *The Women of Grub Street: Press, Politics, and Gender in the London Literary Marketplace 1678–1730* (Oxford: Clarendon Press, 1998), 113–14; Harriet Guest, "Eighteenth-Century Femininity: 'A Supposed Sexual Character,' " in Vivien Jones (ed.), *Women and Literature in Britain* (Cambridge: Cambridge University Press, 2000), 46–68.
3. See Amanda Vickery, "Golden Age to Separate Spheres? A Review of the Categories and Chronology of English Women's History," *The Historical Review* 36 (1993): 383–414. Vickery makes her argument at greater length, and on the basis of several case studies of eighteenth-century women's lives, in *The Gentleman's Daughter: Women's Lives in Georgian England* (New Haven and London: Yale University Press, 1998). Vickery's views have strongly influenced later scholarship such as Lawrence E. Klein, "Gender and the Public/Private Distinction in the Eighteenth Century: Some Questions about Evidence and Analytical Procedure," *Eighteenth-Century Studies* 29 (1995): 97–109; Robert B. Shoemaker, *Gender in English Society 1650–1850: The Emergence of Separate Spheres?* (New York and London: Longman, 1998).
4. Laetitia Pilkington, *Memoirs*, ed. A.C. Elias, Jr., 2 vols. (Athens and London: University of Georgia Press, 1997), 1:209–10; Charlotte Charke, *A Narrative of the Life of Mrs. Charlotte Charke* (London, 1755; facs. repr. Gainsville: Scholars Facsimiles, 1969), 28.
5. Laurence Sterne, *A Sentimental Journey* (1768), ed. Ian Jack (Oxford and New York: Oxford University Press, 1968), 54.
6. West, *Letters to a Young Lady*, 1:143.
7. *Ibid.*, 1:182.
8. According to the radical Mary Hays in *Appeal to the Men of Great Britain, in Behalf of Women* (London, 1798; facs. repr. New York and London: Garland, 1974), men "in general . . . are averse from women acquiring knowledge of almost any sort" (94). Yet this claim seems inconsistent with even conservative conduct books by men, as we will see.
9. Porter, *English Society*, 164.
10. See Isobel Grundy, "Samuel Johnson as Patron of Women," *Age of Johnson* 1 (1987): 59–77; James G. Basker, "Dancing Dogs, Women Preachers and the Myth of Johnson's Misogyny," *Age of Johnson* 3 (1990): 63–90; Kremmerer, *"A Neutral Being Between the Sexes."*

11. Boswell, *Life*, 1:463. For Johnson's views on chastity, see 2:56 and 457, 5: 209.
12. On Johnson's lasting popularity in English women's culture, see Basker, "Dancing Dogs," 64–5, and "Radical Affinities: Mary Wollstonecraft and Samuel Johnson," in James G. Basker and Alvaro Ribeiro, S.J. (eds.), *Tradition in Transition: Women Writers, Marginal Texts, and the Eighteenth-Century Canon* (Oxford: Clarendon Press, 1996), 41–55. See also John Halpern, *The Life of Jane Austen* (Baltimore: Johns Hopkins University Press, 1984), 232; David Nokes, *Jane Austen: A Life* (London: Fifth Estate, 1997), 104 and 124; Elizabeth Barrett Browning, *Letters to Mary Russell*, 3 vols., ed. Meredith B. Raymond and Mary Rose Sullivan (Winfred, KS: Armstrong Browning Library of Baylor University, The Browning Institute, and Wellesley College, 1983), 1:344 and 355; George Eliot, *Letters*, ed. Gordon S. Haight, 9 vols. (New Haven and London: Yale University Press, 1954–78), 5:238.
13. See Anon. ("a Lady"), *The Whole Duty of a Woman* (2nd edn, London, 1696); John Shirley, *The Accomplished Ladies Rich Closet* (London, 1687); Samuel Torshell's *The Woman's Glorie: A Treatise, First, Asserting the Due Honour of that Sexe* (2nd edn, London, 1650); John Heydon's *Advice to a Daughter* (London, 1658).
14. *Paradise Lost*, bk. 4, ll. 296–8, quoted from John Milton, *Paradise Lost* (1674), ed. Merritt Y. Hughes (Indianapolis: Odyssey Press, 1962).
15. Samuel Johnson, *Life of Milton*, in *Lives of the English Poets*, ed. G.B. Hill, 2 vols. (Oxford: Clarendon Press, 1905), 1:157. This edition hereafter referred to as *Lives of the English Poets*.
16. George Savile, Marquis of Halifax, *The Lady's New-Years Gift* (1688; 5th edn, London, 1696), 27.
17. Kenneth Charlton, *Women, Religion, and Education in Early Modern England* (New York and London: Routledge, 1999), 153.
18. Richard Allestree, *The Lady's Calling* (Oxford, 1673), 109.
19. Mary Evelyn, *The Ladies Dressing-Room Unlock'd* (London, 1700), sigs. $A2^v$–$A3^r$.
20. *Ibid.*, sig. $A4^r$.
21. *Ibid.*, 9.
22. *The Rape of the Lock*, canto 5, ll.15–16. Quoted from *The Poems of Alexander Pope*, ed. John Butt (New Haven: Yale University Press, 1963).
23. *The Connoisseur* No. 44 (November 28, 1754), 2:63.
24. Eliza Haywood, *Selections from "The Female Spectator"* (1744–46), ed. Patricia Meyer Spacks (New York and Oxford: Oxford University Press, 1999), 57–8. See Henry Fielding's very similar complaints in *Enquiry*, 83.
25. Anon., *The Female Aegis or, the Duties of Women* (London, 1798; facs. repr. New York and London: Garland, 1974), 71–2.
26. On the range of social activities open to both men and women, see Dorothy Marshall, *Dr. Johnson's London* (New York, London, and Sydney: John Wiley & Sons, 1968), 149–89; George Rudé, *Hanoverian London 1714–1808* (London: Secker & Warburg, 1971), 64–81; Terry Castle, *Masquerade and Civilization:*

The Carnivalesque in Eighteenth-Century English Culture and Fiction (Stanford: Stanford University Press, 1986), 1–51; Porter, *English Society*, 214–50; Kristen Olsen, *Daily Life in 18th-Century England* (Westport, CT, and London: Greenwood Press, 1999), 151–8.

27. *The Connoisseur* No. 60 (March 20, 1755), 2:191.
28. More, *Strictures*, in *Works*, 1:330.
29. *Ibid.*, 1:324.
30. Anon., *The Female Aegis*, 159.
31. Defoe, *Complete English Tradesman*, 1:308.
32. Shirley, *The Accomplished Ladies Rich Closet*, 211.
33. *Ibid.*, 216.
34. John Essex, *The Young Ladies Conduct, or Rules for Education* (London, 1722), 50.
35. Wetenhall Wilkes, *A Letter of Genteel and Moral Advice to a Young Lady* (Dublin, 1740), 126.
36. *Ibid.*, 126.
37. Erasmus Jones, *Luxury, Pride and Vanity, the Bane of the British Nation* (4th edn, London, 1736), 38.
38. *The Spectator*, ed. Donald F. Bond, 5 vols. (1711–12; Oxford: Clarendon Press, 1965), 1:283.
39. James Fordyce, *Sermons for Young Women*, 2 vols. (3rd edn, London, 1766; facs. repr. London: William Pickering, 1996), 2:5.
40. See *ibid.*, Sermon VII ("On Female Virtue, with Intellectual Accomplishments"), 1:266–308.
41. *Ibid.*, 1:43.
42. *Ibid.*, 1:246.
43. Wilkes, *A Letter of Genteel and Moral Advice to a Young Lady*, 96–7.
44. Anon., *The Female Aegis*, 104.
45. Anna Laetitia Barbauld, Letter to Mrs. J. Taylor (June 7, 1786), in *Works*, 2 vols. (London, 1825), 2:103.
46. See David Hume, "Of Essay Writing," in *Essays, Moral, Political, and Literary*, ed. T.H. Green and T.H. Grose, 2 vols. (1742–70; London, New York, Bombay, and Calcutta: Longman, Green and Co., 1912), 2:369–70.
47. Fordyce, *Sermons for Young Women*, 1:60.
48. Boswell, *Life*, 3:3.
49. Vicesimus Knox, *Essays, Moral and Literary* (London, 1779; facs. repr. New York: Garland, 1972), 356.
50. See Samuel Johnson, *Life of Savage*, in *Lives of the English Poets*, 2:322–4. Besides the story in *Rambler* Nos. 130 and 133 of Victoria, whose smallpox leaves her disdained by her mother, see *Rambler* No. 55, where a widowed mother rejects her daughter as a competitor in the pursuit of men.
51. *Life of Milton*, in *Lives of the English Poets*, 1:157.
52. *Works* (1825), 5:362.
53. Knox, *Essays, Moral and Literary*, 332–3.
54. Fordyce, *Sermons for Young Women*, 1:24.

55. Thomas Gisborne, *An Enquiry into the Duties of the Female Sex* (London, 1797), 12–13.
56. More, *Works*, 1:313. For similar opinions see Hester Chapone, *Letters on the Improvement of the Mind* (Dublin, 1773; facs. repr. London: William Pickering, 1996), 121; Priscilla Wakefield, *Reflections on the Present Condition of the Female Sex* (London, 1798; facs. repr. New York and London: Garland, 1974), 69–70. The role of women in "civilizing" men is excellently discussed by G.J. Barker-Benfield in *The Culture of Sensibility: Sex and Society in Eighteenth-Century Britain* (Chicago: University of Chicago Press, 1992).
57. Ellis, *The Women of England*, 18.
58. *Ibid.*, 13.
59. *Ibid.*, 342.
60. See Nokes, *Jane Austen*, 124.
61. See Harriet Guest, *Small Change: Women, Learning and Patriotism 1750–1810* (Chicago and London: University of Chicago Press, 2000).
62. Fielding, *Enquiry*, 77.
63. Anon., *The Tryal of Lady Allurea Luxury, before the Lord Chief Justice Upright* (London, 1757), 67.
64. *Ibid.*, 92.
65. *Ibid.*, 17.
66. Edward Watkinson, *Essay upon Oeconomy* (1762; 8th edn, York: 1767), 11.
67. *Ibid.*, 11.
68. See, e.g., Mary Evelyn, *The Ladies Dressing Room Unlock'd*, sigs. A2^{v}–A3^{r}.
69. Chapone, *Letters on the Improvement of the Mind*, 147.
70. Brown, *Estimate*, 198.
71. Samuel Fawconer, *An Essay on Modern Luxury* (London, 1765), 45.
72. *Ibid.*, 32.
73. Brown, *Estimate*, 45.
74. Kowaleski-Wallace, *Consuming Subjects*, 4–5. On women in the consumer economy, recently a popular topic, see also Pamela Sharpe, *Adapting to Capitalism: Working Women in the English Economy 1700–1850* (Basingstoke: Macmillan, 1996); Gillian Skinner, *Sensibility and Economics in the Novel: the Price of a Tear* (London: Macmillan, 1999); Guest, *Small Change*, 70–92.
75. Jones, *Luxury*, 28.
76. Brown, *Estimate*, 51.
77. Bernard Mandeville. *The Fable of the Bees or, Private Virtues, Publick Benefits*, ed. F.B. Kaye, 2 vols. (1711–34; Oxford: Clarendon Press, 1924), 1:70.
78. John Gregory, *A Father's Legacy to his Daughters* (Dublin, 1774), 22–3.
79. Fordyce, *Sermons for Young Women*, 1.75.
80. Hume,"Of the Refinement of the Arts," in *Essays*, 1:299. This essay bore the title "Of Luxury" in editions of 1742 and 1758.
81. *Ibid.*, 1:301–2.
82. See Adam Ferguson, *An Essay on the History of Civil Society* (Edinburgh, 1767; fasc. repr. New York: Garland, 1971), 375–82; Millar, *Observations concerning the Distinction of Ranks* (London, 1771), 180–6.

83. Millar, *Observations concerning the Distinction of Ranks*, 21.
84. See also anon., *The Female Aegis*, 6.
85. See Sir James Steuart, *An Inquiry into the Principles of Political Oeconomy*, ed. Andrew Skinner, 2 vols. (Chicago: University of Chicago Press, 1966), preface, 1:3–4. Steuart is the earliest author cited in the *OED* under "economy" in its modern disciplinary sense.
86. Boswell, *Life*, 2:218.
87. Brown, *Estimate*, 198.
88. See Clifford, *Dictionary Johnson*, 204–8.
89. Wakefield, *Reflections on the Present Condition of the Female Sex*, 63.
90. *Ibid.*, 58.
91. *Ibid.*, 100.
92. *Ibid.*, 124.
93. *Ibid.*, 118.
94. More, *Strictures*, in *Works*, 1:313.
95. *Ibid.*, 1:362.
96. *Ibid.*, 1:364.
97. See Boswell, *Life*, 1:447–8.
98. Catherine Macaulay, *Letters on Education* (London, 1790; facs. repr. London: William Pickering, 1996), preface, v–vi.
99. Mary Wollstonecraft, *A Vindication of the Rights of Woman*, in *The Works of Mary Wollstonecraft*, 7 vols., ed. Janet Todd and Marilyn Butler (London: William Pickering, 1989), 5:213.
100. *Ibid.*, 5:144. "It is not by a squandering of alms that the poor can be relieved, or improved – it is by the fostering of the sun of kindness, the wisdom that finds them employment calculated to give them habits of virtue, that meliorates their condition" (*Vindication of the Rights of Men*, in *Works*, 5:56).
101. Hays, *Appeal to the Men of Great Britain*, 239.
102. *Ibid.*, 241.
103. Ellis, *The Women of England*, sig. A2^{v}.
104. Elizabeth Langland, *Nobody's Angels: Middle-Class Women and Domestic Ideology in Victorian Culture* (Ithaca and London: Cornell University Press, 1995), 9.
105. In the words of Harriet Taylor in *Enfranchisement of Women* (1851), "For the first time in the world, men and women are really companions" (John Stuart Mill and Harriet Taylor Mill, *Essays on Sex Equality*, ed. Alice S. Rossi [Chicago and London: University of Chicago Press, 1970], 156.)

CHAPTER 3

1. See Brian W. Hill, *The Growth of Parliamentary Parties* (Hamden, CT: Archon Books, 1976), and *The Early Parties and Politics in Britain, 1688–1832* (Basingstoke: Macmillan, 1996); Frank O'Gorman, *The Emergence of the British Two-Party System 1760–1832* (London: Edward Arnold, 1982); Eric

J. Evans, *Political Parties in Britain, 1783–1864* (London: Methuen, 1985); Stephen Ingle, *The British Party System* (Oxford and New York: Basil Blackwell, 1987).

2. See Linda Colley, *In Defiance of Oligarchy* (Cambridge: Cambridge University Press, 1982); Eveline Cruikshanks, *Political Untouchables: the Tories and the '45* (London: Duckworth, 1979); J.C.D. Clark, *English Society 1688–1832: Ideology, Social Structure, Political Practice during the Ancien Regime* (Cambridge: Cambridge University Press, 1985). Another study of the Patriot Opposition that insists on the separate identity of the Tories is Christine Gerrard's *The Patriot Opposition to Walpole: Politics, Poetry, and National Myth 1725–1742* (Oxford: Clarendon Press, 1994).
3. Greene, *Politics*, 6–13.
4. See Clarke, *English Society 1688–1832*, 30–2; Cruikshanks, *Political Untouchables*, 41–5.
5. Howard Erskine-Hill, "Johnson the Jacobite?," 11.
6. See Colley, *In Defiance of Oligarchy*, 41–2.
7. John Perceval, Earl of Egmont, *Faction Detected by the Evidence of Facts* (London, 1743), 5–6.
8. Anon. ("Petronius"), *Party Distinctions the Bane and Misery of the British Nation* (London, 1744), 16.
9. Anon., *The Balance: or the Merits of Whig and Tory exactly weigh'd and fairly determin'd* (London, 1753), 3.
10. Horace Walpole, *A Letter to the Whigs, occasion'd by A Letter to the Tories* (London, 1748), 22.
11. George Lyttelton, *A Letter to the Tories* (1747; 2nd edn, London, 1748), 12.
12. Anon., *The Loyal or Revolutionary Tory* (London, 1733), 17.
13. Anon., *Opposition more Necessary than Ever* (London, 1742), 47.
14. See Clark, *Samuel Johnson*, 211–37.
15. Compare *ibid.*, 99 with 166–7.
16. *Old England* (January 7, 1744).
17. *Old England* (January 28, 1744).
18. On the press campaign of the Broad-bottom Opposition, their political maneuvering and their relationship with the Tories, see John B. Owen, *The Rise of the Pelhams* (London: Methuen & Co., 1957), 185; Archibald S. Foord, *His Majesty's Opposition 1714–1830* (Oxford: Clarendon Press, 1964), pp. 219–60; Robert Harris, *A Patriot Press: National Politics and the London Press in the 1740s* (Oxford: Clarendon Press, 1993), 122–77.
19. Lord Chesterfield and Edmund Waller, *The Interest of Hanover Steadily Pursued since the A____n* (London, 1743), 13.
20. *Ibid.*, 28.
21. See e.g., *ibid.*, 30.
22. *Old England* (December 1, 1744).
23. Anon., *The Honest Grief of a Tory, expressed in a Genuine Letter from a Burgess of ____, in Wiltshire, to the Author of the Monitor, Feb 17, 1759* (London, 1759), 16.

24. John Shebbeare, *A Sixth Letter to the People of England on the Progress of National Ruin* (London, 1757), 41 and 58.
25. See *ibid*, 8–9. Yet J.C.D. Clark takes Boswell's remark on the similarity of Johnson and Shebbeare in *Life*, 4:113, as more evidence that Johnson was a Jacobite. See Clark, *Samuel Johnson*, 244.
26. John Perceval, Earl of Egmont, *Things as They Are* (London, 1758), 86–7.
27. Israel Mauduit, *Considerations on the Present German War* (1760; 4th edn, London, 1761), 42. On the amazing popularity of Mauduit's pamphlet, which went though three imprints in three months, see Marie Peters, *Pitt and Popularity: The Patriot Minister and London Opinion during the Seven Years' War* (Oxford: Clarendon Press, 1980), 183.
28. See Owen, *Rise of the Pelhams*, 197.
29. *The North Briton* No. 11 (August 14, 1762), 34.
30. Boswell, *Life*, 2:341–2.
31. See *ibid.*, 3:315.
32. See below, chapter 5, 144–5.
33. Sir John Hawkins, *The Life of Samuel Johnson*, 3. Yet Hawkins later argues that Johnson's politics derived from Hooker rather than Filmer and that he was ideologically close to Benjamin Hoadly, one of the most provocative Whigs of the early century (504). Note as well that even Hawkins assumes that Johnson left Oxford due to lack of money (17), not because he refused to take the oath of allegiance to George II, contradicting one of J.C.D. Clark's pivotal speculations about Johnson.
34. See David Hume, "The Parties of Great Britain," in *Essays Moral, Political and Literary*, 1:139. Hume believed that English Tories were "partisans" of the Stuart family, an opinion that Linda Colley bluntly dismisses as "wrong" (*In Defiance of Oligarchy*, 115). But Hume was not saying that English Tories were Jacobites, for he draws a clear distinction between them and Scottish Tories, who were Jacobites, he said, by definition. His opinion was that the Tory nostalgia for the Stuarts was limited by their commitment to "liberty," and in that sense Tories and Whigs did not differ drastically in their political outlooks.
35. Anon., *The Loyal or Revolutionary Tory*, 18.
36. Henry St. John, Viscount Bolingbroke, *A Dissertation upon Parties*, in *Political Writings*, ed. David Armitage (Cambridge: Cambridge University Press, 1997), 88.
37. Anon., *Opposition More Necessary than Ever*, 51–2.
38. Anon., *The Sentiments of a Tory, in respect to a late Important Transaction* (London, 1741), 20.
39. *Ibid.*, 6.
40. *The Gentleman's Magazine* 13 (1743): 181.
41. See Greene, *Politics*, 133–5. Greene does summarize the arguments of *Sentiments of a Tory* in Appendix B, 272–9. He neglects to consider, however, that the evidence of that pamphlet indicates that Johnson had *not* changed his heart towards Walpole, but was objecting to the legality of the parliamentary proceedings against him.

42. *The Gentleman's Magazine* 13 (1743): 173.
43. See *Lives of the English Poets*, 2:191–3.
44. *Works* (1825), 10:438. See also Johnson's presentation of debate on a Patriot motion to suspend the right of witnesses to remain silent on evidence that would condemn themselves (roughly what Americans now know as "pleading the Fifth Amendment") in their investigation of Walpole's alleged corruptions (*Works*, 11:68–9). Here as elsewhere, Johnson is clearly on the side of *law* over either vengeance against Walpole or the demands of the "people."
45. *Works* (1825), 11:372.
46. On the composition of the debates, see G.B. Hill's long "Appendix A" in *Life*, 1:501–12; Thomas Kaminski, *The Early Career of Samuel Johnson* (New York and Oxford: Oxford University Press, 1987), 123–6.
47. See, e.g., Anon., *Characters of Parties in British Government* (London, 1782), 75; Thomas Bigge, *Considerations on the State of Parties, and the Means of Effecting a Reconciliation between them* (London, 1793), 29; Anon., *A Letter upon the State of Parties* (London, 1797), 7–8.
48. Boswell, *Life*, 3:221.
49. For example, Boswell clearly expected an ardent defense of the Tory John Shebbeare, but Johnson failed to take the bait (*Life*, 3:314–15); he expected Johnson to condemn the "too great indulgence of Government" in April 1783, and got only qualified and equivocal agreement (*Life*, 4:200).
50. *Ibid.*, 1:141.
51. See *ibid.*, 4:223.
52. On Johnson's place in the history of conservatism, see Anthony Quinton, *The Politics of Imperfection: The Religious and Secular Tradition in England from Hooker to Oakshott* (London: Faber and Faber, 1978), 51–5; James Sack, *From Jacobite to Conservative: Reaction and Orthodoxy in Britain, c. 1760–1832* (Cambridge: Cambridge University Press, 1993), 91–4; Hudson, "The Nature of Johnson's Conservatism."
53. For Dodsley's connections with both Johnson and the Chesterfield circle, see Reddick, *The Making of Johnson's Dictionary*, 16–24. Harry M. Solomon, *The Rise of Robert Dodsley: Creating the New Age of Print* (Carbondale and Edwardsville: Southern Illinois University Press, 1996), 77–80 and 121.
54. See Foord, *His Majesty's Opposition*, 240.
55. Boswell, *Life*, 1:133.
56. See Samuel Shellabarger, *Lord Chesterfield and his World* (Boston: Little, Brown and Company, 1951), 121.
57. Boswell, *Life*, 2:173.
58. Cited in Foord, *His Majesty's Opposition*, 247.
59. See Isaac Kramnick, *Bolingbroke and his Circle: The Politics of Nostalgia in the Age of Walpole* (Cambridge, MA: Harvard University Press, 1968). J.G.A. Pocock assails Kramnick's reading of Bolingbroke in *Virtue, Commerce, and History: Essays in Political Thought and History, Chiefly in the Eighteenth Century* (Cambridge: Cambridge University Press, 1985), 242. See also Owen, *Rise of the Pelhams*, 75.

60. Bolingbroke, *A Dissertation upon Parties*, in *Political Writings*, 64.
61. See below, chapter 5, 137.
62. John Wilkes, *A Letter to Samuel Johnson, L.L.D.* (London, 1770), 43–4.
63. Bolingbroke, *A Dissertation upon Parties*, in *Political Writings*, 37.
64. Bolingbroke, *The Idea of a Patriot King*, in *Political Writings*, 261.
65. Anon., *Sentiments of a Tory*, 5.
66. Anon., *Observations on the Conduct of the Tories, Whigs, and the Dissenters* (London, 1739), 39.
67. See Thomas R. Cleary, *Henry Fielding: Political Writer* (Waterloo, Ontario: Wilfred Laurier University Press, 1984), 173–4.
68. Henry Fielding, *A Full Vindication of the Dutchess Dowager of Marlborough* (London, 1742), 33–4
69. "Review of *The Account of the Dutchess of* Marlborough," in *Works* (1825), 6:7.
70. See DeMaria, "The Politics of Johnson's *Dictionary*," 64–74.
71. Bolingbroke, *The Idea of a Patriot King*, in *Political Writings*, 257–8.
72. The reader may recall Johnson's definition of "Gallicism" in the *Dictionary*: "A mode of speech peculiar to the French language: such as . . . may be found in the pages of *Bolingbroke*." On Johnson's attack on Bolingbroke's anti-Christianity, see Boswell, *Life*, 1:268.
73. Bolingbroke's political works are cited, for example, under "indolency" and "mines."
74. See *Works* (1825), 11:420–6. In these *Works*, the speech is wrongly attributed to Carteret ("Quodrert") rather than Chesterfield ("Castroflet").
75. See Boswell, *Life*, 3:351 and note. As Hill clarified, there were actually three speeches attributed to Chesterfield from *The Gentleman's Magazine*, only two of them by Johnson.
76. See *Works* (1825), 11:496–7.
77. Chesterfield's disdain for the merchant class of the City can be gauged for example by his derisive portrait of vulgar City readers in *The World*, No. 111 (February 13, 1755): 669.
78. Walpole, *Letter to the Whigs*, 17.
79. See Solomon, *The Rise of Robert Dodsley*, 121.
80. *Old England* (December 3, 1743).
81. Anon., *An Apology for a Late Resignation* (London, 1748), 24.
82. On Johnson's views on the press and war, see Greene, *Politics*, 144–5 (on the press) and 266–7 (on war).
83. This letter, first published in *The Gentleman's Magazine*, is cited in Greene's *Politics*, 267.
84. Anon., *A General View of the Present Politics and Interests of the Principle Powers of Europe* (London, 1747), 25–6.
85. See Daunton, *Progress and Poverty*, 10–11. Not all shared this pessimism. See for example, Anon., *The State of the Nation for the Year 1747 and respecting 1748* (Dublin, 1748), a pamphlet that is typical of the jingoistic drum-beating of Lord Carteret and his supporters.
86. *The Remembrancer* No. 11 (February 20, 1748): 73.

87. These were the original ll. 61–2.
88. See *Works* (1825), 6:9.
89. *Ibid.*, 5:191.
90. *Lives of the English Poets*, 2:360–1.
91. Anon., *Sentiments of a Tory*, 6.
92. Hume, "The Parties of Great Britain," in *Essays Moral, Political and Literary*, 1:134.
93. Anon., *Characters of Parties*, 29.
94. See Bigge, *Considerations on the State of Parties*. For an excellent discussion of the growing acceptance of party during the 1760s, see John Brewer, *Party Ideology and Popular Politics at the Accession of George III* (Cambridge: Cambridge University Press, 1976), 39–95.
95. See Edmund Burke, *Thoughts on the Cause of the Present Discontents*, in *Writings and Speeches*, 2:241–322.
96. Hester Lynch Piozzi, *Anecdotes of the late Samuel Johnson, L.L.D.* (Dublin, 1786), 83.
97. *Life of Granville*, in *Lives of the English Poets*, 2:294.
98. Boswell, *Life*, 4:118.
99. *Ibid.*, 2:223.
100. See, e.g., Anon., *The Coalition; or an Essay on the Present State of the Parties* (London, 1783).
101. Burke, *Reflections on the Revolution in France*, in *Writings and Speeches*, 6:140.
102. This argument is set out in a number of places in Pocock's writing, but nowhere more effectively than in "The Varieties of Whiggism from Exclusion to Reform: A History of Ideology and Discourse," in *Virtue, Commerce, and History: Essays in Political Thought and History, Chiefly in the Eighteenth Century* (Cambridge: Cambridge University Press, 1985), 215–310.
103. *The Champion* No. 311 (November 7, 1741).
104. Henry Fielding, *Joseph Andrews*, ed. Douglas Brooks-Davies and Martin C. Battestin, rev. Thomas Keymer (Oxford: Oxford University Press, 1999), bk. 3, chap. 1, 165.
105. Anon., *Merit: A Satire. Humbly Addressed to His Excellency the Earl of Chesterfield* (Dublin, 1746), 10.
106. Henry Jones, *Merit. A Poem: inscribed to the Right Honourable Philip Earl of Chesterfield* (London: Robert Dodsley, 1753), 22.
107. *The Museum* (August 1, 1747), 385.
108. Robert Dodsley, *A Muse in Livery, or, the Footman's Miscellany* (London, 1732), 1.
109. *Ibid.*, 138.
110. Paul Whitehead, *Manners: A Satire* (London, 1739), 7 and 11.
111. James Thomson, "Liberty," in *Poetical Works*, ed. J. Logie Robertson (London, New York, and Toronto: Oxford University Press, 1908), part 5, l. 245.
112. *True Patriot* No. 2 (November 12 1745), in *The True Patriot and Related Writings*, ed. W.B. Coley (Oxford: Clarendon Press, 1987), 118.
113. *Letters*, 1:95.

114. See *True Patriot* No. 1 (November 5, 1745), 108–9.
115. *Lives of the English Poets*, 2:180 and 190.
116. The term used, for example, to describe Fanny in *Joseph Andrews*, bk 2, chap. 12.
117. See *Lives of the English Poets*, 2:363 and 392.
118. *Ibid.*, 2:401.
119. See also *Rambler* No. 72, 4:14–15.
120. James Burgh, *The Dignity of Human Nature* (London, 1754), 27–8.
121. Boswell, *Life*, 1:440.
122. Concerning Johnson's identity as the "respectable Hottentot" mocked by Chesterfield, see Boswell's *Life*, 1:266–7. The editor G.B. Hill famously argues here that Chesterfield meant not Johnson but Lyttelton, but the label stuck to Johnson for the century after the publication of Boswell's biography.
123. Boswell, *Life*, 1:442.

CHAPTER 4

1. See Aytoun Ellis, *The Penny Universities: A History of the Coffee-Houses* (London: Secker and Warburg, 1956), 69.
2. J.C.D. Clark, *The Dynamics of Change: The Crisis of the 1750s and English Party Systems* (Cambridge: Cambridge University Press, 1982), 10.
3. See Brewer, *Party Ideology*, 139–60; H.T. Dickinson, *The Politics of the People in Eighteenth-Century Britain* (New York: St. Martin's Press, 1995); Nicholas Rogers, *Whigs and Cities: Popular Politics in the Age of Walpole and Pitt* (Oxford: Clarendon Press, 1989); Daunton, *Progress and Poverty*, 198–200; Kathleen Wilson, *The Sense of the People: Politics, Culture, and Imperialism in England, 1715–1765* (Cambridge: Cambridge University Press, 1995); Hannah Barker, *Newspapers, Politics, and Public Opinion in Late Eighteenth-Century England* (Oxford: Clarendon Press, 1998).
4. See Anon., *Private Virtue and Publick Spirit Display'd* (London, 1751).
5. *The Museum* No. 8 (July 5, 1746), 1:282.
6. John Dennis, *An Essay on Publick Spirit; being a Satyr in Prose upon the Manners and Luxury of the Times* (London, 1711), 1. See also Anon., *The Livery Man: or Plain Thoughts on Public Affairs* (London, 1740), 1.
7. Anon., *The Present Necessity of Distinguishing Publick Spirit from Party* (London, 1736), 4.
8. *Ibid.*, 4.
9. *Ibid.*, 14. See also James Hodges, *Essays on Several Subjects, viz. Discouragements Private Men meet with in Promoting Publick Good* (London, 1710), 1–2.
10. *Old England* (December 1, 1744).
11. *The Monitor* No. 26 (January 31, 1756), 234.
12. *The Monitor* No. 22 (January 3, 1756), 190.
13. *North Briton*, special issue (April 7, 1763). This is the unnumbered issue that immediately preceded the suppressed No. 45.
14. Anon., *Unity and Public Spirit* (London, 1780), 20.

15. *Ibid.*, 31.
16. *Works* (1825), 6:308.
17. Greene claimed that "there is no evidence that [Johnson], speaking for himself, ever wrote or said anything disparaging about Walpole and his administration later than May 1739, when the *Vindication of the Licensers* was published" (*Politics*, 134). See also Gerrard, *The Patriot Opposition to Walpole*, 244–5.
18. See Boswell, *Life*, 2:128.
19. Dennis, *An Essay on Publick Spirit*, 1. See also Anon., *Livery Man*, 1.
20. Mandeville, "An Enquiry into the Origin of Moral Virtue," in *The Fable of the Bees*, 1:48.
21. Mandeville, Preface to *Fable of the Bees*, 1:3. E. J. Hundert rightly stresses this Dutchman's French roots in a Cartesian skepticism *sans* any social pineal gland harboring an immaterial soul. See E.J. Hundert, "Bernard Mandeville and Enlightenment Maxims of Modernity," *Journal of the History of Ideas* 39 (1978): 119–24. On the relationship between the private and public in eighteenth-century political discourse, see Peter N. Miller, *Defining the Public Good: Empire, Religion, and Philosophy in Eighteenth-Century Britain* (Cambridge: Cambridge University Press, 1994).
22. Boswell, *Life*, 3:292.
23. Fielding, *The True Patriot* No. 2 (November 12, 1745), 118.
24. See Hudson, *Samuel Johnson and Eighteenth-Century Thought*, 66–85.
25. Johnson's analysis is very close to that of John Brown in his better-known *An Estimate of the Manners and Principles of the Time*, published the next year (see p. 140).
26. *The Monitor* No. 16 (November 22, 1755), 137.
27. See Jürgen Habermas, *The Structural Transformation of the Public Sphere: An Inquiry into a Category of Bourgeois Society*, tr. Thomas Burger and Frederick Lawrence (Cambridge, MA: MIT Press, 1989).
28. For a good overview of some of the principal objections against Habermas's theory of the public sphere, see Craig Calhoun (ed.), *Habermas and the Public Sphere* (Cambridge, MA, and London: MIT Press, 1992), 1–48.
29. See Ralph Nevill, *London Clubs: Their History and Treasures* (London: Chatto and Windus, 1911), 3–4; Ellis, *The Penny Universities*, 115–17, 154.
30. The extensiveness of public mobilization in London streets is one of the striking phenomena of eighteenth-century social history. See George Rudé, *The Crowd in History: A Study of Popular Disturbances in France and England 1730–1848* (London: John Wiley & Son, 1964); Robert B. Shoemaker, "The London Mob in the Early Eighteenth Century," in Peter Borsay (ed.), *The Eighteenth-Century Town*, 188–222.
31. See Laurence Hanson, *The Government and the Press 1695–1763* (Oxford: Oxford University Press; London, Humphrey Milford, 1936), 10. Hanson's old book remains the main source of information on press censorship in the eighteenth century.
32. *The Daily Gazetteer* No. 767 (December 9, 1737).
33. Anon., *A New System of Patriot Policy* (London, 1756), 62.

34. *Works* (1825), 11:229.
35. Francis Squire, *A Faithful Report of a Genuine Debate concerning the Liberty of the Press* (London, 1740), 44.
36. *Ibid.*, 46.
37. *The Daily Gazetteer* No. 767 (December 9, 1737).
38. *Works* (1825), 10:368.
39. *Ibid.*, 10:430.
40. See Perceval, *Faction Detected,* 1 and 58.
41. See, e.g., Anon., *An Historical View of the Principles, Character, Persons &c of Political Writers in Great Britain* (London, 1740), 9 and 23.
42. See Anon., *The Craftsman's Doctrine of the Liberty of the Press, Explain'd to the Meanest Capacity* (London, 1732).
43. See, e.g., Fielding's comments on the "illiterate Rabble" in *The Champion* (December 4, 1739), 60. The ignorance of the "mob" is a common theme as well in *Tom Jones*, where the neighboring people are easily swayed by malicious gossip against the hero.
44. *Common-Sense* No. 16 (May 21, 1737).
45. *The Craftsman* (July 30, 1737).
46. See Walpole, *Letter to the Whigs*, 5 and 17.
47. *Con-test* No. 5 (December 18, 1757): 30.
48. See Kaminski, *The Early Career of Samuel Johnson*, 59.
49. *Common-Sense* No. 101 (January 6, 1737).
50. *Common-Sense* No. 116.
51. *Works* (1825), 5:191.
52. See, for example, *Lives of the English Poets*, 2:186–7.
53. Dudley Pope has given us an account of Byng's military debacle from the admirably informed and detailed perspective of a naval *aficionado*. Rather simplified, Byng halted his flag-ship when the French had shot to splinters the preceding British ships-of-the-line. See *At Twelve Mr. Byng was Shot* (London: Secker & Warburg, 1987).
54. *Con-test* No. 15 (February 16, 1757): 86.
55. John Shebbeare, *Appeal to the People, containing the Genuine and Entire Letter of Admiral Byng to the Secr. Of the Ad____y* (London, 1756), 76
56. David Mallet, *The Conduct of the Ministry Impartially Examined* (London, 1756), 55.
57. John Shebbeare, *An Answer to the Pamphlet, call'd The Conduct of the Ministry Impartially Examined* (London, 1756), 91.
58. *Ibid.*, 97.
59. Boswell, *Life*, 4:113, and n. 2.
60. *Ibid.*, 3:315.
61. Paul Whitehead, *A Letter to a Member of Parliament in the Country, from his Friend in London, relative to the Case of Admiral Byng* (London, 1756), 1. Interestingly, Johnson almost certainly knew Whitehead, an old Patriot whose poem "Manners" (1739) had led to the imprisonment of their mutual friend, the publisher Robert Dodsley.

62. Boswell, *Life*, 2:60.
63. *Ibid.*, 2:170.
64. See *The Letters of Junius*, ed. John Cannon (Oxford: Clarendon Press, 1978), Letter 42 (January 20, 1771).
65. See *Life*, 3:376.
66. *Ibid.*, 15–16.
67. Perceval, *Faction Detected*, p. 72.
68. See Hudson, *Samuel Johnson and Eighteenth-Century Thought*, 223–51.
69. See *Thoughts on . . . Falkland's Islands* (10:378); Boswell, *Life*, 1:131, 5:339.
70. See *Works*, 8:704.
71. *Lives of the English Poets*, 2:132.

CHAPTER 5

1. Boswell, *Life*, 2:348.
2. DeMaria, *The Life of Samuel Johnson*. See also Clement Hawes's argument for Johnson's "soft" or "cosmopolitan" nationalism in "Johnson's Cosmopolitan Nationalism," in Smallwood, ed., *Johnson Re-Visioned*, 37–63.
3. See Benedict R. Anderson, *Imagined Communities: Reflections on the Origin and Spread of Nationalism* (London: Verso Editions / NLB, 1983).
4. *The Remembrancer* No. 11 (Feburary 20, 1748), p. 76.
5. Boswell, *Life*, 5:339.
6. The view of England as a quintessentially commercial nation is argued by Langford, *A Polite and Commercial People*, 3–4 and *passim*, and *Englishness Identified* (Oxford: Clarendon Press, 2000), 77; Colley, *Britons*, 55–100. On Protestantism as a nationalist creed, see *ibid.*, 11–54. That francophobia lies at the roots of English nationalism, see *ibid.*, 24–5, 33–5, and 88–90, and Gerald Newman, *The Rise of English Nationalism: A Cultural History 1740–1830* (New York: St. Martin's Press, 1987), 123–48. Newman links francophobic patriotism with hatred of the aristocracy. As I have argued, however, the emergent middle class that did so much to forge modern English nationalism widely regarded the aristocracy as a important bulwark against plebeian "patriotism."
7. See Murray G. A. Pittock, *Inventing and Resisting Britain: Cultural Identities in Britain and Ireland, 1685–1789* (New York: St. Martin's Press, 1997), 9, 45–6.
8. Daniel Defoe, "The True-Born Englishman" (1700; 21st edn, Dublin, 1728), 8. On the popularity of Defoe's poem, see Paula R. Backscheider, *Daniel Defoe: His Life* (Baltimore and London: Johns Hopkins University Press, 1989), 75–6.
9. Patrick Abercromby, *The Martial Atchievements of the Scots Nation*, 2 vols. (Edinburgh, 1711), 1:2 and 76.
10. See *ibid.*, 1:76–7.
11. As most famously in *The Ancient Constitution and the Feudal Law: A Study of English Historical Thought in the Seventeenth Century* (Cambridge: Cambridge University Press, 1957).

12. See Willliam Petyt, *The Antient Right of the Commons of England Asserted; or, a Discourse Proving by Records and the Best Historians, that the Commons of England were ever an Essential Part of Parliament* (London, 1680).
13. James Tyrrell, *The General History of England*, 4 vols. (London, 1697–1704), 1: xxx.
14. Henry St. John, Viscount Bolingbroke, *Remarks on the History of England* (1752; 3rd edn, London 1780), 55–6.
15. Joseph Addison, *Cato* (1713), in *Works*, 6 vols. (London: George Bell and Sons, 1893), III, iii, 1:209.
16. See John Wilkes, *The History of England from the Revolution to the Accession of the Brunswick Line* (London, 1768), 38 and *passim*. See also Catherine Macaulay Graham, *The History of England from the Accession of James I to that of the Brunswick Line*, 8 vols. (London, 1763), introduction, 1:vii, xi–xiv.
17. John Wilkes, *A Letter to Samuel Johnson, L.L.D.*, 43–4.
18. See Pocock, "Burke and the Ancient Constitution: A Problem in the History of Ideas," in *Politics, Language and Time: Essays on Political Thought and History* (Chicago: University of Chicago Press, 1989), 202–32.
19. Robert Brady, *An Introduction to the Old English History* (London, 1684), 11.
20. William Temple, *An Introduction to the History of England* (1695; 3rd edn, London, 1708), 86.
21. See Thomas Carte, *General History of England*, 4 vols. (London: 1747–55), 1:388–450. Belief in the ancient practice of anointing the King authorized Carte's advocacy of touching for the King's Evil, and Carte is mentioned in this connection by Boswell (*Life*, 1:42, and n.). Nevertheless, Carte's huge work did not begin to appear until three decades after the young Johnson was touched for scrofula by Queen Anne.
22. Boswell, *Life*, 4:311.
23. *Ibid.*, 2:344.
24. See especially the opening pages of Section the Third ("Of the Laws of England") in Sir William Blackstone's *Commentaries of the Laws of England*, ed. Wayne Morrison, 4 vols. (1765–9; London and Sydney: Cavendish Publishing Limited, 2001), 1:47–62.
25. Carte, *A General History of England*, 1:318.
26. Boswell, *Life*, 1:177.
27. See Sir Robert Chambers and Samuel Johnson, *A Course of Lectures on the English Law*, ed. Thomas M. Curley, 2 vols. (wr. 1767–73; Madison: University of Wisconsin Press, 1986), 1:100–2.
28. *Ibid.*, 1:103.
29. Daniel Defoe, *An Essay at Removing National Prejudices against a Union with Scotland* (Edinburgh, 1706), 28.
30. Anon., *The True-Born Britain* (London, 1707), 4.
31. See Daniel Defoe, *The History of the Union of Great Britain* (Edinburgh, 1709), 2.
32. Cited from Thomson, *Poetical Works*, ll. 17–20.
33. David Mallet and James Thomson, *Alfred: A Masque* (Dublin: 1740), 8.

34. *Ibid.*, 34–5.
35. See Pope, "Windsor Forest," in *Poems*, l. 46 and ll. 377–410.
36. See J.C.D. Clark, *Samuel Johnson*, 159–65; Erskine-Hill, "Johnson the Jacobite?," 11–12. Even Donald Greene seemed unable to avoid the anti-Hanoverian (if not Jacobite) aura of this piece. See his introduction to *Marmor Norfolciense* in *Works*, 10:19–21 and his last major assault on the thesis of Johnson's Jacobitism, "Johnson: the Jacobite Legend Exhumed," in *Age of Johnson* 7 (1996): 70–1.
37. See Murray G. H. Pittock, *Celtic Identity and the British Image* (Manchester and New York: Manchester, 1999), 19.
38. See Brean S. Hammon, *Professional Imaginative Writing in England 1670–1700: "Hackney for Bread"* (Oxford: Clarendon Press, 1997), 132. Blackmore's *Prince Arthur* (1695) realized a plan considered but finally rejected previously by John Milton.
39. *Works* (1825), 5:21.
40. *Ibid.*, 5:24 and 25.
41. Chambers and Johnson, *Course of Lectures*, 1:133.
42. Katie Trumpener, *Bardic Nationalism: The Romantic Novel and the British Empire* (Princeton: Princeton University Press, 1997), 69–70.
43. See Donald M'Nicol, *Remarks on Dr. Samuel Johnson's Journey to the Hebrides* (London, 1779; facs. repr. New York and London: Garland, 1974), 41, 78, 148.
44. Howard Gaskill (ed.), *Ossian Revisited* (Edinburgh: Edinburgh University Press, 1991), introduction, 14; Richard B. Sher, "Percy, Shaw, and the Ferguson 'Cheat': National Prejudice and the Ossian Wars," in *ibid.*, 224.
45. M'Nicol, *Remarks on Dr. Samuel Johnson's Journey to the Hebrides*, 176.
46. Gaskill (ed.), *Ossian Revisited*, introduction, 14. Fiona J. Stafford refers similarly to "the virtual destruction of [the Highlander's] native community" in "'Dangerous Success': Ossian, Wordsworth, English Romantic Literature," in *ibid.*, 65.
47. Colin Kidd, *Subverting Scotland's Past: Scottish Whig Historians and the Creation of an Anglo-English Identity, 1689–c. 1830* (Cambridge: Cambridge University Press, 1993), 268.
48. See Richard B. Sher, *Church and University in the Scottish Enlightenment* (Edinburgh: Edinburgh University Press, 1985), 213–41.
49. Boswell, *Life*, 5:149.
50. Anon., *Belhaven's Vision: or his Speech in the Union-Parliament November 2, 1706* (Edinburgh, 1732), 8.
51. William Wright, *The Comical History of the Marriage-Union betwixt Fergusia and Heptarchus* (London?: 1706), 3.
52. *Ibid.*, 7.
53. See Pittock, *Celtic Identity*, 114. For a good discussion of the contrast between essentially two different kinds of nationalism at the time of the Union, the progressive vision of England and the historically based identity of Scotland, see Leith Davis, *Acts of Union: Scotland and the Literary Negotiation of the British Nation, 1707–1830* (Stanford: Stanford University Press, 1998), 19–45.

54. See M'Nicol, *Remarks on Dr. Samuel Johnson's Journey to the Hebrides*, 78.
55. William Lloyd, *An Historical Account of Church-Government as it was in Great-Britain and Ireland, when they First Received the Christian Religion* (London, 1684), sig. A6[r]. Lloyd's book was subsequently defended by William Stillingfleet, then Dean of St. Paul's Cathedral, in the preface to *Origines Britannicae, or The Antiquities of the British Churches* (London, 1685).
56. Lloyd, *Historical Account of Church-Government*, sig. A7[r].
57. Sir George Mackenzie, *A Defence of the Antiquity of the Royal Line of Scotland* (London, 1685), 7.
58. Boswell, *Life*, 5:40. This interpretation of the Union lasted into the nineteenth century even among authors who ardently supported the Union. See, e.g., Walter Scott, *Tales of a Grandfather*, in *The Prose Works of Sir Walter Scott*, 30 vols. (Edinburgh: Adam and Charles Black, 1870), 25:70.
59. James Macpherson, *The History of Great Britain from the Restoration to the Accession of the House of Hanover*, 2 vols. (London, 1775), 2:361.
60. Anon., *Remarks on a Voyage to the Hebrides, in a Letter to Samuel Johnson, L.L.D.* (London, 1775; facs. repr. New York and London: Garland, 1974), 21. See also M'Nicol, *Remarks on Dr. Samuel Johnson's Journey to the Hebrides*, 123.
61. See Kidd, *Subverting Scotland's Past.*
62. David Hume, *The History of England*, 8 vols. (1754–62; 4th edn, London, 1778), 1:24, 26.
63. Hume, "On the Authenticity of the Ossian Poems," in *Essays Moral, Political and Literary*, 2:416. David Raynor points out that Hume wrote virtually the same words in a letter to Edward Gibbon, whose historical skepticism is comparable to Hume's. See Raynor, "Ossian and Hume," in Gaskill (ed.), *Ossian Revisited*, 162, n. 10.
64. William Robertson, *The History of Scotland*, 2 vols. (1759; 14th edn, London, 1794), 1:1–2.
65. *Ibid.*, 1:2.
66. *Ibid.*, 1,5.
67. *Ibid.*, 2:41.
68. *Ibid.*, 2:306.
69. See Thomas Pennant, *A Tour of Scotland. MDCCLXIX* (Chester, 1771), 63, 70, 87–9, 121–2, 165, 180.
70. Pennant, *Tour of Scotland*, 179.
71. See M'Nicol, *Remarks on Dr. Samuel Johnson's Journey to the Hebrides*, 24–5, 55–6, 358.
72. John Clark, *An Answer to Mr. Shaw's Inquiry* (Edinburgh, 1781), 28.
73. Quoted from Boswell's private papers by Potkay, *The Passion for Happiness*, 10.
74. M'Nicol regarded the aimless bellicosity of ancient Highlanders as a lost virtue: "Battle seems always to have more their object, than the rewards of victory" (*Remarks on Dr. Samuel Johnson's Journey to the Hebrides*, 357).
75. See Adam Potkay, "Eloquence and Manners in Macpherson's *Poems of Ossian*," in *The Fate of Eloquence in the Age of Hume* (Ithaca and London: Cornell University Press, 1994), 189–225.

76. This is the point made by John Dwyer in "The Melancholy Savage: Text and Context in the *Poems of Ossian*," in Gaskill (ed.), *Ossian Revisited*, 164–206.
77. James Macpherson, *The Works of Ossian, the Son of Fingal* (1762), in *The Poems of Ossian and Related Works*, ed. Howard Gaskill (Edinburgh: Edinburgh University Press, 1996), 43.
78. *Ibid.*, 47.
79. *Ibid.*, 44.
80. Even Sir George Mackenzie had regarded the Scots and Picts as separate peoples. See *Defence of the Antiquity of the Royal Line of Scotland*, 20. Macpherson nonetheless seems to have launched a precedent for talking about "Caledonians" as a homogeneous Scottish race. See John Macpherson, *Critical Dissertations on the Origins, Antiquities, Government, Manners, and Religion of the Antient Caledonians* (Dublin, 1768). Boswell read John Macpherson's *Critical Dissertations* during his trip to the Highlands with Johnson, and was "disgusted by the unsatisfactory conjectures as to antiquity, before the days of record" (*Life*, 5:159).
81. See, e.g., Macpherson, *The Works of Ossian*, 420, n. 6; 421, n.31.
82. In the "Dissertation" appended to the 1765 "translation" of *Temora, Works of Ossian*, 211. Here Macpherson finally gets around to denying directly, without proof, the well-founded evidence that the Scots originally came from Ireland, claiming instead that Ireland was peopled by the Scots (210–11). Equally without evidence, he denies that the Picts were a separate people from the Scots (208).
83. Macpherson, *The Works of Ossian*, 44.
84. See John Whitaker, *The Genuine History of the Britons Asserted* (London, 1773).
85. See Hugh Blair, *A Critical Dissertation on the Poems of Ossian, the Son of Fingal* (1763), in Macpherson, *The Poems of Ossian and Related Works*, 370 and 377.
86. Macpherson, *The Poems of Ossian*, 216.
87. Blair, *A Critical Dissertation on the Poems of Ossian, the Son of Fingal*, in *ibid.*, 351.
88. *Ibid.*, 345.
89. *Ibid.*, 362–3.
90. See Kidd, *Subverting Scotland's Past*, 234.
91. Scott, *Tales of a Grandfather*, in *Prose Works*, 26:400–1.
92. *Ibid.*, 26:402.
93. Ferguson, *An Essay on the History of Civil Society*, 114.
94. *Ibid.*, 116.
95. See Hume, "Of National Characters," in *Essays Moral, Political and Literary*, 1:244–57. The idea of national character developed by Ferguson and Hume dismissed climate as the primary source of varying dispositions among nations, the ancient theory carried into the eighteenth century by many authors, including Montesquieu and Rousseau. The idea of "national character" as founded rather on an inherited tradition of customs and practices, perhaps influenced as well by language and even by racial biology, led to a new sub-discipline represented by, for example, Richard Chenevix's *An Essay upon National Character*,

ed. Percy Knox, 2 vols. (London, 1832), Arthur Bryant's *The National Character* (London, New York, and Toronto: Longmans, Green and Co., 1934) and even Paul Langford's recent *Englishness Identified.*

96. Boswell, *Life*, 5:167.
97. *Ibid.*, 5:223
98. As the Yale editor indicates with regard to this passage, the final question mark should be regarded as a point of emphasis, like an exclamation mark.
99. See his letter to John Taylor upon returning from Wales: "The mode of life is entirely English," he complained (*Letters*, 2:151).
100. See Boswell, *Life*, 2:91–2, 2:28, 3:107, 5:443, 1:321–2.
101. See *Letters*, 3:354–5.
102. Boswell, *Life*, 3:273.
103. *Letters*, 3:114.
104. Boswell, *Life*, 1:554.
105. Thomas Percy, *Reliques of Ancient English Poetry* (1765; 2nd edn, London, 1767), viii–ix.
106. See Mallet and Thomson, *Alfred*, 34.
107. Thomas Warton, *History of English Poetry* (1774), 4 vols. (facs. edn, with introduction by David Fairer, London and New York: Routledge/Thoemmes Press, 1998), 1: i.
108. As Howard Weinbrot has well described, the *celebration* of Britain's mixed literary and social ancestry became an important feature of British literary consciousness, particularly in the era of *Ossian*. See *Britannia's Issue: The Rise of British Literature from Dryden to Ossian* (Cambridge: Cambridge University Press, 1993), 477–571
109. See Tom Nairn, *The Break-Up of Britain: Crises and Neo-Nationalism* (London: NLB, 1977), 162–9.
110. Murray G. H. Pittock, *The Invention of Scotland: The Stuart Myth and the Scottish Identity, 1638 to the Present* (London and New York: Routledge, 1991), 103.
111. This untitled pamphlet by "Antiquary" is published along side one by Edward Hine, *The Anglo-Saxon Riddle* (London: W.T. Allen, 1873), 282. Hine became notorious for his energetic promotion of the belief that the Anglo-Saxons were the true "chosen people" indicated in the Hebrew Scriptures. On the rising cult of Anglo-Saxonism in nineteenth-century England, see Langford, *Englishness Identified*, 18–19.
112. Pittock, *Celtic Identity*, 130.
113. Boswell, *Life*, 5:20.
114. Lorenzo Fowler, *"John Bull" and "Brother Jonathan": Their National Peculiarities* (London, 1866), 6–7.
115. See John Arbuthnot, *The History of John Bull* (1712), ed. Alan W. Bower and Robert A. Erickson (Oxford: Clarendon Press, 1976).
116. John Lingard, *The History of England,* 10 vols. (1819–30; 5th edn, London: Charles Dolman, 1849), 1:2
117. *Ibid.*, 1:11.

CHAPTER 6

1. Edward W. Said, *Culture and Imperialism* (New York: Alfred A. Knopf, 1993), 9–11.
2. Laura Brown, *Ends of Empire: Women and Ideology in Early Eighteenth-Century English Literature* (Ithaca and London: Cornell University Press, 1993), 172.
3. Bridget Orr, *Empire on the English Stage 1660–1714* (Cambridge: Cambridge University Press, 2001), 8. D. George Boyce dates English imperial ambition back as far as King Alfred. See *Decolonization and the British Empire, 1775–1997* (Houndsmills: Macmillan; New York: St. Martin's, 1999), 5.
4. Greene, *Politics*, 165.
5. Thomas M. Curley, "Johnson and America," *Age of Johnson* 6 (1994): 38.
6. Clement Hawes, "Johnson and Imperialism," in Clingham (ed.), *Cambridge Companion to Samuel Johnson*, 119.
7. See C.C. Eldridge, *Disraeli and the Rise of the New Imperialism* (Cardiff: University of Wales Press, 1996), 26–7.
8. Research on the ideological bases of British imperialism in the eighteenth century remain, in fact, the preserve of a small group of good studies. See particularly Anthony Pagden, *Lords of All the World: Ideologies of Empire in Spain, Britain and France, c. 1500 to c. 1800* (New Haven: Yale University Press, 1995); Jack P. Greene, "Empire and Identity from the Glorious Revolution to the American Revolution," in *The Oxford History of the British Empire*, vol. 2, *The Eighteenth Century*, ed. P.J. Marshall, assisted by Alaine Low (Oxford and New York: Oxford University Press, 1998), 2:208–30; David Armitage, *The Ideological Origins of the British Empire* (Cambridge: Cambridge University Press, 2000).
9. T.H. Breen, "An Empire of Goods: The Anglicization of Colonial America, 1690–1776," *Journal of British Studies* 25 (1986): 467–99. See also *The Oxford History of the British Empire*, editor's introduction, 7 and 12.
10. J.R. Seeley, *The Expansion of England* (1883), ed. John Gross (Chicago and London: University of Chicago Press, 1971), 206.
11. Charles Davenant, *Essays upon I. The Balance of Power. II. The Right of Making War . . . III . Universal Monarchy* (London, 1701), 235.
12. *Ibid.*, 38.
13. *Ibid.*, 75, 235–6.
14. Anon., *The State of the British and French Colonies in North America* (London, 1755), 14.
15. Hume, "Of the Balance of Power," in *Essays Moral, Political and Literary*, 1:353. But compare "Of the Jealousy of Trade" (1758), 1:345.
16. Davenant, *Essays*, 3.
17. See Daniel Defoe, *The Ballance of Europe* (Edinburgh, 1711).
18. See Anon., *The State of the British and French Colonies in North America*, 119.
19. See Peters, *Pitt and Popularity*, 12–15.
20. *The Monitor* No. 16 (November 22, 1755): 135.

21. Sir William Keith, *The History of the British Plantations in America* (London, 1738), 8–9.
22. *Ibid.*, 12.
23. George Lillo, *The London Merchant*, ed. William H. McBurney (1731; Lincoln and London: University of Nebraska Press, 1965), III, i, ll. 11–19. As the editor notes in his introduction, "During Lillo's lifetime, *The London Merchant* was staged seventy times and (using Garrick's opening of the new Drury Lane Theatre as a convenient date) ninety-six times between 1731 and 1747" (xii).
24. John Selden, *Of Dominion, or Ownership of the Sea*, trans. Marchamont Nedham (London, 1652), 1.
25. Sir Josiah Child, *A Discourse about Trade* (London, 1689), 189.
26. Whitehead, *Manners: A Satire,* 16.
27. Sir Dalby Thomas, *An Historical Account of the Rise and Growth of the West-India Collonies* (London, 1690), 34.
28. Richard Copithorne, *The English Cotejo: or, the Cruelties, Depredations, and Illicit Trade Charg'd upon the English in a Spanish Libel lately Published* (London, 1739), 8.
29. *Craftsman* No. 644 (November 11, 1738), 1.
30. Archibald Kennedy, *The Importance of Gaining and Preserving the Friendship of the Indians to the British Interest Considered* (New York, 1751), 6.
31. William Clarke, *Observations on the Late and Present Conduct of the French, with regard to their Encroachments upon the British Colonies in North America* (London, 1755), 10 and 53–4.
32. Anon., *The State of the British and French Colonies in North America*, 82.
33. *Ibid.*, 24.
34. *Works* (1825), 6:293.
35. *Ibid.*, 6:297.
36. *Ibid.*, 6:357.
37. *Ibid.*, 6:365.
38. *The Gentleman's Magazine* No. 8 (1738), 286.
39. *Ibid.*, 285–6.
40. Charles Louis de Secondat, Baron de Montesquieu, *Reflections on the Grandeur and Declension of the Romans* (London, 1734), 87.
41. See Edward Gibbon, *The History of the Decline and Fall of the Roman Empire*, ed. David Womersley, 3 vols. (London: Allen Lane, 1994), 1:38.
42. See Francis Hutcheson, *A System of Moral Philosophy*, 2 vols. (1734–1; London, 1755; facs. repr. New York: Augustus M. Kelly, 1968), 2:309.
43. Seeley, *Expansion of England*, 207.
44. *Ibid.*, 56.
45. See *ibid.*, 143.
46. Adam Smith, *Wealth of Nations*, 2:558.
47. *Ibid.*, 2:594 and 584.
48. See R.P Thomas and D.N. McCloskey, "Overseas Trade and Empire 1700–1860," in Floud and McCloskey (eds.), *Economic History of Britain since 1700*, 87–102; John Rule, *The Vital Century: England's Developing Economy 1714–1815*

(London and New York: Longman, 1992), 263; Stanley L. Engerman, "Mercantilism and Overseas Trade," in *The Economic History of the British Empire*, ed. Roderick Floud and Donald McCloskey, 3 vols. (2nd edn, Cambridge: Cambridge University Press, 1994), 1:182–204; Patrick K. O'Brien, "Inseparable Connections: Trade, Economy, Fiscal State, and the Expansion of Empire, 1688–1815," in *Oxford History of the British Empire*, 2:53–77.

49. Davenant, *Essays*, 255.
50. John Oldmixon, *The British Empire in America* (London, 1708), xix.
51. See, e.g., Davenant, *Essays*, 250.
52. Thomas, *An Historical Account of the Rise and Growth of the West-India Colonies*, 2.
53. *Ibid.*, 9.
54. Oliver Goldsmith, *The Citizen of the World* , in *Collected Works*, ed. Arthur Friedman, 5 vols. (Oxford: Clarendon Press, 1966), 2:108.
55. Child, *Discourse about Trade*, 164–5.
56. *Ibid.*, 183.
57. Hume, "Of the Balance of Trade," in *Essays Moral, Political and Literary*, 1:332.
58. Joshua Gee, *The Trade and Navigation of Great-Britain Considered* (London, 1729), 61.
59. *Ibid.*, 147.
60. John Knox, *A View of the British Empire* (London, 1784), ix.
61. Keith, *History of the British Plantations in America*, 11.
62. John Cary, *An Answer to Mr. Molyneux his Case of Ireland's Being Bound by Acts of Parliament in England* (London, 1698), 11. See William Molyneux, *The Case of Ireland's Being Bound by Acts of Parliament* (Dublin, 1698). John Locke's great friend and correspondent, Molyneux drew his argument entirely from Locke's chapter "Of Conquest" in *Two Treatises of Civil Government* (1690), ed. Peter Laslett (2nd edn, New York: Cambridge University Press, 1963), bk. 2, ch. 16.
63. William Atwood, *The History and Reasons of the Dependency of Ireland upon the Imperial Crown* (London, 1698), 47–8.
64. See Hume, "Of the Balance of Power," in *Essays Moral, Political and Literary*, 1:330–56; Adam Smith, *Wealth of Nations*, bk. 4, ch. 6 ("Of Colonies"). As David Armitage points out, Hume "rejoiced" in the dissolution of the British Empire in the mid-Atlantic right up to his death in 1776 (*The Ideological Origins of the British Empire*, 194). See also J.G.A. Pocock, "Hume and the American Revolution: The Dying Thoughts of a North Briton," in *Virtue, Commerce, and History*, 124–41.
65. See Josiah Tucker, *The True Interest of Britain, Set Forth in Regard to the Colonies* (Philadelphia, 1776). Compare this to Goldsmith's *Citizen of the World* (1760), in *Works*, 2:108. Even previous to Goldsmith, authors had worried that the drift of colonies towards independence was inevitable. See Hutcheson, *System of Moral Philosophy*, 2:309.
66. See in particular "Speech on Conciliation with America" (March 27, 1775), in Burke, *Writings and Speeches*, vol. 3.

67. Grenville's speech is printed along with Pitt's reply in *The Celebrated Speech of a Celebrated Commoner* (London, 1766), 9–10.
68. See Smith, *Wealth of Nations,* bk. 4, ch. 7, 2:573; Tucker, *True Interest of Britain,* 4.
69. James Macpherson, *The Rights of Great Britain asserted against the Claims of America* (1775; 3rd edn, London, 1776), 74.
70. *Ibid.*, 4. See also Arthur Young, *Political Essays concerning the Present State of the British Empire* (London, 1772), 36.
71. John Wesley, *A Calm Address to our American Colonies* (London, 1775), 5–6.
72. *Ibid.*, 7.
73. *Ibid.*, 2.
74. Davenant, *Essays,* 48.
75. See Daunton, *Progress and Poverty,* 482.
76. Johnson himself cites Anon., *An Appeal to the Justice and Interestes of the People of Great Britain, in the Present Dispute with America, by an Old Member of Parliament* (Almon, 1774). See also Anon., *Tyranny Unmasked,* 39; Anon., *An Answer to a Pamphlet entitled Taxation No Tyranny* (London, 1775), 7. Something closer to Johnson's position on the analogy between America and Ireland is taken by Arthur Young in *Political Essays,* 40.
77. Cary, *Answer to Mr. Molyneux,* 29.
78. Chambers and Johnson, *Course of Lectures,* 1:287–8.
79. *Ibid.*, 1:282.
80. *Life of the King of Prussia,* in *Works* (1825), 6:463.
81. Donald Greene suggests that Johnson could not seriously have been proposing to force the Americans to obey British law, as their independence was already a *fait accompli* (10:402). But this opinion does not appear to have been shared in the pamphlet literature of the time. See, e.g., Anon., *A Plan for Conciliating the Jarring Interests of Great Britain and her North American Colonies* (London, 1775); Anon., *A Short Appeal to the People of Great-Britain* (London, 1776); Macpherson, *Rights of Great Britain asserted,* 82. Others such as the moderate Josiah Tucker in *True Interest of Britain* and the Pittite Arthur Lee in *An Appeal to the Justice and Interests of the People of Great Britain* (1775; 4th edn, London, 1776), counseled against the strategy of suppressing 3 million colonists at the point of a sword.
82. "Junius," *Letters,* Letter XLII (January 30, 1771), 218–21.
83. *Ibid.*, Letter XLIII (February 6, 1771), 227. "Philo-Junius" was replying to "Anti-Junius" in *The Public Advertiser*, February 4, 1771.
84. Boswell, *Life,* 2:121.
85. Tucker attacked the British restriction on Irish commerce in *A Brief Essay,* 47–8.
86. Smith, *Wealth of Nations,* bk. 4, ch. 7, 2:640.
87. Anon., *The Crisis; or, Immediate Concernments of the British Empire* (London, 1785), 1.
88. Richard Knolles, *The Turkish History, from the Original of that Nation to the Growth of the Ottoman Empire* (6th edn, London, 1687), sig. A1^{r}.

89. *Ibid.*, sig. A1[r].
90. *Ibid.*, sig. A1[r-v].
91. *Works* (1825), 5:21.
92. *Ibid.*, 5:249 and 252.
93. Boswell, *Life*, 1:359.
94. W.J. Bate, "Johnson and Satire Manqué," in *Eighteenth-Century Studies in Honor of Donald F. Hyde*, ed. W.H. Bond (New York: The Grolier Club, 1970): 145–60.
95. *Works* (1825), 5:219.
96. *Ibid.*, 5:221.
97. *Ibid.*, 5:219.
98. *Ibid.*, 5:221.
99. Greene, *Politics*, 167.
100. Cited in Eldridge, *Disraeli and the Rise of a New Imperialism*, 91–2.
101. See C.A. Bayly, *Imperial Meridian: The British Empire and the World* (London and New York: Longman, 1989), 121–6.
102. *Works* (1825), 5:219.
103. Bayly, *Imperial Meridian*, 177.
104. See, e.g., Anon., *The Crisis*, 16–17.
105. See, e.g., Uday Singh Mehta, *Liberalism and Empire* (Chicago and London: University of Chicago Press, 1999). Mehta advances the interesting thesis that the liberal-rationalist tradition, as exemplified by James and John Stuart Mill, is inherently more imperialistic than the anti-rationalist conservative tradition embodied by Burke. But the distinction between these two traditions is not nearly so complete and clean-cut. Burke scholars agree that he supported imperialism, though in a more humane form. See, e.g., Frederick G. Whelan, *Edmund Burke and India: Political Morality and Empire* (Pittsburgh: University of Pittsburgh Press, 1996), 6–41; P.J. Marshall, "Burke and Empire," in Richard Connors, Clyve Jones, and Stephen Taylor (eds.), *Hanoverian Britain and Empire: Essays in Memory of Philip Lawson* (Woodbridge: Boydell Press, 1998), 288–98. And we will consider whether a conservative like Johnson is not, in fact, fairly close to the authoritarian attitudes of authors like the Mills.
106. For a detailed summary of the charges against Hastings, see Whelan, *Edmund Burke and India*, 64–187. With regard to the Nandakumar affair, Hastings has had his defenders since the Victorian age. See Sir James Fitzjames Stephen, *The Story of Nancomar and the Impeachment of Sir Elijah Impey*, 2 vols. (London, 1885); Sophia Weizman, *Warren Hastings and Sir Philip Francis* (Manchester: Manchester University Press, 1929), 36. Whelan, however, generally upholds Hastings's guilt (see *Edmund Burke and India*, 64–187).
107. Burke, "Speech on Fox's India Bill," in *India: Madras and Bengal*, ed. P.J. Marshall (Oxford: Clarendon Press, 1981), vol. 5 of Burke, *Writings and Speeches*, 441.
108. See, e.g., Francis Plowden, *A Short History of the British Empire during the Last Twenty Months, viz. From May 1792 to the Close of the Year 1793* (London, 1794).

109. Burke, "Speech on Conciliation with America," in *Writings and Speeches*, 3:125.
110. *Letters*, 2:135 and 137.
111. See Thomas M. Curley, *Samuel Johnson and the Age of Travel* (Athens: University of Georgia Press, 1976), 135–7. I am indebted to the same source (132–8) for the following information on Johnson's relations with the Vansittart brothers and Joseph Fowke.
112. *Letters*, 2:136.
113. *Works* (1825), 5:219.
114. Stephen Greenblatt, *Marvelous Possessions: The Wonder of the New World* (Chicago: Chicago University Press, 1991). See also Richard Drayton, "Knowledge and Empire," in *Oxford History of the British Empire*, 2:231–52.
115. Boswell, *Life*, 4:66.
116. *Ibid.*, 4:213–14. This is very close to reasoning used by Hastings himself during his trial. See Whelan, *Edmund Burke and India*, 219–20.
117. Boswell, *Life*, 2:343.
118. *Ibid.*, 3:20.
119. *Letters*, 2:41.
120. *Ibid.*, 2:86.
121. *Ibid.*, 2:160.
122. *Ibid.*, 2:351.
123. *Ibid.*, 3:323–4.
124. *Ibid.*, 4:129.
125. See Johnson's letter to Thomas Cadell on April 16, 1783, *ibid.*, 4:123.
126. *Ibid.*, 4:248.
127. *Ibid.*, 4:248. See also Johnson's letter to Chambers on January 22, 1767, in *ibid.*, 1:277–8.
128. *Ibid.*, 4:129.
129. *Ibid.*, 4:248.
130. *Ibid.*, 2:137.
131. *Ibid.*, 4:277.
132. See *ibid.*, 4:403.
133. See James Mill, *The History of British India* (1817–58; 4th edn, London, 1840–8), 4:519–21.
134. Sujit Bose, *Attitudes to Imperialism: Kipling, Forster and Paul Scott* (Delhi: Amar Prakashan, 1990), 3.
135. Burke, "Speech on Conciliation with America," in *Writings and Speeches*, 3:139.
136. See Hudson, *Samuel Johnson and Eighteenth-Century Thought*, 169–71.
137. Homi K. Bhabha, *The Location of Culture* (London: Routledge, 1994), 105–6.
138. See Nicholas Hudson, "From 'Nation' to 'Race': The Origin of Racial Classification in Eighteenth-Century Thought," *Eighteenth-Century Studies* 29 (1996): 247–64.
139. Bayly, *Imperial Meridian*, 100.

CONCLUSION

1. John Rule, *The Vital Century: England's Developing Economy 1714–1815* (London and New York: Longman, 1992), 28.
2. For more detailed discussion of Johnson's role in this decade, see Nicholas Hudson, "Discourse of Transition: Johnson, the 1750s, and the Rise of the Middle-Class," *Age of Johnson* 13 (2002): 31–52.
3. Boswell, *Life*, 5:305. Similar statements can be found in *ibid.*, 2:133, 2:337, and 3:253. On Johnson's intellectual and literary relationship with London, see Nicholas Hudson, "Samuel Johnson, Urban Culture and the Geography of Post-Fire London."

Bibliography

WORKS BY JOHNSON

A Dictionary of the English Language on CD Rom (1st edn, 1755 and 4th edn, 1773). Ed. Anne McDermott (Cambridge: Cambridge University Press, 1995).

Johnsonian Gleanings. Ed. Aleyn Lyell Reade. 10 vols. (New York: Octogon Books, 1968).

Letters. Ed. Bruce Redford. 5 vols. (Princeton: Princeton University Press, 1992–4).

Lives of the English Poets. Ed. G.B. Hill. 2 vols. (Oxford: Clarendon Press, 1905).

Works. 12 vols (Oxford: Talboys and Wheeler; London: W. Pickering, 1825).

The Yale Edition of the Works of Samuel Johnson. Gen. eds. A.T. Hazen and J.H. Middendorf. 16 vols. (New Haven and London: Yale University Press, 1958–)

MANUSCRIPT SOURCES

Edwards, Thomas. Letter to Daniel Wray, 23 May, 1755, Oxford, Bodleian Library, Bodleian MS 1012, 208.

EIGHTEENTH-CENTURY JOURNALS

Briton, The (1762–3).

Champion, The; or, British Mercury (1739–40).

Common-Sense; or, the Englishman's Journal (1737–41).

Connoisseur, The (1754–6).

Con-test, The (1756–7).

Country Journal, The; or, the Craftsman (1727–50).

Daily Gazetteer, The (1735–46).

Gentleman's Magazine, The (1731–1907).

Journal Britannique (1750–55)

Monitor, The; or, the British Freeholder (1755–65).

Museum, The; or, the Literary and Historical Register (1746–7).

North Briton, The (1762–3).

Old England; or, the Broad Bottom Journal (1746–7).

Public Advertiser, The (1752–94).

Remembrancer, The; or, National Advocate (1751).

Spectator, The. Ed. Donald F. Bond, 5 vols. (1711–12; Oxford: Clarendon Press, 1965).
True Patriot, The. Ed. W.B. Coley (1745–6; Oxford: Clarendon Press, 1987).
World, The (1753–6).

SOURCES: PRE-1900

Anon., *An Answer to a Pamphlet entitled Taxation No Tyranny* (London, 1775).
Anon. *An Apology for a Late Resignation* (London, 1748).
Anon. *An Appeal to the Justice and Interestes of the People of Great Britain, in the Present Dispute with America, by an Old Member of Parliament* (Almon, 1774).
Anon. *The Balance: or the Merits of Whig and Tory exactly weigh'd and fairly determin'd* (London, 1753).
Anon. *Belhaven's Vision: or his Speech in the Union-Parliament November 2, 1706* (Edinburgh, 1732).
Anon. *The Celebrated Speech of a Celebrated Commoner* (London, 1766).
Anon. *Characters of Parties in British Government* (London, 1782).
Anon. *The Coalition; or an Essay on the Present State of the Parties* (London, 1783).
Anon. *The Craftsman's Doctrine of the Liberty of the Press, Explain'd to the Meanest Capacity* (London, 1732).
Anon. *The Crisis; or, Immediate Concernments of the British Empire* (London, 1785).
Anon. *The Female Aegis or, the Duties of Women* (London, 1798; facs. repr. New York and London: Garland, 1974).
Anon. *An Historical View of the Principles, Character, Persons &c of Political Writers in Great Britain* (London, 1740).
Anon. *The Honest Grief of a Tory, expressed in a Genuine Letter from a Burgess of ____, in Wiltshire, to the Author of the Monitor, Feb 17, 1759* (London, 1759).
Anon. *A General View of the Present Politics and Interests of the Principle Powers of Europe* (London, 1747).
Anon. *A Letter upon the State of the Parties* (London, 1797).
Anon. *The Livery Man: or Plain Thoughts on Public Affairs* (London, 1740).
Anon. *The Loyal or Revolutionary Tory* (London, 1733).
Anon. *Merit: A Satire. Humbly Addressed to His Excellency the Earl of Chesterfield* (Dublin, 1746).
Anon. *A New System of Patriot Policy* (London, 1756).
Anon. *Observations on the Conduct of the Tories, Whigs, and the Dissenters* (London, 1739).
Anon. *Opposition more Necessary than Ever* (London, 1742).
Anon. ("Petronius"). *Party Distinctions the Bane and Misery of the British Nation* (London, 1744).
Anon. *A Plan for Conciliating the Jarring Interests of Great Britain and her North American Colonies* (London, 1775).
Anon. *The Present Necessity of Distinguishing Publick Spirit from Party* (London, 1736).
Anon. *Private Virtue and Publick Spirit Display'd* (London, 1751).

Anon. *Remarks on a Voyage to the Hebrides, in a Letter to Samuel Johnson, L.L.D.* (London, 1775; facs. repr. New York and London: Garland, 1974).
Anon. *The Sentiments of a Tory, in Respect to a Late Important Transaction* (London, 1741).
Anon. *A Short Appeal to the People of Great-Britain* (London, 1776).
Anon. *The State of the British and French Colonies in North America* (London, 1755).
Anon. *The State of the Nation for the Year 1747 and respecting 1748* (Dublin, 1748).
Anon. *The True-Born Britain* (London, 1707).
Anon. *The Tryal of Lady Allurea Luxury, before the Lord Chief Justice Upright* (London, 1757).
Anon. *Tyranny Unmasked: An Answer to a Late Pamphlet entitled Taxation No Tyranny* (London, 1775).
Anon. *Unity and Public Spirit* (London, 1780).
Anon. ("a Lady"). *The Whole Duty of a Woman* (1695; 2nd edn, London, 1696).
Abercromby, Patrick. *The Martial Atchievements of the Scots Nation.* 2 vols. (Edinburgh, 1711).
Addison, Joseph. *Works.* 6 vols. (London: George Bell and Sons, 1893).
Allestree, Richard. *The Lady's Calling* (Oxford, 1673).
Arbuthnot, John. *The History of John Bull* (1712). Ed. Alan W. Bower and Robert A. Erickson (Oxford: Clarendon Press, 1976).
Atwood, William. *The History and Reasons of the Dependency of Ireland upon the Imperial Crown* (London, 1698).
Barbauld, Anna Laetitia. *Works.* 2 vols. (London, 1825).
Barclay, James. *A Treatise of Education: or, an Easy Method of Acquiring Language, and Introducing Children to the Knowledge of History, Geography, Mythology, Antiquities &c.* (Edinburgh: 1743).
Beattie, James. *Essays on the Nature and Utility of Truth* (Edinburgh, 1776; facs. repr. New York: Garland, 1971).
Bigge, Thomas. *Considerations on the State of Parties, and the Means of Effecting a Reconciliation between them* (London, 1793).
Blackstone, Sir William. *Commentaries of the Laws of England.* Ed. Wayne Morrison. 4 vols. (1765–9; London and Sydney: Cavendish Publishing Limited, 2001).
Bolingbroke, Henry St. John, Viscount. *Remarks on the History of England* (1752; 3rd edn, London 1780).
Political Writings. Ed. David Armitage (Cambridge: Cambridge University Press, 1997).
Bolton, Edmund. *The Cities great Concern, in this Case or Question of Honour and Arms, whether Apprenticeship Extinguisheth Gentry* (London, 1674).
Boswell, James. *Life of Johnson* (1791). Ed. G.B. Hill, rev. L.F. Powell. 6 vols. (Oxford: Clarendon Press, 1934–50).
London Journal, 1762–1763. Ed. Frederick A. Pottle (New York, London, and Toronto: McGraw-Hill, 1950).
Bouhours, Dominique. *Entretiens d'Ariste et d'Eugène* (Amsterdam, 1671).
Brack, O.M. Jr. and Kelley, Robert E. (eds.). *The Early Biographies of Samuel Johnson* (Iowa City: University of Iowa Press, 1974).

Brady, Robert. *An Introduction to the Old English History* (London, 1684).
Brathwait, Richard. *The English Gentleman* (London, 1630).
Brokesby, Francis. *Of Education with Respect to Grammar Schools* (London, 1701).
Brown, John. *An Estimate of the Manners and Principles of the Times* (London, 1757).
Browning, Elizabeth Barrett. *Letters to Mary Russell.* Eds. Meredith B. Raymond and Mary Rose Sullivan. 3 vols. (Winfred, KS: Armstrong Browning Library of Baylor University, The Browning Institute, and Wellesley College, 1983).
Bryant, Arthur. *The National Character* (London, New York, and Toronto: Longmans, Green and Co., 1934).
Burgh, James. *The Dignity of Human Nature* (London, 1754).
Burke, Edmund. *Works*, 12 vols. (Boston: Little, Brown and Company, 1899).
Writings and Speeches of Edmund Burke. Gen. ed. Paul Langford. 9 vols. (Oxford: Clarendon Press, 1980–).
Callender, James Thomson. *A Critical Review of the Works of Johnson* (Edinburgh, 1783; repr. New York and London: Garland Press, 1974).
Campbell, Archibald. *Lexiphanes: A Dialogue* (London, 1767).
Campbell, George. *Philosophy of Rhetoric.* Ed. Lloyd F. Bitzer (1776; Carbondale: Southern Illinois University Press, 1963).
Campbell, R. *The Complete London Tradesman* (1725–7; London, 1747; facs. repr. New York: Augustus M. Kelley, 1969).
Carlyle, Thomas. *On Heroes, Hero-Worship, and the Heroic in History.* Eds. Michael K. Goldberg, Joel J. Brattin, and Mark Engel (1841; Berkeley, Los Angeles, and Oxford: University of California Press, 1993).
Carte, Thomas. *General History of England.* 4 vols. (London: 1747–55).
Cary, John. *An Answer to Mr. Molyneux his Case of Ireland's Being Bound by Acts of Parliament in England* (London, 1698).
Chambers, Sir Robert and Johnson, Samuel. *A Course of Lectures on the English Law.* Ed. Thomas M. Curley. 2 vols. (wr. 1767–73; Madison: University of Wisconsin Press, 1986).
Chapone, Hester. *Letters on the Improvement of the Mind* (Dublin, 1773; facs. repr. London: William Pickering, 1996).
Charke, Charlotte. *A Narrative of the Life of Mrs. Charlotte Charke* (London, 1755; facs. repr. Gainsville: Scholars Facsimiles, 1969).
Chenevix, Richard. *An Essay upon National Character.* Ed. Percy Knox. 2 vols. (London, 1832).
Chesterfield, Philip Dormer Stanhope, Lord, and Waller, Edmund. *The Interest of Hanover Steadily Pursued since the A____n* (London, 1743).
Child, Sir Josiah. *A Discourse about Trade* (London, 1689).
Clark, John. *An Answer to Mr. Shaw's Inquiry* (Edinburgh, 1781).
Clarke, John. *An Essay upon the Education of Youth* (1720; 3rd edn, London, 1740).
Clarke, William. *Observations on the Late and Present Conduct of the French, with regard to their Encroachments upon the British Colonies in North America* (London, 1755).

Constable, John. *The Conversation of Gentlemen* (London, 1738).

Copithorne, Richard. *The English Cotejo: or, the Cruelties, Depredations, and Illicit Trade Charg'd upon the English in a Spanish Libel lately Published* (London, 1739).

Cornish, Joseph. *An Attempt to Display the Importance of Classical Learning* (London: 1783).

Darrell, William. *A Gentleman Instructed* (London, 1704).

Davenant, Charles. *The True-Born Englishman* (1700; 21st edn, Dublin, 1728).

Essays upon I. The Balance of Power. II. The Right of Making War . . . III. Universal Monarchy (London, 1701).

Defoe, Daniel. *An Essay at Removing National Prejudices against a Union with Scotland* (Edinburgh, 1706).

The History of the Union of Great Britain (Edinburgh, 1709).

The Ballance of Europe (Edinburgh, 1711).

The Complete English Tradesman. 2 vols. (1725–27; 2nd edn, London, 1727; facs. repr. New York: Augustus M. Kelley, 1969).

The Compleat Gentleman. Ed. Karl D. Bülbring (n.d.; London: David Nutt, 1890).

Dennis, John. *An Essay on Publick Spirit; being a Satyr in Prose upon the Manners and Luxury of the Times* (London, 1711).

Dodsley, Robert. *A Muse in Livery, or, the Footman's Miscellany* (London, 1732).

Eden, Sir Frederic Morton. *The State of the Poor: or, an History of the Labouring Classes in England*. 3 vols. (London, 1797).

Eliot, George. *Letters*. Ed. Gordon S. Haight. 9 vols. (New Haven and London: Yale University Press, 1954–78).

Ellis, Sarah Stickney. *The Women of England, Their Social Duties and Domestic Habits* (1839; 21st edn, London and Paris: 1847).

Elphinston, John. *Education, in Four Books* (London, 1763).

Essex, John. *The Young Ladies Conduct, or Rules for Education* (London, 1722).

Evelyn, John. *The Writings of John Evelyn*. Ed. Guy de la Bédoyère (Woodbridge: The Boydell Press, 1995).

Evelyn, Mary. *The Ladies Dressing-Room Unlock'd* (London, 1700).

Fawconer, Samuel. *An Essay on Modern Luxury* (London, 1765).

Fell, John. *An Essay towards an English Grammar* (London, 1784; repr. Menston: Scholar Press, 1967).

Ferguson, Adam. *An Essay on the History of Civil Society* (Edinburgh, 1767; fasc. repr. New York: Garland, 1971).

Fielding, Henry. *A Full Vindication of the Dutchess Dowager of Marlborough* (London, 1742).

Joseph Andrews. Eds. Douglas Brooks-Davies and Martin C. Battestin. Rev. Thomas Keymer (1742; Oxford: Oxford University Press, 1999).

Enquiry into the Causes of the Late Increase of Robbers. Ed. Malvin R. Zirker (1751; Oxford: Clarendon Press, 1988).

Fordyce, James. *Sermons for Young Women*. 2 vols. (3rd edn, London, 1766; facs. repr. London: William Pickering, 1996).

Fowler, Lorenzo. *"John Bull" and "Brother Jonathan": Their National Peculiarities* (London, 1866).
Gee, Joshua. *The Trade and Navigation of Great-Britain Considered* (London: 1729).
Gibbon, Edward. *The History of the Decline and Fall of the Roman Empire*. Ed. David Womersley. 3 vols. (London: Allen Lane, 1994).
Gisborne, Thomas. *An Enquiry into the Duties of Men in the Higher and Middle Classes in Great Britain*. 2 vols. (1794; 2nd edn, London, 1795).
An Enquiry into the Duties of the Female Sex (London, 1797).
Goldsmith, Oliver. *Collected Works*. Ed. Arthur Friedman. 5 vols. (Oxford: Clarendon Press, 1966).
Graham, Catherine Macaulay. *The History of England from the Accession of James I to that of the Brunswick Line*. 8 vols. (London, 1763).
Greenwood, James. *An Essay towards a Practical English Grammar* (London, 1711).
Gregory, John. *A Father's Legacy to his Daughters* (Dublin, 1774).
Halifax, George Savile, Marquis of. *The Lady's New-Years Gift* (1688; 5th edn, London, 1696).
Hawkins, Sir John. *The Life of Samuel Johnson* (London, 1787).
Hays, Mary. *Appeal to the Men of Great Britain, in Behalf of Women* (London, 1798; facs. repr. New York and London: Garland, 1974).
Haywood, Eliza. *Selections from "The Female Spectator."* Ed. Patricia Meyer Spacks (1744–6; New York and Oxford: Oxford University Press, 1999).
Heydon, John. *Advice to a Daughter* (London, 1658).
Higford, William. *Institutions or Advice to his Grandson* (London, 1658).
Hine, Edward. *The Anglo-Saxon Riddle* (London: W.T. Allen, 1873).
Hodges, James. *Essays on Several Subjects, viz. Discouragements Private Men meet with in Promoting Publick Good* (London, 1710).
Hume, David. *The History of England*. 8 vols. (1754–62; 4th edn, London, 1778).
Essays, Moral, Political, and Literary. Ed. T.H. Green and T.H. Grose. 2 vols. (1742–70; London, New York, Bombay, and Calcutta: Longman, Green and Co., 1912).
Hutcheson, Francis. *A System of Moral Philosophy*. 2 vols. (1734–7; London, 1755; facs. repr. New York: Augustus M. Kelly, 1968).
Jones, Erasmus. *Luxury, Pride and Vanity, the Bane of the British Nation* (4th edn, London, 1736).
Jones, Henry. *Merit. A Poem: inscribed to the Right Honourable Philip Earl of Chesterfield* (London: 1753).
"Junius." *The Letters of Junius*. Ed. John Cannon (Oxford: Clarendon Press, 1978).
Keith, Sir William. *The History of the British Plantations in America* (London, 1738).
Kennedy, Archibald. *The Importance of Gaining and Preserving the Friendship of the Indians to the British Interest Considered* (New York, 1751).
Knolles, Richard. *The Turkish History, from the Original of that Nation to the Growth of the Ottoman Empire* (1603; 6th edn, London, 1687).
Knox, John. *A View of the British Empire* (London, 1784).
Knox, Vicesimus. *Essays, Moral and Literary* (London, 1779; facs. repr. New York: Garland, 1972),

Liberal Education: or, a Treatise on the Methods of Acquiring Useful and Polite Learning (1781; 5th edn, London: 1783).

Lee, Arthur. *An Appeal to the Justice and Interests of the People of Great Britain* (1775; 4th edn, London, 1776).

Lillo, George. *The London Merchant*. Ed. William H. McBurney (1731; Lincoln and London: University of Nebraska Press, 1965).

Lingard, John. *The History of England.* 10 vols. (1819–30; 5th edn, London: Charles Dolman, 1849).

Lloyd, William. *An Historical Account of Church-Government as it was in Great-Britain and Ireland, when they First Received the Christian Religion* (London, 1684).

Locke, John. *Two Treatises of Civil Government* (1690). Ed. Peter Laslett (2nd edn, New York: Cambridge University Press, 1963).

Lyttelton, George. *A Letter to the Tories* (1747; 2nd edn, London, 1748).

Macaulay, Catherine. *Letters on Education* (London, 1790; facs. repr. London: William Pickering, 1996).

Mackenzie, Sir George. *A Defence of the Antiquity of the Royal Line of Scotland* (London, 1685).

M'Nicol, Donald. *Remarks on Dr. Samuel Johnson's Journey to the Hebrides* (London, 1779; facs. repr. New York and London: Garland, 1974).

Macpherson, James. *The History of Great Britain from the Restoration to the Accession of the House of Hanover.* 2 vols. (London, 1775).

The Rights of Great Britain asserted against the Claims of America (1775; 3rd edn, London, 1776).

The Poems of Ossian and Related Works. Ed. Howard Gaskill (Edinburgh: Edinburgh University Press, 1996).

Macpherson, John. *Critical Dissertations on the Origins, Antiquities, Government, Manners, and Religion of the Antient Caledonians* (Dublin, 1768).

Mallet, David. *The Conduct of the Ministry Impartially Examined* (London, 1756).

Mallet, David and Thomson, James. *Alfred: A Masque* (Dublin: 1740).

Malthus, Thomas. *An Essay on the Principle of Population, as it Affects the Future Improvement of Society* (London, 1798).

Mandeville, Bernard. *The Fable of the Bees or, Private Virtues, Publick Benefits*. Ed. F.B. Kaye. 2 vols. (1714–39; Oxford: Clarendon Press, 1924).

Mattaire, Michael. *The English Grammar* (London, 1712; repr. Menston: Scholar Press, 1967).

Mauduit, Israel. *Considerations on the Present German War* (1760; 4th edn, London, 1761).

Miège, Guy. *The Present State of Great Britain and Ireland* (1707; 8th edn, revised, London, 1738).

Mill, Harriet Taylor and Mill, John Stuart. *Essays on Sex Equality*. Ed. Alice S. Rossi (Chicago and London: University of Chicago Press, 1970).

Mill, James. *The History of British India* (1817–58; 4th edn, London, 1840–8).

Millar, John. *Observations concerning the Distinction of Ranks in Society* (London, 1771).

Milton, John. *Paradise Lost*. Ed. Merritt Y. Hughes (1674; Indianapolis: Odyssey Press, 1962).
Molyneux, William. *The Case of Ireland's Being Bound by Acts of Parliament* (Dublin, 1698).
Montesquieu, Charles Louis de Secondat, Baron de. *Reflections on the Grandeur and Declension of the Romans* (London, 1734).
More, Hannah. *Works*. 2 vols. (New York: Harper & Brothers, 1835).
Oldmixon, John. *The British Empire in America* (London, 1708).
Peachum, Henry. *The Compleat Gentleman* (London, 1634).
Pennant, Thomas. *A Tour of Scotland. MDCCLXIX* (Chester, 1771).
Perceval, John, Earl of Egmont. *Faction Detected by the Evidence of Facts* (London, 1743).
Things as They Are (London, 1758).
Percy, Thomas. *Reliques of Ancient English Poetry* (1765; 2nd edn, London, 1767).
Petyt, Willliam. *The Antient Right of the Commons of England Asserted; or, a Discourse Proving by Records and the Best Historians, that the Commons of England were ever an Essential Part of Parliament* (London, 1680).
Pilkington, Laetitia. *Memoirs*. Ed. A.C. Elias, Jr. 2 vols. (Athens and London: University of Georgia Press, 1997).
Piozzi, Hester Lynch. *Anecdotes of the late Samuel Johnson, L.L.D.* (Dublin, 1786).
Plowden, Francis. *A Short History of the British Empire during the Last Twenty Months, viz. From May 1792 to the Close of the Year 1793* (London, 1794).
Pope, Alexander. *Poems*. Ed. John Butt (New Haven: Yale University Press, 1963).
Priestley, Joseph. *Rudiments of English Grammar* (London, 1761; repr. Menston: Scholar Press, 1969).
An Essay on a Course of Liberal Education (London, 1765).
Quintilian, *Institutio Oratorio*. Trans. H.E. Butler. Loeb Classical Library. 4 vols. (Cambridge, MA: Harvard University Press; London: Heinemann, 1930).
Ramsey, William. *The Gentleman's Companion* (London, 1672).
Robertson, William. *The History of Scotland*. 2 vols. (1759; 14th edn, London, 1794).
Ruskin, John. *Works*. 39 vols. Eds. E.T. Cook and Alexander Wedderburn (London: George Allen; New York: Longman, Green and Co., 1903–12).
Scott, Sir Walter. *The Miscellaneous Prose Works*. 6 vols. (Edinburgh, 1827).
The Prose Works of Sir Walter Scott. 30 vols. (Edinburgh: Adam and Charles Black, 1870).
Seeley, J.R. *The Expansion of England*. Ed. John Gross (1883; Chicago and London: University of Chicago Press, 1971).
Selden, John. *Of Dominion, or Ownership of the Sea*. Trans. Marchamont Nedham (London, 1652).
Shebbeare, John. *An Answer to the Pamphlet, call'd The Conduct of the Ministry Impartially Examined* (London, 1756).
Appeal to the People, containing the Genuine and Entire Letter of Admiral Byng to the Secr. Of the Ad____y (London, 1756).
A Sixth Letter to the People of England on the Progress of National Ruin (London, 1757).

Shirley, John. *The Accomplished Ladies Rich Closet* (London, 1687).
Smith, Adam. *An Inquiry into the Nature and Causes of the Wealth of Nations* (1776). Eds. R.H. Campbell, A.S. Skinner, and E.B. Todd. 2 vols. (Oxford: Clarendon Press, 1976).
Squire, Francis. *A Faithful Report of a Genuine Debate concerning the Liberty of the Press* (London, 1740).
Stephen, Sir James Fitzjames. *The Story of Nancomar and the Impeachment of Sir Elijah Impey*. 2 vols. (London, 1885).
Sterne, Lawrence. *A Sentimental Journey*. Ed. Ian Jack (1768; Oxford and New York: Oxford University Press, 1968).
Steuart, Sir James. *An Inquiry into the Principles of Political Oeconomy*. Ed. Andrew Skinner. 2 vols. (Chicago: University of Chicago Press, 1966).
Stevenson, William. *Remarks on the Very Inferior Utility of Classical Learning* (Manchester, 1796).
Stillingfleet, William. *Origines Britannicae, or The Antiquities of the British Churches* (London, 1685).
Stockdale, Percival. *An Examination of the Important Question, Whether Education at a Great School or by Private Tuition is Preferable* (London, 1782).
Swift, Jonathan. *A Proposal for Correcting, Improving, and Ascertaining the English Tongue*. Eds. Herbert Davis and Louis Landa (Oxford: Blackwell, 1957).
Temple, William. *An Introduction to the History of England* (1695; 3rd edn, London, 1708).
Thomas, Sir Dalby. *An Historical Account of the Rise and Growth of the West-India Collonies* (London, 1690).
Thomson, James. *Poetical Works*. Ed. J. Logie Robertson (London, New York, and Toronto: Oxford University Press, 1908).
Torshell, Samuel. *The Woman's Glorie: A Treatise, First, Asserting the Due Honour of that Sexe* (1645; 2nd edn, London, 1650).
Tucker, Josiah. *A Brief Essay on the Advantages and Disadvantages which respectively attend France and Great Britain with regard to Trade* (1749; 2nd edn, London, 1750).
An Humble Address and Earnest Appeal to those Respectable Personages in Great Britain and Ireland who, by their Great Permanent Interest in Landed Property, their Elevated Rank and Enlarged Views, are the Ablest to Judge, and the Fittest to Decide, whether a Connection with, or a Separation from the Continental Colonies of America, be most for the National Advantage, and the Lasting Benefit of those Kingdoms (Gloucester, 1775).
The True Interest of Britain, Set Forth in Regard to the Colonies (Philadelphia, 1776).
Tyrrell, James. *The General History of England*. 4 vols. (London, 1697–1704).
Vaugelas, Claude Favre de. *Remarques sur la langue française*. 2 vols. (1647; Versailles: Cerg; Paris: Baudry, 1880).
Wakefield, Priscilla. *Reflections on the Present Condition of the Female Sex* (London, 1798; facs. repr. New York and London: Garland, 1974).
Walker, John. *A Critical Pronouncing Dictionary* (London, 1791).

Walpole, Horace. *A Letter to the Whigs, occasion'd by A Letter to the Tories* (London, 1748).

Warton, Thomas. *History of English Poetry*. 4 vols. (1774; facs. edn with introduction by David Fairer, London and New York: Routledge/Thoemmes Press, 1998).

Watkinson, Edward. *Essay upon Oeconomy* (1762; 8th edn, York, 1767).

Wesley, John. *A Calm Address to our American Colonies* (London, 1775).

West, Jane. *Letters to a Young Lady*. 3 vols. (1806; 4th edn, London, 1811; facs. repr. London: William Pickering, 1996).

Whitaker, John, *The Genuine History of the Britons Asserted* (London, 1773).

Whitehead, Paul. *Manners: A Satire* (London, 1739).

A Letter to a Member of Parliament in the Country, from his Friend in London, relative to the Case of Admiral Byng (London, 1756).

Wilkes, John. *The History of England from the Revolution to the Accession of the Brunswick Line* (London, 1768).

A Letter to Samuel Johnson, L.L.D. (London, 1770).

Wilkes, Wetenhall. *A Letter of Genteel and Moral Advice to a Young Lady* (Dublin, 1740).

Wollstonecraft, Mary. *The Works of Mary Wollstonecraft*. 7 vols. Eds. Janet Todd and Marilyn Butler (London: William Pickering, 1989).

Wright, William. *The Comical History of the Marriage-Union betwixt Fergusia and Heptarchus* (London?, 1706).

Young, Arthur. *Political Essays concerning the Present State of the British Empire* (London, 1772).

SOURCES: POST-1900

Anderson, Benedict R. *Imagined Communities: Reflections on the Origin and Spread of Nationalism* (London: Verso Editions / NLB, 1983).

Armitage, David. *The Ideological Origins of the British Empire* (Cambridge: Cambridge University Press, 2000).

Armstrong, Nancy. *Desire and Domestic Fiction* (New York and Oxford: Oxford University Press, 1987).

Backscheider, Paula R. *Daniel Defoe: His Life* (Baltimore and London: Johns Hopkins University Press, 1989).

Bailey, John. *Dr. Johnson and his Circle* (London: Williams and Norgate, 1913).

Barker, Hannah. *Newspapers, Politics, and Public Opinion in Late Eighteenth-Century England* (Oxford: Clarendon Press, 1998).

Barker-Benfield, G.J. *The Culture of Sensibility: Sex and Society in Eighteenth-Century Britain* (Chicago: University of Chicago Press, 1992).

Barrell, John. *English Literature in History, 1730–80: An Equal, Wide Survey* (London: Hutchinson, 1983).

Basker, James G. "Dancing Dogs, Women Preachers and the Myth of Johnson's Misogyny." *Age of Johnson* 3 (1990): 63–90.

"Samuel Johnson and the African-American Reader." *The New Rambler* (1994–5): 47–57.

and Ribeiro, Alvaro, S.J. *Tradition in Transition: Women Writers, Marginal Texts, and the Eighteenth-Century Canon* (Oxford: Clarendon Press, 1996).

Bate, W.J. *The Achievement of Samuel Johnson* (New York: Oxford University Press, 1955).

Samuel Johnson (New York: Harcourt, Brace, Jovanovich; London: Macmillan, 1977).

Bayly, C.A. *Imperial Meridian: The British Empire and the World* (London and New York: Longman, 1989).

Bhabha, Homi K. *The Location of Culture* (London: Routledge, 1994).

Bond, W.H. (ed.). *Eighteenth-Century Studies in Honor of Donald F. Hyde* (New York: The Grolier Club, 1970).

Borsay, Peter. *The English Urban Renaissance: Culture and Society in the Provincial Town 1660–1770* (Oxford: Clarendon Press, 1989).

(ed.). *The Eighteenth-Century Town: A Reader in English Urban History* (London and New York: Longman, 1990).

Bose, Sujit. *Attitudes to Imperialism: Kipling, Forster and Paul Scott* (Delhi: Amar Prakashan, 1990).

Bourdieu, Pierre. *Language and Symbolic Power*. Ed. John B. Thompson. Trans. Gino Raymond and Matthew Adamson (Cambridge, MA: Harvard University Press, 1991).

The Field of Cultural Production: Essays on Art and Literature. Ed. Randal Johnson (Cambridge: Polity Press, 1993).

Boyce, D. George. *Decolonization and the British Empire, 1775–1997* (Houndsmills: Macmillan; New York: St. Martin's Press, 1999).

Breen, T.H. "An Empire of Goods: The Anglicization of Colonial America, 1690–1776." *Journal of British Studies* 25 (1986): 467–99.

Brewer, John. *Party Ideology and Popular Politics at the Accession of George III* (Cambridge: Cambridge University Press, 1976).

and Porter, Roy (eds.). *Consumption and the World of Goods* (London and New York: Routledge, 1993).

Brown, Laura. *Ends of Empire: Women and Ideology in Early Eighteenth-Century English Literature* (Ithaca and London: Cornell University Press, 1993).

Calhoun, Craig (ed.). *Habermas and the Public Sphere* (Cambridge, MA, and London: MIT Press, 1992).

Cannadine, David. *Class in Britain* (New Haven and London: Yale University Press, 1998).

Cannon, John. *Samuel Johnson and the Politics of Hanoverian England* (Oxford: Clarendon Press, 1994).

Castle, Terry. *Masquerade and Civilization: The Carnivalesque in Eighteenth-Century English Culture and Fiction* (Stanford: Stanford University Press, 1986).

Chapin, Chester. *The Religious Thought of Samuel Johnson* (Ann Arbor: University of Michigan Press, 1968).

Charlton, Kenneth. *Women, Religion, and Education in Early Modern England* (New York and London: Routledge, 1999).

Clark, Alice. *Working Life of Women in the Seventeenth Century* (London: Routledge, 1919).

Clark, Anna. *Struggle for the Breeches: Gender and the Making of the British Working Class* (Berkeley, Los Angeles, and London: University of California Press).

Clark, J.C.D. *The Dynamics of Change: The Crisis of the 1750s and English Party Systems* (Cambridge: Cambridge University Press, 1982).

English Society 1688–1832: Ideology, Social Structure, Political Practice during the Ancien Regime (Cambridge: Cambridge University Press, 1985).

Revolution and Rebellion: State and Society in England in the Seventeenth and Eighteenth Centuries (Cambridge: Cambridge University Press, 1986).

Samuel Johnson: Literature, Religion and English Cultural Politics from the Restoration to Romanticism (Cambridge: Cambridge University Press, 1994).

Clarke, M.L. *Classical Education in Britain 1500–1900* (Cambridge: Cambridge University Press, 1959).

Cleary, Thomas R. *Henry Fielding: Political Writer* (Waterloo, Ontario: Wilfred Laurier University Press, 1984).

Clifford, James L. *Dictionary Johnson* (New York: McGraw-Hill, 1979).

Clingham, Greg (ed.). *The Cambridge Companion to Samuel Johnson* (Cambridge: Cambridge University Press, 1997).

Colley, Linda. *In Defiance of Oligarchy* (Cambridge: Cambridge University Press, 1982).

Britons: Forging the Nation (New Haven and London: Yale University Press, 1992).

Connors, Richard, Jones, Clyve and Taylor, Stephen (eds.). *Hanoverian Britain and Empire: Essays in Memory of Philip Lawson* (Woodbridge: Boydell Press, 1998).

Corfield, Penelope J. (ed.). *Language, History and Class* (Oxford: Basil Blackwell, 1991).

Crowley, Tony. *Language in History: Theories and Texts* (London and New York: Routledge, 1996).

Cruikshanks, Eveline. *Political Untouchables: the Tories and the '45* (London: Duckworth, 1979).

Curley, Thomas M. *Samuel Johnson and the Age of Travel* (Athens: University of Georgia Press, 1976).

"Johnson and America." *Age of Johnson* 6 (1994): 31–73.

Daunton, M.J. *Progress and Poverty: An Economic and Social History of Britain 1700–1850* (Oxford: Oxford University Press, 1995).

Davidoff, Leonore and Hall, Catherine. *Family Fortunes: Men and Women of the English Middle-Class 1780–1850* (Chicago and London: University of Chicago Press, 1987).

Davis, Leith. *Acts of Union: Scotland and the Literary Negotiation of the British Nation, 1707–1830* (Stanford: Stanford University Press, 1998).

DeMaria, Robert. *Johnson's "Dictionary" and the Language of Learning* (Chapel Hill and London: University of North Carolina Press, 1986).

"The Politics of Johnson's *Dictionary*." *PMLA* 104 (1989): 64–74.

The Life of Samuel Johnson: A Critical Biography (Oxford: Blackwell, 1993).
Dickinson, H.T. *The Politics of the People in Eighteenth-Century Britain* (New York: St. Martin's Press, 1995).
Earle, Peter. *The Making of the English Middle Class* (Berkeley and Los Angeles: University of California Press, 1989).
Eldridge, C.C. *Disraeli and the Rise of the New Imperialism* (Cardiff: University of Wales Press, 1996).
Ellis, Aytoun. *The Penny Universities: A History of the Coffee-Houses* (London: Secker and Warburg, 1956).
Erskine-Hill, Howard. "Johnson the Jacobite?" *Age of Johnson* 7 (1996): 3–26.
Evans, Eric J. *Political Parties in Britain, 1783–1864* (London: Methuen, 1985).
Floud, Roderick and McCloskey, Donald (eds.). *The Economic History of Britain Since 1700*. 2 vols. (Cambridge: Cambridge University Press, 1981).
The Economic History of the British Empire. 3 vols. (2nd edn, Cambridge: Cambridge University Press, 1994).
Foord, Archibald S. *His Majesty's Opposition 1714–1830* (Oxford: Clarendon Press, 1964).
Gaskill, Howard (ed.). *Ossian Revisited* (Edinburgh: Edinburgh University Press, 1991).
Gerrard, Christine. *The Patriot Opposition to Walpole: Politics, Poetry, and National Myth 1725–1742* (Oxford: Clarendon Press, 1994).
Graff, Harvey J. (ed.). *Literacy and Social Development in the West: A Reader* (Cambridge: Cambridge University Press, 1981).
Grafton, Anthony and Jardine, Lisa. *From Humanism to the Humanities* (London: Duckworth, 1986).
Gray, James. *Johnson's Sermons: A Study* (Oxford: Clarendon Press, 1972).
Greenblatt, Stephen. *Marvelous Possessions: The Wonder of the New World* (Chicago: University of Chicago Press, 1991).
Greene, Donald J. *The Politics of Samuel Johnson* (New Haven: Yale University Press, 1960).
"Johnson: the Jacobite Legend Exhumed." *Age of Johnson* 7 (1996): 70–1.
Grundy, Isobel. "Samuel Johnson as Patron of Women." *Age of Johnson* 1 (1987): 59–77.
Guest, Harriet. *Small Change: Women, Learning and Patriotism 1750–1810* (Chicago and London: University of Chicago Press, 2000).
Habermas, Jürgen. *The Structural Transformation of the Public Sphere: An Inquiry into a Category of Bourgeois Society*. Trans. Thomas Burger and Frederick Lawrence (Cambridge, MA: MIT Press, 1989).
Halpern, John. *The Life of Jane Austen* (Baltimore: Johns Hopkins University Press, 1984).
Hammon, Brean S. *Professional Imaginative Writing in England 1670–1700: "Hackney for Bread"* (Oxford: Clarendon Press, 1997).
Hans, Nicholas. *New Trends in Education in the Eighteenth Century* (London: Routledge & Kegan Paul, 1951).

Hanson, Laurence. *The Government and the Press 1695–1763* (Oxford: Oxford University Press; London: Humphrey Milford, 1936).
Harris, Robert. *A Patriot Press: National Politics and the London Press in the 1740s* (Oxford: Clarendon Press, 1993).
Hart, Kevin. *Samuel Johnson and the Culture of Property* (Cambridge: Cambridge University Press, 2000).
Hill, Brian W. *The Growth of Parliamentary Parties* (Hamden, CT: Archon Books, 1976).
The Early Parties and Politics in Britain, 1688–1832 (Basingstoke: Macmillan, 1996).
Hill, Bridget. *Women, Work and Sexual Politics in Eighteenth-Century England* (Oxford: Basil Blackwell, 1989).
Hollis, Christopher. *Dr. Johnson* (New York: Henry Holt and Company, 1929).
Holmes, Geoffrey. *Augustan England: Professions, State and Society* (London: George Allen & Unwin, 1982).
Hudson, Nicholas. *Samuel Johnson and Eighteenth-Century Thought* (Oxford: Clarendon Press, 1988).
"From 'Nation' to 'Race': The Origin of Racial Classification in Eighteenth-Century Thought." *Eighteenth-Century Studies* 29 (1996): 247–64.
"The Nature of Johnson's Conservatism." *ELH* 64 (1997): 925–43.
"Johnson's *Dictionary* and the Politics of 'Standard English.'" *Yearbook of English Studies* 28 (1998): 77–93.
"Discourse of Transition: Johnson, the 1750s, and the Rise of the Middle-Class." *Age of Johnson* 13 (2002): 31–52.
"Samuel Johnson, Urban Culture and the Geography of Post-Fire London." *Studies in English Literature* 42.3 (2002): 577–600.
Hundert, E.J. "Bernard Mandeville and Enlightenment Maxims of Modernity." *Journal of the History of Ideas* 39 (1978): 119–24.
Hunt, Margaret R. *The Middling Sort: Commerce, Gender, and the Family in England 1680–1780* (Berkeley, Los Angeles, and London: University of California Press, 1996).
Ingle, Stephen. *The British Party System* (Oxford and New York: Basil Blackwell, 1987).
Jones, Vivien (ed.). *Women and Literature in Britain* (Cambridge: Cambridge University Press, 2000).
Kaminski, Thomas. *The Early Career of Samuel Johnson* (New York and Oxford: Oxford University Press, 1987).
Kelly, Gary. *Women, Writing, and Revolution 1790–1827* (Oxford: Clarendon Press, 1993).
Kernan, Alvin. *Print Technology, Letters and Samuel Johnson* (Princeton: Princeton University Press, 1987).
Kidd, Colin. *Subverting Scotland's Past: Scottish Whig Historians and the Creation of an Anglo-English Identity, 1689–c. 1830* (Cambridge: Cambridge University Press, 1993).

Klein, Lawrence E. "Gender and the Public/Private Distinction in the Eighteenth Century: Some Questions about Evidence and Analytical Procedure," *Eighteenth-Century Studies* 29 (1995): 97–109.

Kowaleski-Wallace, Elizabeth. *Consuming Subjects: Women, Shopping, and Business in the Eighteenth Century* (New York: Columbia University Press, 1997).

Kramnick, Isaac. *Bolingbroke and his Circle: The Politics of Nostalgia in the Age of Walpole* (Cambridge, MA: Harvard University Press, 1968).

Kremmerer, Katherine. *"A Neutral Being between the Sexes": Samuel Johnson's Sexual Politics* (Lewisburg: Bucknell University Press, 1998).

Langford, Paul. *A Polite and Commercial People: England 1727–1783* (Oxford: Clarendon Press, 1989).

Englishness Identified (Oxford: Clarendon Press, 2000).

Langland, Elizabeth. *Nobody's Angels: Middle-Class Women and Domestic Ideology in Victorian Culture* (Ithaca and London: Cornell University Press, 1995).

Englishness Identified (Oxford: Clarendon Press, 2000).

Laslett, Peter. *The World We Have Lost* (2nd edn, London: Methuen, 1971).

Lynn, Steven. *Samuel Johnson after Deconstruction: Rhetoric and "The Rambler"* (Carbondale: Southern Illinois University Press, 1992).

McDermott, Anne. "Johnson's *Dictionary* and the Canon: Authors and Authority." *Yearbook of English Studies* 28 (1998): 44–65.

McDowell, Paula. *The Women of Grub Street: Press, Politics, and Gender in the London Literary Marketplace 1678–1730* (Oxford: Clarendon Press, 1998).

McIntosh, Carey. *Common and Courtly Language: The Stylistics of Social Class in 18th-Century English Literature* (Philadelphia: University of Pennsylvania Press, 1986).

McKendrick, Neil, Brewer, John, and Plumb, J.H. *The Birth of a Consumer Society: the Commercialization of Eighteenth-Century England* (Bloomington: Indiana University Press, 1982).

McKeon, Michael. "Historicising Patriarchy: The Emergence of Gender Difference in England, 1660–1760." *Eighteenth-Century Studies* 28 (1995): 295–322.

Marshall, Dorothy. *Dr. Johnson's London* (New York, London, and Sydney: John Wiley & Sons, 1968).

Marshall, P.J. (ed.). Assisted by Low, Alaine. *The Eighteenth Century*. Vol. 2 of *The Oxford History of the British Empire* (Oxford and New York: Oxford University Press, 1998).

Mazzocco, Angelo. *Linguistic Theories in Dante and the Humanists* (Leiden, New York, and Cologne: E.J. Brill, 1993).

Mehta, Uday Singh. *Liberalism and Empire* (Chicago and London: University of Chicago Press, 1999).

Miller, Peter N. *Defining the Public Good: Empire, Religion, and Philosophy in Eighteenth-Century Britain* (Cambridge: Cambridge University Press, 1994).

Mingay, G.E. *English Landed Society in the Eighteenth Century* (London: Routledge and Kegan Paul; Toronto: University of Toronto Press, 1963).

Morris, R. J. *Class and Class Consciousness in the Industrial Revolution, 1780–1850* (London and Basingstoke: Macmillan, 1979).

Myers, Sylvia Harcstark. *The Blue-Stocking Circle: Women, Friendship and the Life of Mind in Eighteenth-Century England* (Oxford: Clarendon Press, 1990).

Nairn, Tom. *The Break-Up of Britain: Crises and Neo-Nationalism* (London: NLB, 1977).

Neale, R.S. *Class in English History* (Oxford: Basil Blackwell, 1981).

Nevill, Ralph. *London Clubs: Their History and Treasures* (London: Chatto and Windus, 1911).

Newman, Gerald. *The Rise of English Nationalism: A Cultural History 1740–1830* (New York: St. Martin's Press, 1987).

Nokes, David. *Jane Austen: A Life* (London: Fifth Estate, 1997).

O'Day, Rosemary. *Education and Society 1500–1800* (London and New York: Longman, 1982).

O'Gorman, Frank. *The Emergence of the British Two-Party System 1760–1832* (London: Edward Arnold, 1982).

Olsen, Kristen. *Daily Life in 18th-Century England* (Westport, CT, and London: Greenwood Press, 1999).

Orr, Bridget. *Empire on the English Stage 1660–1714* (Cambridge: Cambridge University Press, 2001).

Owen, John B. *The Rise of the Pelhams* (London: Methuen & Co., 1957).

The Oxford History of the British Empire (Oxford and New York: Oxford University Press).

Padley, G.A. *Grammatical Theory in Western Europe 1500–1700*, 2 vols. (Cambridge: Cambridge University Press, 1985–8).

Pagden, Anthony. *Lords of All the World: Ideologies of Empire in Spain, Britain and France, c. 1500 to c. 1800* (New Haven: Yale University Press, 1995).

Perkin, Harold J. *The Origins of Modern English Society, 1780–1880* (London: Routledge and Kegan Paul; Toronto: University of Toronto Press, 1969).

Peters, Marie. *Pitt and Popularity: The Patriot Minister and London Opinion during the Seven Years' War* (Oxford: Clarendon Press, 1980).

Pinchbeck, Ivy. *Women Workers and the Industrial Revolution, 1750–1850* (1930; London, Virago, 1981).

Pittock, Murray G. A. *The Invention of Scotland: The Stuart Myth and the Scottish Identity, 1638 to the Present* (London and New York: Routledge, 1991).

Inventing and Resisting Britain: Cultural Identities in Britain and Ireland, 1685–1789 (New York: St. Martin's Press, 1997).

Celtic Identity and the British Image (Manchester and New York: Manchester, 1999).

Pocock, J.G.A. *The Ancient Constitution and the Feudal Law: A Study of English Historical Thought in the Seventeenth Century* (Cambridge: Cambridge University Press, 1957).

Virtue, Commerce, and History: Essays in Political Thought and History, Chiefly in the Eighteenth Century (Cambridge: Cambridge University Press, 1985).

Politics, Language, and Time: Essays on Political Thought and History (Chicago: University of Chicago Press, 1989).

Pope, Dudley. *At Twelve Mr. Byng was Shot* (London: Secker & Warburg, 1987).

Porter, Roy. *English Society in the Eighteenth Century* (rev. edn, London: Penguin, 1990).

Potkay, Adam. *The Fate of Eloquence in the Age of Hume* (Ithaca and London: Cornell University Press, 1994).

The Passion for Happiness: Samuel Johnson and David Hume (Ithaca and London: Cornell University Press, 2000).

Quinlan, Maurice J. *Samuel Johnson: A Layman's Religion* (Madison: University of Wisconsin Press, 1964).

Quinton, Anthony. *The Politics of Imperfection: The Religious and Secular Tradition in England from Hooker to Oakshott* (London: Faber and Faber, 1978).

Raleigh, Walter. *Six Essays on Johnson* (Oxford: Clarendon Press, 1910).

Reddick, Allen. *The Making of Johnson's Dictionary 1746–1773* (2nd edn, Cambridge: Cambridge University Press, 1996).

Richetti, John. "Class Struggle without Class: Novelists and Magistrates." *The Eighteenth Century: Theory and Interpretation* 32 (1991–2): 203–18.

Ricken, Ulrich. *Linguistics, Anthropology and Philosophy in the French Enlightenment.* Trans. Robert E. Norton (New York and London: Routledge, 1994).

Rogers, Nicholas. *Whigs and Cities: Popular Politics in the Age of Walpole and Pitt* (Oxford: Clarendon Press, 1989).

Rudé, George. *The Crowd in History: A Study of Popular Disturbances in France and England 1730–1848* (London: John Wiley & Son, 1964).

Hanoverian London 1714–1808 (London: Secker & Warburg, 1971).

Rule, John. *The Vital Century: England's Developing Economy 1714–1815* (London and New York: Longman, 1992).

Rummel, Erika. *The Humanist-Scholastic Debate in the Renaissance and Reformation* (Cambridge, MA, and London: Harvard University Press, 1995).

Robbins, R.H. *A Short History of Linguistics.* (2nd edn, London: Longman, 1979).

Sack, James. *From Jacobite to Conservative: Reaction and Orthodoxy in Britain, c. 1760–1832* (Cambridge: Cambridge University Press, 1993).

Said, Edward W. *Culture and Imperialism* (New York: Alfred A. Knopf, 1993).

Saintsbury, George. *A Short History of English Literature* (London: Macmillan and Co., 1925).

Seccombe, Thomas. *The Age of Johnson (1749–1798)* (London: George Bell and Sons, 1900).

Sharpe, Pamela. *Adapting to Capitalism: Working Women in the English Economy 1700–1850* (Basingstoke: Macmillan, 1996).

Shellabarger, Samuel. *Lord Chesterfield and his World* (Boston: Little, Brown and Company, 1951).

Sher, Richard B. *Church and University in the Scottish Enlightenment* (Edinburgh: Edinburgh University Press, 1985).

Shoemaker, Robert B. *Gender in English Society 1650–1850: The Emergence of Separate Spheres?* (New York and London: Longman, 1998).

Skinner, Gillian. *Sensibility and Economics in the Novel: the Price of a Tear* (London: Macmillan, 1999).

Smallwood, Philip (ed.). *Johnson Re-Visioned: Looking Before and After* (Lewisburg: Bucknell University Press; London: Associated University Presses, 2001).

Smith, Olivia. *The Politics of Language 1791–1819* (Oxford: Clarendon Press, 1984).

Solomon, Harry M. *The Rise of Robert Dodsley: Creating the New Age of Print* (Carbondale and Edwardsville: Southern Illinois University Press, 1996).

Speck, W.A. *Stability and Strife: England 1714–1760* (London: Edward Arnold, 1977).

Stephen, Sir Leslie. *English Literature and Society in the Eighteenth Century* (London: Duckworth, 1903).

Stone, Lawrence. "Social Mobility in England, 1500–1700." *Past and Present* 33 (1966): 16–55.

Taylor, Daniel J. *Declension: A Study of the Linguistic Theory of Marcus Terentius Varro* (Amsterdam: Benjamins, 1974).

Thompson, E.P. *The Making of the English Working Class* (New York: Vintage Books, 1966).

"Eighteenth-Century English Society: Class Struggle without Class?" *Social History* 3 (1978): 133–65.

Thompson, F.M.L. *The Rise of Respectable Society: A Social History of Victorian Britain 1830–1900* (London: Fontana, 1988).

Thompson, Richard S. *Classics or Charity? The Dilemma of the 18th-Century Grammar School* (Manchester: Manchester University Press, 1971).

"English and English Education in the Eighteenth Century." *Studies in Voltaire and the Eighteenth Century* 167 (1977): 65–79.

Trumpener, Katie. *Bardic Nationalism: The Romantic Novel and the British Empire* (Princeton: Princeton University Press, 1997).

Veblen, Thorstein. *The Theory of the Leisure Class: An Economic Study of Institutions* (London: George Allen & Unwin, 1925).

Vickery, Amanda. "Golden Age to Separate Spheres? A Review of the Categories and Chronology of English Women's History." *The Historical Review* 36 (1993): 383–414.

The Gentleman's Daughter: Women's Lives in Georgian England (New Haven and London: Yale University Press, 1998)

Vincent, David. *Literacy and Popular Culture in England 1750–1914* (Cambridge: Cambridge University Press, 1989).

Wahrman, Dror. *Imagining the Middle Class: The Political Representation of Class in Britain c. 1780–1840* (Cambridge: Cambridge University Press, 1995).

Watt, Ian. *The Rise of the Novel* (Berkeley and Los Angeles: University of California Press, 1956).

Wechselblatt, Martin. *Bad Behavior: Samuel Johnson and Modern Cultural Authority* (Lewisburg: Bucknell University Press, 1998).

Weinbrot, Howard D. *Britannia's Issue: The Rise of British Literature from Dryden to Ossian* (Cambridge: Cambridge University Press, 1993).

Weizman, Sophia. *Warren Hastings and Sir Philip Francis* (Manchester: Manchester University Press, 1929).

Whelan, Frederick G. *Edmund Burke and India: Political Morality and Empire* (Pittsburgh: University of Pittsburgh Press, 1996).

Williams, Raymond. *The Long Revolution* (London: Chatto & Windus, 1961).

Wilson, Angus. *The Strange Ride of Rudyard Kipling* (London: Secker and Warburg, 1977).

Wilson, Kathleen. *The Sense of the People: Politics, Culture, and Imperialism in England, 1715–1765* (Cambridge: Cambridge University Press, 1995).

Wimsatt, W.K. Jr. *Philosophical Words: A Study of the Style and Meaning in the "Rambler" and "Dictionary" of Samuel Johnson* (New Haven: Yale University Press, 1948).

Wrigley, E.A. "A Simple Model of London's Importance in Changing English Society and Economy, 1650–1750." *Past and Present* 37 (1967): 44–70.

Index

Abercromby, Patrick 136, 151
Act of Succession 84
Adams, William 140
Addison, Joseph 94, 131, 137, 141
Africa 131, 169, 183, 207, 210
Akenside, Mark 7, 91, 103
Alexander the Great 173, 203
Alfred the Great 7, 140, 142–3, 144, 257
Allestree, Richard 47, 48
America 6–7, 17, 24, 83, 117, 134, 135, 136, 172, 174, 178–9, 181, 185, 186, 187, 189–98, 205, 207, 209, 210, 211, 212, 217, 225, 260
native peoples 158, 160, 172, 177–9, 182–3, 193–4, 198, 206, 207, 208, 219
War of Independence 186, 188–93
ancient constitution, the 137–8, 139, 146, 188, 190, 192, 201
Anderson, Benedict 133
Anglicanism 85–6, 99, 100, 107, 129, 135, 167, 209, 210, 214–15
Anglo-Saxons 8
Anne, Queen 91, 97, 122
antiquarianism 8, 144, 150, 164–7
Antoinette, Marie 29
Arabs (*see* Middle East)
Arbuthnot, John 168
Armitage, David 259
Arnauld, Antoine 38
Arthur, King 145, 167
Astell, Mary 50, 52, 67
Astle, Daniel 139
Astle, Thomas 164
Atterbury, Francis 80
Atwood, William 187, 192
Austen, Jane 46, 60
Australia 209

Barbauld, Anna Laetitia 52, 53
Barclay, James 18
Barrell, John 32–3, 38
Bate, W.J. 204, 223
Baumgarten, Alexander Gottlieb 131
Bayly, C.A. 220
Beattie, James 27
Belhaven, Lord 151
Belize 177
Bembo, Pietro 38
Bengal (*see* India)
Bhabha, Homi K. 219
Bible, the 47, 194, 256
Bigge, Thomas 98
Birmingham 8
Blackmore, Sir Richard 145
Blackstone, Sir William 139
Blair, Hugh 37, 149, 158–9
Blake, Admiral Robert 112, 113, 125, 172, 176
Boece, Hector 136, 151, 154
Bolingbroke, Henry St. John, Lord 85, 91–2, 94, 98, 100, 103, 104, 107, 111, 122, 123, 135, 137, 139, 145, 246
Bolton, Edmund 16
Boswell, James 1, 3, 9, 18–20, 22, 25, 32, 34, 53, 65, 79, 84, 88, 91, 99, 106, 110, 115, 126, 127, 129, 133, 134, 138–40, 150, 152, 162–4, 167–8, 197, 204, 214–15, 219, 222, 223, 245, 255
Bouhours, Dominique 38
Bourdieu, Pierre 22
Brady, Robert 138
Breen, T.H. 171
Brett, John 123
Brewer, John 109
Bristol 8
Britons 136, 137, 139, 144, 145, 146, 155–7, 168, 196
Broad-bottom coalition 7, 36, 78–9, 82, 90–100, 102, 104, 106, 111, 115, 127, 224
Bromley, John 175
Brooke, Henry 81, 124
Brown, John 9, 62–3, 66, 67, 135, 149, 166, 249
Brown, Laura 170
Browning, Elizabeth Barrett 46
Buchanan, George 136, 151, 154

Burgh, James 105
Burke, Edmund 6–7, 28–42, 59, 89, 99–100, 101, 128, 137, 173, 189, 190, 191, 197, 207, 209, 211–12, 217, 218, 219, 261
Bute, John Stuart, Lord 112
Byng, Admiral John 113–14, 125–8, 224, 250
Byzantine Empire 200–1

Callender, James Thomson 236
Camden, William 152
Campbell, Archibald 37–8
Campbell, George 40
Canada 3, 178, 208, 209
  Nova Scotia 111
  Quebec 199, 208
Cantemir, Demetrius 200
capitalism and commerce 8, 23, 27, 66, 105, 108–16, 117, 119, 143, 150, 155–6, 160, 166, 191, 204–5, 209, 214–15, 225
Carlyle, Thomas 4, 218
Carte, Thomas 139, 140
Carter, Elizabeth 9, 45
Carteret, John, Lord 87, 90, 95, 103, 133, 246
Casas, Bartolomé de las 177
Castiglione, Baldassarre, conte 38
Cataline 203
Cave, Edward 12, 20–1, 22, 24, 32, 88
Ceylon 210
Chambers, Sir Robert 139–40, 146, 192–3, 197, 211, 214–16
Champion, The 101
Chapone, Hester 62, 66
Charke, Charlotte 44
Charles I 14, 93, 115
Charles II 93, 138
Charles XII (of Sweden) 202, 203, 204, 207
Chester 192
Chesterfield, Philip Dormer Stanhope, Lord 7, 33, 36–7, 40, 79, 82, 90–1, 93, 94–7, 101–3, 106, 122, 123, 135, 146, 203, 235
Child, Sir Josiah 176, 185–6, 187, 198
Christianity 2, 111, 113, 115, 136, 139, 172, 180, 199, 207–8, 210, 218, 225
Cicero 94
Civil Wars 14, 47, 98, 129, 143
Clarendon, Edward Hyde, Lord 94
Clark, J.C.D. 78, 79, 81–2, 85, 109, 110, 244
Clark, John 156–7
Clarke, John 19, 232–3
Clarke, William 178
Clarkson, Thomas 209
Clive, Robert 211
coffee-houses 108
Colbert, Jean Baptiste 118
Colden, Cadwallader 178, 182
Cole, W.A. 5
Colley, Linda 78, 80, 244
Columbus, Christopher 203
Common-Sense 122, 123
Connoisseur, The 48, 49, 224
Constable, John 16–17, 26
Con-test, The 123, 125
Copithorne, Richard 177
Coram, Thomas 111, 112
Corderius 232
Cornish, Joseph 27
Cornwall 196
Cotton, Sir John Hynde 80, 90
Craftsman, The 58, 122, 123, 177
Croker, John Wilson 3
Cromwell, Oliver 14, 155–6, 161, 176, 214–15
Crowe, Eyre 1, 10
Cruikshanks, Eveline 78
Cumberland, Henry Frederick, Duke of 154
Curley, Thomas M. 171, 213
Curzon, George, Lord 171

Daily Gazetteer, The 121, 122
Danes 136, 139, 142, 155–6
Darrell, William 15, 18, 21
Davenant, Charles 173–4, 184, 191, 192
Davidoff, Leonore 43
Davis, Leith 253
Defoe, Daniel 15–16, 18, 19, 21, 50, 136, 140–1, 144, 146, 174
DeMaria, Robert 10, 94, 133
Demosthenes 94
Dennis, John 111, 114–17, 119, 145
Dicey, Edward 209
Dickinson, H.T. 109
Disraeli, Benjamin 3, 7, 171, 209, 218
dissenters 39, 83
Dodington, George Bubb 90
Dodsley, Robert 7, 36, 79, 90, 95, 96, 101–2, 103, 104, 111, 177, 250
Donne, John 181
Drake, Sir Francis 113, 125, 172, 176
Drummond, William 164
Dryden, John 94, 138
Durham 192
Dutch, the 83, 173, 176, 182, 210

Earle, Peter 44
East India Company, the 173, 198, 210, 211, 212, 216, 218, 219
Eden, Sir Frederic M. 30
education 1, 15, 17–18, 19, 22, 27–8, 31, 45–6, 47, 51–2, 53, 54–6, 58–9, 63, 119, 150, 166, 225
Edward III 206
Edwards, Thomas 37

Egmont, Lord (*see* John Perceval)
Eliot, George 46
Elizabeth I 39, 143, 147, 177, 180
Ellis, Sarah Stickney 31, 59–60, 65
Elphinston, James 19
England (material data)
  economics 4–5, 11, 184, 221, 222
  population 4
  urbanization 4
Enlightenment, the 115, 161, 166, 185, 212, 219
Erskine-Hill, Howard 78, 79, 81
Essex, John 51
Evans, Lewis 182
Evelyn, John 14, 47

Falconer, Samuel 62
Falkland Islands 128
farmers 185, 190
Ferguson, Adam 64, 149, 160–1, 166, 255
Fielding, Henry 7, 36, 79, 82, 91, 95, 96, 97, 101, 115, 122
  Enquiry into the Causes of the Late Increase of Robbers 13–14, 24, 25, 60
  Full Vindication of the Dutchess Dowager of Marlborough 93
  Joseph Andrews 101, 102, 103
  Tom Jones 32, 82, 102–4, 106, 110, 112, 138, 250
Filmer, Robert 244
Ford, Cornelius 90
Fordyce, James 52, 58, 59, 64
Fowke, Francis 212, 215
Fowke, Joseph 212, 213, 215–16
Fowler, Lorenzo 168
Fox, Charles James 100, 216
France 4, 12, 17, 28–9, 38, 52, 61, 82, 109, 115, 118, 120, 124–5, 135, 139, 140–1, 143, 165, 168, 171, 172, 173–5, 176, 178–9, 182–3, 186, 187, 188, 189, 191, 193–4, 201, 204–6, 210, 211, 212, 219, 223, 224, 249
  French Revolution 6, 7, 11, 31, 32, 39
Frederick, Prince of Wales 92–3, 104
Frederick the Great 193
Froude, James 218

Gaskill, Howard 148
Gauls 139
Gay, John 15
Gee, Joshua 186, 187, 198
gentleman, the (*see also* social class: untitled gentry) 12–14, 16, 17, 19–20, 26, 27, 31, 32–3, 41, 52, 105, 166, 195, 223, 224, 233
Gentleman's Magazine, The 18, 19, 20, 32, 34, 86, 92, 112, 180, 181
George II 82, 84, 143, 244
George III 78, 79, 83, 84, 88, 94, 100, 165, 195
Germany (*see also* Hanover) 4, 82, 83, 85, 145, 157, 219
Gibbon, Edward 181, 198, 200, 254
Gisborne, Thomas 28, 31, 58–9, 120
Gladstone, Sir William 171, 209
Glorious Revolution, the 79, 86, 92, 138
Godwin, William 30
Goldsmith, Oliver 65, 67, 185, 189
Gower, John-Leveson-Gower, Lord 90
Greece 176, 203, 213
Greenblatt, Stephen 213
Greene, Donald J. 3, 6, 22, 78, 87, 89, 113, 171, 208, 244, 249, 253, 260
Greenwood, James 38, 39
Gregory, John 64
Grenville, George, Lord 189
Grey, Jemima Campbell, Marchioness 37
Guatemala 177
Guest, Harriet 60

Habermas, Jürgen 109, 120–1, 128
Halifax, Charles Montagu, Lord 46, 47
Hall, Catherine 43
Hammond, James 91
Hanover 82, 83–5
Hanoverian Succession, the 39, 79, 82, 85, 87, 88, 144, 145
Harley, Edward (3rd Earl of Oxford) 86, 87, 88, 97
Harley, Robert (1st Earl of Oxford) 87, 97
Hastings, Warren 6–7, 172, 211–19, 226, 261
Hawes, Clement 171
Hawkesworth, John 34
Hawkins, Sir John 85, 233, 244
Hays, Mary 56, 59, 74
Haywood, Eliza 49
Henry II 102
Henry V 206
Heydon, John 46
Higford, William 13–14
Hill, George Birkbeck 248
Hill, Sir Rowland 164
Hoadly, Benjamin 103, 244
Hogg, James 107, 166
Hollis, Christopher 3
Home, John 155–6
Hooke, Nathaniel 93
Hooker, Richard 244
Hoole, John 216, 217
humanism 38, 133, 136, 236
Hume, David 8, 38, 52, 64, 67, 85, 98, 139–41, 149, 154–7, 159, 161, 174, 186, 188, 198, 211, 236, 244, 255, 259
Hundert, E.J. 249
Hunt, Margaret 44

Hutcheson, Francis 181
imperialism 2, 3, 5, 7, 8–9, 96, 111, 135, 140–1, 143, 148, 161, 167, 168–9, 170–220, 221
Impey, Sir Elijah 211, 214–15
Incas 177
India 7, 34, 172, 183, 192, 198, 200, 209, 210–19
Indians (*see* America: native peoples)
Indonesia 210
industrial revolution 4, 5
Ireland 8, 30, 135, 157, 158, 164, 167, 172, 175, 187, 188, 192–3, 197, 255
Islam 199, 200, 213
Italy 4, 39

Jacobitism 3, 78, 79–85, 87, 89, 99, 139, 141, 144, 145, 148, 159, 223, 244, 253
James I 176, 182
James II 79, 82, 83, 138
Jenyns, Soame 22
John Bull 4, 18, 152, 163–8
Johnson, Michael 20, 22, 32, 200
Johnson, Samuel
Adventurer, The 223, 224
No. 67 66, 219
No. 99 203
No. 131 59
No. 138 130
Bravery of the English Soldier, The 205
Catalogue of Harleian Miscellany 124
Compleat Vindication of the Licensers of the Stage 113–14, 123–4
Course of Lectures on the English Law ("Vinerian Lectures") 139–40, 192–3, 197
Debates in the Senate of Lilliput 86–8, 97, 181
Dictionary of the English Language 11–12, 32–42, 49, 61, 67, 86, 90, 93, 95, 140, 146, 167, 223
False Alarm, The 24, 94, 109, 116, 117, 134, 137
Further Thoughts on Agriculture 191
Idler, The 19–20, 56, 223, 224
No. 5 58
No. 8 124
No. 13 66
No. 22 206
No. 30 124
No. 37 67
No. 39 69
No. 53 70
No. 55 240
No. 57 104
No. 72 105
No. 73 25
No. 81 208
No. 86 21
No. 87 58
No. 100 66
No. 142 66
Introduction to *A New Dictionary of Trade and Commerce* 204
Introduction to the Political State of Great Britain 146
Introduction to *The World Displayed* 206–8, 213
Irene 57, 59, 172, 181, 199–202
Journey to the Western Islands of Scotland 23, 147–8, 155–6, 162–3, 166, 214–15
Letters 103, 213, 215–17, 256
Life of Blake 113, 146, 180
Life of Drake 113, 146, 180–1
Life of the King of Prussia 193
Lives of the English Poets 91, 131, 161, 167, 215–16
Life of Addison 131
Life of Granville 99
Life of Pope 91
Life of Prior 87, 103
Life of Savage 56, 103–4, 106, 138
"London" 79, 84, 90, 95, 102, 143–5, 146, 147, 180, 206
Marmor Norfolciense 79, 82, 84–5, 123, 144–5, 165
Observations on the Present State of Affairs 194, 205
"Origin and Importance of Certain Small Tracts and Fugitive Pieces" 97, 124
Patriot, The 113–14, 129, 134
Plan of an English Dictionary 102, 146, 203
Plays of Shakespeare, The 167
preface 130, 140–1, 145
Project for the Employment of Authors 58
Rambler, The 18, 223–4
No. 4 131
No. 12 55, 70
No. 23 129
No. 27 113–14
No. 34 57
No. 39 21
No. 51 53
No. 68 107
No. 70 59
No. 71 36
No. 75 55
No. 84 53
No. 95 99
No. 97 49, 54
No. 99 93, 99, 104
No. 113 54
No. 115 54
No. 118 26
No. 122 199
No. 123 19

No. 130 56
No. 132 21
No. 133 56
No. 142 27, 66
No. 145 33
No. 170 70
No. 171 70
No. 173 37, 53
No. 182 72
No. 188 105
No. 191 55
No. 192 26
No. 193 105
No. 197 66
No. 198 66
Rasselas 9, 54, 67–9, 183
Review of *Account of the Conduct of the Duchess of Marlborough* 92–3, 97
Review of *An Analysis of a General Map of the Middle British Colonies* 194
Review of *A Letter to a Member of Parliament* 126
Sermon 6 106
Sermon 7 116
Sermon 14 115
Sermon 23 115, 117
Sermon 24 26, 117–29
Taxation No Tyranny 114, 188, 190, 196–7, 198, 207, 209
Thoughts on the Late Transactions Respecting Falkland's Islands 128, 129, 188, 194–6
Vanity of Human Wishes, The 54, 84, 90, 97, 117, 133, 172, 202–3, 223
Vision of Theodore 90
Jones, Erasmus 51, 63, 67
Julius Caesar 168, 203
Junius 101, 128, 137, 195
Juvenal 204

Kant, Immanuel 131
Keith, Sir William 175, 187
Kennedy, Archibald 178, 182
Kerr, Sir James 153
Kidd, Colin 148, 154
King, William 123
Kipling, Rudyard 3, 171, 218
Knolles, Richard 199, 202, 213
Knox, John 186, 210
Knox, Vicesimus 27, 54, 58
Korshin, Paul 18
Kowaleski-Wallace, Elizabeth 63
Kramnick, Isaac 91

Laing, Malcolm 159
Lancelot, Claude 38
Langland, Elizabeth 75
Lansdowne, George Granville, Lord 99
Laslett, Peter 12
Lee, Arthur 260
Lennox, Charlotte 9, 45
Liberals 171, 221
Lichfield 133
Lillo, George 176
Lingard, John 168–9
Literary Magazine, The 204, 224
Lloyd, William 152
Locke, John 94, 137, 187, 188, 190, 192–3
London 8, 59, 102, 110, 133, 146, 219, 223, 224, 263
Louis XIV 118
luxury 5, 8–9, 14, 17, 48, 60–9, 111, 115, 150, 166, 201, 226, 229
Lyttelton, Sir George 7, 37, 79, 80, 82, 91, 103, 122, 123, 248

Macaulay, Catherine 27, 56, 73
Macaulay, Thomas Babington 3, 140–1
Macclesfield, Countess of 56
Machiavelli, Nicolo 184, 211
McKendrick, Neil 5
Mackenzie, Sir George 152, 159
Mackenzie, Henry 110, 166
McLeod, Emilia Brodie, Lady 162, 253
Macpherson, James 148, 149, 150, 152, 153, 154, 155–6, 159, 160, 166, 190, 191, 255
M'Nicol, Donald 149, 156–7, 254
Magna Carta 146
Mallet, David 113–14, 126, 142
Malory, Sir Thomas 145
Malthus, Thomas 30, 31, 120
Mandeville, Bernard 9, 63–4, 65, 67, 114
manners 105–6
Marlborough, Charles Spencer, Duke of 205
Marlborough, Sarah Jennings Churchill, Duchess of 73, 92–3
Mattaire, Michael 38–9
Marx, Karl 6, 11–13, 23, 68, 73, 91, 222
Maxwell, William 197
Mauduit, Israel 83
Mehta, Uday Singh 261
mercantilism 186, 211
merchants (*see* social class: commercial community)
merit 91, 100–7, 129
Methodism 210
Mexico 177–8
Middle East, the 28–42, 54, 199–201, 212
Miège, Guy 13, 16
Mill, James 218, 261
Mill, John Stuart 261
Millar, John 23–4, 25, 64

Milton, John 46–7, 57
Molyneux, William 187, 188, 192
Monboddo, James Burnet, Lord 219
Monitor, The 112, 118, 174
Monmouth, James Scott, Duke of 138
Montagu, Elizabeth 49
Montesquieu, Charles Louis de Secondat, Baron de 181, 200, 255
More, Hannah 9, 41, 45, 46, 49, 51, 56–9, 66, 72–3, 219
Museum, The 102, 111

Nairn, Tom 167
Namier, Sir Lewis 77, 89
Nandakumar, Maharaja 211, 215–16, 261
Napoleon III 171
nationalism 2, 5, 7–8, 111–19, 133–69, 220, 253
  English nationhood 3, 60, 131–2, 133–69
  patriotism 7, 78, 110, 112–14, 118, 127, 133–5, 141, 144, 163, 168, 225, 251
Netherlands 4
Newberry, John 18
Newcastle, Thomas Pelham-Holmes, Lord 125
Non-jurors 80, 228
Normans 136, 138–9, 142, 161
  Norman conquest 140–2
North, Frederick, Lord 100, 190, 195
North Briton, The 83, 84, 112

Observer, The 209
O'Connor, Charles 164
Old England 82, 95, 97, 112
Oldmixon, John 175, 184, 185
Orient, the (*see* Middle East)
Owen, John B. 83
Oxford University 81

Paine, Thomas 29
Paley, William 209
party 5, 77–107, 110, 111, 224
patriotism (*see* nationalism)
Patriots 80, 86–7, 95, 103, 111, 114, 115, 122, 123, 127, 129, 133–4, 137, 139, 140, 142, 145–6, 165, 180, 181, 182, 185, 188, 191, 195, 245
Peachum, Henry 14
Peace of Utrecht 103, 143, 182
pedantry 37–8, 52, 53
Peel, Sir Robert 228
Pelham, Henry 87, 90, 91
Pennant, Thomas 155–6
Perceval, John, Lord Egmont 80, 83, 86, 122, 129
Percy, Thomas 164–5
Peter the Great 203
Petyt, William 137, 138, 139
Pilkington, Laetitia 44
Piozzi, Hester Lynch 99
Pitt, William (the elder) 82, 93, 98, 112, 123, 125, 171, 174, 188, 191, 195, 210, 224
Pitt, William (the younger) 171, 210
Pittock, Murray G.A. 135, 145, 167, 168
Pocock, J.G.A. 92, 100–1, 107, 136, 137
Pope, Alexander 48, 91, 94, 98, 102, 110, 143, 144
Porter, Roy 45
Porteus, Beilby 209
Portugal 207
post-colonial studies 170
Potkay, Adam 155–7
press, liberty of the 95, 121–30, 226
print culture 1, 35, 133
Prior, Matthew 103
Priestley, Joseph 39–40, 223
Protestantism 135, 138
public, the 5, 6–7, 43–60, 63–4, 97–8, 108–32, 220, 221, 226
Public Advertiser, The 128
public spirit 110–19, 123, 125
Pulteney, William 86, 87, 90, 95, 103, 123, 133

Quintilian 38

racial science 178, 219, 255
Radcliffe, Ann 164
Raleigh, Walter 4
Ralph, James 82, 97, 101, 133
Ramsay, James 209
Ramsey, William 15, 18, 21
Raynor, David 254
Reform Bill (1832) 31, 109
Remembrancer, The 72, 97, 134
Renaissance, the 3, 17, 38, 60, 133, 225, 236
Restoration, the 39, 47
Rhees, David ap 164
Richardson, Samuel 48–9, 54
  Clarissa 54
Robertson, William 8, 140–1, 149, 154–5, 156–7, 159
Rogers, Nicholas 109
Rolt, Richard 204
Roman Catholicism 138, 153
Romanticism 150, 164
Rome 136, 137, 142, 144, 151, 152, 157, 161, 169, 171, 173, 175, 176, 181, 201, 203, 209
Rousseau, Jean-Jacques 214–15, 219, 255
Rule, John 221
Ruskin, John 218
Russia 135

Sacheverell, Henry 85–6
Said, Edward W. 170
Sandys, Samuel 86

Savage, Richard 56, 98, 104, 138
Saxons 122, 135–40, 142, 144–5, 146, 157, 159, 164, 167, 256
Scholastics 236
Scotland 7–8, 9, 22–3, 37, 64, 66, 132, 135, 136, 140–1, 146, 147–69, 175, 185, 187, 192, 193, 214–15
Scott, Sir Walter 3, 24, 150, 166
Seccombe, Thomas 4
Seeley, J.R. 170, 171, 172, 183
Selden, John 176
Seven Years' War, the 118–19, 124, 165, 172, 174–5, 179, 180, 186, 187, 191, 194, 195, 199, 200, 204–8, 218, 219, 224
Shaftesbury, Anthony Ashley Cooper, Lord 115
Shakespeare, William 130, 148, 161
Sharpe, Granville 209
Shaw, William 164, 236
Shebbeare, John 83, 84, 126, 245
Sher, Richard 148, 149
Shippen, William 88
Shirley, John 46, 50–1
Shrewsbury, Charles Talbot, Duke of 103
slavery 2, 172, 209–10
Smith, Adam 37, 64–5, 67, 166, 173, 184, 188, 189, 198, 207, 211
social class 2, 5–6, 11–32, 77, 220, 221, 224
  aristocracy and titled gentry 6, 11, 12, 14, 17, 21, 25, 28, 29, 32, 35–8, 39, 41, 43–6, 47–8, 49, 50, 61, 89, 91, 108, 109, 120, 134, 135, 150, 221, 251
  commercial community 8, 11, 12, 14, 15, 16, 17–18, 22, 26, 27–8, 29, 32, 33–5, 43, 44, 49, 50, 51, 61, 63, 67, 91, 95, 117, 118, 122, 131, 135, 171, 172, 173, 175, 177, 183–4, 185, 190, 195, 197, 198, 199, 204, 211, 217, 223, 224, 230, 231, 246
  lower, service and working classes 5, 11, 16, 19, 28, 30, 31, 33, 35, 37, 60, 61, 102, 120, 134, 224
  middle class 3, 6–7, 11–32, 33, 41, 43, 105, 108–9, 120, 220, 221, 224, 230, 251
  professionals 12, 14, 43, 184, 185, 198, 225, 230
  untitled gentry (traditional "gentlemen") 43, 184, 185, 230
Spain 113–14, 142, 143, 171, 173, 174, 175, 176, 177, 180–1, 182, 185, 186, 187, 188, 191, 193, 194–6, 201
Spectator, The 51
Squire, Francis 121
Stamp Act 188
Steele, Sir Richard 51
Stephen, Sir Leslie 3
Sterne, Laurence 44
Steuart, James 58–65, 67, 166
Stevenson, William 28
Stillingfleet, William 152
Stockdale, Percival 27
Stone, Lawrence 230
Sweden 219
Swift, Jonathan 39, 94, 113–14, 138, 159–60, 221

Tate, Nahum 131
Tatler, The 51
Taylor, Harriet 242
Taylor, John 93, 106, 216, 217, 256
Temple, Sir William 138
Tennyson, Alfred Lord 145
Theatrical Licensing Act 121, 122, 123, 124
Thomas, Sir Dalby 177, 185
Thomson, James 32, 91, 103, 142, 176
Thrale, Henry 113–14, 134, 225
Thrale, Hester (*see* Piozzi, Hester Lynch)
Tindal, Nicholas 200
Tories 2, 3, 77–90, 91–2, 93–4, 98–100, 111, 113, 127, 128, 138–9, 140–1, 221, 223, 224, 226
Torshell, Samuel 46
Trumpener, Katie 147, 167
True Patriot, the 83, 103, 115
Tucker, Josiah 17, 29, 189, 197, 198
Turks (*see* Middle East)
Tyrell, James 137, 139

United States, the (*see* America)
Universal Chronicle, The 205
Universal Visitor, The 58

Valla, Lorenzo 38
Vansittart, Henry 213
Vansittart, Robert 213
Varro 39
Vaugelas, Claude Fauve de 38
Vernon, Admiral Edward 176
Vickery, Amanda 44
Victoria, Queen 167, 218
Virgil 55
Veblen, Thorstein 233

Wahrman, Dror 31
Wales 8, 61, 135, 142, 145, 155–6, 163–4, 167, 175, 192, 256
Waller, Edmund 82
Walpole, Horace 80, 95, 110, 121, 122, 164, 199, 245
Walpole, Sir Robert 78, 86–7, 90, 91, 93, 95, 96, 101, 102, 103, 104, 112, 114, 115, 121, 122, 127, 129, 142, 143, 144, 181, 195, 244, 249
War of Austrian Succession 82, 84, 96, 203, 205
War of Jenkins' Ear 32, 124, 142, 143, 172, 174, 175, 177, 180, 186, 187

Warburton, William 7, 91
Warton, Thomas 165
Watkinson, Edward 62
Weinbrot, Howard D. 256
Wesley, John 190, 209, 219
West, Jane 41, 44, 45, 56
Wetherill, Lorna 233
Whigs 3, 6, 29, 77, 78, 79, 80, 81, 83, 85, 86, 87, 89, 90, 91–2, 93–4, 97, 98, 99, 101, 107, 117, 134, 136–8, 139, 140–1, 165, 173, 182, 187, 188, 190, 195, 201, 209, 216, 221, 223, 244
Whitaker, John 158
Whitehead, Paul 91, 95, 103, 127, 177, 250
Wilberforce, William 209
Wilkes, John 8, 11, 12, 24, 29, 83, 84, 92, 112, 127, 137
Wilkes, Wetenhall 51, 52
Wilkins, John 40
William the Conqueror 137, 138–9, 151
William III 93, 138, 143
Williams, Anna 45
Williams, Raymond 6
Wolfe, James 208
Wollstonecraft, Mary 46, 47, 56–7, 59, 120, 242
women 2, 15, 24, 36, 43–76, 108–9, 111, 220, 221, 223, 225
  domesticity 9, 43–60, 108
  gender studies 1, 5, 9, 43–6, 61
World, The 36–7, 224
Woolf, Virginia 46
Wright, William 151–2
Wynn, Sir William Watkins 80, 90

Xerxes 203

Yearsley, Ann 72
Young, Arthur 210, 260